THE TAX SCHEDULE

A GUIDE TO TAX WARRANTIES AND INDEMNITIES

THIRD EDITION

by Eile Gibson, CTA, Solicitor

First published by Spiramus Press in 2012.

This third edition published October 2016.

© Spiramus Press Ltd, 2016

102 Blandford Street, London, W1U 8AG.

ISBN hardback 978 1910151 28 0

ISBN digital   978 1910151 29 7

British Library Cataloguing-in-Publication Data.

A catalogue record for this book is available from the British Library.

Typeset by: Spiramus Press Ltd

Printed by Grosvenor Group, London

Preface to the third edition

The rate of new tax legislation is unabating. Since January 2014, the date of the second edition, we have witnessed continued erosion of the powers of the tax evasion industry including a new Targeted Anti-Avoidance Rule (TAAR), draconian penalties and new HMRC powers, major changes the taxation of UK property for non-UK residents and non-UK domiciles, and a recently introduced investors' relief, similar to entrepreneurs' relief but which is available to non-employees and directors.

For transactions, as always the devil is in the detail – both in respect of UK tax legislation and the drafting of the commercial documents involved in the sale of a company or business. Unfortunately the author's experience is that standard precedents for the tax schedule are virtually unchanged since 2012, which was the date of the first edition of this publication, and that few tax advisors are aware of the three cases which should be compulsory reading for any corporate tax professional involved in sale transactions, namely *Drachs Investment No.3 Limited v Brightsea UK Limited* [2011] EWHC 1306; *Porton Capital Technology Funds and Others v 3M UK Holdings Limited and another [2011] EWHC 2895;* and *Teeside Power Holdings Limited v Elctrabel International Holdings BV & GDF International SAS* [2012] EWHC 33.

This edition contains an extended glossary, details of new investor relief schemes and changes in legislation as announced as at 15 September 2016.

Preface to the first edition

I was introduced to my first tax schedule at the beginning of my career as a tax lawyer. It was totally impenetrable and my senior colleagues appeared to be unwilling or unable to explain the principles behind it. It was what it was and the junior tax associate was thrown in at the deep end. This was in the late-1990s when there were only two text books on the subject: – *Tax Indemnities & Warranties* by Sanders & Ridgway and the Hammond publication *Tax Aspects of the Purchase and Sale of a Private Company's Shares.* Both of these excellent publications remained secretly hidden in the top drawer of the desk of a colleague, and it was at least six months into my training when I realised the existence of these books. Over a period of time and involving many transactions I painstakingly taught myself, with their help, the real issues behind the many obscurities contained in tax deeds.

I am convinced that current market practice in drafting the tax schedule has strayed from commercial principles and common sense – the concept of *caveat emptor* for the buyer is rarely considered, and often the negotiation of the tax schedule ignores the responsibility for the buyer to carry out proper due diligence on the target. Additionally, the cost for the clients and time in negotiating the tax schedule in transactions involving the sale and purchase of companies and businesses can be, in my view, out of all proportion to their significance in terms of the overall deal. More frustrating is an all too frequent argument from the other side when arguing against a particularly obscure issue that 'this is standard practice'. Whilst this may have gradually become the case from the tax lawyers' perspective, it is unlikely to cover an issue which the clients have agreed on commercial grounds, nor is necessarily one which is in a party's interest.

I have always been cautious about what might happen if a dispute arises relating to the tax deed and what attitude a judge might take when considering some of the standard provisions in a tax deed. Now we know. Similar to the experience of waiting for a number 36 bus for an interminable period of time, and then having three arrive simultaneously, after a considerable period during which there has been no reporting of litigation involving the tax deed two cases in 2011 and one in early 2012 were reported on – *Drachs Investment No. 3 Limited v Brightsea UK Limited* [2011] EWHC 1306[1]; *Porton Capital Technology Funds and Others v 3M UK Holdings Limited and another* [2011] EWHC 2895[2]; and *Teesside Power Holdings Limited v Electrabel International Holdings BV & GDF International SAS [2012] EWHC 33[3]*. And parts of the judgments have confirmed my views on so-called 'standard' tax schedule provisions. Whilst not having seen the tax deeds in question in these cases, which

[1] Before His Honour Judge Chambers QC (sitting as a Judge of the High Court)
[2] Before Mr Justice Hamblen
[3] Before His Honour Judge Chambers QC

were the basis of each of the disputes (all unrelated however), it is clear that the judge in each case had difficulty in interpreting the drafting of certain provisions. Whether one agrees with the findings of the courts, at the heart of the disputes were interpretation issues involving conflicting provisions. These cases are discussed in greater detail at paragraphs 4.6.4, 10.10 and 10.13 but should be reference points for anyone involved in negotiating a tax schedule. They are required reading for all tax specialists.

This book is intended to be used by tax lawyers and tax accountants but also for non-tax specialists including finance directors, corporate advisors, and buyers and sellers of businesses and companies. Therefore, I have attempted to include detailed background technical information wherever possible. The **Glossary** and the **Warranties** chapter, as well as the appendices are intended to be sources of quick reference directing the reader quickly to the statutory source.

The tax schedules and warranties in Appendices 1 to 4 are included on a disk for use as templates. These are provided in PDF format (which cannot be amended), and as Word documents. Any person using the templates for the tax schedule should expect to amend them to reflect the circumstances of the target, the commercial agreement and intentions of the parties. My advice is to consider also the issues raised in the first two chapters – **The Transaction Process** and **Due Diligence** before the negotiation process.

Acknowledgements

My grateful thanks to the following people who have assisted me in reviewing parts of the book and providing me with such helpful comments, as well as my patient publisher Carl Upsall. However all errors, omission, views and opinions are my own and for which I take full responsibility -

Fiona Bell of RSM
Louise Eldridge of Bristows
Ann Fairpo, barrister at Atlas Chambers
Nick Gould of Gunner Cooke
Ann Humphrey of Ann L Humphrey Solicitors
Melanie List of Lupton Fawcett and
Matthew Peppitt of EY

I also thank all my clients for whom I have acted in transactions and my colleagues, as well as tax lawyers acting for the other side. Every transaction has been different, interesting, sometimes entertaining but always increasing my knowledge of the subject.

Table of contents

Table of authorities

Cases

Statutes

Glossary

accounting period	the period for which a company's accounts are drawn up as required under statute
ACT	advanced corporation tax (abolished for distributions made after 5 April 1999)
advance pricing agreement/APA	advance pricing agreements whereby taxpayers enter into a binding agreement with a Tax Authority relating to certain Taxation issues, and in the United Kingdom under TIOPA 2010 Part 5 (sections 218 to 230)
AIM	the market of that name administered by the LSE
approved CSOP option	an option issued under an approved CSOP scheme under ITEPA Schedule 4 (discussed in **Chapter 7**)
associated company	there are a number of definitions, including CTA 2010 section 25 relevant for the small profits rate, and CTA 2010 section 449 for close company purposes – generally a company is associated with another company if one controls the other or both are under the control of the same person or persons
ASB	the Accounting Standards Board, an autonomous board which issues accounting standards including the FRS
business and asset sale	the sale of an ongoing business through the acquisition of a bundle of assets by another party
ATED	annual tax on enveloped dwellings, the provisions for which are contained in Part 3 FA 2013 (ss 94 to 174)
CA 2006	the Companies Act 2006
CAA 2001	the Capital Allowances Act 2001
CAP 1 (Clearances and Approvals)	replacing COP 10 and VAT Notice 700/6: VAT rulings. Sets out how HMRC deal with non-business customers or customers or

	their advisors who have a query about non-business activities and want advice on HMRC's interpretation of recent tax legislation (generally passed during the last four years) or on a completed or future transaction
capital goods scheme	a scheme within the VAT provisions and relevant in respect of certain computer equipment and property assets of certain values – see SI 1995/2518 regulations 112 – 116 – and discussed in **Chapter 3 (Tax Warranties)** at 3.37.3
careless/carelessly	failure to take reasonable care or failure to inform HMRC of an inaccuracy – see FA 2007 Schedule 24 paragraph 3(1)(a)
CGT	capital gains tax
chargeable assets	in UK tax legislation this refers to the assets in question being subject to UK capital or chargeable gains tax
CIS	the construction industry scheme – see FA 2004 sections 57 to 77 and SI 2005/2045 and as discussed in **Chapter 3** at 3.13
Class 1A NIC	NIC payable by employers and certain third parties on taxable benefits provided to employees, and calculated as a % of the cash equivalent of the benefits
Class 1B NIC	NIC payable by employers who enter into any PAYE Settlement Agreement with HMRC (PSA)
close company	an unquoted UK resident company which is under the control of five or fewer participators or any number of directors who are participators – CTA 2010 section 439
code of practice	codes published by HMRC setting out how some of its departments work or deal with certain matters and which the taxpayer should be able to rely on

company reorganisation	any reorganisation or reduction in a company's share capital or a reconstruction involving a transfer of a business, under which the provisions of TCGA Chapter II (section 126 to 140) can apply
completion	refers to completion of the transaction in question – usually by the signing of the SPA
completion accounts	accounts drawn up to the date of completion, ordinarily using the same accounting treatment as for the last set of accounts drawn up by the target company
connected	see definitions in ITA section 993, TCGA section 286, CTA 2009 sections 58B and 1316 , CTA 2010 section 1122 , CAA section 575 , ITTOIA sections 50B, 103 and 179
consortium	for corporation tax relief purposes as set out in CTA 2010 section 153
consortium relief	relief for corporation tax available between members of a consortium, as referred to in the provisions under CTA 2010 sections 129 to 149 and discussed in **Chapter 9 (Group Issues)** at paragraph 9.2.2
construction industry scheme (CIS)	the scheme whereby contractors or deemed contractors are required to deduct income tax from payments, primarily set out in SI 2005/2045
control	see definitions under CAA section 574, sections 69 and 719 ITEPA, ITA section 995, CTA 2009 section 472 , CTA 2010 sections 450 and 1124
controlled foreign company/CFC	a non-UK resident company controlled by UK resident persons which satisfies certain criteria under ICTA sections 747 to 756 for accounting periods beginning before 1 January 2013. A new regime came into effect after that date and is contained in TIOPA Part 9A (ss 371AA to 371VJ
COP 10	code of practice 10 (now replaced by CAP 1) which set out how HMRC provided

	information or advice including post-transaction rulings and advice on applicable law to a specific transaction – there are separate provisions for business customers seeking non-statutory clearances and discussed in **Chapter 1 (The Transaction Process)** at paragraph 1.2.10
corporate bond	defined in TCGA section 117(1) as a security (defined in TCGA section 132(2)(b)) the debit of which represents a normal commercial loan, expressed in sterling and which has no conversions or redemption provisions
corporation tax	UK corporation tax is charged on profits of a company, meaning income and chargeable gains. Income includes trading and property income; profits also include those arising from loan relationships and derivative contracts and from disposals of know-how and patent rights
Corporation Tax Acts	enactments relating to taxation of income and chargeable gains of companies and of company distributions (including provisions relating to income tax), as defined in ICTA section 831 and Interpretation Act 1978 Schedule 1
corporation tax instalment regime/CT Instalment Regs	the regulations set out in SI 1998/3175 requiring a company to pay corporation tax by quarterly instalments
CVS	the Corporate Venturing Scheme which provides relief against corporation tax on investments by companies in small 'high risk' trading companies, under the provisions set out in FA 2000 Schedule 15 and discussed in **Chapter 8 (Venture Capital Schemes)**
debenture	An acknowledgement of indebtedness, usually a bond of a company or corporation acknowledging a debt and providing for interest payments; for tax purposes there is

	no statutory definition, but a debenture is likely to be considered to be a security
deferred tax	an accounting concept whereby provisions must be provided for in the accounts for tax assets or liabilities which might arise sometime in the future- they normally reflect timing differences and often don't become payable
degrouping charge	a charge to tax arising from a company leaving a group, and relating to withdrawal of intra-group tax relief – see TCGA section 179, CTA 2009 sections 780 & 795 , CTA 2009 sections 344 to 346 , TCGA Schedule 7AC paragraph 38 , and FA 2003 Schedule 7 paragraph 3 & 9
demerger	under CTA 2010 section 1074, certain transactions which divide the trading activities of a single company or group so that they are subsequently carried on by two or more companies not belonging to the same group or by two or more independent groups – they are discussed in **Chapter 1** at paragraph 1.2.1 as well in **Chapter 3** at paragraph 3.16
determination and assessment	HMRC power to determine tax payable by a company if no return is delivered under self-assessment in response to a notice under FA 1998 Schedule 18 paragraph 36
discovery assessment and discovery determination	HMRC powers under FA 1998 Schedule 18 paragraph 41(1) where loss of tax is discovered
discovery determination	a determination as referred to in FA 1998 Schedule 18 paragraph 41(2)
disclosure & transparency rules (DTR)	the disclosure rules apply to an issuer whose financial securities are admitted to a UK regulated market; the transparency rules implement the transparency directive
disguised remuneration rules	rules introduced by FA 2011 intended to counter perceived tax avoidance and

	contained in ITEPA sections 554A to 554AZ21, and discussed in **Chapter 7** at paragraph 7.8[1]
distribution/dividend	as defined in CTA 2010 section 1000
DOTAS	Disclosure of Tax Avoidance Schemes see FA 2004 sections 306 to 319; VATA Sch 11A; SSAA 1992 section 132A; SI 2004/1933; VAT Notice 700/8; SI 2004/1864 – Information regs, SI 2004/1865 – promoters and prescribed circumstances; SI 2004/1868 (prescribed description of arrangements); SI 2006/1543 (prescribed descriptions and arrangements); SI 2007/785 ; SI 2011/170
EIS	the Enterprise Investment Scheme under which individuals can receive income tax relief on investments in small unquoted trading companies under the provisions set out in ITA 2007 sections 156 to 257, with capital gains tax relief also available under TCGA section 150A and 150B and roll-over relief under TCGA Schedule 5B; discussed in **Chapter 8 (Venture Capital Schemes)**
EMI	an enterprise management incentive under ITEPA Schedule 5 (discussed further in **Chapter 7 (Share Scheme Issues))**
employment income	as defined in ITEPA section 7
employment-related loan	a loan made to an employee which satisfies the requirements of ITEPA section 174
employment-related option	securities options acquired by a person where the right or opportunity to acquire it is available by reason of an employment of that person or any other person, as set out in ITEPA section 471
entrepreneurs' relief	relief against capital gains for individuals on disposals of certain business assets on or after 5 April 2008, the provisions for which

[1] HMRC opened a technical consultation which closed for comments 5 October 2016 and therefore after the publication of this book

	are set out in TCGA sections 169H to 169S
Enquiry	HMRC enquiry into a company's tax return (FA 1998 Schedule 18 paragraph 24) by a notice of enquiry; enquiry into a personal or trustee tax return (TMA section 9A)
ESC	extra-statutory concessions are defined by HMRC in Notice 48 (January 2011) as remissions of revenue that allow relief in specific sets of circumstances to all business falling within the relevant conditions and authorised by HMRC when strict application of the law would create a disadvantage or the effect would not be the one intended. This followed Lord Hoffman's judgment in *R v HM Commissioners of Inland Revenue ex p Wilkinson [2005]* UKHL 30, where, discussing section 1 TMA, (agreed under case law to give a wide managerial discretion to HMRC in the efficient collection of the revenue) he stated that if some extra-statutory concessions went beyond such mere management, the commissioners may have exceeded their powers under that section. Following *Wilkinson*, HMRC have withdrawn a number of concessions
ESSU	the Employees Share Scheme Unit of HMRC is involved in policy on the employment-related securities legislation and tax advantaged employee share scheme legislation (namely HMRC approved share schemes), and provides technical support and advice on the application of the legislation, as well as handling operational work on the approval and monitoring of HMRC approved share award and share option schemes
EU	means the European Union (formerly referred to as the European Economic

	Community/ EEC);
exempt distribution	defined in CTA 2010 sections 1075 to 1078 and relating to a demerger
FA	followed by a number means the Finance Act of that year
FCA/the Financial Conduct Authority	the organisation which regulates the financial securities industry in the UK – together with the PRA it replaced the FSA (the Financial Services Authority); It has rule making, investigative and enforcement powers and is accountable to the Treasury
fire sale	a sale of a business or company in distressed circumstances usually for a low price and usually requiring a quick completion
fraudulent and negligent conduct	this concept was repealed as from 1 April 2011 and replaced with the concepts of careless inaccuracy, deliberate but not concealed inaccuracy and deliberate and concealed inaccuracy and discussed further **in Chapter 3 (Warranties)** at paragraph 3.30 (Penalties Regime) and in **Appendix 1 (Penalties & Errors)**
financial reporting standards/FRS	accounting standards developed by the Accounting Standards Board/ASB
FSA	the Financial Services Authority, being the competent authority under FSMA Part VI – is also referred to as the UK Listing Authority or UKLA – it is the securities regulator focussed on companies which issue securities traded on financial markets
FSMA	the Financial Services and Markets Act 2000
FRSSE	the Financial Reporting Standard for Smaller entities
GAAP	generally accepted accounting practices – unlisted UK companies can choose to report using UK GAAP or IFRS
GAAR/Generally Anti-Abuse Rule	enacted under FA 2013 ss 206 to 215 with effect from 17 July 2013

group payment arrangements	arrangements permitted at HMRC's discretion under TMA section 59F to 59H whereby members of a group may nominate one of its members to pay their corporation tax, and discussed further at **Chapter 9 (Group Issues)** at paragraph 9.3
group relief	ordinarily refers to intra-group relief for corporation tax purposes (discussed in **Chapter 9 at** paragraph 9.2) – namely amounts eligible for relief from corporation tax and which may be surrendered or claimed under CTA 2010 sections 97 to 128
heads of terms	the initial terms agreed by the parties to a transaction, usually conditional and often not binding – also referred to as the deal sheet
HMRC	Her Majesty's Revenue & Customs
IA 1986	Insolvency Act 1986
IAS	international accounting standards issued by the IASB and which , replaced by international financial reporting standards (IFRS)
IASB	the International Accounting Standards Board
ICAP Securities and Derivatives Exchange	owned by ICAP Group Holdings plc, it is regulated by the FCA and has two equity markets – the ISDX Growth Market and the ISDX Main Market
ICTA	the Income and Corporation Taxes Act 1988
IFRS	international financial reporting standards – as from 1 January 2005 the consolidated accounts of European listed companies must report using IFRS
IHT	inheritance tax
IHTA	the Inheritance Tax Act 1984
Income Tax Acts	the enactments relating to income tax, including any provisions of the Corporation Tax Acts which related to income tax under

	ICTA section 832; Interpretation Act 1978 Schedule 1 defines the Income Tax Acts as all enactments relating to income tax; section 1 ITA refers to the following acts making provision about income tax – ITEPA, ITTOIA, ITA, TIOPA Part 2 (*double taxation relief*), CAA 2001 and FA 2004 Part 4 (*Pension schemes, etc*)
indexation allowance	introduced in 1982 and now relevant only to UK companies or non-UK companies with a permanent establishment in the UK, the allowance increases the amount of deductible allowable expenditure when calculating the chargeable gain on the relevant capital asset disposal
insolvency arrangements	arrangements under which a person acts as a liquidator, provisional liquidator, receiver, administrator, or administrative receiver as well as voluntary arrangements as referred to in Insolvency Act 1986 Part I and discussed in **Chapter 6 (Special Situations)**
IPO	an Initial Public Offering whereby a company lists its shares for the first time either on a regulated market of LSE or on AIM
IR35	now covered under ITEPA sections 48 to 61 (*Applications to provisions to workers under arrangements made by intermediaries*) these are provisions designed to counter tax avoidance of NIC through the use of an intermediary by a person who would otherwise be considered to be an employee of the ultimate client
ITA	the Income Tax Act 2007
ITEPA	the Income Tax (Earnings & Pensions) Act 2003
ITTOIA	the Income Tax (Trading and Other Income) Act 2005
limited company	a company in respect of which the liability

	of its members is limited by its constitution – it may be limited by shares or limited by guarantee as defined under CA 2006 section 3(1)
Listing Regime	operated by the FCA whereby the Listing Rules must be complied with
Listing Rules	issued by UKLA which provide general guidelines for listings
LLP	a limited liability partnership under the LLP Act
LLP Act	the Limited Liability Partnership Act 2000
loan relationship provisions	where a company is either a debtor or creditor in respect of an underlying money debt, and whereby the taxation of loan relationships treat all profits and losses by the companies as income items, with the provisions set out in CTA 2009 sections 292 to 476
LSE	the London Stock Exchange, an RIE owned by the London Stock Exchange Group plc
main market	the main equity market of the LSE reserved for established companies, and which has stricter requirements than the rules for an AIM or ISDX Growth Market listing for example
market value	as defined in TCGA section 272, the price which an asset might reasonably be expected to fetch on a sale in the open market
MBO	a management buy-out, usually involving the managers of a business or company
merger	a reorganisation where activities of two or more companies are merged and carried on by a successor company – can involve a transfer of assets from one company to another or share exchanges but not involving any cash consideration; see also TCGA section 181; also EC Merger Directive (Council Directive 2009/133/EC); and SI

	2004/2199 for VCT mergers
newco	abbreviation for a new company set up specifically for a transaction to acquire a business or another company
NICs	national insurance contributions
NOMAD	a nominated advisor approved by AIM – it is obligatory for AIM listed companies to have a NOMAD
non-statutory clearance	a non-statutory clearance is written confirmation of HMRC's view of the application of tax law to a specific transaction or event that a customer can rely on in most circumstances – information and guidance set out in the HMRC Non-statutory Clearance Guidance Manual
Notice	a notice of guidance published by HMRC but which does not have statutory force
notice of assessment	a notice of assessment as referred to in FA 1998 Schedule 18 paragraph 47(1)
notice of enquiry	a notice under FA 1998 Schedule 18 paragraph 24 whereby HMRC can enquire into a company's tax return and under TMA section 9A whereby HMRC may enquire into a personal or trustee tax return
OECD	the Organisation of Economic Co-operation and Development
official rate of interest	the rate of interest applicable under FA 1989 section 178 which gives the Treasury the power to set the rate
official UK list	the definitive record as to whether a company's securities are officially listed in the UK, and which is maintained by the FCA, defined under FSMA sections 72 to 103
option	a right to acquire something, thereby representing a chose in action
option to tax	the provisions of VATA Schedule 10 paragraphs 1 to 34 which enable persons to

	tax supplies of land they make which would ordinarily be exempt supplies for VAT purposes
Panel on Takeovers and Mergers	established in 1968 by statute and now as provided in CA 2006 its main function is to issue and administer the City Code on Takeovers and Merger (the Takeover Code/the Code)
participator	a person who has a share or interest in the capital or income of a close company including certain loan creditors, as defined in CTA 2010 section 454
Patent Box Regime	introduced as from 1 April 2013, and set out in CTA 2010 Part 8A, the regime allows a company with profits from qualifying patents to claim a 10% rate of corporation tax
PAYE	the pay-as-you-earn system of accounting for income tax and NIC whereby an employer deducts amounts from employees' wages and salaries on their behalf under ITEPA sections 682 to 712 and SI 2003/2686 (*Income Tax (Pay As You Earn) Regulations*)
PAYE Settlement Agreement (PSA)	a formal agreement between HMRC and an employer whereby the employer accounts for tax on certain expenses and benefits provided to employees paid in one lump sum at the end of the tax year, and which would normally be a Class 1 or Class 1A liability
P/E multiple	a price/earnings multiple being a company's share price divided by its predicted earnings for the relevant year in question and a standard measure for valuing a company by stock markets
phoenix company	a 'successor' company – common in insolvencies when the previous owners will start up a new company in the same business and with some of the old assets

PLC	a public limited company under Companies Act 2006 section 4(2)
PRA/the Prudential Regulation Authority	part of the Bank of England and responsible for the prudential regulation and supervision of banks, building societies, credit unions, insurers and major investment firms
pre-pack	a pre-packaged administration discussed in **Chapter 6 (Special Situations)** at paragraph 6.1.4
private company	defined as a company which is not a public company under CA 2006 section 4(1)– see also CA 2006 sections 755 to 760 with further provisions prohibiting private companies from making an offer to the public
Prospectus Rules	the rules which set out what a prospectus must contain, and which must be approved prior to securities being offered to the public in the UK or admitted to a regulated UK market
public company	under CA 2006 section 4(2) defined as a company which is limited by shares or by guarantee, which has a share capital, its certificate of incorporation states that it is a public company and in respect of which the registration requirements have been complied with – CA 2006 section 781 to 767 sets out the minimum share capital requirements and related matters
qualifying corporate bonds	defined in TCGA section 117 as being an asset representing a loan relationship of a company and in respect of which the definition of a corporate bond applies
quarterly instalment payment regimes	the regime requiring large companies to pay their estimated corporation tax by quarterly instalments (see SI 1998/3175 regulation 3) and discussed in **Chapter 3 (Tax Warranties)** at paragraph 3.15.1

readily convertible asset/RCA	as defined in ITEPA section 702 an asset which is, amongst other things, capable of being sold or otherwise realised on certain exchanges including a recognised investment exchange, an asset consisting of certain rights relating to a money debt or being realised in money, or an asset in respect of which there are trading arrangements in existence
recognised investment exchange/RIE	defined in FSMA section 285 as an investment exchange in relation to which a recognition order by the FCA is in force – in the UK those markets which deal in securities are the LSE and the ICAP Securities and Derivatives Exchange Ltd; important under ITEPA section 702(1)(a) for the purposes of the definition of a readily convertible asset
recognised stock exchange/RSE	defined in ITA 2007 section 1005 for tax purposes only for the purpose of the Income Tax Acts as being a market of a recognised investment exchange designated as such by HMRC and any market outside the United Kingdom which is also designated – HMRC's website will provide a list of UK and overseas recognised exchanges
reconstruction	a company reconstruction to which TCGA sections 136 and 139 apply
revenue determination	a determination and assessment under FA 1998 Schedule 18 paragraph 36
reverse premium	a payment received by a person as an inducement to enter into a transaction – usually in respect of leases
roll-over relief	roll over of tax under TCGA section 152
SAYE scheme	an approved save-as-you-earn (SAYE) option scheme under ITEPA Schedule 3 (discussed further in **Chapter 7 (Share Scheme Issues)** at 7.6.2 and in **Appendix 8**

	at 8.4)
SCE	*Societas Cooperativa Europaea* – a European co-operative company which may operate throughout the EU
scheme of reconstruction	a merger, division or other restructuring with reference to TCGA sections 136, 139 and Schedule 5AA– it results with a business being owned by the same persons which owned it prior to the reconstruction
SE	means a *Societas Europaea*, a type of European company under Council Regulation (EC) No 2157/2001, and if based in the UK treated like a public limited company
secondary tax liability	a liability to tax which falls on a party as a result of the failure of a connected person (including another member of a group in which the company was or is a member) to pay a tax liability, including liabilities arising under CTA 2010 sections 706 to 718, TCGA section 190; FA 2003 Schedule 7 paragraph 12; CTA 2009 section 795 and joint and several liability in respect of VAT
section 198 election	an election under CAA section 198 entered into by a seller and buyer on the disposal of an asset on which capital allowances can be claimed by the buyer going forward (discussed **in Chapter 5 (Sale and Purchase of a Business)** at paragraph 5.2.1)
Seed Enterprise Investment Scheme (SEIS)	introduced from April 2012 this scheme provides 50% income tax relief for investments up to £100,000 in small trading companies and set out in ITA 2007ss 257A to 257J– the SEIS provisions are discussed in **Chapter 8**
self-assessment	the system for self-assessing taxation by persons under the provisions of FA 1998 Schedule 18
SI	followed by a number means a statutory

	instrument of the relevant year
small company	defined in Annex EU comm. 2003/361/EC]
small profits rates	corporation tax rate charged on a company's total taxable profits and set out in CTA 2010 CTA 2010 sections 18 to 34
SME	a small or medium sized enterprise and using the definition in Commission Recommendation (EC) No 2003/361 as follows: small – less than 50 headcount, turnover or balance sheet total less than or equal to 10 million Euros medium – less than 250 headcount and turnover of not greater than 50 million Euros or a balance sheet total of not more than 43 million Euros
SIP	an approved share incentive plan under ITEPA Schedule 2 (discussed further in **Chapter 7 (Share Scheme Issues)** at paragraph 7.6.3 and in **Appendix 8** at paragraph 8.1
SP	a Statement of Practice issued by HMRC which sets out its interpretation of legislation and the way it applies the law in practice. A taxpayer may nevertheless have a right to argue a different interpretation at Tribunal
SPA	a sale and purchase agreement
Sponsor/Sponsor Firms	every company listed on the main market of the LSE involving an IPO must have a sponsor approved by the UKLA, and kept on a register held by the FSA; their responsibilities are contained in the Listing Rules
SSAP	a Statement of Standard Accounting Practice, issued by the ASB
SSAP 13	UK GAAP accounting standard for research and development

stamp duty	duty imposed primarily under the Stamp Act 1891 and which currently only applies to instruments relating to stock or marketable securities by virtue of FA 2003 section 125
stamp duty land tax/SDLT	a tax chargeable on the acquisition of a chargeable interest in UK land under FA 2003 sections 43 to 217
stamp duty reserve tax/SDRT	a stamp charged in a transaction where there is an agreement between two people to transfer chargeable securities for consideration in money or money's worth, and governed by the provisions in FA 1986 sections 86 to 114
substantial shareholdings exemption	set out in TCGA Schedule 7AC an exemption from corporation tax arising on a capital gain from the disposal of shares in a company by another company, subject to the 10% holding requirement and discussed in **Chapter 9 (Group Issues)** at paragraph 9.8
Takeover Code	the City Code on Takeovers & Mergers – administered by the Panel on Takeovers and Mergers, which applies to takeovers intended to ensure that shareholders in offeree companies are treated fairly, and to ensure an orderly framework as to how takeovers are conducted in the United Kingdom
Takeover Panel	the Panel on Takeovers and Mergers – see explanation above
taper relief	relief for the purposes of computing capital gains and available on the disposal of assets by individuals but which was withdrawn in April 2008 and is not available for disposals after that date
target	refers to the target company or target business which is the subject of an acquisition in an transaction

tax assets	often defined as 'tax reliefs', they represent reliefs from or a reduction in taxation or an entitlement to a payment of taxation
tax equalisation	these are commonly arrangements between a UK employer and a foreign national who comes to the UK to work and there is an agreement that the employee will receive specified net cash earning and/or benefits, with the employer undertaking to meet the income tax; the employer usually provides an advisor to deal with the employee's UK tax affairs; it also covers arrangements where an individual performs duties for a UK employer whilst employed by an overseas employer; each year HMRC provides a 'Help Sheet'
taxpayer notice	a notice from HMRC under paragraph 1 FA 2008 Schedule 36 requiring a taxpayer to produce information or a document
TCGA	the Taxation of Chargeable Gains Act 1992
thin capitalisation	investments in an associated enterprise involving excessively high interest bearing debt which at arm's length would have taken the form of equity
TIOPA	Taxation (International and Other Provisions) Act 2010
TMA	the Taxes Management Act 1970
transfer of a going concern/TOGC	a transfer of a going concern under VATA section 49 and discussed further in **Chapter 5 (Sale and Purchase of a Business)** at paragraph 5.5
transfer pricing regime	set out in TIOPA Part 4 (sections 146 to 217) applying to transactions between connected persons not made on arm's length principles
TUPE Regulations	the Transfer of Undertakings (Protection of Employment) Regulations, which protects employees' terms and conditions of employment when a business transfers
undertaking	means the business or trade of a company

	and referred to in FA 2003 Schedule 7 paragraphs 7 & 8 for SDLT relief and FA 1986 sections 75 & 76 for stamp duty relief
unapproved option	an option which does not satisfy the requirements of UK legislation for approved options and whereby there will be no tax reliefs in the UK
UKLA	the UK Listing Authority a division of the FCA – it is responsible for the admission of securities to the Official UK List; it produces the Listing Rules, the Prospectus Rules and the Disclosure and Transparency Rules in addition to a number of other publications
unlimited company	a company in respect of which there is no limit on the liability of its members as defined under CA 2006 section 3(4)
VAT	value added tax
VAT group	see definition at **Chapter 9 (Group Issues)** paragraph 9.9.1
VATA	the Value Added Taxes Act 1992
venture capital schemes	the Enterprise Investment Scheme (EIS), the Venture Capital Trust Scheme (VCT Scheme), the Corporate Venturing Scheme (CV Scheme) and relief for venture capital loss (VC Loss Relief) and discussed further in **Chapter 8 (Venture Capital Schemes)** at 8.2
VCT Scheme	a Venture Capital Trust scheme under ITA sections 258 to 332 and discussed further in **Chapter 8** at 8.2
warrant	a right to subscribe for and be issued with shares or loan notes and therefore identical to an option and representing a chose in action
warranty	an undertaking as to ownership or quality of something sold, hired, etc; often accepting responsibility for defects
Valuation Office	the department within HMRC which *inter*

| Agency/VOA | *alia* provides agreed share valuations for CGT and IHT purposes |
| yield | a measurement whereby the amount a company pays in dividends is divided by its market capitalisation |

1 THE TRANSACTIONAL PROCESS

1.1 Background Issues

The fundamental principle when negotiating a tax schedule is that it is a commercial document unique to the transaction at hand and should be treated as such – in other words, there are no rules which set a tax deed apart from any other commercial document.

In any arm's length commercial transaction involving the sale and purchase of a company or business there should be a willing buyer and a willing seller and the parties will want the deal transacted as efficiently and cost-effectively as possible. Legal advisors are required to act in the best interests of their clients to avoid future problems arising from the transaction, but few clients will appreciate lawyers who take a confrontational approach with their opposite number early on in the transactional process.

Background issues requiring clarification for the tax advisor at an early stage in a transaction include the following:

- what due diligence has and/or will be carried out (discussed more fully in **Chapter 2 (Due Diligence)**);
- what clearances are required (see paragraphs 1.2 and 1.3 below and **Appendix 7**);
- which party will provide the first draft of the sale and purchase agreement and the tax schedule and what additional documents will be required;
- what banking documents will be produced;
- whether any of the seller's liabilities/assets remain with the target following completion;
- how the purchase price is to be structured and whether the seller has taken relevant tax advice (see paragraph 4.6 below which discusses the main issues);
- whether there are post-completion issues; and
- whether there will be completion accounts or a completion working capital statement?

1.2 Pre-completion Clearances

When, or shortly after, the heads of terms are agreed the tax advisors should agree whether HMRC clearances are required and which party should be responsible for their submission. **Appendix 7** summarises statutory clearances.

It is standard practice for the party responsible for seeking the clearances to circulate the draft applications and all related correspondence to all parties for comments and input before submission. While the standard time limit for HMRC to respond is 30 days from the date of receipt of the application, if further information is required or the proposed structuring undergoes changes the response period can begin again from the date the new information is received by HMRC.

A word of warning: Restructuring, including demergers, company reconstructions and schemes of reconstructions, will have different tax consequences for both the shareholders and the companies concerned if not structured properly, and therefore specialist tax advice should be taken before considering and adopting such schemes and arrangements. A pre-completion reconstruction can involve advance clearance in respect of several taxes, for example corporation tax on chargeable gains/capital gains tax, stamp duty and, possibly, SDLT.

The main clearance procedures likely to be relevant in the sale and purchase of a company (and sometimes a business) are briefly discussed below.

1.2.1 CTA 2010 section 1091 – advance clearance relating to a demerger and exempt distribution under CTA 2010 section 1075

A demerger is a reorganisation whereby trading activities carried on by a group or a company are transferred (either as a trade or involving the transfer of the shares if the trade is held a company) directly to the shareholders of the transferring or distributing company[1]. The transfer of shares in the transferee company is referred to as an exempt distribution and will not be taxed as a distribution for income tax purposes, and there will not be a chargeable gain at the time of the distribution for the purposes of TCGA section 122 by virtue of TCGA section 192.

---

[1] CTA 2010 section 1074

A clearance can be sought under CTA 2010 section 1091 prior to a demerger, for confirmation that the distribution will be exempt.

The distributing company must have available distributable reserves equal to the assets or shares being transferred. The anti-avoidance degrouping charges under TCGA section 179 and CTA 2009 section 780 (in respect of intangible assets) will not apply to the company leaving a group solely as a result of the demerger.

The following transactions fall within the demerger provisions:

- a distributing company transfers to all its shareholders its shareholding (or substantially the whole of its shareholding) in a 75% subsidiary, so long as the shares are not redeemable shares (referred to as a direct demerger);
- a distributing company transfers all of a trade to another company (transferee company) and the transferee company issues shares to shareholders of the distributing company (an indirect demerger);
- a distributing company transfers to a transferee company all of its shares (or substantially all of its shares) in a 75% subsidiary and the transferee company issues shares to the shareholders of the distributing company (an indirect demerger).

Further requirements for a demerger include the following:

- the distributing company, the subsidiary, and the transferee company must be UK resident at the time of the distribution;
- the distributing company must be a trading company or a member of a trading group at the time of the distribution;
- the 75% subsidiary whose shares are transferred must be either a trading company or the holding company of a trading group at the time of the transfer;
- the transfers must not be for tax avoidance purposes; and
- advance clearance from HMRC is obtained.

The importance of needing to know whether the target company has been involved in a demerger is that CTA 2010 section 1086 will apply if, within five years of an exempt distribution having been made, a 'chargeable payment' is made by any company concerned in the distribution. If so, a charge to tax on the recipient will arise, which will not be deductible for corporation tax purposes.

A chargeable payment is defined[2] as being any payment made otherwise than for *bona fide* commercial reasons, or forming part of a scheme or arrangement for the avoidance of tax and which is:

- made by any company concerned with an exempt distribution directly or indirectly to a member of that company or of any other company concerned in that distribution; and
- made in connection with, or with any transaction affecting, the shares in that or any such company; and
- not a distribution or exempt distribution or made to another company which belongs to the same group as the company making the payment.

A buyer is unlikely to consider that any distribution made by the target after its acquisition will not be for *bona fide* commercial reasons or that it would be made for tax avoidance purposes but if, say, a restructuring was to be effected within the buyer's group post-completion and intra-group dividends or other payments were to be made, these provisions might bite.

See paragraph **1.3.3** regarding clearances for a chargeable payment. Any company making a chargeable payment which consists of a transfer in money or money's worth within the five year period must provide details to HMRC within 30 days of the transfer, and whether a payment is a chargeable payment would need consideration under self-assessment.

1.2.2 TCGA section 138 – advance clearance for an exchange of securities for those in another company under TCGA section 135

If the transaction involves the sale of a company, and as part of the purchase price shares or debentures in the buyer are to be issued and exchanged for some or all of the target's ordinary shares, advance clearance from HMRC is normally sought under TCGA section 138. However, TCGA section 135 can apply equally to an intra-group reorganisation prior to a third party sale.

There are three different scenarios under TCGA section 135:

1. the buyer will hold more than 25% of the target's ordinary share capital;

---

[2] CTA 2010 section 1088

2. the buyer issues the shares or debentures in exchange for shares as a result of a general offer made to the target's shareholders or any class of them, and made on a condition that if it were satisfied the buyer company would have control of the target; or

3. the buyer will hold the greater part of the voting power in the target.

There are no UK residency requirements for either party. If any of the above situations apply, the effect is that the newly issued shares in the buyer will be treated as if they were the original shares in the target, no chargeable gain arises on the target's shareholders at the time the new shares are issued and the base cost of the original shares becomes the base cost of the new shares for capital gains purposes[3].

The relief is mandatory so long as all the conditions are met and there is no requirement for the taxpayer to make a claim for the relief. Under TCGA section 138, on application for clearance to HMRC they will confirm that they are satisfied that the exchange of shares will be effected for *bona fide* commercial reasons and not as part of an arrangement to avoid corporation tax or capital gains tax (which are conditions under section 135(6) TCGA). It will remain the parties' responsibility to ensure that all the conditions of TCGA section 135 are satisfied in order for the CGT treatment to apply. If the parties do not want the roll-over treatment to apply they should structure the transaction so as not to satisfy the requirements of TCGA section 135.

An unconnected buyer of a company commonly offers shares as consideration on commercial grounds in circumstances: when it does not have available cash to pay upfront on completion; when it wishes the sellers to retain a stake in the merged companies; when the sellers prefer to be given securities rather than cash for timing purposes to minimise the chargeable gain; and on the grounds that a share-for-share deal will be less dilutive than cash for the buyer's shareholders.

---

[3] TCGA sections 127 to 131

1.2.3 TCGA section 138 – advance clearance for a scheme of reconstruction involving issue of securities under TCGA section 136

TCGA section 136 applies where there is a reconstruction of a company or group (company A) under an arrangement between the company and its shareholders and/or debenture holders, whereby another company (company B) issues shares or debentures to company A shareholders in proportion to their holdings in company A, and the shares or debentures in company A are either retained by those shareholders or are cancelled. The procedure involves putting a newco on top of the group with the shareholders remaining the same, resulting in a new holding company which can thereafter dispose of the original company. A section 136 reorganisation will be used in preparation for selling off a company to a third party.

TCGA section 136 can apply to any scheme of reconstruction defined in TCGA Schedule 5AA[4] (which is only concerned with ordinary share capital), including a demerger or division as well as a voluntary winding up under an insolvency procedure (see **Chapter 6 (Special Situations)**) and a court-approved reduction of capital under the Companies Act, and extends to fixed-rate shares, loan note and debentures.

Where TCGA section 136 applies, the shareholders are treated as exchanging their holdings in company A for the shares or debentures in company B, and company A and company B will be treated as if they were the same company. This roll-over treatment is mandatory with no provisions to disapply the treatment.

An application for HMRC clearance under TCGA section 138 can be made for the confirmation that the arrangements are *bona fide* and not for tax avoidance purposes.

1.2.4 TCGA section 138 clearance – advance clearance for a reconstruction involving transfer of a business under TCGA section 139

TCGA section 139 provides that where there is a scheme of reconstruction involving a transfer of the whole or part of a

---

[4] TCGA section 136(4)

company's business to another company, so long as the transferor receives no consideration for the transfer apart from the transferee taking over whole or part of the business's liabilities, and the transferee is UK resident or the assets become chargeable assets immediately after the transfer, the transaction will be treated for corporation tax purposes as having been carried out on a no gain/no loss basis and no chargeable gains will arise on the transferring company. These provisions will cover any scheme of reconstruction as defined in TCGA Schedule 5AA.[5]

A section 139 reconstruction differs from a section 136 reconstruction in that it can involve ring-fencing assets to be packaged into a newco and thereafter sold to a third party.

The use of the word 'business' rather than 'trade' means the legislation is more widely drawn although the term business should not be interpreted as merely a group of assets. A business can comprise shares of a subsidiary.

A clearance application should be made under TCGA section 138, that the arrangements are not designed to avoid corporation tax on chargeable gains, capital gains tax or income tax. However, TCGA section 139 will not apply to the transfer of trading stock or to transfers to unit trust schemes.[6]

The relief is mandatory so long as the conditions are satisfied, and there are no provisions to disapply the relief, for example to crystallise a loss or if the transferor wants to use the substantial shareholdings exemption[7].

If an avoidance purpose is subsequently found, any tax charge which cannot be claimed from the transferor can be charged to the transferee.[8] So, if the transferee is to be the target company it is essential that the buyer scrutinises the clearance application and requires an indemnity from the transferring company or, in respect of any such tax charge, from the seller in a transaction (assuming the seller and the transferor are within the same group).

---

[5] TCGA section 139(9) referring to TCGA section 136

[6] TCGA sections 139(2) & (4)

[7] TCGA Schedule 7AC paragraph 6(1)(a) excludes no gain or loss disposals

[8] TCGA sections 139(5) to (7)

There are similar provisions for such transfers involving EU companies. These are referred to below at paragraph **1.3**.

1.2.5 CTA 2009 section 831 – clearance for a transfer of business or trade involving intangible assets under CTA 2009 section 818

These provisions are similar to those in TCGA section 139, and relate to any genuine reconstruction, transfer or merger. If there is a scheme of reconstruction[9] involving chargeable · intangible assets[10] in the transfer of the whole or part of the business of one company to another company and the transferor receives no part of the consideration for the transfer (otherwise than by the transferee taking over the whole or part of the liabilities of the business), it will be tax-neutral. Exclusions include transfers within a group or if incorporated friendly societies or dual resident investing companies are involved.[11]

The intangible assets are those acquired or created by the company for use on a continuing basis in the course of the company's activities on or after 1 April 2002. Excluded intangible assets are defined in CTA 2009 Part 8 Chapter 10.[12]

There are provisions covering European cross-border transfers of business and mergers under CTA 2009 sections 819 to 823 – see paragraphs **1.4.2** to **1.4.4**.

Clearance by HMRC requires the reconstruction, transfer or merger to have been effected for genuine commercial reasons with no tax avoidance purposes.[13]

1.2.6 FA 1986 section 75 (Acquisition relief for stamp duty)

If a company acquires the whole or part of an undertaking of another company in a scheme for the reconstruction of that other company ('target company') no stamp duty will be chargeable on any instrument executed in connection with the transfer so long as

---

[9] As defined in TCGA section 136

[10] They must be chargeable both before and after the transfer

[11] CTA 2009 sections 818(3) & (4)

[12] CTA 2009 sections 800 to 816

[13] Tax is defined as corporation tax, capital gains tax or income tax.

THE TAX SCHEDULE

the following conditions are met: the consideration for the acquisition must consist of or include the issue of non-redeemable shares in the acquiring company to all the shareholders of the target company and include nothing else other than the assumption or discharge by the acquiring company of liabilities of the target company, and the acquisition must be for *bona fide* commercial reasons and not for tax avoidance purposes.[14] After the acquisition of the target company each shareholder of each of the companies is a shareholder of the other and after the acquisition the proportion of shares of one of the companies held by any shareholder is the same as the proportion of shares of the other company held by that shareholder ('mirror image' requirement).

Application to HMRC Birmingham Stamp Office to have the instrument stamped denoting that it is not chargeable to any duty is required. If an application is not made HMRC warn that the full amount of stamp duty will be payable.[15]

1.2.7 FA 1986 section 77 (Stamp duty relief involving acquisition of target's share capital)

Stamp duty is not payable on the transfer of shares in a company (target company) to another company if the following conditions are met: the acquiring company must acquire the whole of the issued share capital of the target company, which is effected for *bona fide* commercial reasons and not for tax avoidance purposes; the consideration consists only of the issue of shares in the acquiring company; following the acquisition the shares in the acquiring company's shares and shareholdings mirror that of the target company immediately before the acquisition.

The transfer instrument must be sent to the Birmingham Stamp Office to be stamped that no stamp duty is chargeable is required, otherwise the full amount of stamp duty will be payable.

---

[14] Being stamp duty, income tax, corporation tax or capital gains tax – see FA 1986 section 75(5)(a)

[15] www.gov.uk/guidance/stamp-duty-on-shares#reliefs-and-exemptions

1.2.8 CTA 2010 section 748 and ITA section 701 advance clearance – cancellation of tax advantages from certain transactions in securities

As a result of the Anti-Avoidance Simplification Review published on Budget Day 2008, the somewhat obscure and complicated provisions relating to tax avoidance involving transactions in securities were substantially amended by the Finance Act 2010 for transactions effected on or after 24 March 2010. These provisions also cover transactions which took place before that date and on which an income tax advantage arises after that date. Where previously any reorganisation under TCGA sections 135 and 136 involving a clearance application would be worded so as to cover clearance under the anti-avoidance provisions for transactions in securities, there are now separate provisions for transactions involving companies and individuals, with the latter substantially re-written.

ITA sections 682 to 712 set out the provisions as they relate to income tax advantages for individuals. These include the requirement that the person must be a party to the transaction,[16] the burden of proof is on HMRC[17] and there is a positive exemption[18] as discussed below. 'Transaction in securities' remains widely defined as being a transaction of whatever description relating to securities. In order for the anti-avoidance provisions to apply the following conditions must be met:

- the main purpose or one of the main purposes of the person who is a party to the transaction is to obtain an income tax advantage;
- the person obtains an income tax advantage as a result of the transaction; and
- either of the following applies:
  o the person receives relevant consideration in respect of:
    ▪ the distribution, transfer or realisation of assets of a close company,

---

[16] ITA section 684(1)(a)

[17] ITA section 695

[18] That no counteraction notice ought to be served

THE TAX SCHEDULE

- the application of assets of a close company in a discharge of liabilities, or
- the direct or indirect transfer of assets of a close company to another close company,

and he or she does not pay income tax on the consideration; OR

o the person receives relevant consideration in respect of the transaction and
- two or more close companies are concerned in the transaction, and
- the person does not pay income tax on the consideration.

The Finance Act 2016 extended the provisions to cover any income tax advantage which might arise if a shareholder takes money out of a company such that CGT would be paid rather than at the rate income tax on dividend and discussed in **Chapter 6 (Special Situations)** at paragraph 6.1.2.7.

It is difficult to envisage any of the above circumstances applying in an arm's length commercial transaction where a person sells his or her interest in a company to a third party for cash or shares, or a mixture of both.

The anti-avoidance provisions do not apply if, immediately before the securities transaction the person holds shares in the close company and there is a fundamental change of ownership of the close company,[19] namely:

- 75% of its ordinary share capital is beneficially held by an unconnected person and who has not been connected with the company within the period of two years ending on the date of the transaction, or it is held by persons none of whom are connected within that period; and
- the shares held in the close company carry an entitlement to at least 75% of the distributions it might make and at least 75% of the voting rights.

The corporation tax provisions set out in CTA 2010 sections 731 to 751 are largely unchanged from the original ICTA provisions, but with amendments to the circumstances where the cancellation of a

---

[19] ITA section 686 – excluded circumstances: fundamental change of ownership

corporation tax advantage may arise. These apply if the company is in a position to obtain or has obtained a corporation tax advantage from:

- receipt of consideration representing company's assets, future receipts or trading stock;
- receipt of consideration in connection with relevant company distribution; and
- receipt of assets of relevant company.

The anti-avoidance provisions will not apply if the company can show that the transaction meets either of the following conditions:

- it was effected for genuine commercial reasons or in the ordinary course of making or managing investments; AND
- a tax advantage was not the main object of the transactions.

HMRC have provided a list of transactions[20] which might fall within the anti-avoidance provisions in ITA 2007 and CTA 2010 as follows:

- the sale of share or securities by a seller to another company in which the seller has a substantial interest;
- the payment of a substantial dividend by the company before the sale of its shares, combined with an agreement whereby some or all of the shareholders waive their dividend rights in return for a greater share in the sale proceeds;
- the sale by a significant shareholder in a close company of part of its holding, to the trustees of a pension scheme of which the seller is a member or to the trustees of an employee benefit trust which is funded by a contribution from the company;
- the transfer by a company of its assets or business to another company having some or all of the same shareholders, followed by liquidation of the transferring company or the sale of shares in either company (i.e. a standard form of reorganisation involving a demerger using section 110 of the Insolvency Act 1986);
- receipt of capital consideration by shareholders of a company or group following a demerger or scheme of reconstruction, from the sale or liquidation of one demerged company where the same shareholders retain an interest via another company

---

[20] See HMRC CTM 36875/CT 3687a

THE TAX SCHEDULE

involved in the transaction (a not uncommon form of restructuring);

- the sale of shares under any agreement whereby the shares or the underlying assets are subsequently reacquired by the seller;
- the acquisition by an individual or company under his/her control of shares in a company with accumulated losses, at the same time as the assignment to him/her at a substantial discount of debts due by the loss-making company, followed by repayments of the assigned debts.

1.2.9 Clearances for Enterprise Investment Schemes (EIS); the Seed Enterprise Investment Scheme (SEIS); the Social Investment Tax Relief Scheme (SITR); and Venture Capital Trusts (VCT)

EIS, SEIS, SITR and VCT issues are discussed in detail in **Chapter 8 (Venture Capital Schemes)** with basic criteria for EIS, SEIS, SITR and VCT investments contained in **Appendix 1** through to **12**.

If the target satisfies the criteria as an investee company or the transaction involves raising funds for the investor companies, the company may (and should) ask HMRC under an informal advance assurance that the shares will qualify for the relevant relief and VCT investment purposes. The criteria can sometimes be quite complex, particularly for newcos which have not started to trade and those involved in research and development. Certainly the target's management will need to confirm that it understands what amounts to a qualifying trade and that the company can meet the time provisions for using the subscription monies and starting to trade if it is a start-up venture before requesting informal advance clearance.

If there is to be a reorganisation of the investee EIS company, and it falls within the provisions of ITA sections 247 to 249 (the issuing company is acquired by a newco on a share for share basis and the issuing company has a compliance certificate) and the rights of the first company roll over into newly issued shares, then clearance (which is mandatory[21]) under TCGA section 138 will apply.

---

[21] ITA section 247(1)(f)

1.2.10 Non-statutory clearances[22]

The regime introduced in 2007 relating to non-statutory business clearances by HMRC now applies to all business taxes. CAP 1 replaced COP 10 and VAT Notice 700/6 in respect of non-business persons.

Under the CAP 1 facility HMRC undertake[23] to provide a clearance in circumstances where there is material uncertainty relating to all business taxes legislation regardless of its date. For legislation which pre-dates FA 2007 the uncertainty must also relate to a commercially significant issue to the business itself, determined by reference to the scale of the business and the impact of the issue upon the business. Pre-transaction clearances will be considered where the transaction is genuinely complicated. HMRC undertake to make a clearance to business customers within 28 days regarding material uncertainty for all taxes arising within four finance acts of the introduction of any new legislation but other complex cases may take longer.[24] A clearance is a written confirmation of HMRC's view of the application of the tax law in question to a specific transaction or event. Some clearances will involve statutory and non-statutory components, in which case HMRC advise[25] that they should be submitted separately.

HMRC state that non-statutory clearance applications will not be accepted in respect of the following situations:[26]

- asking for comment or approval on tax or NIC planning arrangements;
- the application involves a minor variation of a previous application for the same client on the same transaction;
- where HMRC consider the arrangements are primarily to gain a tax or NIC advantage;
- where there is not, in fact, any uncertainty including where the point is covered by published guidance;

---

[22] HMRC Clearances Team , Alexander House 21 Victoria Avenue, Southend on Sea, Essex SS99 1BD

[23] HMRC Non-Statutory Business Clearance Guidance Manual (NBCG Manual) 1200.

[24] NSBCC Manual 1310

[25] NSBCC Manual 2100

[26] NSBCC Manual 2350

- if HMRC have opened an audit or enquiry into a transaction which is the subject of a clearance application;
- where the issue does not involve the interpretation of tax law or its application to particular circumstances, such as asset valuations and transfer pricing;
- where the question relates to the application of customs rules;
- where the question is whether a particular R&D project qualifies for research and development tax incentives;
- in relation to tax consequences of executing trust deeds and settlements and whether ITTOIA Part 5 Chapter 5 applies.[27]

SP1/94 (*Lump sum redundancy payments*) gives guidance for clearances to be given by the relevant HMRC inspector of a company if employees and directors are to be made redundant under a non-statutory redundancy scheme; or if their services are dispensed with before or following completion to confirm that lump sum payments will be taxable only under ITEPA section 401. Application for clearance should be accompanied by the scheme documentation together with the text of any intended explanation of terms to the employees.

1.3   Post-completion clearances

1.3.1   TCGA section 138A(4A) – election for TCGA section 138A treatment[28] not to apply

TCGA section 138A (discussed in detail in **Chapter** 4 **(Sale and Purchase of a Company)** paragraph 4.6.4 (Earn-outs)) provides that if an 'earn-out' right (being a right to be issued with new shares or debentures in the future) is part of the consideration in a share-for-share exchange and so long as the number and value of the shares to be acquired under that right is unascertainable and other conditions are satisfied, the earn-out right is treated as the original security. Therefore, on exercise of the right the new securities issued will be treated as the original securities under TCGA section 135. This treatment is automatic unless the shareholder elects under TCGA sub-section 138(4A) that the earn-

---

[27] Settlements: amounts treated as income of settlor

[28] Use of earn-out rights for exchange of securities

out right shall not be treated as a security of the new company.[29] If an election is made (which will be irrevocable) the earn-out right will be taxable for capital gains purposes at the time of its issue.

A company may make this election within two years from the end of the accounting period in which the right was conferred, and any other person may elect before the first anniversary of 31 January following the year of assessment in which the right was conferred[30]. Depending on an individual seller's entitlement to claim entrepreneurs' relief on the disposal of his or her interest in the target, it may be advisable to make the election. Entrepreneurs' relief is discussed in **Chapter 4 (Sale and Purchase of a Company)** at paragraph **4.3.1** and in relation to earn-outs at paragraph **4.6.4**.

1.3.2   TCGA section 162A – election for TCGA section 162 not to apply

If a person other than a company transfers a business to a company as a going concern and the criteria are met under TCGA section 162 (roll-over relief on a transfer of a business – sometimes called incorporation relief) roll-over relief of any capital gains arising on the transfer of the assets will automatically apply to the shares received by the transferor. TCGA section 162A was introduced in 2002 and allows the transferor to make an election for TCGA section 162 not to apply. A transferor who wishes to have his or her capital gains crystallised (including for the purposes of entrepreneurs' relief) will make this election or alternatively can structure the transfer so that it does not fit within the conditions in TCGA section 162.

The time for making an election under section 162A must be not later than the second anniversary of 31 January following the year of assessment in which the transfer took place[31], or if the transferor has sold the shares by the end of the tax year in which the transfer took place, he or she must make an election by the first anniversary of the 31 January following the tax year of the

---

[29] Available since April 2003

[30] TCGA section 138A(5)

[31] TCGA section 162A(3)

transfer[32]. A seller who wishes to claim entrepreneurs' relief on the disposal of shares in a company following a transfer under TCGA section 162 would need to make such an election.

1.3.3 Section 1092 CTA 2010 – advance clearance for chargeable payments

Demergers and exempt distributions are discussed in more detail in **Chapter 3 (Tax Warranties)** paragraph 3.16 and clearances for an exempt distribution is discussed in paragraph 1.2.1 above.

If within five years before any transaction there has been a demerger involving the target company and an exempt distribution was made, and thereafter a payment has or will be made which might be a chargeable payment, a charge to income tax or corporation tax will arise on the recipient.

A chargeable payment will arise if:
- a payment is made by a company concerned in an exempt distribution and it is made to a member of that company or of any other company concerned in the exempt distribution;
- the payment is made in connection with the shares of such companies, and not for genuine commercial reasons; and
- it forms part of a tax avoidance scheme.[33]

There are separate definitions for chargeable payments involving unquoted companies under CTA 2010 section 1089 based on the same principles. Therefore, before any payment is made within five years of a demerger and an exempt distribution by any company involved or connected with the demerger, an advance clearance of payments application under CTA 2010 section 1092 should be made. This can be done by a company which intends to make the payment or any company which is to make a payment and which becomes connected or ceases to be connected after making the payment. Otherwise, the chargeable payment could become chargeable to income tax or corporation tax.

Due diligence, and disclosure against the appropriate tax warranty, as to whether an exempt distribution has been made relating to a demerger and involving the target company, should

---

[32] TCGA section 162A(4)

[33] See CTA 2010 section 1088

produce the appropriate clearance documentation relating to any payment.

1.4 Transactions and Clearances with EU Dimension

It is not within the scope of this book to provide detailed information regarding mergers,[34] restructuring or transfers involving cross-border EU businesses, and where the EU Merger Directive, treaty relief, accountancy issues and anti-avoidance provisions will also to be in issue. There are also separate rules relating to transfers involving loan relationship assets or liabilities,[35] double taxation relief and European cross-border transfers of business,[36] and derivative contracts.[37] These subjects are also outside the scope of this book. Warranties set out at paragraph **3.11** of **Chapter** 3 should elicit appropriate disclosures if the target company has operations in other EU member states.

1.4.1 TCGA section 140A – transfer or division of UK business – clearance under TCGA section 140B[38]

TCGA section 140A applies where there is a transfer of a UK trade between companies, each of which is resident in a different EU member state, in exchange for shares or debentures. So long as the transfer is for genuine commercial reasons and clearance is provided by HMRC (claimed by both the transferor and transferee) it will be treated on a no gain/no loss basis. The transferee will be deemed to have taken over the assets at their historic costs and the newly issued securities to the transferor will be treated as acquired at their market value at the date of the transaction.

1.4.2 CTA 2009 section 827 – application for roll-over relief on a cross-border transfer involving intangible fixed assets

As an alternative to an application for a transfer to be treated as no gain/no loss, a claim for a postponement of a chargeable gain to be

---

[34] See TIOPA sections 118 to 122 relating to European cross-border mergers

[35] See CTA 2009 sections 421 to 476

[36] See TIOPA sections 116 & 117

[37] See CTA 2009 sections 674 to 681

[38] And whereby TCGA sections 138(2) to (5) shall have effect

THE TAX SCHEDULE

rolled over can be made under CTA 2009 section 827. The transferor company must be UK-resident and the transfer must be in respect of all or part of a business carried on outside the UK through a permanent establishment, together with all the company's assets used in the trade (other than cash). The transferred assets must include intangible fixed assets which are chargeable in the hands of the transferor at the time of the transfer. The transferee company must be non-UK resident and the consideration must be wholly in the form of shares or shares and loan stock issued by the transferred company to the transferor and represent 25% or more of the ordinary share capital of the non-UK company.

An application by the UK transferor company must be made before the transfer and must satisfy the test that the transfer is for genuine commercial reasons and not for avoiding corporation tax, capital gains tax or income tax. The relief effectively allows any gain on the intangible fixed assets transferred to be rolled over against the base cost of the shares in the non-UK company. It can be clawed back on the disposal of securities in the non-UK company and on any subsequent realisation of the intangible fixed assets within six years.

1.4.3 TCGA section 140C – transfer or division of non-UK business – clearance under TCGA section 140D

This provision allows a UK resident company to transfer part of a business which is established in an EU member state other than the UK, to a company or companies, one of which is resident in an EU member state other than the UK, in exchange wholly or partly for the issue of shares or debentures in the transferee. A claim for an anti-avoidance clearance must be made by the transferor. The assets transferred must represent the whole of the assets used in the business or part-business other than cash. The chargeable gains accruing to the transferor on the transfer must exceed the accrued aggregate allowable losses. This provision also applies if the business transferred is carried on in an EU member state other than the UK through a permanent establishment. There are separate provisions if a transparent entity is involved.[39]

1.4.4 Sections 140E and 140F TCGA – merger leaving assets within or outside UK tax charge – clearances under TCGA section 138

These provisions apply where a *Societas Europaea* (SE) or a *Societas Cooperativa Europaea* (SCE) is formed by the merger of two or more companies or cooperative societies effected by the transfer by one or more companies of all their assets and liabilities to a single existing company or by the transfer of all their assets and liabilities to a single new company (other than an SE or an SCE) in exchange for the issue by the transferee to each person holding shares in or debentures of a transferor of shares or debentures. Conditions include each merging company being resident in a member EU state but not all resident in the same state. Where section 140E applies (a merger leaving assets with UK tax charge) qualifying transferred assets shall be treated for corporation tax on chargeable gains as if acquired by the transferee on a no gain/no loss basis. Where section 140F applies (assets outside a UK tax charge) any allowable losses accruing to the UK resident transferor shall be set off against accrued chargeable gains.

1.5 Employee Share Scheme Matters

If the target company operates any HMRC-approved employee incentive plan, discussed in greater depth in **Chapter 7 (Share Scheme Issues),** as from 6 April 2014 companies have been required to register and self-certify and provide annual declarations online which would include changes in control of a company and falling outside the scheme's legislative requirements.

If the deal involves a listed company (which for these purposes would, at the time of writing, include trading on AIM) the procedure for protecting the target's option holders (regardless of whether the schemes are HMRC-approved or not) is complex, often with voluminous documentation. Generally, the tax advisors should attend to the rights of option holders early on in the

---

[39] TCGA section 140I, and 'transparent entity' is defined in TCGA section 140L(1)(c)

transaction in order not to interfere with completion if problems come to light relating to the scheme in question (see some examples discussed in **Chapter 7**, paragraph 7.1).

1.6 Buyer's Issues

The fundamental rationale for any buyer acquiring a company or business is the intention that the target will produce a return on the investment and enhance the buyer's future earnings. The reasons for choosing the target may include any of the following:

- to prevent the competition acquiring the target;
- to expand the buyer's business including by entering a new business area or new geographical location;
- there are strong synergies between the target and the buyer or buyer's group;
- the buyer regards the target's break-up value as being attractive;
- there are turnaround opportunities particularly if the target is loss-making; or
- a combination of the above.

A corporate buyer will wish to avoid dilution of its earnings, particularly if its shares are publicly held – tax issues relating to a target company (including but not limited to its profitability) will have a bearing on this issue. As discussed elsewhere, the greatest protection against any unexpected tax liability in the target is comprehensive due diligence by the buyer and an appropriate consideration price which reflects any risks. However, as an alternative, there are very few tax issues which can arise from acquiring a transferred business and accordingly no tax indemnity from the seller will be necessary in these transactions.

The buyer's tax advisor should be told of the buyer's post-completion plans for the target to ensure that they will not interfere with the buyer's rights to sue the seller for any pre-completion tax liability. This could occur if there is a hive-up of the business of the target company following completion which could interfere with carried forward trading losses and corporation tax relief relating to employment-related securities, or if there are changes which might be treated as a fundamental change in the business. As post-completion reorganisation of some kind is likely in most transactions, it would be reasonable for the seller's tax indemnity to limit the seller's liability which might be connected with post-completion actions of the target company or the buyer. However, from a seller's perspective if the terms of the consideration include an earn-out dependent on post-completion events, it will be equally important that any post-completion reorganisation cannot interfere with the possibility of the earn-out being paid.

The purpose of the tax indemnity in the sale and purchase of a company, as well as protecting the buyer from any undisclosed tax liabilities of the target, is also to draw a line which allocates responsibilities for the target's tax affairs – usually on a pre- and post-completion basis if there are to be completion accounts. If the transaction is an 'accounts only' deal nothing should be transacted outside the ordinary course of business after the accounts date, which begs the question what is outside the ordinary course of business. This issue is often fudged, with a list provided as to what is not in the ordinary course (such as any payment of dividends and a sale of a capital asset) but rarely is there a statement of what might represent the ordinary course of business of the target. A reasonable definition which is often contained within the body of the SPA would be 'the business of *[refer to the business set out in the accounts or heads of terms]* as carried on at Completion' followed by what will be outside the ordinary course of business.

If the target's management will be staying with the target company and continues, at least initially, to be responsible for its day-to-day administration including in respect of its tax affairs, at the very least the buyer's due diligence team should have formed some view of its capabilities and competence during due diligence, and may be one of the factors behind the acquisition.

A buyer should require the following standard protections and rights under the tax schedule for the purchase of a company:

- full protection from any tax liability of the target arising pre-completion save as provided for in the target's most recent accounts or any completion accounts;

- full protection from any tax liability of the target arising outside the ordinary course of business from the accounts date up to completion if there are to be no completion accounts;
- full protection for costs and expenses which may arise on the target and the buyer if the seller wishes to dispute or appeal a tax assessment of the HMRC arising in respect of a pre-completion period – the parties may wish to argue whether this extends to the buyer's internal management time and if so, the basis of computing these costs;
- an unfettered right to sue under the tax indemnity for any pre-completion tax liability of the target so long as HMRC have a right to make an assessment against the target under FA 1998 Schedule 18 paragraph 46 ;[40]
- an absolute right to sue the sellers under the tax indemnity in circumstances where any tax liability of the target arises from deliberate error, fraud or tax evasion pre-completion, not limited by time except as provided for under statute – however, this would need to be subject to a high level of proof of such conduct;
- an ultimate right to have the conduct of any tax claim by a tax authority subject to reasonable input by the seller;
- limits on the seller's ability to appeal an assessment or determination on the target when a dispute with a tax authority would disrupt the target's business or relationship with the tax authority or where on the balance of probabilities there is no likelihood of an appeal being successful.

1.7 Seller's Issues

The seller may wish to dispose of its investment in the target company or business in any of the following circumstances:

- the shareholders who also manage the company want to retire;
- shareholders wish to realise capital investment gains;
- there is a shareholders' dispute;
- the management of the target wishes to buy out the shareholders;
- the target needs new funding;

---

[40] The time limit being not more than four years after the end of the accounting period to which the assessment relates

- the target is loss-making and there aren't sufficient internal financial resources or available outside funding to effect a recovery;
- there is no synergy between the target and the rest of the seller's group;
- the seller needs to realise cash;
- a difficult competitive environment necessitates a merger or stronger parent for the target with sufficient financial resources;
- it may be a liquidator's sale;[41]
- the venture capitalist shareholders want to realise their investments.

For a corporate seller, corporation tax on any chargeable gain should not arise if substantial shareholding relief is available.[42] Individual sellers may be entitled to entrepreneurs' relief so long as the target company or business satisfies the various requirements[43] and if so, capital gains tax of 10% will be payable so long as the gains are within the shareholder's lifetime limit of £10 million.[44]

The main pitfalls for any seller of a competently managed and profitable company which has a good tax compliance record will arise if the accounts or completion accounts do not accurately provide for tax liabilities at the relevant date or if an expected tax relief which the seller has warranted does not become fully available. A seller should require joint if not full responsibility of preparing the completion accounts, and provisions for revisiting the calculations in the event of any disagreement with the buyer (and not merely restricted to obvious error in their preparation) and the tax advisor will need to provide input into the completion accounts schedule to cover these issues.

If a management buy-out of a company is involved, the seller is justified in resisting any demand to provide a tax indemnity, although the buyer's bank or other financier may initially not

---

[41] Discussed further in **Chapter 6 (Special Situations)**

[42] See **Chapter 9 (Group Issues)** at paragraph **Error! Reference source not found.**

[43] See **Chapter** 0 paragraph **4.3.1** for details of entrepreneurs' relief for shares and **Appx 8**

[44] Effective for disposals made on or after 6 April 2011

agree to this. However, it is standard for exiting venture capitalists to refuse to provide tax indemnities and sellers in any management buy-out should take a similar strong position as a condition of agreeing to the deal. If the financing entity has a charge on the target or the buyers following completion, the seller can legitimately argue that the bank should have carried out a requisite amount of due diligence on the MBO team and the target. These are issues for the seller's financial and corporate advisors to provide guidance on at the heads of terms stage (while taking a robust stance in favour of the sellers). If a tax indemnity is required it should be extremely limited in time (no more than two years) and in substance, and not covering anything which the MBO team had knowledge of or should have had knowledge of.

In standard transactions involving the sale of a company a seller will want the following provisions in the tax schedule:

- limitations of its liabilities for the target's tax relating to time reflecting HMRC's ability to make an assessment under FA 1998 Schedule 18 paragraph 46[45] and limitations relating to quantum – in practice this is usually never greater than the consideration received;
- control and conduct relating to the tax affairs of the target company before completion including the preparation of accounts and filing of tax returns following completion if the tax indemnity attaches to them;
- rights to be informed, comment, dispute and appeal any tax assessment or determination by a tax authority relating to the target company's pre-completion tax affairs covered by the tax indemnity – whether such rights should be unfettered will be a negotiation point with the buyer;
- full protection against any tax liability which falls on the seller and arises from the actions or inactions of the target or the buyer following completion including any post-completion restructuring involving the target;
- limitations for any tax liability of the target which the parties have agreed will be paid by the target or the buyer following

[45] Being not more than four years after the end of the accounting period to which an assessment relates

completion, usually provided for in the last accounts of the target or any completion accounts, but also any other specific liabilities as agreed.

1.8 Negotiating the Tax Schedule

1.8.1 Required background information

Strength in any negotiation is acquired through knowledge of the subject matter. It is preferable that the tax advisor is involved in the transactional process at the earliest opportunity but this is often not the case, with that person being brought in only at the drafting stages of the sale and purchase agreement. The first step for the tax advisor, regardless of which party he or she is acting for, is to organise copies of the following documents:

- the heads of terms and deal sheet and any related correspondence;
- the report and accounts of the target company for the previous four years if available;
- details of any employee share and incentive schemes of the target and copies of any rules and related documentation;
- any available due diligence report prepared on the target;
- a printout of background information on the target from its website or available elsewhere on the internet; and
- the basic package of information on the target available at Companies House including:
  - date of incorporation;
  - list of directors;
  - filing history;
  - charges register; and
  - if a private company, the shareholders' register.

Before drafting the tax warranties and the tax indemnity and before any negotiations with the other side the tax advisors for each party should compile specific information on the target and the target's group including the following:

- the nature of its businesses and trading operations;
- details of its share capital;
- details of its territories of operations and its subsidiaries (relevant for overseas tax issues);
- the approximate number of both UK and non-UK employees;

- its sales, profits and/or losses, and dividend history (preferably covering the last previous four years);
- the most recent management accounts;
- information on the assets and liabilities, gearing and working capital as at the most recent financial year end;
- what rate of tax the target has been paying, and details of any deferred taxation, if any;
- the amount of any losses – past or ongoing;
- whether there are outstanding share options and if so the number of shares currently under option and the terms of exercise; and
- whether any clearances have been made or may be required.

By understanding the target's operations, the tax advisors should be able to agree certain issues relating to the tax warranties and the tax indemnity without prolonged and unnecessary arguments.

Similarly, basic information on the buyer should also be compiled (again, regardless of whether you are acting for the buyer or the seller) including most of the following if available:

- the nature of its business and recent accounts information;
- whether it has employee share schemes and whether roll-over options can be issued to employees and officers staying with the target;
- its cash resources and gearing;
- details of its share capital;
- its acquisition history;
- what post-completion reorganisation involving the target it intends to carry out.

No two deals will be identical and the requirements for tax warranties and the tax indemnity will differ substantially depending on the nature of the target's business, operations and other circumstances and the commercial terms of the deal. Issues arising when the target is a stand-alone company with only UK operations and a limited track record and, say, currently loss-making, will be different from those which may arise if the target has internationally-based subsidiaries, and a considerable track record (either profitable or loss-making) or if the target company is leaving a group or there are other group issues involved.

1.8.2 The purpose of the tax schedule

The heads of terms are likely to require that the seller provides a *'standard set of tax warranties and a tax indemnity'* and it will be up to the tax advisors to agree what is standard. In the author's view, there is no such thing as a 'standard' tax deed, although there should be little argument that the tax indemnity should set out which tax liabilities of the target's should be for the account of the seller following completion of a transaction, and how and when the seller's liabilities cease and the buyer takes on the risk and rewards from acquiring the target.

It is trite to argue that a further purpose of the tax schedule is to be fair to both parties – an uneasy concept when dealing with a commercial transaction and probably of little use to either party to the transaction. From a seller's perspective a useful analogy is the *caveat emptor* principle, with the argument that it should be up to the buyer to carry out thorough and proper due diligence before completion of the transaction, and that only in circumstances where deliberate error or fraud is involved should there be any comeback on the seller for any tax liability of the target. In a seller's market or a locked-box transaction[46] the seller's argument may prevail but often not in other circumstances, particularly when there is third party funding of the acquisition by the buyer. Banks will want wide protection for their client's investment.

The buyer's advisors may argue that something may not be market practice and that any reasonable seller should be willing to provide a standard tax indemnity protecting the buyer from any pre-completion tax liabilities of the target – the argument being that if the seller has provided full tax warranties on which the buyer will be relying, why should the seller not be willing to back up those warranties with a tax indemnity.

The major tax-related risk for the buyer when acquiring a company is past incorrect accounting for tax and reporting failures before completion (whether due to a mistake, bad judgement or deliberate error on the part of the seller or the target company's management) and which will be required to be put right post-

---

[46] See **Chapter 6 (Special Situations)** at paragraph 6.2

completion when under the new ownership of the buyer. Ideally, during a comprehensive due diligence and disclosure process such errors will have come to light, the parties will be aware of the possible tax liabilities and quantum, and provisions should be made to reflect them, either in a reduced purchase price or a retention, as well as agreement relating to post-completion conduct to sort out the problem. If this is the case, and the consideration has been adjusted, then the seller's liability should be limited accordingly with a specific carve-out for the liability in question. If warranties and a tax indemnity have been refused by the seller, the purchase price should reflect the risk which the buyer is taking on.

1.8.3   Clarity in the tax schedule

The four essentials features of a well-drafted tax schedule are as follows:

- the provisions should clearly reflect the commercial agreement reached between the buyer and the seller;
- clarity in all respects such that the commercial parties understand the extent of and possible repercussions arising from all the provisions;
- there must be no conflict with the provisions in the main body of the sale and purchase agreement and its other schedules including those dealing with limitations, completion, post-completion conduct, and the completion accounts (if relevant); and
- the possibility of future litigation is kept to a minimum.

Anything which is not set out in clear English or is obscure and cannot be understood by the signatories of the tax schedule should be rejected, regardless of how often they may be included in standard documentation or related text books. Further tests for including or rejecting a provision in the tax schedule which might be helpful in the drafting process are as follows:

- Does the tax advisor understand precisely what tax issue underlies the provision in question?
- Will the client fully understand, now and in the future, what the provision covers?

- Has the client properly considered whether a claim could arise under the provision?
- Would a judge be able to understand fully what the provision means if litigation arises or is the wording so vague or conceptually inarticulate that it is meaningless for the purposes of the litigation?

For example:

- How can an *'omission'* be included in the definition of *'event'* which in itself requires an action of some sort?
- What pre-completion tax issues could arise and what circumstances can satisfy the so-called *'combined events'* clause, often included under the following wording:

  'an event occurring before completion outside the ordinary course of business and an event occurring after completion inside the ordinary course of business',

  and could the finance director of the target company explain and undertake to the sellers that no claim by the buyer could arise under such a provision?
- What tax liability can arise on the target company in respect of the pre-completion period for which it is not primarily liable (i.e. a *'secondary'* tax liability) if it is not a member of a group?
- What actions or events arising in the ordinary course of business of the target company post-completion could trigger a pre-completion tax liability, and if there are any why should the seller be liable?

There are often provisions in tax schedules which are meant to cover any unexpected tax liability arising out of unknown factors and events which might have a bearing on the target company (either for the benefit of the seller or the buyer, whatever they might be and regardless of how unlikely they are to arise). These should be refused point blank by the affected party's tax advisor. The better course is to provide in plain English for the specific issue which concerns the relevant tax advisor.

In a recent case heard in the High Court, involving the provisions of tax deeds in *Teeside Power Holdings Limited*[47] (an acquisition

---

[47] *Teeside Power Holdings Limited* [2012] EWHC 33

involving a consideration price in the region of £340 million), the issue involved post-completion payments by the buyer to the seller relating to repayments of tax to the target by HMRC and whether interest paid by HMRC on the repayment was to be included in the refund to the seller. Even though the definition of Tax included *'interest connected therewith'* the judge declined to include the interest in the definition of Refund referred to in the tax deed – on the grounds that the definition, in the view of the judge, clearly referred to interest paid by the company as opposed to interest paid by HMRC[48] and who in part based his argument on what the parties did or did not intend a Refund to include. Regardless of whether the judge was correct in his conclusions regarding tax schedules and his findings, the case is a salutary lesson that all definitions must be cross-checked with specific provisions, and the commercial intentions of the parties must be clearly set out in the tax schedule with no leeway for one of the parties to rely on conflicting provisions to defeat a claim.

1.8.4   Negotiating tactics

In an ideal transaction, before drafting or marking up the tax schedule the tax advisor should seek full instructions from the client, although in practice this can be difficult as potential tax issues can take second place to more immediate commercial issues in the sale and purchase agreement and the due diligence process. Also, when dealing with owners of small and medium sized enterprises who may not have accounting and financial experience, they will assume that their advisors will volunteer the appropriate advice as it arises. This goes without saying, but nevertheless a tax advisor cannot do this in a vacuum. The preferred course is for the tax advisors to agree a reasonable and balanced tax schedule, and seek instructions on major disputes, rather than getting stuck on less material issues at the initial stages of the negotiation process.

The spectrum for taking a negotiating stance is broad and includes the following:

---

[48] At paragraph 59

- agree the other side's position in its entirety – it is not unknown for a client to tell its tax advisor that he or she should negotiate the tax schedule as he or she thinks fit but that the client will eventually agree the other side's requirements in their entirety (however unwise this might seem to be);
- agree the other side's position so long as it is reasonable subject to taking client's instructions;
- seek a compromise to the issue at stake and seek to substitute unreasonable provisions with more reasonable wording;
- strenuously argue against any compromise, subject to client's instructions and seek to win the point;
- refuse to agree any further compromise and explain the underlying issues to the client;
- advise your corporate colleagues and the client to pull out of the transaction.

Needless to say, the last two options are drastic and could lead to grief from your client and other colleagues on the transaction, in view of the underlying assumptions that the clients wish to do the deal. The tax advisors' job is to negotiate the tax schedule not wreck the transaction.

A tax advisor will have failed in the negotiating process if negotiations break down due to trivial issues or they become unduly prolonged and expensive. In the author's view, a major role of the tax advisors is to ensure that a future claim under the tax schedule does not arise – this should be in the forefront of their minds throughout the negotiating process. Serious tax-related issues which come to light during due diligence require robust advice and ideally they should be covered and signed off by the client in email correspondence or at least documented in attendance notes. Often the client wants the deal done as quickly as possible and in these circumstances a diligent tax advisor must provide the requisite health warning to limit any future comeback if there is a dispute between the parties.

A word of warning: when potential tax issues come to light during the course of a transaction the tax advisor must resist any pressure from bullying corporate colleagues who want to let the matter drop or fudge the issue with dubious legal practices. Proposals can range from be asked to have documents post-dated, being less than frank with a tax authority, failing to notify the client's other advisors of the issue at stake, and failing to provide robust advice to the client as to what it will be required to do to fix properly the problem.

1.8.5 No conflict with the SPA

The tax schedule is subsidiary to the sale and purchase agreement and should not conflict with the provisions in the body of the SPA and its other schedules. The tax schedule should never be agreed until the commercial issues in the sale and purchase agreement have been fully agreed and it is in its final draft, regardless of any pressure to do otherwise.

Except in exceptional circumstances, the following provisions should be the same for the tax schedule and the rest of the SPA:

- the maximum liability of the seller under all claims;
- whether there can be recovery from a third party and if so on what terms;
- if there are completion accounts, whether any credit will be given to the seller for any overprovisions for tax and any tax relief if a claim arises – this issue will be partly determined by the constituents of the consideration (but see paragraph 10.11 in **Chapter 10** regarding overprovisions);
- what amounts to the ordinary course of business or trade of the target; and
- interest provisions for late payments.

Due to the nature of procedures under UK tax statute and the likelihood in most cases that a claim under the tax schedule will be triggered by an enquiry from HMRC, the tax schedule should have separate and discrete provisions relating to the following issues:

- time limits for bringing a claim under the tax schedule mirroring time limits of a tax authority to bring an enquiry, or raise an assessment or determination against the target (both ordinarily and in exceptional circumstances).[49] See also **Appendix 6**;

---

[49] See FA 1998 Schedule 18 paragraphs 24, 36 and 46

- procedure for the buyer to notify the seller of any possible tax claim and the rights of the seller relating to conduct of disputes and making an appeal;
- post-completion responsibilities relating to the target's tax affairs for the accounting period in which completion falls;
- whether or not any *de minimis* shall apply to a claim under the tax schedule.

Again, even though it may be argued that a 'standard' tax schedule provides for common provisions in one particular party's favour (usually the buyer's), a good tax advisor should not accept them on that argument alone and should be prepared to reject unreasonable provisions, however standard in market practice it is purported that they are.

1.9 Completion Issues

The tax indemnity and tax warranties should be self-contained, in a schedule which forms part of the SPA. That way, there is one less document which needs signatures, and it also helps to ensure that the tax advisors are party to any late changes being made to the sale and purchase agreement which may have affected the tax schedule. If the tax schedule is a separate document (usually in the form of a deed) all boiler plate clauses need careful checking to ensure they mirror the wording in the SPA.

The tax advisors must review the provisions of the final versions of the disclosure letter and the schedule for any completion accounts or working capital statement, which in practice are often the last documents agreed. Last minute changes to them may require further amendments to the tax schedule and, therefore, ideally the tax advisors should be present at the final pre-completion meeting when the sale and purchase agreement is agreed.

1.9.1 Option and share scheme matters[50]

It will be important to have any exercise of options unconditionally effected before the day of completion to preserve any corporation tax relief relating to employment-related

---

[50] See **Chapter 7 (Share Scheme Issues)** for discussion of further issues

securities[51]. If that relief is not an issue then options should be capable of being exercised on the completion date. However, the relevant documentation should be signed by the option holders before completion with agreement from the option holders that they be dated on or immediately prior to completion under powers of attorney provided to the target's directors. Any cashless exercise of options may technically fall within the disguised remuneration rules and, therefore, should be avoided, although HMRC Manuals[52] appear to give their blessing to cashless exercise (meaning that enough shares are sold on exercise to cover income tax and NIC arising on the exercise) – however, HMRC practice can change without notice so should never be completely relied upon.

Documents for execution at completion relating to share options (on the assumption that corporation tax relief will be an issue) will include:

- powers of attorney enabling directors of the target to date any documents relating to the exercise of share options and sign the sale and purchase agreement and accept all terms on behalf of the option holder-come-shareholders;
- deeds of exercise of share options signed by option holders before completion which should include the terms of payment by option holders of the exercise price and any related tax, with instructions to deduct under PAYE if the shares are readily convertible assets;[53]
- if roll-over options are to be granted to employees and officers of the target a copy of the buyer's board minutes authorising their issue and ideally the relevant documentation effecting their grant or, otherwise, some form of binding commitment by the buyer;
- if the buyer does not have an option scheme in place at completion enabling it to grant roll-over options, but it intends to put an option scheme in place, the notice of exercise of the target's share options should contain terms and

---

[51] See **Chapter 7** paragraph 7.2

[52] See ESSU 41105 and ERSM 20410

[53] See the **Glossary** for the definition

conditions that new options will be granted by the buyer or a member of its group following completion and which should be executed as a deed by the option holders, the target and the buyer to ensure legal enforceability;

- a copy of the target's shareholders' register as at a date before completion which includes the names of the option holders who have exercised their options and received the target's shares if corporation tax relief is relevant, and a copy of the relevant board minutes;

- indemnities given to the target by option holders relating to any income tax and related PAYE arising on the exercise of the options and the issue of the target's shares, and related consideration shares or securities to be issued under the terms of the SPA;

- relevant directions that the target and any relevant subsidiary company which may be the employer within the target group is reimbursed for the exercise prices and tax deductible under PAYE on the exercise of share options either directly from payments made by the option holders (including their salaries) or as deductions from cash consideration paid by the buyer.

1.9.2   Partly-paid shares

All partly-paid shares on the target's shareholder register should be fully paid for and the receipts banked by the target company before entering into the sale and purchase agreement, and not merely credited as being paid out of the proceeds of their sale at completion. Otherwise, a tax charge could arise if HMRC argues that a deemed loan has been waived.

1.10 Post-completion Matters

The transactional process does not stop at completion and the tax advisors should provide their clients with a list of post-completion issues requiring action by either the target or the buyer.

1.10.1 Approved share schemes

If the target operated approved employee share schemes, either the target or the buyer must report online the reportable event that the target is now under the control of the buyer.

1.10.2 Roll-over options

If the buyer is offering roll-over options under an established scheme already in place, HMRC must be provided with full details of the terms of the new options if this has not been done before completion. If the buyer has no such scheme then it needs to adopt a relevant scheme (normally within six months of change of control of the target for UK schemes) and, if necessary, apply for HMRC approval of the relevant rules and terms of the roll-over options (see **Chapter 7 (Share Scheme Issues)** for the relevant procedure). If the options in question (either in the target or in respect of roll-over options) are unapproved options no approval by HMRC is needed.

1.10.3 Reporting for matters relating to options and shares

There are annual online reporting requirements for both the target and the buyer by 6 July following the tax year in which the transaction took place, in respect of reportable events for shares and other forms of securities which were obtained by reason of employment, and to be filed with the Employees Share Schemes Unit at HMRC. The main reportable events will arise in respect of the following:

- options over shares in the target company were exercised by employees;
- options and shares are issued to employees and officers of the target company;
- a notional loan relating to securities acquired for less than market value is discharged.

1.10.4 VAT degrouping issues

If the target is leaving a VAT group on completion, HMRC must be notified within 30 days of the change of its ownership.[54] Removal from a VAT group does not automatically apply on the date of change of control. Therefore, the notice should request removal on the completion date to which, ordinarily, HMRC are likely to agree. However, it is preferable that the representative member of the target's VAT group or the buyer notifies HMRC in advance of the change of control and requests removal from the

---

[54] Regulation 5(2) SI 1995/2518 (Value Added Tax Regulations 1995)

completion date. The notification should be made using forms VAT 50 and 51.

1.10.5 Degrouping and withdrawal of stamp duty land tax relief (SDLT)

If stamp duty land tax relief was given under FA 2003 Schedule 7 in respect of intra-group transfers of UK land and property, and there has been a degrouping whereby some or all of the relief will be clawed back (which essentially will arise within three years of the relief having been granted), notification of the relevant event must be made in writing to the relevant HMRC office (at the time of writing, the Birmingham Stamp Office) within 30 days. The form of notification includes a letter and self assessment of the tax due together with a cheque for the relevant amount.

1.10.6 Post-Completion Clearances

These are discussed at paragraph **1.3** above and primarily concern the seller.

2 DUE DILIGENCE

2.1 Overview

This chapter provides a brief overview of tax issues arising out of the due diligence process, which all too frequently in transactions is rather cursory. Unless stated otherwise, there is an assumption throughout that the buyer is a corporate and that the target is a company. Paragraph **2.6** covers brief details of issues relating to the sale and purchase of a business as does **Chapter 5**. In view of the significance of the due diligence in commercial transactions, persons involved in the process should also refer to specialist publications on the subject.[1]

Due diligence is primarily carried out by accountants, and it rarely if ever involves the tax advisor dealing with tax issues in negotiating the tax schedule. However, the first thing a tax advisor should ask for when beginning the process of drafting and negotiating the tax schedule is sight of any due diligence report on the target. If there is none, the representative for the buyer should proceed with caution, on the assumption that the buyer may be lacking in diligence!

Ideally, the due diligence process involved in the sale and purchase of a company should include a written due diligence report by professional advisors independent of the party commissioning it (most commonly the buyer), and further information about the target provided by the seller during the disclosure process to be summarised in the disclosure letter. In standard transactions the due diligence process should provide the basis for setting and agreeing the purchase price, and supplying both the buyer and any lender with essential information on the target. The seller will want to ensure that the best offer is received for the sale and a positive sign-off based on information compiled during the due diligence should, in theory, underpin the seller's valuation and asking price for the target. The directors of the buyer will need to produce objective evidence that they have made

---

[1] see *Tax Due Diligence*, by Matthew Peppitt (Spiramus Press)

proper enquiries into the target's business and affairs and that the proposed purchase price is justifiable.

It is best practice is for the buyer to commission a due diligence report unless the buyer is fully informed about the target – this is only likely if the transaction is a management buy-out. Additionally, the seller will be asked to provide a full set of warranties against which it will make disclosures as necessary. The seller, in turn, will be able to limit its liability in respect of any warranty claims where it has made sufficient disclosure against a particular warranty. The disclosures will enable the buyer to identify the nature of potential problems although, depending on the basis of the purchase price, the seller is likely to remain liable for tax liabilities of the target under the tax indemnity. However, in certain circumstances, including management buy-outs, a sale by an administrator or a venture capitalist or merely when the seller is in the stronger bargaining position, it may refuse to provide comprehensive warranties and/or a tax indemnity. In these circumstances in-depth due diligence by the buyer is extremely important.

The sellers should be aware of the provisions in FSMA section 397 (*Misleading statements and practices*), whereby there are financial penalties and imprisonment if a person makes misleading, false or deceptive statements or conceals material facts (recklessly or dishonestly) involving the entering into a relevant agreement under the act. This would be relevant if the target company or group is listed or its shares are dealt or are to be dealt on a market.

The due diligence process may be started by the seller providing a report compiled by independent advisors to be issued to potential buyers. This is standard (but need not be restricted to) in an auction or locked-box transactions (see **Chapter 6 (Special Situations)** – paragraphs **6.2** and **6.3** for more detailed information). In any event the process is likely to extend over a period (often protracted) beginning soon after the heads of terms stage and ending just before completion with the compilation and agreement of the disclosure letter. Invariably, once the heads of terms have been agreed the parties set an unreasonably short time table for completing the transaction.

2.2   The Buyer's Tax Due Diligence Report

The role of the buyer's advisors in compiling the due diligence report (DD Report) requires accuracy in information-gathering, with their brief being the consideration of potential pitfalls and essential weaknesses of the target, making conclusions about the fact-finding and providing written advice regarding the necessary remedial actions, some of which may relate to tax issues.

The report should represent an independent objective review (regardless of the advisors having knowledge of the target or otherwise) and should cover the following tax issues:

- past tax compliance and practice including a review of self-assessment documentation and tax computations;
- details of any HMRC audits, correspondence and investigations;
- overseas tax issues reviewed by local tax advisors;
- the target's practice and compliance for PAYE and VAT;
- tax risks relating to pre-completion periods;
- tax issues for the target going forward including recommended remedial actions;
- a summary of issues needing specific reference under both the tax warranties (to elicit further disclosure) and for protection under the tax indemnity.

In addition, the report should meet, if relevant, compliance obligations under FSMA and any listing authority, and provide all the information which may be required by the buyer's bankers involved in the funding of the acquisition.

The report should include information and advice relating to the following:

- the target's internal systems and procedures relating to tax and tax compliance, their adequacy or otherwise;
- the expertise and qualification of the target's tax personnel;
- any perceived problems between the target and the relevant tax authorities;
- any cross-border tax issues which might arise following completion;

- full analysis of tax reliefs which may or should be available at completion, their scope and potential, and whether or how they might be withdrawn following completion;
- full details of any deferred tax of the target and any crystallisation events;
- the likely tax rate of the target following completion;
- specific assessments of the target's PAYE and VAT compliance.

Depending on whether, following completion, the target will operate as a stand-alone operation within the buyer's group or as an integral part of the buyer's group, there may or may not be savings opportunities relating to its tax function following completion. In any event a managerial issue is likely to involve integration of the target's tax function in some manner within the new group.

It would be unusual for a report to provide an opinion on the proposed purchase price but it should ensure that the risks and liabilities are clearly highlighted as well as their quantum and whether they are significant enough to require the buyer to reconsider the purchase price and the structure of the deal.

Reading a due diligence report on a company together with its past report and accounts is an easy way to learn about its business, strengths and weaknesses and is required reading for the advisor dealing with negotiation the tax schedule.

2.3   The Seller's Tax Due Diligence Report

If a report is carried out on behalf of the seller its purpose is to provide potential buyers with a reasonably comprehensive review of the target's tax record. It should:

- seek to confirm that the target's tax compliance has been adequate, that its tax affairs are in order, and that no remedial actions are required;
- if the transaction is an auction sale, provide an up-to-date balance sheet and profit and loss account which the seller can warrant is true and comprehensive and can be relied upon;
- meet compliance obligations under FSMA and for any listing authority (if the target is listed); and
- provide all the information normally sought by the buyer's bankers.

The author of the seller's report may also:

- identify potential issues which could arise on the disposal of the target, both in respect of other group companies (if relevant) and in respect of the seller's liabilities under the tax schedule and the sale and purchase agreement; and
- provide advice to the seller relating to any pre-transactional restructuring which may be required, particularly as it relates to group tax issues;

but these are matters of private interest to the seller and should not be part of the report issued to potential buyers.

If the seller's report advises that remedial action is required it would be best effected before completion. If this is not possible, then the tax advisors should negotiate, as part of agreeing the tax schedule, post-completion conduct issues to ensure that the proper action is taken by the relevant party, with risk apportionment, conduct and costs agreed accordingly. As the target will be under the control of the buyer following completion, the buyer and target may need the assistance of the seller's management and it will be in the seller's interest that the issue is properly resolved with the relevant tax authority as a matter of priority, particularly if there has been a retention of the purchase price pending resolution of the issue.

2.4   The Disclosure Process

There are two stages:

- the buyer and seller negotiate the warranties; and then
- the seller discloses against those warranties.

The sale and purchase agreement will usually provide for the seller to be protected against claims for breach of warranty by making disclosures against them. If there are no warranties or they are not sufficiently comprehensive, this will result in limited disclosure and as a fact-finding exercise the disclosure process will have limited value for the buyer. This will be the buyer's argument for asking for a comprehensive set of warranties. However, a seller is entitled to argue that a responsible buyer should carry out adequate and comprehensive due diligence and that tax warranties should be specific to the target's affairs and limited in number and time.

It is not uncommon for a buyer's lawyer to ask for tax warranties for the previous six years – an onerous time-consuming obligation for the seller save where there are only a few warranties. The seller should refuse this request and offer a compromise of warranties for the previous four tax years save for specific warranties relating to concerns arising from the due diligence. The four year period mirrors the four year period for HMRC to make assessments under TMA section 34 and paragraph 46 FA 1998 Schedule 18 (see also **Appendix 6 – Time Limits for Assessments and Claims**).

The disclosure process can be painful for both the commercial parties and their advisors, and is often hotly negotiated up to the point of completion. Specific issues identified in the buyer's due diligence report should form the basis of disclosure questions put to the seller which will be an ongoing process. The seller will be expected to respond quickly.

In most transactions the seller is expected to provide factual information on the target accompanied by relevant evidence accumulated into numerous bundles which passes to the buyer at completion. The disclosures and further requests to responses, and responses relating to tax matters should be reviewed, for both the seller and the buyer, by the persons who will be negotiating the tax schedule.

Depending on the size of the target and the value of the transaction there may or may not be a data room, where the seller provides copy documentation relating to the target which the buyer is entitled to investigate as part of the general due diligence process. Rules and reasonableness relating to the data room vary, with the seller usually dictating when the room will be available to the buyer, the hours of attendance, what documents will be provided, whether documents can be copied, and when it will close finally to further visits. Strict time limits should be imposed to ensure that the transaction is completed within a timetable and not become unduly protracted.

Virtual data rooms, which are now standard for international transactions involving multi-jurisdictional operations, are useful for the parties involved, allowing the buyer quick access to documents without physically having to visit a data room and enabling the seller to add data progressively. If the virtual data room is properly organised, the seller can keep better control on which party views which documents throughout the process. Uploading the documentation should take no longer than photocopying them for a physical data room and updating the information for viewing should be faster. The main problem is security and confidentiality which cannot be fully protected even with passwords.

A common tactic in transactions is for the seller to seek to include in the disclosure letter as a general disclosure, all documents provided or made available to the buyer and its advisers as part of the due diligence process. Accordingly, the seller will disclose a myriad of documents so that the buyer is overwhelmed with information, not all of which is relevant but which is intended to protect the seller for breach of warranties. The buyer's advisor should refuse to accept both the disclosure and inclusion of documents not produced within good time for proper consideration.

During the disclosure process time pressure can be intense for the seller (who will be providing documentation and answers to the disclosure questions in addition to continuing to run the company) as well as for the seller's advisors who will be collating the information they receive from their client which will be the basis for the finally agreed disclosure letter. The buyer's tax advisor will need to liaise closely with the buyer's lawyer responsible for the disclosure process to ensure that any tax issues of the target which come to light are properly provided for in the tax indemnity. Given disclosure against the warranties will usually have the effect of protecting the seller from any claim for breach in transactions, where there is to be no tax indemnity or it is limited, it is very important that the buyer is properly advised of the risk to the buyer arising from the tax disclosures, and to carve out the protections for the more serious risks.

In practice, the disclosure letter is invariably late – sometimes as a tactical ploy, sometimes because requests for information have been onerous or simply because of the size and complicated nature of the transaction. It is important, albeit sometimes unpopular, that the buyer's tax advisor should only agree the tax schedule after seeing the final draft of the disclosure letter.

2.5 Measuring the Risk

Relevant issues include the identification of tax compliance failings and maladministration which would have certain or highly probable negative tax consequences for the target; regulatory issues which will require post-completion actions; issues so fundamental as to justify a retention of a proportion of the consideration or renegotiation of the purchase price; tax issues which require reconsideration that the transaction should be a business sale rather than a share sale or ultimately consideration of a withdrawal by the buyer from the transaction.

The following table sets out a number of different scenarios beginning with high probability/low risk and concluding with low probability/high risk together with possible actions.

Different Scenarios	Possible Action
Commercial parties agree there is a hypothetical but low risk that HMRC might raise a query or make an assessment on the target regarding an insubstantial tax issue.	Seller or buyer should seek an HMRC business ruling if possible; the issue is highlighted in the indemnity which the buyer can rely on if HMRC makes a successful claim against the target company.
Medium risk of an assessment by HMRC against the target company regarding a more than nominal tax liability.	The issue is highlighted in the tax indemnity; the buyer requires a retention of the purchase price and either pre- or post-completion the situation is regularised with HMRC by either buyer or seller (buyer and target being fully indemnified by seller for costs).
Buyer believes there to be a high risk of an assessment by HMRC against target but seller wants to sell target company not merely its assets and business.	The issue is highlighted in the tax indemnity; the buyer renegotiates terms of the purchase price which could involve a retention and buyer regularises target's situation with HMRC immediately following completion (buyer and target being fully indemnified by seller for costs).

Acknowledgement by commercial parties that there is a very high likelihood of an assessment by HMRC against the target and that tax liability is significant.	Renegotiate terms of the transaction so that buyer acquires assets and business of the target or renegotiate purchase price to take account of the tax liability including a retention until the matter is agreed with HMRC.
Robust advice from buyer's advisors that the target's tax liabilities are significant, and/or that recklessness/fraud may be issues, and refusal by seller to acknowledge such liabilities or renegotiate terms of the deal.	Buyer to consider withdrawing from the transaction unless the transaction can be the purchase of the business only.

Whilst all identified risks and issues which come to light during the due diligence process may be theoretically covered by the tax indemnity, in order to avoid a claim or future litigation it is essential that the parties consider and resolve the outstanding tax issues before completion. Furthermore, a right to sue another party is a valuable redress only if the respondent is easily located, has the relevant funds and is accordingly worth pursuing. A winding up of the seller following completion is not uncommon, and in such cases a right to sue would have very limited purpose without specific protections against the seller's shareholders. Avoiding future litigation by dealing with the problem before completion is essential in circumstances when any of the sellers stay with the target and become directors or employees within the buyer's group following completion. Finally, it should be noted that litigation is a last resort and is rarely in the best interests of a buyer and its shareholders and should be avoided. Therefore, a major purpose of the due diligence is to avoid litigation.

If potential tax issues come to light during the due diligence process, both the buyer and the seller, as well as the target, will have been put on notice that any past error must be regularised by the target. Often, because the parties are eager to complete the transaction, they may ignore their advisors' advice on the potential tax consequences of the issues raised, in which case the advisor should try as best as he or she can to provide the relevant protections in the tax documentation (with the support of its client's accountant). This can have disadvantages as well advantages. The seller's advisor may argue that disclosure should be effective against the tax indemnity as the buyer has been made aware of the potential liability (in the author's experience this is rarely accepted except in an MBO or a 'fire sale') or alternatively if the issue has resulted in a lower purchase price the seller should not be penalised further by the issue being carved out of the tax indemnity. If the parties view the tax risk as being minimal the seller's tax advisor should carve out any interest and/or penalties arising from delay or inaction of the buyer to regularise the situation post-completion if the issue has been disclosed.

2.6   Due Diligence in the Purchase of a Business

Chapter 5 (Sale and Purchase of a Business) comprehensively covers this type of transaction. Essentially, the seller will be disposing of a basket of assets which represents a business, rather than selling the corporate entity which owns the business. No tax liabilities of the company can transfer, so an inclusive tax indemnity is not necessary. Specific but limited tax warranties are commonly provided relating to PAYE and VAT and sometimes SDLT but nevertheless the buyer's due diligence should be thorough to avoid later litigation for a breach of warranties, which can be involved, costly and will require mitigation by the seller (see **Chapter 3 (Warranties)**).

Because the risks of acquiring any UK tax liabilities on the purchase of a business and assets are minimal, tax due diligence should focus on the following issues:

Tax	Investigation
VAT on a transfer of a going concern (TOGC)	1. Is all or part of the business being transferred?
	2. Has there been a significant break in trading at any time before completion?
	3. Has there been a previous transfer of the business?
	4. Is the seller VAT registered?
	5. Is the business currently ongoing?
	6. Has the seller opted to tax the land and property?
	7. Is there a transfer of the freehold in a 'new' or partially completed building or civil engineering

	work? 8. Does the capital goods scheme apply to any land and property or computer equipment? If 'yes' what input tax was incurred on the original purchase and how much of the adjustment period remains?
PAYE	1. Are PAYE records correct and up-to-date? 2. Has PAYE been properly applied in respect of employees transferring under TUPE? 3. Are there any consultants who might in fact be employees? 4. What PAYE audits have taken place and what were the outcomes? 5. Has Real Time Information (RTI regime) been complied with?
SDLT	1. Are all documents relating to UK property properly stamped?[2] 2. Has any SDLT relief been claimed and will it be clawed back on completion?
Overseas Assets	1. What tax issues could arise on transfer? 2. What permissions and registration are required?
Inheritance Tax	Could any person have a charge over any of the assets under IHTA section 212?

2.7   Tax Due Diligence in the Purchase of a Company

The purchase of a company is discussed in detail in **Chapter 4 (Sale and Purchase of a Company)**. Tax issues requiring investigation and comments by the buyer's advisors during the due diligence process are set out in the following table:

Tax	Investigation
Corporation Tax	1. Are past computations correct? 2. Is past treatment of all revenue expenditure and related issues tenable and reasonable? 3. If the target was paying small companies tax rate,

---

[2] Proper due diligence on SDLT is by no means simple – it includes, for example, requiring documentary evidence to support the market value of the land and property in question at the time of the land transaction and on which the SDLT charge has been paid

Tax	Investigation

	were there any associated companies which might affect the rate?[3]
	 4. Comment on available tax reliefs:-
	   a. capital or trading losses carried forward;
	   b. capital allowances;
	   c. will relief under CTA 2009 sections 1001 to 1038 be available (corporation tax relief for employee related securities and options)?
	   d. has the target complied with all self-assessment requirements?
	 5. Is there a history that corporation tax has been paid on time? Does the target pay corporation tax on a quarterly basis? Will it be required to do so after completion?
	 6. Are there any deferred tax provisions? If so, what are they and what are the chances they will become payable?

Accounting	1. Does the target use UK GAAP or IAS? 2. Any other comments on the target's accounting policies and practices? 3. Does the target recognise tax assets? 4. Have incentive schemes been properly accounted for under IFRS12 or equivalent UK GAAP?
SDLT	1. What intra-group UK property transactions will be effected before completion? 2. Will any SDLT group relief be withdrawn on completion?
VAT	1. Is the target VAT registered and if so does it have a good track record of being VAT compliant? 2. Does the target make exempt supplies and, if so, what proportion of total turnover do they account for? 3. Has VAT been properly computed in respect of

[3] This is no longer an issue with the rates of corporation tax for large companies and small companies now the same

Tax	Investigation
	input and output tax and are records up to date?
	4. Has the target been the subject of penalties, interest or a surcharge?
	5. Has the target been involved in VAT avoidance schemes?
PAYE	1. Are PAYE records in order and up to date?
	2. Has PAYE been properly applied, including in respect of directors and other person under contracts for services to the target?
	3. Has the target entered into any compromise agreements with past employees?
	4. Has the target been the subject of penalties and interest relating to PAYE?
	5. Has the target been involved in any tax avoidance arrangements relating to income tax and NIC?
	6. Has the target company implemented any redundancy programmes in the past?
	7. Has the RTI regime been complied with?
Management Accounts	Is it likely that the target will have sufficient working capital to cover its current tax obligations following completion?
Restructuring	What restructuring has been or will be carried out prior to completion and have the necessary related clearances been obtained?
Tax Avoidance	Has the target been involved in any schemes or arrangements requiring disclosure to any tax authority?

THE TAX SCHEDULE

3   WARRANTIES

3.1   Overview

A warranty is a representation of fact on which another party (usually the buyer in a transaction involving the purchase of a business or company) will rely when agreeing to enter into the transaction. If it transpires subsequently that the warranty statement is untrue, the buyer can sue under a damages claim.

The procedure for pursuing a damages claim can be onerous for the claimant who must prove that:

- the claimant has suffered a financial loss arising from the misrepresentation or untrue statement;
- the loss is directly connected with the claimant having relied on the representation; and
- the loss is not too remote.

Additionally, the claimant has a duty to mitigate so as to reduce the amount of the loss it suffers.

The measurement of the loss will be the amount required to put the claimant in the position it would have been if the warranty had been true – not without its difficulty. A claim under an indemnity does not impose these same obligations on the claimant, who will be paid on a successful indemnity claim on a pound-for-pound basis so long as the indemnity is correctly worded. Therefore, when the tax schedule includes tax warranties and a wide-ranging tax indemnity, it will be usual for the claimant to sue under the tax indemnity for any tax liability arising from the same circumstances as for a warranty breach. There are several tax liabilities which can arise which may not be covered by a tax indemnity, in which case the claimant must sue for breach of warranties.

3.2   Warranties in Due Diligence

Tax warranties go hand-in-hand with the disclosure process, in that without the warranties there will be nothing to disclose against. **Chapter 2 (Due Diligence)** discusses in more depth the due diligence process although this chapter repeats some of the same issues as they apply to the tax warranties.

WARRANTIES

The primary purpose of requiring the seller to warrant certain tax issues is to gather information, as part of a buyer's due diligence on the target (whether the target is a business or a company) rather than, primarily, as a protection mechanism for the buyer. Ordinarily, the buyer will sue for damages for breach of warranty when the tax liability is not covered by the tax indemnity or where a seller refuses to provide a tax indemnity as a commercial term of the deal. It is standard practice to provide that any disclosure against warranties will disbar a claim for breach of warranties. If no tax indemnity is given, the seller might be relatively relaxed about providing warranties so long as it is so protected under the disclosure process, but in these circumstances a buyer should be certain there are no significant liabilities or adjust the consideration accordingly.

Potential tax liabilities which would not normally fall within the provisions of a general tax indemnity include chargeable gains arising post-completion and relating to the following:

- crystallisation of roll-over relief on capital assets;[1]
- a balancing charge on the disposal of an asset on which capital allowances have been claimed;[2]
- clawback of SDLT reconstruction or acquisition relief involving UK land and property;[3] and
- crystallisation of roll-over relief in respect of any compulsory acquisition of land[4] or part disposal of land.[5]

The tax indemnity should, therefore, specifically provide for protection against these potential tax liabilities rather than rely purely on the relevant tax warranties.

The accountants for both the seller and buyer involved in the due diligence process as well as the parties' financial officers involved in the transaction should provide details to the tax advisors of any particular tax and accounting issues in the target. In an ideal

---

[1] See TCGA section 152

[2] Including under CAA sections 61 to 64

[3] FA 2003 Schedule 7, paragraphs 9 & 11

[4] TCGA section 247

[5] TCGA section 243

transaction the seller's tax advisor should go through each tax warranty requested, with the client, and ensure that the warranty can be given, as a preliminary step to negotiating the tax schedule, but often this is not possible. Depending on the consideration at stake, the size of the target's business operations and its trading history, warranties involving an excessive amount of time to confirm or negate should be resisted by the seller as being onerous. The buyer will be protected with the indemnity, and the seller should require that the number of warranties are reasonable.

Unfortunately, tax warranties are often treated by the seller as a mere formality and not a priority compared with other pre-completion issues. In order to make appropriate disclosure, the seller must investigate its past tax affairs and consider each tax warranty separately. It is recommended that certain warranties are put in the alternative (see 'group warranties' under paragraphs 3.22 and 3.37.1 as examples) – if the seller client does not strike out one of the two alternatives, it is clear that it has not considered the warranties properly and the tax advisor must correct the situation.

In circumstances where the buyer's tax advisor suspects that its client has not properly considered the disclosures against the tax warranties provided by the other side, he or she needs to explain precisely how the tax indemnity will apply and identify those warranties which will not fall under the indemnity but in respect of which the seller will be protected.

The extent and number of tax warranties will be a negotiating issue between the parties' tax advisors. However, a refusal to agree to a warranty by the seller's advisor is likely to be met with a response from the buyer's advisor that there must be an issue which the seller is disguising, and therefore it is all the more important for the warranty to remain.

3.3   Disclosures against Tax Warranties[6]

If acting for the buyer, disclosure against the tax warranties should be requested as a matter of priority early in the transaction, and the tax schedule should never be agreed before receipt of the final

---

[6] This subject is also discussed in **Chapter 2 (Due Diligence)** and therefore there may be some repetition of some points

disclosure letter. Unfortunately, in practice the disclosure letter is often agreed very late in the transaction process (often on the eve of completion) but the buyer and its corporate lawyer should insist on the disclosure process being one of priority.

The tax advisor should be working closely with both the corporate lawyer compiling the disclosures and the client's accountants involved in the due diligence process. The buyer should have carried out some due diligence independently but there are likely to be issues which require disclosure and the best way to achieve this is to draft warranties broadly and in the alternative. The process of disclosure against the warranties is therefore fundamental for any buyer, whether the target is commercially strong or in straitened circumstances. The buyer's tax advisor should not back down when requiring relevant broadly-worded warranties particularly those relating to administration and tax compliance set out in paragraph 3.5 below.

Specific indemnities against material tax issues should be included, regardless of whether these are covered under the general wording of the tax indemnity, unless there has been a reduction in the purchase price to reflect the liability, in which case the liability will be included in the limitation clause, discussed in detail in **Chapter 10** at paragraph 10.8.

Disclosure against a tax warranty relating to tax compliance should trigger the immediate attention of the buyer and its advisors as to whether pre- or post-completion rectification by the target will be needed. It could be a matter which, on the balance of probabilities, is not material financially but against which the buyer would want protection under the tax indemnity, or it could be an issue which could have commercial significance. The buyer will need to consider, in addition to whether any disclosure requires an adjustment to the purchase price or a retention, if it will have obligations to remedy the underlying issue disclosed (it probably will) once ownership of the target has been transferred. A seller would be entitled to argue that if the buyer does not remedy any disclosed tax compliance issues it should not be entitled to claim under the indemnity (see limitation 3.1(g) of the long form tax schedule in **Appendix 1**) which relates to this issue.

A similar principle arises where a disclosure has been made and the buyer has taken a commercial decision not to renegotiate the purchase price – it would be illogical for the buyer then to be entitled to sue under the tax indemnity. In these circumstances, the seller should seek to carve out the issue by including it in the limitations in the tax indemnity in the form referred to in the above paragraph.

In this chapter most of the warranties are broadly worded to gain as much information about the target as possible via disclosure. The buyer's tax advisor should be prepared to ask more detailed follow-up questions relating to disclosures and must communicate the relevance of all disclosures to the corporate advisors and the client.

The paragraphs which follow discuss in detail and provide warranties for the major tax issues which should always be considered when drafting the tax schedule. Not all of them will be required in each transaction and before drafting warranties, the buyer's tax advisor should consider both the history and the business the target (see paragraph 1.8.1 in **Chapter 1 (The Transactional Process)**) to ensure that the warranties are relevant and necessary.

All capitalised words in the following warranties will be defined at the beginning of the tax schedule.

3.4   Accounts, Tax Computations and Payments

The last accounts prepared before completion will be the basis for the most recent corporation tax returns and, unless there are to be completion accounts, the 'accounts date' will be the reference date at which the seller's liabilities for the target's tax liabilities will cease, in most transactions. Depending on when the accounts date falls in relation to the date on which the transaction is completed, the corresponding tax returns (which ordinarily should be filed under self-assessment within twelve months of the end of the accounting period[7]) may not have been filed. (Further issues relating to self-assessment and corporation tax are discussed in paragraphs 3.34 and 3.15 respectively of this chapter.) The

---

[7] FA 1998 Schedule 18, paragraph 14

warranties under paragraph 3.5 below (Administration and Tax Compliance) may cover these issues and, therefore, there is overlap with the warranties in this paragraph, which are intended to direct the seller's attention to the current accounting period and result in specific disclosure. Whilst the tax schedule should deal with the parties' separate obligations and rights for compiling and filing any pre-completion tax returns, warranties relating to these tax returns should also be given.

The tax schedule will normally limit the seller's liability for any tax liabilities provided for in the accounts but if there are no specific provisions because, for example, the accounts are abbreviated, this issue can be addressed by a disclosure setting out the company's tax liabilities as at the accounts date. In this situation, if there are to be no completion accounts then the limitation provisions in the tax schedule should refer to the amount disclosed, the principle being that the seller will be covered for taxation relating to the target's taxable profits (both capital and trading) at the end of the relevant period, for which the buyer will be acquiring and receiving the benefit.

The preparation of the tax returns is dependent on the preparation of the accounts, as is the payment regime for corporation tax. Payment is required not later than nine months from the end of the accounting period for a small company.[8] For large companies the corporation tax instalment provisions apply which are discussed in paragraph 3.15.1 (the quarterly instalment payments).[9]

The following warranties, in addition to standard accounting warranties in the body of the main SPA, should be provided by the seller. A buyer should not accept disclosure against them by the seller merely providing copies of past accounts and tax returns.

a) **"The Accounts which have been prepared on a basis consistent with previous accounts and under generally accepted accounting principles fully and accurately provide for all Tax Liabilities of the Company as at the Accounts Date**

---

[8] TMA section 59D

[9] See regulation 3 SI 1998/3175 for definition of large companies

THE TAX SCHEDULE

including full provisions for contingent and/or Deferred Tax at such a date."

b) "Since the Accounts Date no Tax Liability of the Company has arisen other than in the ordinary course of business of the Company."

c) "The Company is not a large company for the purposes of the Corporation Tax (Instalment Payments) Regulations 1998 ("SI 1998/3175") and has correctly made payment of its corporation tax arising in the accounting period ending on the Accounts Date under TMA section 59D."[10]

3.5 Administration and Tax Compliance

Warranties relating to tax compliance matters are arguably the most important from a buyer's perspective. In giving the warranties the seller is indicating that the target has had no disputes with the tax authorities, its tax affairs are in order and it has complied with the requirements of the relevant tax statutes including under self-assessment, PAYE and VAT, and payment of taxes. Alternatively, the seller should reveal any failings, exceptions and errors through disclosures in which case, the buyer will be put on effective notice to remedy any previous or outstanding failures or omissions of the target with the relevant authorities following completion. It would follow that the seller's advisor should provide a relevant limitation in the tax schedule.

From the buyer's perspective, the following warranties should not be the subject of negotiation and should apply for at least a four year period ending with the accounts date.

a) "The Company has complied with all requirements and obligations relating to its liabilities to tax under all Tax Statutes and as required under the Companies Acts [since incorporation] [during the past four years] [at all times] including but not limited to:

    (i)   proper preparation and submission of the Accounts of the Company to the relevant Tax Authorities;

    (ii) proper filing of all Tax Returns, notices, computations, assessments (including self-assessment), amendments,

---

[10] Within nine months from the end of the accounting period

registrations and de-registrations together with relevant correspondence with the relevant Tax Authorities;

(iii) timely and correct remittances of Tax by the Company to the relevant Tax Authorities;

(iv) proper maintenance of all records and correspondence relating to the Company's tax affairs (including Tax Returns) as required, including for the avoidance of doubt relevant documentation relating to the computation for Taxation of the Company."

b) "All Tax Returns including any amended Tax Returns filed by the Company [since incorporation] [during the past four years] were true and accurate in all [material] respects (including computations relating to claims for Relief), have not been and [so far as the seller is aware] are not likely to be the subject of any enquiry or investigation or dispute with any Tax Authority."

c) "All disclosures and statements provided to any Tax Authorities relating to the Company's Tax affairs were complete, true and accurate in all respects."

d) "No arrangements have been entered into by the Company with any Tax Authority for the postponement or reduction of, or any dispensation relating to, the payment of any Tax by the Company and the Company has not at any time benefited from any Relief relating to its Tax affairs for which it is not entitled under Tax Statute."

e) "All Tax Liabilities of the Company as at Completion will have been correctly and duly paid and no outstanding fines, penalties and/or surcharges have arisen before nor will arise as at Completion."[11]

f) "There are no ongoing proceedings with any Tax Authority involving the Company including any which could adversely affect the Seller's ability to enter into this Agreement."

---

[11] It would be expected that a disclosure should be made under this warranty relating to PAYE, VAT and possibly corporation tax – if not perhaps the seller has not considered the warranties in which case its tax advisor should press for a response

3.6   Advance Corporation Tax (ACT)

The payment of ACT was a process by which, as the name suggests, a UK company paid tax based on the amount of any qualifying distribution[12] it made, at the time the distribution was made. That advance payment of tax could be set off under the pay-and-file regime against corporation tax paid in an earlier accounting period, surrendered to a 51% subsidiary or set off against corporation tax payable for the current accounting period. If the ACT could not be set off, it could be carried forward for future set-off in a similar manner. ACT was abolished for distributions made after 5 April 1999, when the quarterly payment regime for larger corporate entities[13] was introduced. Therefore, if warranties are suitably limited to four years or even six years preceding the date of the transaction, no warranties relating to ACT should be necessary except warranties relating to 'shadow ACT'.

Shadow ACT will be relevant only in respect of companies which had unrelieved surplus ACT (that is, ACT which had not been set off as described above and which would have been eligible for carry- forward) on 5 April 1999. The shadow ACT regulations[14] provide for the unrelieved surplus ACT as at 5 April 1999 to be used as if ACT had not been abolished. The rules for computing shadow ACT treat the ACT as having been paid on distributions made by the company in accounting periods after 5 April 1999, capped at 20%. If the shadow ACT does not exhaust the 20% limit in the accounting period, the unrelieved surplus ACT carried forward can be set off against the liability to corporation tax for that accounting period[15]. In the rare circumstances where shadow ACT may remain an issue (which will be for the benefit of the target) it is unlikely to be a major negotiating factor.

A suitable warranty if target's history goes back to 1999 is as follows:

---

[12] Defined in CTA 2010 section 1136

[13] See paragraph 3.34 (Self-assessment)

[14] Corporation Tax (Treatment of Surplus Advance Corporation Tax) Regulations 1999 (SI 1999/358)

[15] SI 1999/358 paragraph 14(4)

"There is neither unrelieved surplus ACT nor any shadow ACT for the Company or any Group Company as at the date of this Agreement."

3.7 Anti-avoidance

The UK rules on tax avoidance are wide-ranging, under case law and increasingly under statute. The concept of tax avoidance ranges from valid tax planning and tax mitigation to (illegal) tax evasion. Therefore, any general warranty referring to tax avoidance without a specific reference to the mischief involved is unlikely to be useful to the buyer and could be dangerous to the warrantor. It would be unwise for a seller to disclose against such a warranty although most sellers are likely to be comfortable with warranting that there has been no tax evasion.

A myriad of legislation to counter specific tax avoidance schemes and practices has been enacted over the years and this area of statutory enactment is likely to continue to develop with extensions to the scope of tax avoidance schemes brought in by FA 2004 (Disclosure Of Tax Avoidance Schemes/DOTAS – see paragraph 3.18 below). The Finance Act 2013 introduced the GAAR (General Anti-Abuse Rule) under sections 206 to 215. This targets tax avoidance arrangements in which it would be reasonable to believe that the relevant tax provisions are being misused and not used as intended when enacted. It will now be standard for any tax advisor to consider whether any tax arrangements might fall within the GAAR when providing advice.

Under DOTAS, whilst avoidance schemes reported to HMRC are not deemed to be illegal at the time of any reporting, it would be reasonable to expect that anti-avoidance legislation could follow to curtail some reported schemes – thus a buyer will need to know if target has been involved in any DOTAS-reported schemes and ask for a specific indemnity to cover any future potential tax liability.

Relevant anti-avoidance warranties specific to separate tax issues are included in the various sections within this chapter. If acting for a seller, the tax advisor should reject any warranty baldly asking whether the target has been involved in tax avoidance, without specific parameters as to what comprises tax avoidance – a compromise position would be to substitute the reference to 'tax avoidance' with 'tax evasion'. Alternatively, a general anti-avoidance warranty intended to cover something more than tax mitigation as follows should be argued for:

"The Company has never been involved in any arrangement or arrangements which included a pre-conceived or pre-ordained series of transactions, which had no commercial purpose other than tax [avoidance] [evasion] including any reportable under DOTAS and/or which could fall within the GAAR and/or the TAAR."

3.8 Associated Companies

A company with profits of no more than £300,000 (the lower limit)[16] was entitled to the small profits rate of corporation tax so long as the company is UK resident in the relevant accounting period, it was not a close investment-holding company and its augmented profits did not exceed the lower limit.[17] That rate for the financial year 2013 (i.e. the year ending 31 March 2014) was 20% compared with the main rate of 23%, but by 2015 the main rate was 20% and to fall to 17% by 1 April 2019. Therefore, the small profits rate is immaterial for corporation tax purposes. Previously, the existence of any associated companies required the small company profits band to be divided by the number of associated companies in existence during the relevant tax year. This could result in the worst position for a company if it moved into the marginal corporation tax rate band.

Any two companies are associated if at a given time in an accounting period one of the two companies has control of the other or both are under the control of the same person or persons.[18] Dormant companies can be disregarded but overseas companies are included. Control for the purposes of CTA 2010 section 25(4) is defined under CTA 2010 section 450 and arises when a person exercises, is able to exercise or entitled to acquire direct or indirect control over a company's affairs. Control is therefore not merely by virtue of share capital ownership, or

---

[16] CTA 2010 section 24

[17] CTA 2010 sections 3(2) & 18

[18] CTA 2010 section 25(4)

voting rights, or entitlement to distributions and/or assets on a winding up but also covers arrangements resulting in control. The consequences of a company having an associated company in the past was that it might not have been entitled to the small profits rate for corporation tax and could be liable to the main rate of corporation tax from the date of the companies became associated, together with interest and penalties and possibly becoming subject to the quarterly instalment payment regime (see paragraph 3.15.1 which discusses this regime).

It is not uncommon in a company purchase transaction for this issue to arise in respect of the pre-2015 period during the due diligence process, where a higher corporation tax charge will have arisen on the target company unwittingly due to the existence of an another company, not known to most of target's directors and shareholders, which is unconnected with the target except for being under the control of one of the shareholders. If the issue arises, the buyer will have been put on notice to regularise the situation with the target's corporation tax office following completion with respect to back payment of taxes, interest and penalties, if this has not been put into effect by the seller before completion for the pre-2015 period.

Extra-statutory concession C9 had provided that HMRC would not treat one company as being under the control of another or companies as being associated, in four rather detailed circumstances including a restricted definition of a relative being a spouse, civil partner and minor child, and where there is no substantial interdependence between them. FA 2011 section 55 amended CTA 2010 section 27[19] for accounting periods ending on or after 1 April 2011 and provides that a person can only have rights and powers of being associated if there is a substantial commercial interdependence.

The following warranty should always be asked for if the target company has at any time been subject to the small profits rate:

a) **"There are no, nor have there been any, companies which are under the control of the same person or persons which**

---

[19] Attributions to persons of rights and powers of their associates

control the Company such that the Company was not entitled to the small profits rate of tax for corporation tax purposes."

b) "There have been no circumstances when the Company relied on ESC C9 relating to control of the company by associated persons ("Associated Companies")."

3.9 Capital Allowances

Capital allowances are a form of tax depreciation available for computing corporation tax for a company and applicable in respect of the purchase of certain capital assets by a business. The Capital Allowances Act 2001 (CAA) was consolidating legislation but the Finance Act 2008 brought in major changes for capital expenditure incurred by companies on or after 1 April 2008 with the rates further reduced under FA 2011.

The CAA provides for annual allowances to be given in respect of capital expenditure under the following categories:[20]

- plant and machinery;
- business premises renovation;[21]
- flat conversions for expenditure incurred prior to 1 April 2013 but withdrawn from that date;[22]
- mineral extraction[23];
- research and development;[24]
- know-how;[25]
- patents;[26]
- dredging;[27]
- assured tenancies.[28]

The changes brought in by FA 2008 and FA 2011 included the following:

---

[20] CAA section 1

[21] CAA section 360A – to be extended for a further five years from 2012

[22] CAA section 393A – abolished after 2012

[23] CAA section 394

[24] CAA section 437

[25] CAA section 452

[26] CAA section 464

[27] CAA section 484

[28] CAA section 490

- reduced writing down allowances on expenditure on plant and machinery (25% p.a. before April 2008 but reduced to 18% (standard rate) and 8% (special rate) from April 2012);
- 100% first-year allowances for energy-saving plant or machinery,[29] cars with low CO_2 emissions,[30] zero-emission goods vehicles,[31] plant or machinery for certain refuelling stations[32], and environmentally beneficial plant or machinery;[33]
- allowances on the pool of long-life assets (those with a useful life of more than 25 years) – in 2011 they went from 6% p.a. to 10% p.a.;
- the introduction of a new separate classification of features integral to a building ('special rate expenditure'[34]), initially with an annual 10% allowance, but which was reduced to 8% in FA 2011;
- phased withdrawal of industrial buildings allowances (IBA) and agricultural buildings allowances (ABA) with the effective rate of allowances falling to 3% from 1 April 2008; 2% from 1 April 2009; 1% from 1 April 2010 and full withdrawal taking effect on 1 April 2011;
- the introduction of new rules enabling companies to surrender losses derived from enhanced capital allowances (ECA) which will apply to certain environmentally beneficial types of plant and machinery, in return for a cash payment;
- the introduction of the annual investment allowance (AIA).[35] From 1 January 2013 to 31 December 2014 it was £250,000; £500,000 for 2014/2015 and £200,000 from 1 January 2016.

In most transactions involving the purchase of a company, warranties relating to capital allowances for plant and machinery are likely to be the most relevant, as well as, possibly, R&D, know-how and patents – these are discussed in paragraph 3.31 below.

---

[29] CAA section 45A – 45C

[30] CAA section 45D

[31] CAA section 45DA

[32] CAA section 45DE

[33] CAA sections 45H–45J

[34] CAA sections 104A to 104G

[35] For 2011 to 2012 the maximum AIA was £100,000

Companies have been entitled to claim capital allowances for computing corporation tax under self-assessment for accounting periods ending after 30 June 1999[36] (therefore relevant for the usual time periods for most tax warranty provisions) with the ability to amend or withdraw such claims within certain time periods. A company need not make use of available capital allowances, and can either make a partial claim or not make any claim, in circumstances where it can use trading losses by the various standard available means.[37] On the disposal of an asset for which capital allowances have been claimed, a balancing charge or allowance may arise depending on whether the disposal price is greater or less than the asset's written-down value. If the target company disposes of any asset following completion and a balancing charge arises the liability will not be covered by the standard tax indemnity unless there is a specific provision.

In acquiring a company the buyer will want information on the following capital allowances issues:

- details of the capital allowance pools (the 'main' pool, any single asset pool, any 'small' pool, and any class/special rate pool);
- whether the target is involved in leasing or other financing transactions (in which case specific anti-avoidance provisions apply to related capital allowances);
- whether there are unclaimed allowances available for carry forward at completion (and possibly representing a relief for the purposes of the tax schedule if its availability has been taken into account when agreeing the purchase price between the commercial parties).

A seller may be reluctant or unable to provide detailed information relating to its asset pools, which could be onerous, and may refer to details of capital allowance claims as contained in the target's tax returns. Set out below are suggested warranties but they need careful reflection as to which ones will be relevant for the target company:

---

[36] FA 1998 Schedule 12, paragraphs 78 to 83

[37] Carry back, group relief, set off against current year profits or carry forward

a) "The Company has made no claims under self assessment relating to capital allowances during the past [four] years, including in respect of the following:
   (i)   plant and machinery;
   (ii)   industrial buildings;
   (iii)   [business premises renovation;]
   (iv)   [agricultural buildings;]
   (v)   [flat conversions;]
   (vi)   [mineral extraction;]
   (vii)   [research and development;]
   (viii) know-how;
   (ix)   patents;
   (x)   [dredging;]
   (xi)   [assured tenancies.]"

b) "The Company has always made claims for capital allowances under self-assessment using the maximum available relief under the relevant Tax Statutes in each of the past [four] years and there are no unutilised capital allowances as at the date of this Agreement nor will there be at the Completion Date."

c) "Neither a balancing allowance nor a balancing charge in respect of capital allowances would arise on the Company on the disposal of a capital asset or discontinuance of a qualifying activity as at the date of this Agreement."[38]

d) "All available capital allowance claims made by the Company have been made correctly under self-assessment and under the relevant legislation and records have been maintained relating to such claims (including but not restricted to records kept as required under Self-Assessment) which provide full and accurate information including the dates when the relevant capital expenditure was incurred."

e) "The Company has only one plant and machinery pool."

---

[38] This could be rejected by the seller as being onerous if it has a large asset base. If so and there is concern by the buyer about potential future balancing charges, a tax indemnity should be included in the tax schedule referring to any capital allowance balancing charge arising on the sale of an asset following completion, but it would need to carve out any capital allowances claimed following the buyer's purchase of the target company

f) **"The Company has never participated or been involved in arrangements relating to capital allowances which could be perceived as tax avoidance."**

g) **"The Company has never been involved in financial transactions involving capital allowances including those involving finance leases or operating leases."**

3.10 Chargeable Gains

Issues relating to proper accounting for the tax treatment of capital assets and corporation tax for any chargeable gains or losses arising before completion are covered under the Administration and Compliance Warranties at (a) and (b) in paragraph 3.5 above. However, the important issues relating to chargeable gains about which a buyer will want information are whether degrouping charges might arise on completion if the target company is leaving a group, whether latent chargeable gains could crystallise on the sale of an asset due to roll-over relief, and if there are carried forward capital losses.

There are three separate scenarios relevant to chargeable gains issues:

- the target is a stand-alone entity;
- the target is leaving a group;
- the target is the holding company of a group.

3.10.1 Chargeable gains – single corporate entity

If the target company has no subsidiaries and has never been part of a group the warranties relating to chargeable gains requesting confirmation or disclosures will relate to:

- any past reconstructions or re-organisations;
- close company issues (see 3.12 below);
- what roll-over relief has been claimed in the past;
- the availability of capital losses as at completion; and
- whether target has been part of a consortium.

Set out as follows are reasonable warranties when target is a single entity.

a) **"The Company is not and never has been, nor has been deemed to be part of a group for Tax purposes including in respect of chargeable gains."**

b) "No capital assets owned by the Company as at the date of this Agreement have been acquired whereby roll-over relief under TCGA sections 152 to 158 (*Replacement of business assets*) has been claimed and there are no capital assets of the Company in respect of which a charge to tax could crystallise at any time under those provisions."

c) "The Company has properly assessed chargeable gains and losses for corporation tax purposes on all disposals of any of its capital assets, and has in its possession all records relating to all disposals of capital assets including all relevant computations and assessments including the basis for any valuation and relevant for Substantial Shareholdings Exemption."

d) "The Company has never been involved in any reorganisation and/or reconstruction including under sections 135 TCGA (*Exchange of securities for those in another company*), 136 TCGA (*Scheme of reconstruction involving issue of securities*), or 139 TCGA (*Reconstruction involving transfer of business*)."

e) ["HMRC have never issued any notices to the Company under section 184I TCGA relating to avoidance arrangements involving losses under TCGA section 184G (*Avoidance involving losses: schemes converting income to capital*) and 184H TCGA (*Avoidance involving losses: schemes securing deductions*)."][39]

f) "The Company had no capital losses available to be carried forward as at the Accounts Date nor will it have at Completion."

g) ["The Company has never transferred any of its assets other than by way of a bargain made at arm's length nor have the provisions of TCGA section 125 (*"Shares in close company transferring assets at an undervalue"*) been applicable."][40]

---

[39] Include only if there is an indication during due diligence that it might be relevant

[40] Do not include if the target company is clearly not a close company

THE TAX SCHEDULE

h) "The Company has never received a capital distribution from a connected party whereby a chargeable gain will have accrued and in respect of which it could be subject to unpaid corporation tax of the connected party under section 189 TCGA (*Capital distribution of chargeable gains recovery from the shareholder*)."

3.10.2 Chargeable gains – target leaves a group

If the target company is leaving a group, issues requiring disclosure or confirmation, in addition to those covered in warranties (b) to (h) in paragraph 3.10.1 above will relate to whether:

- the target has at any time been a member of another group or a member of more than one group at the same time;
- the target has been involved in any transfer of assets on a no-gain or no-loss basis under TCGA section 171 or in respect of any election under TCGA section 171A;
- there have been any transfers trading stock within the group involving the target company under TCGA section 173;
- there has been any replacement of business assets within the group under TCGA section 152 to 158 whilst the target was a member; and
- a charge under TCGA section 179 could arise on target on Completion.

In addition to warranties (b) to (h) in paragraph 3.10.1 above the following warranties should be required from the seller:

i) "The Company has never been nor deemed to be a member of any group other than the Group nor a member of more than one group of companies, however defined."

j) "The Company has never been involved in any transfer of capital assets on a no gain/no loss basis under TCGA section 171 (*Transfers within a group*) nor has it been a party to any elections under TCGA section 171A (*Election to reallocate gain or loss to another member of the group*);

k) "The Company has neither acquired nor disposed of an asset whilst being a member of the Group whereby TCGA section 173 (*Transfers within a group: trading stock*) could apply."

l) "The Company has not been a party to any claim for roll-over relief under TCGA sections 152 to 158 whilst being a member of the Group and whereby TCGA section 175 (*Replacement of business assets by members of a group*) would apply."

m) "No charge to tax is capable of arising on the Company under TCGA section 179 (*Company ceasing to be member of group: post-appointed day cases*) at any time including on Completion."

n) "The Company has neither received nor paid any consideration for a transfer of any capital asset from or to any member of the Group."

3.10.3 Chargeable gains – target a holding company

If the target company is a holding company the buyer will want disclosures for the following issues:

- what intra-group transfers of assets have been made, have elections been made under TCGA section 171A and if so which company owns the capital assets;
- what payments have been made for intra-group transfers of capital assets;
- details of claims for roll-over relief;
- whether there have been any intra-group transfers involving trading stock;
- details of any re-organisation or restructuring including under TCGA sections 135, 136 and 139;
- what group relief claims have been made for losses relating to capital asset disposals;
- whether any degrouping charges could arise under TCGA section 190 (*Tax recoverable from another group company or controlling director*);
- what disposals by any Group member has been subject to the substantial shareholdings relief (discussed in **Chapter 9 (Group Issues)** paragraph 9.8?

Set out as follows are reasonable warranties relating to chargeable gains when a group of companies is being acquired:

o) "There have been no transfers of capital assets within the Group on a no gain/no loss basis under TCGA section 171 (*Transfers within a group*) nor have any Group Members made any election under TCGA section 171A (*Election to reallocate gain or loss to another member of the group*);

p) "There have been no transfers within the Group whereby TCGA section 173 (*Transfers within a group: trading stock*) could apply."

q) "There have been no claims for roll-over relief under TCGA sections 152 to 158 whereby TCGA section 175 (*Replacement of business assets by members of a group*) would apply."

r) "No charge to tax is capable of arising on any Group Member under TCGA section 179 (*Company ceasing to be member of group: post-appointed day cases*) at any time including on Completion."

s) "There have been no payments made between Group Companies for any transfer of any capital asset from or to any member of the Group."

t) "There have been no disposals by the Company whereby exemption from chargeable gains arose under the Substantial Shareholdings regime nor in respect of which paragraph 38 TCGA Schedule 7AC (*Degrouping*) could apply."

3.11 Clearances

The buyer will want full details of all clearances sought by the target, whether statutory or under the non-statutory business clearance procedure. The relevant correspondence with HMRC should provide sufficient background information on past restructuring or in respect of issues which involved uncertainty or commercial significance for which the target has sought HMRC assurance.

The main clearances which could be relevant in a sale and purchase of a company is discussed in **Chapter 1 (The Transaction Process)** at paragraph 1.2 and also listed in **Appendix 7**.

Suitable warranties to cover any past clearances are set out as follows:

a) "The Company has never submitted an application to any Tax Authority during the past [four] years whether required under statute or otherwise, whereby the Tax Authority was required or able to provide a ruling, clearance, guidance and/or opinion relating to any transaction, arrangements or schemes effected or entered into by the Company."

b) "There have been no transactions or arrangements entered into by the Company for which a clearance application could or should have been made to a Tax Authority but which was not made by the Company including any transaction having an EU dimension."

3.12 Close Companies

The anti-avoidance provisions for close companies essentially attach a tax charge on deemed distributions and certain loans made to controlling shareholders, directors and participators, and remove the benefit of any small profits tax rate for close companies which do not carry on a trade. In addition, there are issues relating to inheritance tax and capital gains tax.

The relevant legislation is contained in:

- CTA 2010 sections 438 to 465 (the re-write of ICTA sections 414 to 422) which set out the main provisions for close companies for income tax and corporation tax purposes;
- CTA 2010 section 34 (*Close-investment holding companies*);
- TCGA section 13 (*Attribution of gains of non-resident companies to UK shareholders*); and
- IHTA sections 94 and 101 (*Charge on participators, & Companies' interests in settled property*) relating to inheritance tax issues.

A close company is defined as an unquoted UK-resident company which is under the control of five or fewer participators or under the control of participators who are directors (i.e. regardless of their number).[41] Control is widely defined under CTA 2010 sections 450 and 451 as is the concept of a director under CTA 2010 section 452. A participator[42] is a person having a share or interest in the capital or income of the company and includes persons

---

[41] CTA 2010 section 439

[42] CTA 2010 section 454

entitled to acquire such rights, any loan creditor of the company, any person who possesses or is entitled to acquire a right to receive distributions of the company and any person entitled to secure that income or assets of the company will be applied directly or indirectly for his benefit.

Subsidiaries are not treated as close companies, nor are companies under the control of two or more non-close companies, nor are quoted companies. A company is quoted so long as not less than 35% of the voting shares (excluding shares with a fixed rate dividend) have been unconditionally allotted or acquired and held by the public and such shares have been dealt and listed on a recognised stock exchange within the preceding 12 months. The **Glossary** provides the statutory references as to what amounts to a recognised stock exchange. At the time of writing it does not include AIM.

Under CTA 2010 section 455, if a close company lends or advances money to a participator who is an individual or to his or her associate[43] other than in the ordinary course of its business of lending money, 32.5% of the amount of the loan or advance will be assessed on the company as if it were corporation tax chargeable for the accounting period during which the loan or advance was made. The rate changed with effect from 6 April 2016, from 25% to the upper dividend rate and applies under section 464A as well. These provisions apply also where the participator incurs a debt to the close company or a debt due from that person to a third party is assigned to the close company. On any repayment or writing off of the loan the close company can make a claim for relief in respect of the corporation tax paid. If such a loan is released or written off by the company, the participator will be subject to income tax at the dividend ordinary rate on the amount of the debt released or written off, grossed up by that amount of tax[44]. However, under

---

[43] CTA 2010 section 448 defines 'associate' as including any relative or partner of the participator, the trustees of any settlement in relation to which the participator is, or any relative of his (living or dead) is or was a settlor

[44] ITTOIA section 416

THE TAX SCHEDULE   75

CTA 2010 section 456 these provisions will not apply to a loan to a director or employee of a close company[45] if:

- the amount of the loan together with other outstanding loans does not exceed £15,000;
- the borrower does not have a material interest in either the close company or any associated company; and
- the borrower works full-time for the company or any of its associate companies.

A person with or without one or more associates will have a material interest if he or she owns more than 5% of the ordinary share capital of the company or has an entitlement to 5% of the assets in a winding up.[46]

FA 2013 introduced further measures to counteract avoidance schemes with a charge to tax arising in the following circumstances:

- on loans or advance, made by an intermediary when the participator has an interest in the intermediary;
- if a close company is, at any time, a party to tax avoidance arrangements resulting in a benefit conferred on an individual who is a participator or on his or her associate;
- if, during any 30 day period, loans of more than £5,000 are repaid to the company and (new) loans or amounts of £5,000 or more are paid to the participant;
- if, at any time, there are loans or amounts outstanding of more than £15,000.

A close company must include details of any loans it makes to an individual participator which remains outstanding at the end of any accounting period under self assessment, and therefore this issue will be technically covered under the warranty relating to Administration and Tax Compliance at paragraph 3.5. However, to ensure the seller of a company which might be a close company has its attention drawn to the issue, the following warranties should be given:

---

[45] Or a director or employee of an associated company of the close company

[46] CTA 2010 section 457

a) "The Company has made no loans or advances to, or been assigned any debt in respect of, any shareholder or director, or employee benefit trust including but not limited to under CTA 2010 section 455 (*Charge to tax in case of loans to participators*) in respect of which the Company could or did become liable to a corporation tax charge."

b) "The Company has not at any time released or written off or waived any loans it has made to any person."

c) "The Company has properly accounted for corporation tax purposes under self-assessment all loans and deemed loans it has made to participators, shareholders and directors under CTA 2010 section 455 (*Charge to tax in case of loans to participators*) and all tax and other liabilities arising on the Company have been properly accounted for within the required time period."

Certain benefits provided by a close company to participators and directors will be treated as distributions and the benefits will not qualify as trading expenses for the purposes of the company's taxable profits.[47] These deemed distributions are widely drawn to include any expense incurred by the company in connection with the provision for any participator of living or other accommodation, of entertainment, of domestic or other services, or of other benefits or facilities of whatever nature. If the recipient of the benefit is an individual he will be subject to income tax on the cash equivalent of the benefit received less any amount made good to the company. Excluded from these deemed distributions are benefits-in-kind provided to individuals which are taxed as employment-related income.

Appropriate warranties for deemed distributions made by a close company are as follows:

d) "The Company has provided no benefit in connection with any shareholder or director or a participator (as defined under CTA 2010 section 454) which would not be allowable as a trading expenses for the purposes of corporation tax such

---

[47] CTA 2010 section 1064

benefit to include the provisions of living accommodation, of entertainment, of domestic services, and/or the use of company assets."

e) "All benefits provided by the Company to any employee, director, shareholder and persons associated to such persons under CTA 2010 section 1064 (*Distribution to include certain expenses of close companies*) which would be treated as a distribution, have been properly accounted for under self-assessment [and the Company is fully indemnified by such persons in respect of any income tax arising from the provisions of such benefits]."

3.12.1.1 Close Investment-holding Companies

Under CTA 2010 section 34 a close company will be a close-investment company unless it exists wholly or mainly for a number of 'permitted' purposes including the following:

- carrying on a trade or trades on a commercial basis;
- making investments in land, or estates or interests in land where the land is or is intended to be, let commercially;
- holding shares in and securities of, or making loans to, one or more companies each of which is a qualifying company;
- co-ordinating the administration of two or more qualifying companies.

Prior to the disappearance of the small profits rate of corporation tax it a close investment-holding company was not entitled to claim it, and was charged to the main rate of corporation tax (when these rates differ). A suitable warranty is as follows:

f) "The Company has at no time been a close investment-holding company as defined under CTA 2010 section 34 and has at all times existed wholly or mainly for the purposes of carrying on its trade of [   ] on a commercial basis."

3.12.1.2 Inheritance tax issues for a close company

When a close company makes a transfer of value for inheritance tax purposes,[48] under IHTA section 94 (*Charge on participators*) that

---

[48] A transfer of value being, under IHTA section 3 a disposition made by a person resulting in the value of his estate immediately after the disposition being less than it would be but for the disposition

value is apportioned between the participators for IHT purposes. A transfer of value could include a non-arm's length transaction, or an undervalue transaction not treated as a distribution, but would not include genuine commercial transactions made at arm's length. Apportionment would only be in respect of participators with an interest or entitlement of more than 5% in the close company.

IHTA section 98 provides that if there is an alteration of a close company's share or loan capital (not being quoted[49] shares or securities) and there is an alteration (including extinguishment) in any rights attaching to the unquoted shares or debentures of the close company, the alteration will be treated as a disposition by the participators. As the disposition cannot be treated as a potentially exempt transfer by virtue of IHTA section 98(3), it will therefore be treated as a transfer of value and IHTA section 94 will apply.

Under IHTA section 202(1), the close company making the transfer of value is primarily liable for the tax, but if it remains unpaid the participators become liable. Payment is due within six months from the end of the month in which the transfer was made.

g) "There have been no transfers made by the Company other than on an arm's length basis and for commercial purpose and the Company has never made nor could be deemed to have made a transfer of value whereby apportionment to the participators was required under IHTA section 94 (*Charge on participators*) and no charge to tax has arisen or could arise on the Company under section 202(1) IHTA (*Close companies*)."

h) "The Company has properly assessed for all transfers of value under which tax has arisen on the Company under IHTA section 202."

i) "There have been no alterations to the share capital and the loan capital of the Company."

3.13 The Construction Industry Scheme (CIS)

The CIS, which underwent revision in 1999 and more recently in 2007, involves obligations on contractors who make payments to

---

[49] IHTA section 272 defines quoted as being listed on a recognised stock exchange

sub-contractors to deduct income tax from those payments. The current legislation is contained in FA 2004 sections 57 to 77 and SI 2005/2045 (*The Income Tax (Construction Industry Scheme) Regulations 2005*). Failure to comply with the CIS regulations results in a penalty for the contractor. The CIS does not apply to employed workers.

Between 1999 and April 2007 a contractor was obliged to deduct a certain percentage from payments made to a sub-contractor (the rate was 18% as from 6 April 2000) and pay the deduction to HMRC, unless the sub-contractor met the conditions for receiving the payment gross of tax. The sub-contractor was required to have a valid registration card and the contractor was required to ensure that the card-holding sub-contractor was the person it said he was. Tax warranties should therefore refer to these provisions if they are to extend to years prior to 2007.

The current CIS now requires a contractor to:
- register as a contractor with HMRC;
- verify the registration status of the sub-contractor in addition to ensuring that he is self-employed;
- determine whether the sub-contractor should be paid gross or net of tax (determinable by the sub-contractor's registration status with HMRC); and
- pay over any deduction payments and make periodic returns to HMRC.

HMRC will notify the contractor whether it can pay a sub-contractor gross, net of deduction at the standard rate of 20% if the person is registered or net of deduction at the higher rate of 30% if the person is not registered.[50]

Clearly if the target company is involved in property or the construction industry, warranties relevant to the CIS should be required. However, the CIS has an extremely wide remit with the definition of contractor including:
- any person carrying on a business which includes construction operations – 'mainstream contractors';

[50] See FA 2004 section 61(2),m, (Relevant Percentage) Order, SI 2007/46

- any person whose main business does not include construction operations but whose expenditure on construction operations exceeds certain limits – 'deemed contractors'; and
- any sub-contractor to a contract for construction operations who engages sub-contractors to carry out any of that work.

A sub-contractor includes any person who intends to work within construction and who must register with HMRC – otherwise contractors will be required to deduct tax from all payments made to the sub-contractor at the higher rate of 30%.

Under the CIS, businesses and other concerns whose average annual expenditure on construction work over the previous three years was more than £1 million are considered to be contractors. Therefore, any organisations which regularly carry out or commission construction work on their own premises or investment properties, are likely to be deemed contractors.[51]

Prima facie, in most transactions it should be assumed that the target company may be a deemed contractor for the purposes of CIS at some time and therefore the following warranties should be asked for:

a) **"The Company has never spent more than £1 million on average annually in any three year period on construction or building work."**

b) **"The Company has never been required to operate under any of the provisions of the Construction Industry Scheme at any time and has at no time been a contractor or sub-contractor as defined under such scheme."**

c) **"The Company has at all times properly operated under the provisions within the Construction Industry Scheme including making proper and appropriate deductions for income tax from payments it has made to sub-contractors as required and has never been subject to any penalties under the scheme."**

---

[51] FA 2004 section 59(2)

3.14 Controlled Foreign Companies (CFC)

The anti-avoidance regime relating to CFCs is contained in ICTA sections 747 to 756 for accounting periods beginning before 1 January 2013 with the new regime, set out in TIOPA Part 9A for companies with accounting periods beginning on or after 1 January 2013.

A CFC is any company resident outside the UK, controlled by persons resident in the UK and which essentially is subject to a lower level of taxation in the territory in which it is resident.[52] If a company falls within that definition during an accounting period the anti-avoidance provisions may apply, and a company having at least a 25% interest in the CFC may be subject to an apportionment of the CFC's profits chargeable to UK corporation tax. Any company with a relevant interest in a CFC must self-assess accordingly for each accounting period. Additionally, transfer pricing issues will arise in respect of transactions between a company and any CFC.

The original purpose of the CFC provisions was to prevent UK resident companies structuring their tax affairs in order to keep profits offshore in low tax jurisdictions, thus avoiding UK corporation tax. Pre-TIOPA there was a wide list of exemptions under the CFC legislation as follows:[53]

- an exempt activities test;
- an acceptable distribution policy;
- the excluded companies regulations;
- the *de minimis* exemption;
- a motives test;
- territorial exclusion;[54]
- trading companies with a limited UK connection; and
- a company exploiting intellectual property with a limited UK connection.

---

[52] ICTA section 747; TIOPA section 371AA(1)(a). The TIOPA definition does not refer to low taxation in its definition

[53] See ICTA section 748

[54] See SI 2998/3081 – *Controlled Foreign Companies (Excluded Countries) Regulations*

Under the new rules, which were intended to result in a more competitive international regime and to simplify it, there is a 'gateway' test for the company's profits. This must be satisfied for the tax charges to apply, unless they are excluded by entry conditions, safe harbours or exemptions. Any CFC charge will be reduced by a credit for foreign tax attributable to the apportioned profits. The new rules do not contain a motives test exemption and there are a number of other changes as follows:-

- a low profit exemption;
- a low profit margin exemption;
- there is now no 'exempt activities' test but there are trading income exemptions within the gateway test;
- excluded territories may apply;
- companies operating in high tax territories (previously not CFCs) now have a tax exemption; and
- there is now an exempt period exemption for new acquisitions.

If a company has doubts relating to a non-UK resident company in which it has an interest and which is potentially a CFC it may ask for clearance from HMRC relating to issues under the CFC regime.

A corporation must report any holding of 25% or more in a foreign company controlled in the UK in its corporation tax return and, therefore, the administration and tax compliance warranty will cover these issues. More specific warranties relevant to the CFC regime are set out as follows:

a) **"The Company has at no time held an interest (either directly or indirectly) in another company which is resident outside the United Kingdom which could fall within the definition of a Controlled Foreign Company and whereby profits of such non-UK resident company should have been or were apportioned to the Company."**

b) **"The Company has at no time entered into a transaction or a series of transactions with any other company which is or could be considered to be a Controlled Foreign Company other than on an arm's length basis and has proper and appropriate records which can justify this warranty."**

c) "The Company has properly reported under self-assessment its interests in companies resident outside the United Kingdom which are Controlled Foreign Companies."

d) "The Company has never asked for clearance from HMRC nor has it done so in respect of any other Tax Authority relating to its transactions with companies resident outside the United Kingdom in which the Company has an interest."

3.15 Corporation Tax

Corporation tax is charged on the worldwide profits of a company which is incorporated in the United Kingdom or which is deemed to be UK-incorporated due to its management and control residing in the UK. The tax arises in respect of a company's profits and chargeable gains arising in the relevant accounting period, with profits based on the income of the company but excluding dividends and distributions (both qualifying and non-qualifying). Income is computed on income tax principles, and chargeable gains are computed on capital gains principles but with no special capital gains tax rate available for companies.

If the seller warrants that the target has correctly computed its corporation tax, relevant issues could include the following:

- income relating to loan relationships, overseas income, any property business it may have, and intangible fixed assets;
- chargeable gains or losses;
- loans to participators if the company is a close company;
- cross-border royalties;
- carried forward losses[55] and non-trading deficits;
- correct computation for deductions, management expenses and reliefs;
- any corporate venturing scheme losses;
- any losses from any property business and/or loan relationships, as well as carried forward trading losses;
- capital allowance claims;
- claims for group and/or consortium relief; and

---

[55] Including, as from April 2017, changes to the carried forward losses rules restrictions so that only 50% of profits over £5 million will be able to offset against carried forward losses

- employment tax liabilities.

These issues will be covered in other warranties under specific headings, such as Administration and Tax Compliance, Accounts Tax Computations and Payments, Close Companies, Controlled Foreign Companies, Group Issues, and Self-Assessment. However, a corporation tax warranty should be tailored to include further reference to any of the above specific issues if they are found to be relevant - i.e. if the target is a close company, it has a property business, is a member of a group or consortium or is loss-making.

Common difficulties unearthed during due diligence include disallowable revenue expenses, computation of losses and disallowable claims for tax relief. Often the seller will attempt to disclose with an all-embracing warranty relating to corporation tax by referring to tax returns which have been filed, but which may not provide the buyer with specific information or assurance being sought. Whilst warranties for self-assessment (see paragraph 3.34) cover the relevant issues, the following warranties should result in relevant disclosures relating to a target's corporation tax affairs:

a) **"The Company has never received a Notice of Enquiry, nor has any Tax Authority (including HMRC) amended any tax return or made a Revenue determination relating to any corporation tax return which has been filed by the Company."**

b) **"All copies of correspondence and evidence of communications between the Company and Tax Authorities relating to the corporation tax affairs of the Company have been properly maintained and the Company has in its possession all tax records as recommended by HMRC in its guidance and under relevant statutory requirements."**

c) **"The Company is not, nor has been a member of a group for corporation tax purposes, nor of a consortium."**

3.15.1 Quarterly instalment payment regime

SI 1998/3175 (Corporation Tax (Instalment Payments) Regulations 1998) contains the provisions for corporation tax payments under the quarterly instalment regime, which apply to large companies. A company is large under regulation 3 if its profits chargeable to corporation tax exceed the upper maximum amount which determines the small profits rate of tax in CTA 2010 section 25 (currently £1.5 million). A company is not 'large' if the amount of its total liability for corporation tax for an accounting period does not exceed £10,000 or (where the accounting period is less than 12 months) that amount proportionately reduced.[56] A company is also not a large company if in an accounting period its profits do not exceed £10 million and it was not a large company (by the above criteria) in the previous 12 months.[57]

The quarterly payment system works by the company estimating its corporation tax due for the year and making the first instalment payment not later than six months and 13 days from the start of the accounting period, and the final instalment payment not later than the third month and 14 days from the end of the accounting period, with further instalments due between the first and final at three-month intervals. There will be a series of adjustments at each payment, based on changes to the full year's estimates. If the target is a large company it will have paid corporation tax on account for the period in which completion falls based on estimates, and these amounts should be disclosed. It should be fairly obvious whether the target company is within the regime but a warranty intended to produce any disclosure is set out below:

d) **"The Company has never been within the quarterly instalment payment regime."**

3.16 Deferred tax

Deferred tax is tax which is or may become payable in the future. It is an accounting concept whereby certain taxes are required to be recognised in a company's financial statement. An example of a deferred tax charge is the amount of difference between the carrying value of an asset (being its cost less cumulative depreciation charged in the accounts) and the tax base of an asset (being the cost less accumulative capital allowances claimed). There can, or will be, temporary differences at the end of each year. The taxes at issue may be assets or liabilities, but essentially

---

[56] Regulation 3(2) SI 1998/3175

[57] Regulation 3(3) SI 1998/3175

the provisions are primarily made in respect of future tax payments which *might* arise relating to current or previous period's profits. Deferred tax also applies to:

- share-based payments, namely the difference between their value recognised in equity and recognised in the P & L account;
- investments in subsidiaries or investments in associates, whereby the difference in their carrying value versus their tax base is likely to reverse sometime in the future;
- unused tax losses and tax credits available for use in the future, to the extent that there is a taxable temporary difference.

A seller of a company will want the definition of taxation to include any deferred tax provided for in the accounts, and will want it carved out in the limitations clause. From the buyer's perspective, it will want a breakdown of what comprises the deferred tax and the likelihood of any tax charge arising in the future and the indemnity to include any deferred tax realised after completion. Both tax advisors should ask their client's accountants to provide a breakdown of what comprises any deferred tax and their future particularly if employment-related securities are in issue. It may be that in the event a deferred tax credit will arise in the near future the parties will negotiate which is entitled to the benefit. A suitable warranty to elicit disclosure is as follows:

"There are no deferred taxes which would become payable by the Company in the future and required to be accounted for under Section 28 FRS 102 or any equivalent accounting standard reference."

3.17 Demergers and Exempt Distributions

The demerger provisions are set out in CTA 2010 sections 1073 to 1099 (the re-write of ICTA sections 213 to 218) (see also HMRC guidance under the revised Statement of Practice 13/80).

A demerger involves a reorganisation whereby trading activities carried on by a company or a group are transferred directly to the shareholders of the transferring or distributing company. The shares in the transferee company will be an exempt distribution[58]

---

[58] CTA 2010 section 1075

and neither taxable as a distribution for income tax purposes nor chargeable to capital gains on disposal by virtue of not being treated as a capital distribution for the purposes of TCGA section 122.[59] Advance clearance from HMRC should be sought under CTA 2010 section 1091 before any exempt distribution is made and which is discussed further in **Chapter 1 (The Transactional Process)** at paragraph 1.2.1.

It is important to know whether the target company has been involved in a demerger because the tax avoidance provisions under CTA 2010 section 1086 will apply if, within five years of the demerger, a 'chargeable payment' is made by any company concerned in the distribution, in which case a charge to tax on the recipient will arise which will not be deductible for corporation tax purposes.[60]

A chargeable payment is widely defined,[61] being any payment made otherwise than for *bona fide* commercial reasons, or forming part of a scheme or arrangement for the avoidance of tax, and which is:

- made by any company concerned with an exemption distribution directly or indirectly to a member of that company or of any other company concerned in that distribution; and
- is made in connection with, or with any transaction affecting, the shares in that or any such company; and
- is not a distribution or exempt distribution or made to another company which belongs to the same group as the company making the payment.

Any company making a chargeable payment which consists of a transfer in money or money's worth within the five year period must provide details to HMRC within 30 days of the transfer.

A warranty relating to exempt distributions and demergers is set out as follows:

---

[59] By virtue of TCGA section 192 and TCGA sections 126 to 130 and 136

[60] Under CTA 2009 section 1305

[61] CTA 2010 section 1088

"The Company has never been involved in a demerger and/or an exempt distribution as provided for in CTA 2010 sections 1073 to 1099."

3.18 Disclosure of Tax Avoidance Schemes (DOTAS)[62]

This is the legislation requiring promoters and arrangers of tax avoidance schemes and other involved persons to provide HMRC with details of notifiable arrangements and notifiable proposals, currently covering avoidance of VAT, IHT, income tax, capital gains, corporation tax, SDLT, NIC and ATED. A summary of the legislative provisions is set out in **Appendix 13**.

Broadly, disclosure of schemes and arrangements is required in circumstances where a person might be expected to obtain a tax advantage as one of the main benefits of the arrangements, and the arrangements fall within the prescribed statutory regulations. Disclosures of proposals which if entered into would be notifiable are also required – see FA 2004 section 306(2). The disclosure itself will not automatically have an effect on the tax position of the person who uses it, as the aim of the disclosure procedure is to bring tax avoidance schemes to the attention of HMRC and enable the government to legislate against the mischief in question. Alternatively, HMRC could challenge such schemes under general legal principles without enacting legislation.

The person required to disclose the scheme and provide HMRC with the prescribed information relating to it, will normally be the scheme promoter defined in FA 2004 section 307 as:

- a person in the course of a relevant business who is
    - responsible for the design of the proposed arrangements,
    - makes a firm approach to another person in relation to the notifiable proposal with a view to making it available for implementation, or

---

[62] FA 2004 sections 306 to 319; SI 2004/1864 (*Tax Avoidance Schemes (Information) Regulations 2004*); SI 2004/1865 (*Tax Avoidance Schemes (Promoters and Prescribed Circumstances) Regulations 2004*); SI 2006/1543 (*Tax Avoidance Schemes (Prescribed Descriptions of Arrangements) Regulations 2006*); SI 2007/3104 (*Tax Avoidance Schemes (Penalty) Regulations*); SI 2009/2033 (*Tax Avoidance Schemes (Prescribed Descriptions of Arrangements) (Amendment) Regulations 2009)* and others as set out in the **Glossary**

- who makes the notifiable proposal available for implementation by other persons, and
- in relation to notifiable arrangements which are implemented he is responsible for their design, or their organisation or managements.

Relevant business is defined as any trade, profession or business which involves providing other persons with taxation services, a bank or a securities house.[63]

If there is no promoter, the promoter is based outside the UK or the scheme is an 'in-house' scheme, the person who enters into any transaction forming part of the notifiable arrangements must make the disclosure.[64] Once notified to HMRC, the arrangement or proposal will be given a scheme reference number which must be provided to any other user of the scheme, and the reference number and information on the scheme must be included in the relevant tax return of the user under self-assessment. The promoter is required to provide the client with the reference number, and any person who is a party to a notifiable arrangement must provide the number to HMRC relating to any reference number notified to him and the time when he obtains or expect to obtain the tax advantage.[65] Additionally, under FA 2004 section 313ZA where services are provided in connection with notifiable arrangements, and there is either a reference number or the promoter has failed to notify HMRC of the arrangements under FA 2004 section 308, the promoter must provide HMRC with prescribed information relating to the client.

There are stiff financial penalties for failing to disclose a relevant scheme[66] (set out in **Appendix 12**) but more importantly for a buyer, it will wish to be put on notice as to whether any past tax planning entered into by the target is vulnerable to legislative change in the future or a challenge from HMRC. If the target has engaged in a notifiable arrangement the buyer should ask for a

---

[63] FA 2004 section 307(2)

[64] FA 2004 section 310

[65] See FA 2004 section 313

[66] See **Appendix 12 (Penalties and Errors)**

specific indemnity to cover the target's costs (including management time) relating to any enquiry by HMRC or change in legislation with retrospective effect. If the target company is involved in providing tax advice and planning, and/or in tax avoidance schemes, enhanced due diligence would be required.

Suggested warranties relating to DOTAS are as follows:

a) "The Company has never been involved in any scheme or arrangement which might fall within any provisions requiring reporting of the details of such scheme or arrangement to HMRC or any other Tax Authority, including the disclosure requirements in FA 2004 sections 306 – 319 ("Notifiable Arrangements") including (but not limited to) such schemes or arrangements in respect of the following:

   (i) income tax, capital gains tax and/or corporation tax;

   (ii) national insurance contributions;

   (iii) stamp duty land tax;

   (iv) ATED;

   (v) VAT;

   (vi) IHT;

   (vii) financial products including but not limited to shares and securities.

b) "As far as the Sellers are aware there is no reason why HMRC would be entitled to enquire into any arrangement entered into by the Company which could be a Notifiable Arrangement including where a penalty might arise under TMA section 98C (*Notification under Part 7 of Finance Act 2004*)."

c) "The Company has included under self-assessment the relevant reference number relating to all Notifiable Arrangements it has been involved in."

3.19 Distributions and Dividends

Distributions are widely defined[67] and include the following:

• any dividend paid by the company including a capital dividend;

---

[67] CTA 2010 sections 1000 to 1023

- any distribution out of the assets of a company whether in cash or otherwise but other than a repayment of capital on the shares or relating to new consideration received by the company for the distribution;
- any redeemable share capital issued by the company in respect of securities other than wholly for new consideration;
- any other security issued by the company in respect of shares in, or securities of, the company and otherwise than for new consideration;
- any interest or other distribution out of the assets of the company in respect of securities of the company which are non-commercial securities under CTA 2010 section 1005, except the amount which represents the principal secured by the securities and that which represents a reasonable commercial return for the use of the principal;
- any transfer of assets or liabilities by a company to its members or vice versa whereby the value of the benefit received by the member based on market value exceeds the consideration given;
- any bonus issued following repayment of share capital, under CTA 2010 section 1022;
- certain expenses of a close company treated as a distribution, under CTA 2010 section 1064 (see paragraph 3.12). CTA 2010 section 1136 defines a qualifying distribution as any distribution other than:
  - any redeemable share capital or security issued other than for new consideration; or
  - any security issued by a company in respect of securities in the company otherwise than for consideration.

A company must provide a return for non-qualifying distributions to HMRC under CTA 2010 section 1101 within 14 days from the end of the accounting period in which it was made, or if not made within an accounting period, within 14 days of having been made. A recipient of a qualifying distribution is entitled to request a written statement from the company showing the amount or value of the distribution and the amount of the tax credit would be entitled under CTA 2010 section 1100.

A payment from a subsidiary before a sale or hive-off is a frequent tax planning technique to reduce or avoid capital gains tax on the sale of the subsidiary, although care is needed to avoid falling within the value shifting provisions under TCGA section 31 (discussed further in paragraph 3.38 below).

Warranties relating to distributions include the following:

a) "The Company has made no distributions as set out in CTA 2010 section 1000(1), save for dividends other than a capital dividend."

b) "The Company has made the proper returns within the required period relating to all non-qualifying dividends it has made under CTA 2010 section 1101."

3.20 Dormant Companies

Generally, dormant companies are ignored for tax purposes. The existence of any purported dormant companies within any group requires a warranty that such companies have been dormant for all tax purposes, and that they have not carried on any activities such that a tax charge might arise. The tax indemnity is likely to cover any tax liability of any dormant subsidiary in any case.

a) "There are no, nor have there ever been, any dormant companies within the Group."

b) "Those subsidiaries within the Group classified as being dormant have at all times been dormant and never carried on any activities, including but not limited to trading activities, such that an adjustment to the Company's taxation could be required by any Tax Authority."

3.21 Employment-Related Tax Issues

This area requires particular attention during the due diligence process because of the strict obligations on employers for the collection and payment of income tax and national insurance contributions (NIC) under the pay-as-you-earn system (PAYE). It is an area where companies' compliance is often found to be problematic (sometimes due to deliberate error if the company has cash flow problems but more often due to carelessness, ignorance or wishful thinking). The buyer will also want an exact position of the target company's PAYE position as at completion and assurance that the target has sufficient working capital to meet the current liabilities. NIC is discussed in paragraph 3.28 below and PAYE is discussed further in paragraph 3.29 below.

Income tax arises under the main charging provision of ITEPA section 62, namely *"on any salary, wages or fee, or any gratuity or other profit of incidental benefit of any kind obtained by the employee in money or money's worth or anything else which constitutes an emolument of the employment"*.

ITEPA provides self-contained rules for income tax which can arise in respect of employment-related securities, securities options, benefits-in-kind, and deemed payments and benefits. Tax avoidance in this area has been an industry for many years, with schemes and arrangements devised to avoid the payment of NIC for employed workers through the provision of certain types of benefits-in-kind (although most of the previous blatant loopholes have been closed) and to take workers outside the regime of employment income. These have included arrangements where the individual is purported to be self-employed or the use of a personal services company by the individual contracting with the employer company. These schemes have been curtailed by increasingly robust anti-avoidance legislation including the 'IR35' provisions[68] and the DOTAS regime.

FA 2011 introduced anti-avoidance rules on disguised remuneration[69] which cover situations where benefits are provided to employees by third parties. The benefits can include loans, assets and money, and the third party may include an employer acting as trustee. The rules cover situations where money or another asset held by the third party is earmarked for the employee, or is paid or transferred both directly and indirectly and can include the provisions of security for loans, as well as an asset being made available on terms which would be equivalent to transferring the benefit of ownership. Excluded from the regime are HMRC approved share schemes, certain transactions under

---

[68] ITEPA sections 48 to 61 – *'Arrangements made by intermediaries'*

[69] Contained in ITEPA section 554A to 554Z21 Part 7A – *Employment income provided through third parties*; see also HMRC Manuals starting at EIM 4500

employee benefit packages, the earmarking of deferred remuneration, and pension schemes. If these rules apply, PAYE will be due on the value of the benefit deemed to have been received.

The disguised remuneration legislation will be relevant to employers which have existing:

- employee benefit trusts;
- employer-financed retirement benefits schemes;
- loan arrangements involving employees and third parties; and
- unapproved share and option plans involving a trustee or third party.

A snapshot picture of the target's compliance with the relevant legislative requirements should be contained in any PAYE audit reports by HMRC and, therefore, a negative warranty is the standard way of asking for sight of any such audit. In addition to the standard administration and tax compliance warranty, a buyer will want full information on the following issues relating to the target company's workforce:

- the company has paid proper recognition to the tests and requirements of employed persons;
- all record keeping for the past four year relating to emoluments and benefits provided to employees, directors and officers of the company is in order and up to date;
- details of arrangements entered into with consultants and self-employed persons providing services to the target company;
- whether there are employees who might be subject to dual jurisdictions under double tax treaty agreements;
- what benefits-in-kind employees receive and how they are treated for tax purposes;
- what dispensations under ITEPA section 65[70] have been applied for and are in force;
- what employment-related securities and security options have been granted to employees and officers of the company and

---

[70] Dispensations relating to benefits within provisions not applicable to lower-paid employment

any other individuals including the recently introduced Employee Shareholder Shares (ESS)[71];

- confirmation that directors and officers of the company (including non-executive directors and shadow directors) have been and are properly treated as employees for tax purposes;
- whether there are special arrangements between the company and any tax authority relating to specific employees including those coming to or leaving the UK such as tax equalisation arrangements, and/or in respect of certain benefits and deemed payments;
- what redundancy programmes, if any, the company has operated;
- confirmation that the company has not made any tax-free payments to any individuals;
- what payments were made in respect of any termination of employments purported to fall within the provisions of ITEPA section 401;
- whether the following regimes may apply to the target in any capacity:
    a)   the Managed Service Companies regime;[72]
    b)   IR35 anti-avoidance provisions;[73]
    c)   Agency Worker legislation;[74]
- whether there are any arrangements relating to payments made by the company to offshore employees and directors; and
- what loan arrangements and similar employment-related benefits have been provided to any person by the company.

Set out below is a comprehensive set of warranties covering the issues above. Each warranty needs to be considered, and only included when relevant to the circumstances of the target. If a group is involved the warranties should also cover subsidiaries:

---

[71] Finance Act 2013 Schedule 23

[72] ITEPA sections 61A to 61J

[73] Provisions to workers under arrangements made by intermediaries ITEPA sections 48 to 61

[74] ITEPA sections 44 to 47

a) "All salaries wages fees and benefits in money or money's worth paid by the Company at any time to employees and officers and directors of the Company under ITEPA section 62 have been made subject to deduction of income tax and employees' NIC and the Company has at all times properly complied with all the provisions in respect of the PAYE provisions and similar provisions outside the United Kingdom, including the proper deduction of income tax and other charges on all payments made to persons who supply services to the Company."

b) "The Company has never had a PAYE audit by HMRC or any other Tax Authority relating to PAYE or equivalent system operating outside the United Kingdom to which the Company and any of its Subsidiaries are subject."

c) "The Company has comprehensive and accurate records properly compiled during the past [four] years relating to payments it has made or deemed to have made including emoluments and benefits provided to all its employees and officers and directors and such records will be up to date as at Completion."

d) "The Company has never claimed for dispensations relating to income tax payable on particular expenses payments or benefits of any directors and/or employees under ITEPA section 65 (*"Dispensations"*)."

e) "The Company has full documentation relating to all dispensations under ITEPA section 65 (*"Dispensations"*) applied for and all such applications were properly made and given by HMRC and so far as the Sellers are aware there is no reason for HMRC to withdraw such Dispensations."

f) "The Company has no employees nor any directors or officers who are not UK resident, or who are non-UK domiciled or who might be considered to have dual residency."

g) "The Company has never entered into any arrangements with any Tax Authority relating to employees coming to or leaving the United Kingdom for work purposes including tax-equalisation arrangements."

h) "The Company has no employees, officers or directors based outside the United Kingdom with whom special arrangements have been entered into relating to reduction in income tax, and there are no arrangements relating to payments to employees officers or directors wherever-based whereby payments are made involving offshore jurisdictions including under dual employment contracts."

i) "The Company has at no time employed agency workers to which ITEPA section 688 (*"Agency Workers"*) could apply."

j) "The Company has never been involved in arrangements involving agents and agency workers whereby ITEPA sections 44 to 47 could apply (*"Agency workers provisions"*)."

k) "The Company has at no time been involved in arrangements involving intermediaries (either as a client or as an intermediary) whereby ITEPA sections 48 to 61 (*"Workers under arrangements made by intermediaries"*) could apply."

l) "The Company is not a managed service company nor is it a managed service company provider for the purposes of ITEPA section 61A to 61J (*"Managed Service Companies"*)."

m) "The Company [and its Subsidiaries] has [have] never granted options over its shares or issued shares at any time to any of its employees officers or directors or to their associates nor have there been any transfers of Shares by other persons to such persons."

n) "The Company has agreed in writing with Shares Valuation HMRC the market value of any Shares including ESS which it has issued to its employees officers and directors and their associates and all information supplied by the Company to HMRC in respect of such agreement was accurate and true in all respects."

o) "The Company has never issued shares to employees under the provisions of Finance Act 2013 Schedule 23 (Employer Shareholder Shares/ESS)."

p) "There are no outstanding options over the Company's shares nor will any rights arise whereby a person shall be entitled to acquire shares in the Company on Completion or at any time after Completion and there are no circumstances whereby following Completion a charge to income tax and/or NIC could arise in respect of such shares held by any person or in respect of such options and rights."

q) "The Company has not at any time participated in any scheme or arrangement one of the purposes of which was to avoid or reduce the payment of income tax and/or NIC."

r) "No payments have been made by the Company relating to termination of employment under ITEPA section 401 (*Payments connected with termination of a person's employment*)."

s) "Payments made in respect of termination of employment under ITEPA section 401 have received clearance from HMRC and such payments have been made after the proper deduction of income tax and no liability to NIC can arise in respect of such payments."

t) "The Company has never provided loans to any employee officer and/or director of the Company or to any of their associates."

u) "The Company has never provided any employment-related loans which would be regarded as taxable cheap loans under ITEPA Part 2 Chapter 7 (*Applications of provisions to agency workers*) and no employment-related loans have ever been released or written off."

v) "All payments made by the Company relating to or in connection with (including deemed payments and benefits of any kind) to employees officers and directors were and remain properly allowable as a trading expense and deductible in calculating the profits of the Company."

3.22 Group Issues

Chapter 9 (Group Issues) considers in some depth the tax issues relating to groups – namely chargeable gains groups and groups for corporation tax purposes, intellectual property, loan relationships, stamp taxes and VAT. If the target is a standalone company the only warranty relating to group issues is the following:

a) **"The Company is not and never has been a member of a group for any tax purposes whatsoever."**

If the company is a group or is leaving a group the following warranties relating to corporation tax issues:

b) **"The Company has never claimed or been involved in a claim for group relief referred to in CTA 2010 section 97(2) (including consortium claims and surrenders); has never been involved in group payment arrangements to which the provisions of TMA section 59F may apply; and has never been involved in a surrender of a tax under CTA 2010 section 963."**

The following warranties are relevant to group issues:
- paragraphs 3.10.2 and 3.10.3 cover chargeable gains issues;
- paragraph 3.15(c) refers to corporation tax group issues;
- paragraph 3.27(d) covers loan relationship intra-group transfers;
- paragraph 3.25 covers intellectual property (see warranties at (f), (l), (o) and (m) for group-related issues);
- paragraph 3.33 covers secondary liabilities issues, which can only arise in respect of groups;
- paragraph 3.35(b) (h) and (i) deal with stamp taxes and
- paragraph 3.37.1 cover VAT group issues.

3.23 Inheritance Tax

Inheritance tax can arise on the transfer of property by an individual during his or her lifetime if the individual gifts property which has a value exceeding the nil rate IHT band allowance at the date of the transfer and the individual dies within seven year of the gift. An example would be the transfer of shares for nil consideration or below market value between connected persons. Depending on the circumstances of the transfer, the IHT charge could arise at the time of the transfer or on the death of the transferor. If the tax remains unpaid after it should have been paid, the transferee, or any person in whom the property is vested at any time after its taxable transfer, could be liable.[75] These provisions could also apply to any property for which the sale of the original transferred property was re-invested.[76] In circumstances where these provisions might apply, such as in the sale involving a closely held company a buyer should ask for assurance that the IHT provisions will not apply after the transfer. Generally, IHT warranties should not be required when the shares or assets relate to a corporation which is not a close company, although such warranties are commonly requested regardless of whether a charge could conceivably arise.

It is unlikely that an IHT charge would arise in standard transactions in that any buyer of the property (and any person deriving title from that buyer) will only be liable for any IHT if the property is subject to an 'Inland Revenue charge'.[77] A 'buyer' means a buyer in good faith for consideration in money or money's worth other than a nominal consideration. A buyer will also include a lessee, mortgagee or other person who for consideration acquires in interest in the property in question.

An 'Inland Revenue charge' is widely defined, being any IHT charge which is unpaid after it ought to have been paid. The charge attaches to any property which directly or indirectly represents the property on which the charge arose.[78] However, the exceptions to this charge, when the original property subject to the charge is disposed of, are as follows:

a) land in England and Wales where the charge was not registered as a land charge or was not protected by notice on the register;

b) personal property (not being land) situated in the United Kingdom and any property situated outside the United Kingdom and where the buyer had no notice of the facts giving rise to the charge; and

---

[75] IHTA section 199(1)

[76] IHTA section 199(5)

[77] IHTA section 199(3)

[78] IHTA section 237

c) property to which a certificate of discharge has been given by HMRC.

Additionally the Inland Revenue charge expires at the end of the six years after the date on which the tax became due in circumstances when the property is disposed of to a buyer, as defined above.

If a close company makes a transfer of value that company will be liable for tax chargeable, but if the tax remains unpaid after it ought to have been paid the participators with more than a 5% interest in the company and any individual whose estate was increased by the relevant transfer of value, are liable.[79] (See paragraph 3.12 relating to Close Companies and transfers of values to participators and the relevant protective warranty set out above.)

Suitable protective warranties either in respect of a transfer of assets or the sale of shares are set out as follows:

a) "There is no Inland Revenue charge for unpaid tax as referred to in IHTA section 237 (*Imposition of Charge*) on [any assets of the Company] [on the assets being transferred][on the Shares] which could arise either directly or indirectly."

b) "No person has a limited interest nor has any person the power to sell or mortgage, or create a terminable charge on [any of the assets of the Company] [on any of the assets being transferred] [on the Shares] under IHTA section 212 (*Power to raise tax*)."

c) "The Company, being a close company under IHTA section 202 (*Close Company*), has made no transfer of value whereby a tax charge could arise on a participator in the Company under IHTA section 94 (*Charge on participators*)."

3.24 Insolvency Issues

Insolvency covers a situation where a business does not have sufficient assets to pay its debts, and arrangements are entered into whereby there is a change relating to its control and

---

[79] IHTA section 202

administration. The different formal arrangements include the following:

- a compulsory liquidation;
- a voluntary winding up (either members or creditors);
- the appointment of an administrative receiver;[80]
- a voluntary arrangement between the members and the company's creditors;
- a scheme of arrangement;
- a liquidation (either voluntary or compulsory);
- the company entering into administration;
- liquidation following administration.

Chapter 6 (Special Situations) discusses issues relating to insolvencies in greater depth. However, the following warranties relating to relevant issues are appropriate:

a) **"The Company has at all times had sufficient assets to pay its debts and has never entered into arrangements, either voluntary or involuntary, formal or informal, involving its liquidation or winding up, it being put into administration, the appointment of an administrative receiver, receiver or liquidator, or entering into a scheme of arrangement."**

b) **"The Company has never sought, nor should have sought, at any time protection from its creditors nor has it ever been involved in insolvency arrangements involving its business or the business of another person."**

3.25 Intellectual Property

FA 2002 Schedule 29-30[81] introduced a new corporation tax regime for intangible assets (which includes intellectual property and goodwill), effective from 1 April 2002 and covering intangible assets acquired or created after that date. Companies became entitled to tax relief for relevant costs generally equivalent to the rate of depreciation in their accounts. This legislation was re-

---

[80] Under the Enterprise Act 2002, only a floating charge holder (i.e. lender) can appoint an administrative receiver provided the charge was made before 15 September 2003

[81] Gains and losses of a company from intangible fixed assets

written under CTA 2009 Part 8 (sections 711 to 906)[82] (*Intangible Fixed Assets*) and Part 9 (sections 907 to 930)(*Intellectual property: know-how and patents*) but with very few changes to the FA 2002 provisions. An acquisition of a company which holds intellectual property (IP) assets or is an SPV holding IP assets will require warranties to identify the nature of them, confirm title and ownership (an issue often overlooked and requiring specific due diligence) and stating whether a post-completion tax liability might arise.

Generally, before FA 2002 the tax treatment of intangible assets owned by a company differed substantially from the accountancy treatment, with goodwill taxed as a capital asset and chargeable gains roll-over relief generally restricted to goodwill and IP assets that were considered to be part of goodwill (such as unregistered trademarks). With the current corporate tax regime for IP assets, receipts for IP assets are taxed as income and expenses (and losses) on disposal are deductible against income.

Deductible expenses include those incurred in creating, acquiring and enhancing IP assets, as well as amortisation deductions for acquired IP assets and the costs of registering and maintaining the registration of IP assets. Roll-over relief is available if the proceeds on the disposal of IP assets are reinvested in qualifying replacement intangible assets (although claiming roll-over relief will affect the amortisation deduction available on the replacement asset).

The pre-FA 2002 regime continues to apply to intangible assets owned by a company (or an associated company) held at 1 April 2002, although roll-over relief under the new regime is available on the disposal of pre-FA 2002 assets.

A high proportion of companies and businesses are likely to have intellectual property. Warranties relating to IP rights are set out below. Those listed in paragraph (l) to (o) are only applicable if the target has been a member of a group. The use of the phrase 'IP Assets' should be a defined term in the SPA.

---

[82] For accounting periods after 1 April 2009 for corporation tax and for 2009 to 2010 onwards for income and CGT purposes

a) "The legal situs of the IP Assets is the United Kingdom and all related rights are recognised and protected under UK law and are owned absolutely by the Seller."

b) "The IP Assets were acquired or created by the Company after 1 April 2002 and fall within the definition of 'intangible fixed assets' in CTA 2009 section 711(2)."

c) "None of the IP Assets were created or acquired on or before 1 April 2002."

d) "None of the IP Assets have been acquired or disposed of since the Accounts Date."

e) "Since the Accounts Date no circumstances have arisen as a result of which any IP Assets will need to be revalued."

f) "The Company has not made any election under CTA 2009 section 730 to write down the cost of an intangible fixed asset for tax purposes at a fixed rate."

g) "The Company has not made any claim for roll-over relief under CTA 2009 section 757 in respect of any IP Asset."

h) "The IP Assets are held for the purpose of a trade and none are held for non-commercial purposes."

i) "All receipts received by the Company in respect of the IP Assets have been taxed as income and not as capital."

j) "No payments have been made to any employee of the Company in respect of the IP Assets, the right to receive such a payment being under Patents Act 1977 section 40."

k) "All appropriate withholdings and tax deductions required to be made in respect of payments made by the Company relating to the IP Assets have been made and have been properly accounted for to HMRC."

l) "No IP asset has been transferred to or by the Company on a no gain/no loss basis in a case where the Company and the other company (being either the transferor or the transferee) are members of the same group under CTA 2009 section 775."

m) "The execution or completion of this agreement [or any other Event since the Accounts Date] will not result in any

IP Asset being deemed to have been disposed of and re-acquired by the Company under section 780 CTA (*Deemed realisation and reacquisition at market value*) or CTA 2009 section 785 (*Principal company becoming member of another group*)."

n)   "The Company has not made any claim to postpone a charge on transfer of a trade under CTA 2009 section 827 (*Claims to postpone charge on transfer*)."

o)   "No reallocation of a degrouping charge relating to IP assets has been made within the Group as referred to under CTA 2009 section 792 (*Reallocation of charge within group*)."

p)   "The Company has not entered into any tax avoidance arrangements, the main object or one of the main objects of which was to enable the Company to obtain a debit to which it would not otherwise be entitled or to avoid having to bring a credit into account or to reduce the amount of any such credit."

3.26 Land and Property Issues

CTA 2009 sections 202 to 291 set out the corporation taxation provisions for a company's property business (both UK and overseas). The other specific charges to tax relating to land and property are SDLT and VAT which are discussed separately in paragraphs 3.35 and 3.37 of this chapter. FA 2013 introduced a new annual tax on enveloped dwellings (ATED) which applies to UK dwellings worth more than £500,000 which are owned by a company, partnership or a collective investment scheme. It is conceivable that a private company may own such a property and an annual charge could arise. Reliefs for the tax are for property rental business, property developers, property opened to the public, property traders and financial institutions acquiring dwellings in the course of lending.

A UK property business is defined as a business for generating income from land in the UK and every transaction entered into by the company for that purpose otherwise than in the course of such a business.[83] This covers exploitation of an estate, interest or right in or over land as a source of rents or other receipts.[84] The following activities are not treated as generating income from land[85]:

- farming and market gardening in the UK;
- any other occupation of land;
- mines quarries and other concerns under CTA 2009 section 39.

An overseas property business is defined as every business which the company carries on for generating income from land outside the United Kingdom.[86]

Corporation tax is charged on the profits of a property business in the same way as the profits of a trade, using generally accepted accounting practice[87] but without regard to loan relationships and derivative contracts. There are specific rules relating to receipts of lease premiums, which are generally treated as capital, except for leases of 50 years or less, in which case a portion of the premium will be treated as revenue[88]. CTA 2009 section 250 deals with reverse premiums.

If the target company is a trading company or a holding company of a trading group and unlikely to be a property business the following warranty should be sufficient:

"The Company has no property business, either in the United Kingdom or outside the United Kingdom, and as defined in CTA 2009 sections 204 to 206."

If the target company has a property business the following warranties will be relevant:

a) **"The Company has had a UK property business as defined in CTA 2009 section 205 since incorporation but has never been involved in an overseas property business as defined in CTA 2009 section 206."**

---

[83] CTA 2009 section 205

[84] CTA 2009 section 207

[85] CTA 2009 section 208

[86] CTA 2009 section 206

[87] CTA 2009 section 210

[88] CTA 2009 sections 217 to 235

b) "The Company has at all times properly accounted for the profits of its property business and including for the avoidance of doubt under CTA 2009 sections 210 and 214."

c) "The provisions of CTA 2009 Part 4 Chapter 4[89] (*Profits of property businesses: Lease Premiums etc*) are not and have not been relevant in respect of the Company's property business."

3.27 Loan Relationships

The loan relationship rules were originally contained in FA 1996, amended in FA 2002 Schedule 25 for accounting periods beginning after September 2002 (including anti-avoidance provisions), underwent changes in FA 2004 Schedule 10 to take account of revised UK financial reporting standards for financial instruments, and subsequently re-written in CTA 2009 Parts 5 and 6 (section 292 to 569). Part 5 deals with loan relationships and Part 6 with relationships which are treated as loan relationships. Because of the highly technical and specialised nature of the subject and involving accounting issues, it is not possible to cover it in detail in this publication. Following consultation, the Finance Act 2015 introduced changes to the taxation of corporate debt and derivative contracts including amendments to bring the calculation of taxable amounts in line with the usual approach to the computation of profits, for both commercial and tax purposes. CTA 2009 section 323A excludes taxable amounts which would otherwise arise where arrangements are made to restructure the debts of a company in financial distress with a view to ensuring its continued solvency. Also a regime-wide anti-avoidance rule was to counter arrangements entered into with a main purpose of obtaining a tax advantage by way of the loan relationships or derivative contracts rules.

For corporation tax purposes, all profits arising to a company from its loan relationships are chargeable to tax as income.[90] If the loan relationship arises for the purposes of a trade (and will arise if the company is a party to the creditor relationship in the course of

---

[89] CTA 2009 sections 215 to 247

[90] CTA 2009 section 295

activities forming an integral part of the trade[91]), then credits are treated as receipts of the trade and brought into account in calculating profits, and debits will be treated as expenses of the trade and deductible in calculating those profits.[92]

In respect of non-trading loan relationships, and which will arise for virtually all companies (at the very least from time to time), a company has non-trading profits from its loan relationships if the non-trading credits for the accounting period in question exceed the non-trading debits or there are no debits for the period.[93] A non-trading deficit will arise if non-trading debits exceed the non-trading credits.[94] Non-trading deficits of any accounting period must be carried forward and set off against future non-trading profits of the company unless it can be surrendered as group relief or a claim can be made to set it off against any profits of the company for the deficit period or carried back for set off against profits of an earlier periods under CTA 2009 section 459.[95]

A loan relationship exists when a company stands in the position of a creditor or debtor for any money debt which arises from a transaction for the lending of money.[96] A money debt is a debt which falls to be settled:

- by the payment of money;
- by the transfer of a right to settlement under a debt which is itself a money; or
- by the issue or transfer of any shares in a company,[97]

and includes bank borrowings and deposits, and rights or liabilities attached to securities issued in relation to a debt.[98]

Since 1 January 2005 companies must account for loan relationships using UK GAAP or IAS subject to certain exceptions

---

[91] CTA 2009 section 298(1)

[92] CTA 2009 section 297

[93] CTA 2009 section 301(4)

[94] CTA 2009 section 301(4) & (5)

[95] CTA 2009 section 457

[96] CTA 2009 section 302

[97] CTA 2009 section 303

[98] CTA 2009 section 305

(see CTA 2009 sections 315 to 327). There are provisions for exchange gains and losses to be included in the calculation of profits and losses of loan relationships (see CTA 2009 section 328) and rules for companies ceasing to be a party to loan relations (CTA 2009 section 331 and 332).

CTA 2009 Part 5 Chapter 15 (sections 440 to 455) sets out the anti-avoidance legislation. It covers loan relationships of a company which have an unallowable purpose – being a purpose which is not amongst the business or other commercial purposes of the company[99]. Section 443 provides for restriction of relief for interest where tax relief schemes are involved, and the anti-avoidance provisions cover transactions not at arm's length.

In a transaction involving the sale and purchase of a company whose trade is not that of lending money the following issues justify relevant warranties:

- that the target company has properly accounted for all loan relationships, that it has not entered into any arrangement whereby it would make voluntary payments of interest which could not be relieved under the relevant provisions, and it has only been a party to a loan relationship for a non-trading purposes and not for any unallowable purpose;[100]
- if the target is a close company, it has not entered into a loan relationship with any participator or whereby a participator benefits under any arrangement with a third party, and all loan relationships with connected parties have been entered into on an arm's-length basis;
- if the target is part of a group, whether there have been any intra-group transfers and/or reorganisations (see CTA 2009 Part 5 Chapter 4 sections 335 to 348);
- whether the connected companies relationship provisions under CTA 2009 Part 5 Chapter 5 (sections 348 to 352) have ever applied.

Warranties are set out as follows:

---

[99] CTA 2009 section 442

[100] Also covered under warranty set out in paragraph 3.5(a)

a) "The Company has properly accounted for all loan relationships as defined in CTA 2009 section 302 to which it has been a party."

b) "The Company has never been a party to a creditor relationship for the purposes of a trade."

c) "The Company has not entered into any arrangements relating to loans with a participator (referred to in CTA 2010 sections 455, 459, and 460) nor any arrangements set out in CTA 2010 sections 464A and 464C."

d) "No Group Company has ever been a party to an intra-group transfer of a loan or a reorganisation to which CTA 2009 Part 5 Chapter 4 (section 335 to 347 – *Continuity of treatment on transfers within groups or on reorganisations*) could apply."

e) "The Company has never been a party to a scheme or arrangement involving any loan relationship for the purpose of tax avoidance including for the avoidance of doubt arrangements to which CTA 2009 section 440 to 455A (*Tax Avoidance*) could apply."

f) "The Company has never been involved in a relationship which would fall within the definition of a 'connected companies relationship' as defined under CTA 2009 section 348(2) nor where CTA 2009 Part 5 Chapters 5, 6 and 8 could apply."

3.28 National Insurance Contributions (NICs)

National insurance contributions are taxes in all but name, with class 1 NIC relevant for employers (including companies, businesses/sole traders and partnerships) as it must be collected through PAYE, and classes 2, 3 and 4 for self-employed earners. The tax take from NIC is the second largest source of HMRC receipts after income tax[101] and is therefore of prime importance to the Exchequer in absolute values and in respect of cash flow. However, there is a history of tax avoidance schemes in relation to NIC which have steadily been curtailed through anti-avoidance

---

[101] Office for Budget Responsibility – '*Economic & Fiscal Outlook*' March 2011

legislation including the IR35 legislation and more recently involving DOTAS.

NIC legislation is contained in the Social Security Contributions and Benefits Act 1992, the Social Security Administration Act 1992 and the Social Security Act 1998, together with the main governing regulations namely the Social Security (Contributions) Regulation 2001 (SI 2001/1004). The anti-avoidance DOTAS legislation is contained in SSAA 1992 section 132A(7) and SI 2007/785.

The PAYE warranties contained in paragraph 3.29 below are relevant for NIC because Class 1 NIC is collected under PAYE (save for in certain exceptional circumstances[102]). A number of the warranties contained in paragraph 3.21 (Employment Related Tax Issues) which specifically refer to NIC are also relevant. However, the following issues require clarification through additional NIC warranties:

- the target company has not made payments to third parties on behalf of employees on which NIC could arise;
- NIC has been properly collected and paid in respect of earnings and all other payments made to all employees, office holders and directors (including shadow directors) of the target company;
- no secondary NIC has arisen or will arise in respect of employment-related securities[103] and/or securities options granted by the target to any individual;
- whether or not the target pays Class 1A and/or Class 1B NIC;[104]
- whether the target has any overseas employees who are subject to NIC in the UK.

Appropriate NIC warranties are set out as follows:[105]

---

[102] When the employer company is not resident nor has a place of business in the UK in which case the employee must self-assess – see SI 2001/1004 reg 145(1)(b) and Schedule 4 paragraph 30

[103] Namely, readily convertible assets

[104] Class 1A NIC may arise where an employed earner receives benefits-in-kind which are not subject to Class 1 NIC; Class 1B NICs are payable when an employer enters into a PAYE Settlement Agreement for tax whereby the employer deals with NICs on items in a lump sum after the end of the tax year. Class 1B NICs are payable only by employers and payment does not provide any benefit entitlement for individuals.

THE TAX SCHEDULE

a) "The Company has at all times abided by its legal obligations as an employer in relation to the collection, payment and reporting of NIC to the relevant Tax Authorities, and it has full documentation relating to all such matters in its possession, and no liabilities relating to NIC applicable to any period before Completion will arise on or after Completion including in respect of securities issued and/or securities options granted before or on Completion."

b) "The Company has never made payments to third parties or deemed payments of employment earnings on which NIC could arise nor has it been required to pay Class 1A and/or Class 1B contributions."

c) "The Company has at all times deducted and made the appropriate payments in respect of NIC on all payments made to its directors and office holders, including non-executive directors providing services under a letter of engagement and shadow directors."

d) "There are no employees of the Company who have worked outside the United Kingdom who have been subject to NIC."

e) "The Company has had no involvement in any scheme or arrangement designed to reduce or avoid the payment of or obligations in respect of NIC including any which require reporting under the DOTAS regime."

f) "So far as the Sellers are aware the Company has never entered into any arrangements which could fall within the provisions of the Disguised Remuneration Rules under ITEPA sections 554A to 554AZ21."

3.29 PAYE

The main legislative framework is contained in ITEPA Part 11 (sections 682–712) and the Income Tax (Pay As You Earn) Regulations 2003 (SI 2003/2682) (*PAYE Regulations*), which are the consolidating regulations which took effect from 6 April 2004 and which charge income tax on employment income, pension income

---

[105] Again, if a group is involved the definition of Company should include Subsidiaries

and social security income. For the purposes of this publication we are only concerned with PAYE on employment income.

The subject of what amounts to employment income and its taxation can be an emotive issue and is often the source of dispute between HMRC and the taxpayer, as well as between the tax advisor and his or her client. The due diligence process should carefully focus on whether the target company or business has properly operated PAYE.

Under PAYE, employers operating in the United Kingdom have the following responsibilities:

- to keep proper PAYE employer records;
- to make PAYE employer returns throughout the tax year and at the end of each tax year;
- to make PAYE payments to HMRC in respect of income tax and primary Class 1 NIC deducted from payments made to employees and to pay secondary Class 1 NIC.

These responsibilities are onerous and the rules are strict. If any income tax or NIC is not deducted or paid over, interest and penalties will arise from an employer's failure to properly apply PAYE and with only limited rights for the employer to make up for under-deductions from future payments it makes to the employee.

An employer's responsibilities to pay and recover payments from the employee under PAYE are set out in SI 2003/268 regulation 68. However, an employer can argue under regulation 72A(1), reasonable care and good faith relating to any under-deduction – this might arise if the employer has been given the wrong tax code for an employee by HMRC (by no means a rare occurrence) in which case HMRC may recover the under-payment from the employee. Nevertheless, the employee can appeal to the tax tribunal against a direction notice which HMRC have given to the employer, under regulations 72B and 72C.

Companies may either unwittingly or deliberately fail to apply the PAYE provisions properly, and such errors may only come to light during a PAYE investigation with HMRC. It is not unusual for businesses which are experiencing a cash flow crisis to ignore its obligations under PAYE and delay or fail to make the required payments over to HMRC. If this issue comes to light during due diligence the outstanding tax, NIC, interest and penalties may need to be made up for by a lower purchase price and therefore involve further negotiation of the consideration. It will also require agreement as to which of the parties in the transaction should negotiate with HMRC over the matter and this should be set out in the tax schedule under the conduct clause.

In addition to whether or not the target company has properly applied PAYE on standard salary payments other issues requiring clarification during due diligence include the following:

- whether HMRC have issued to the target any determinations for unpaid PAYE tax;
- whether the target has entered into any PAYE settlement agreement, whereby HMRC agrees special treatment of certain expenses and taxable benefits provided by the employer to employees, the purpose being to allow the employer to omit small items of payments and benefits from returns on forms P11D and essentially allowing the employer to pay the tax in question;
- the findings of any PAYE inspection;
- whether or not the target operates the quarterly tax payment periods under regulation 70;[106] and
- what the target's PAYE position will be at Completion.

Warranties for PAYE, NIC and Employment Related Tax Issues overlap but the following warranties specific to PAYE are recommended:[107]

a) **"The Company has at all times correctly operated the PAYE system, all payroll records of the Company have at all times been properly maintained and are in proper order, all year end returns have been correctly made, all deductions required to be taken from payments and benefits made and provided to employees, officers and directors (full-time, part-time, executive, non-executive and shadow directors) have been properly effected, and the Company is currently**

---

[106] Generally applicable if the employer has reasonable grounds for believing that the average monthly payments will be less than £1,500

[107] The definition of Company should include Subsidiaries unless the target is a standalone company

up to date with all its obligations under the PAYE provisions."

b) "As at Completion the Company will have no outstanding liabilities relating to the PAYE nor will any such liabilities arise after Completion which relate to any period before Completion."

c) "HMRC have never been required to make a determination of unpaid tax in respect of the Company under Regulation 80 SI 2003/2682 (*Income Tax (Pay As You Earn) Regulations 2003*)."

d) "The Company has never had a PAYE inspection by HMRC."

e) "The Company has never operated the quarterly payment regime under Regulation 70 SI 2003/2682 (*Income tax Pay as you earn) Regulations 2003*)."

3.30 Penalties Regime

The current penalties regime was initially set out in FA 2007 Schedule 24 (*Penalties for Errors*) for corporation tax return periods starting on or after 1 April 2008 and covered errors on returns and documents relating to VAT, PAYE, NIC, chargeable gains, income tax, corporation tax and the CIS. FA 2008 extended the regime to environmental taxes, excise duties, IHT, stamp duties, pension schemes and petroleum revenue tax for tax returns for periods commencing on or after 1 April 2009.

FA 2008 Schedule 36 (*Information & Inspection Powers*) provided HMRC with enhanced powers to obtain information and documents, and FA 2008 Schedule 41 (*Penalties: Failure to Notify and Certain VAT and Excise Wrongdoing*) covers penalties for failure to notify and certain VAT and Excise wrongdoing. **Appendix 12** sets out a summary of the consolidated penalties regime.

FA 2007 Schedule 24 defines the degrees of culpability in respect of penalties for errors which includes the following:

• a 'careless' inaccuracy arises if the taxpayer fails to take reasonable care and which can result in a penalty of 30% of the potential lost revenue;

- a 'deliberate but not concealed' inaccuracy arises if the inaccuracy is deliberate but the taxpayers does not conceal it, which can result in a penalty of 70% of the potential lost revenue;
- a 'deliberate and concealed' inaccuracy arises if it is deliberate on the taxpayer's part and the taxpayer makes arrangements to conceal it, and which can result in a penalty of 100% of the potential lost revenue.

If there is an under-assessment by HMRC of a taxpayer's liability to tax, and the taxpayer has failed to take reasonable steps to notify HMRC within 30 days, beginning with the date of the under-assessed assessment, a penalty can be 30% of the potential lost revenue. If there is an inaccuracy in a document given by the taxpayer to HMRC which was neither careless nor deliberate on the taxpayer's part at that time it will be treated as careless if the taxpayer discovers the inaccuracy at some later time and does not take reasonable steps to inform HMRC. In these cases the penalty can be 30% of the potential lost revenue.

As from 1 April 2010 the concept of fraudulent or negligent conduct was repealed.

All taxpayers are expected to take 'reasonable care' in relation to their tax affairs, and may incur a penalty under the new regime if they fail to do so. Penalties will arise in respect of tax returns which contain an inaccuracy which leads to an understatement of a tax liability or a false or inflated statement of a loss or repayment claim relating to tax and where the inaccuracy was careless, deliberate or deliberate and concealed. The onus will be on the taxpayer to demonstrate that it has taken reasonable care to get their tax right. A disclosure of an error as soon as discovered can reduce a penalty.

HMRC consider that what represents 'reasonable care' will differ depending (essentially) on the level of sophistication of the taxpayer, with companies expected to have a higher level of knowledge and expertise than for individuals (for example).

HMRC emphasise the importance of proper record keeping[108] which would include the taxpayer ensuring that:

- accounting records, systems are documented and are in place from 1 April 2008;
- systems and processes are followed;
- it can show the decision-making processes in relation to the tax returns which are submitted; and
- it applies the correct tax treatment in relation to its circumstances or seeks advice from a tax professional or HMRC.

Relevant warranties relating to potential penalties are:

a) **"The Company has always taken reasonable care when dealing with HMRC and its tax affairs, and has never been guilty or accused by HMRC, of negligent or fraudulent or careless behaviour relating to such affairs and the Company has never concealed any error it was responsible for to HMRC nor suffered any penalty relating thereto."**

b) **"The Company has set up and has in place proper systems and procedures (including accounting systems) which cover all applicable taxes and their proper computation, and has all records providing confirmation that the Company has properly considered the proper tax treatment arising in respect of its affairs and has sought and followed advice from tax professionals."**

c) **"There are no issues relating to Taxation which have come to the attention of the Company and/or its officers and directors in respect of which a voluntary disclosure should have been but was not made to HMRC or any other Tax Authority, or in respect of which consultation with HMRC would have been appropriate."**

3.31 Research and Development (R&D)

Tax relief on qualifying expenditure on R&D can be generous, both in respect of capital assets (currently 100% relief – see below)

---

[108] www.hmrc.gov.uk/about/new-penalties/faqs

and revenue expenditure. There are two schemes for corporation tax relief depending on the size of the company.

Research and development ('R&D') is defined by CTA 2010 section 1138 as being activities which fall to be treated as R&D in accordance with generally accepted accounting practice. The relevant GAAP accounting standard is FRS 102 (replacing SSAP 13 for accounting periods from 1 January 2015) and the equivalent International Accounting Standard is IAS 38 (*Accounting for intangible assets*). FRS 102 states that the standard 'accruals' and 'prudence' accounting concepts apply to R&D, including the principle that expenditure should be written off in the period in which it arises save when its relationship to the revenue of a future period can be established with reasonable certainty. The standard refers to three broad categories of activity – pure research, applied research, and development. Additionally, it states that R&D activity is distinguished from non-R&D activity by the presence or absence of an appreciable element of innovation. FRS 102 is a useful reference as to what may or may not amount to R&D.

Expenses of a trading company incurred on research and development which is related to the trade and directly undertaken by or on behalf of the company will be deductible for the purpose of calculating its trading profits under CTA 2009 section 87. Excluded will be expenses on the acquisition of rights in the R&D, but expenses in carrying out, or providing facilities for carrying out, the R&D will be included. Under CTA 2009 section 87(3) research relating to a trade includes R&D which may lead to or facilitate an extension of the trade, and R&D of a medical nature which has a special relation to the welfare of workers employed in the trade.

CTA 2009 Part 13 (*Additional relief for expenditure on research and development*) (sections 1039 to 1142) sets out the separate provisions for R&D relief, which depend on whether a company is a small or medium-sized enterprise (an 'SME') or a large company, and with relief for both categories of companies in respect of vaccine research (vaccine research is not discussed here nor is R&D relief for insurance companies[109]). A 'large' company is any company that is not an SME.[110] Definitions of an SME[111] which includes a larger SME[112] are set out below:

Enterprise category	Headcount	Turnover	Balance Sheet total
Larger SME[113]	< 500	< Euros 100 million	< Euros 86 million
Medium sized[114]	< 250	< Euros 50 million	< Euros 43 million
Small	< 50	< Euros 10 million	<Euros 10 million

These R & D reliefs were available only up to 1 April 2016. FA 2011 introduced a 200% deduction for qualifying expenditure for SMEs so long as total qualifying R&D expenditure is not less than £10,000 for a 12 month qualifying period.[115] A company may either claim the relief or alternatively can claim a trading loss equal to 200% of the qualifying R&D expenditure.[116]

Relief for large companies[117] is available if its R&D expenditure is at least £10,000 for a 12 month accounting period[118] and is either in-house direct R&D expenditure (see CTA 2009 section 1077); contracted out R&D expenditure (see CTA 2009 section 1078); or contributions to independent R&D expenditure (see CTA 2009 section 1079).

100% capital allowances are available in respect of qualifying expenditure on research and development.[119] CAA Part 6 (sections 437 to 451) sets out the provisions for research and development allowances; Part 7 (sections 452 to 463) sets out provisions know-how allowances; Part 8 (sections 464 to 483) covers patent

---

[109] Covered in CTA 2009 section 1080 for insurance companies

[110] CTA 2009 section 1122

[111] By virtue of Commission Recommendation (EC) No 2003/361

[112] CTA 2009 sections 1120 and 1121

[113] CTA 2009 section 1121

[114] CTA 2009 section 1120

[115] CTA 2009 section 1050

[116] FA 2011 section 43

[117] CTA 2009 Part 13 Chapter 5 (sections 1074 to 1080)

[118] CTA 2009 section 1075

[119] CAA 2001 sections 439 & 441

allowances (namely on the purchase of patent rights[120] for the purposes of a trade or for qualifying non-trade expenditure as defined under CAA 2001 section 469).

Qualifying expenditure is incurred by a person on research and development (under the GAAP definition) directly undertaken by a person carrying on a trade when the expenditure is incurred and the R&D relates to that trade or after incurring the expenditure the person sets up and commences a trade connected with the R&D. Expenditure on land is excluded.

A new regime was introduced by FA 2012 and contained in CTA 2010 Part 8A,[121] with effect from 1 April 2013, which enables companies to elect to apply a 10% rate of corporation tax on profits attributable to qualifying patents ('relevant IP profits of a trade'). To qualify the company must hold qualifying IP rights or hold an exclusive licence in respect of qualifying IP rights. Other 'non-qualifying profits' of the company concerned will be taxed at the main rate of corporation tax. If the target company is involved in R&D, detailed specialist due diligence should be carried out on past claims for R&D relief to ensure that the complex legislative requirements were met, with specific warranties relating to any issues or queries arising from the due diligence. For companies not specifically involved in research the following warranties can be asked for:

a) **"No Group Company has made a claim for relief of any sort relating to expenditure on research and development as defined in CTA 2010 section 1138 nor under CTA 2010 Part 8A (*Patent Box Regime*)."**

b) **"The Company is a small or medium-sized companies as referred to in CTA 2009 section 1119, and has maintained full records relating to claims made for corporation tax relief for qualifying expenditure on research and development and all such claims have been properly made under section 87 and CTA 2009 Part 13 (sections 1039 to 1142)."**

---

[120] CAA 2001 section 464

[121] CTA 2010 sections 357A to 357GF

3.32 Residency issues

A UK resident company is subject to UK tax on its worldwide income (subject to double taxation treaty relief) and a non-UK resident company will be outside the scope of UK taxation for all purposes, save for income arising in the UK. Since 1998 a company which has been incorporated in the United Kingdom is UK resident for UK tax purposes (incorporation rule). Additionally, a company which is controlled and managed in the UK regardless of its place of incorporation, could also be considered to be UK resident. Case law has provided a number of tests for such control and management[122] including the issue of where the real decision making takes place and where the real control of the company resides. The incorporation rule can be overridden under the relevant double taxation treaty with the UK, in which case the 'tie-breaker' test will decide the place of residence, determined by where the actual place of management resides – if it is outside the UK then the company will be a 'Treaty non-resident company' for UK tax purposes. A Treaty non-resident company will be considered as non-resident for all tax purposes, in which case there would be consequences for UK tax relief availability.

Warranties relating to residency issues will be relevant if the target company has a major shareholder (either corporate or an individual) and/or connected parties which are based offshore. In the majority of cases, the certificate of incorporation of the target company can be assumed to reflect its residence, but a company can unwittingly be deemed resident elsewhere, because the real place of its control and management is based outside the United Kingdom by virtue of the residence of a controlling shareholder. Additionally, deliberate changes to a company's residence are often used in tax avoidance schemes, including those which want to take chargeable gains outside the UK tax regime. The following warranties are intended to cover these issues:

a) **"The Company has always been resident in the United Kingdom by virtue of its incorporation and its effective**

---

[122] See *De Beers Consolidated Mines Ltd v Howes* (Surveyor of Taxes) [1906] A.C.455 and more recently *Wood v Holden* (HMIT) [2006] EWCA Civ 26 – see also SP1/90 for HMRC guidance and interpretation

management and control has always been situate in the United Kingdom and it has never been deemed to be dual resident for Taxation purposes by virtue of any tax treaty or otherwise."

b) "There are no shareholders of the Company which Control the Company (either alone or together with Connected Parties) [so far as the Seller is aware] which are resident outside the United Kingdom."

3.33 Secondary Tax Liabilities

The possibility of a tax liability of another person becoming a liability of the target company could arise under the following provisions:

- CTA 2009 section 795 (*Recovery of charge from another group company*) relating to intangible fixed assets and discussed in **Chapter 9** at paragraph 9.4.3 (degrouping);
- CTA 2010 section 710 (*Recovery of unpaid corporation tax for an accounting period beginning before a change of ownership*) – see paragraph 3.33.1 below;
- CTA 2010 section 713 (*Recovery of unpaid corporation tax for an accounting period on or after a change in ownership*) – see paragraph 3.33.1;
- TCGA section 190 (*Tax recoverable from another group company or controlling shareholder*) – see paragraph 3.33.2;
- group corporation tax payment arrangements (discussed in **Chapter 9 (Group Issues)**) at paragraph 9.3;
- paragraph 5 FA 2003 Schedule 7 (*recovery of group relief from another group company or controlling director*) in respect of recovery of SDLT group relief (see warranties in paragraph 3.35); and
- VATA group arrangements under VATA section 43 (joint and several liability of members of a VAT group) and discussed in **Chapter 9 (Group Issues)** at paragraphs 9.3 and 9.9).

A seller should only give a warranty referring to the specific statutory provision in question and resist providing an all-embracing indemnity relating to secondary tax liabilities (see paragraph 3.33.3 below). Furthermore, if the target company has never been part of a group it is unlikely to be responsible for another party's tax liabilities unless it has contracted to do so.

3.33.1 Company purchased tax avoidance schemes

ICTA section 767A was introduced in 1994 and section 767AA in 1998 (now replaced with CTA 2010 sections 710 and 713). These provisions were aimed at arrangements between parties involving blatant tax-avoidance in which a profitable company would be stripped of its trade or business, followed by a change of ownership of a company to a third party, while retaining some cash. The third party would then enter into arrangements reducing that company's tax to nil. The provisions are widely drawn and often require explanation to the client as to what might fall within them, but it has become standard that related warranties be provided by the seller in the sale of a company.

To fall within the provisions of CTA 2010 section 710 the following circumstances must apply:

- there must be a change in ownership in a company (X);
- corporation tax is assessed on X for an accounting period beginning before the change of ownership; and either:
  - at any time in the three year period before the change of ownership of X its trading or business activities ceased or became small or negligible and there was no significant revival of those activities before the change of control; or
  - after the change of control of X but under an arrangement made before the change, its trading or business activities ceased or became small or negligible; or
  - at any time during a six year period beginning three years before a change of control of X and ending three years after such change of control there was a major change in the nature or conduct of its trade or business (major change) and there is a transfer of assets of the taxpayer company to a person who had control of the taxpayer company (or a person connected to such person) either before the change of control or after but subject to arrangements entered into before that date, and the major change is attributable to such transfer; and

- corporation tax is assessed on the taxpayer company for an accounting period beginning before the change of control remains unpaid at any time after six months following the assessment date.

If the above highly contrived circumstances apply, the unpaid tax will be payable by any person who is linked to X, namely:

- a person who had control of X at any time during the period of three years before the change of ownership; or
- a company which is controlled by a person who had control of X at any time during the above mentioned three year period.

Tax avoidance arrangements are required for CTA 2010 section 710 to apply. Only if the target company was in control of a company whose trade became negligible or whose assets were transferred to a controlling person under the conditions referred to above, or if the target company and X were under the same control and the tax avoidance arrangements had been effected could a tax liability fall on the target but not otherwise.

The CTA 2010 section 713 provisions cover the following situation:

- there has been a change of ownership of a company (Y);
- corporation tax relating to an accounting period ending on or after the change has been assessed on Y or an associated company;[123]
- the tax remains unpaid at any time after six months following the assessment; and
- it is reasonable to infer from the terms of any transaction entered into in connection with the change of ownership and any other circumstances relating to the change of control, that at least one of the transactions was entered into by one of the parties on the assumption that the potential tax liability would be unlikely to be met or met in full (the expectation condition).[124]

---

[123] Either at the time of assessment or at an earlier time after the change in ownership of Y – a company which has control of Y, it is a company of which Y has control, or it is a company under the same control as Y – CTA 2010 section 718

[124] CTA 2010 section 714

If the target is linked to Y it can be assessed for the corporation tax arising after Y has left a group of companies. Similar to CTA 2010 section 711, blatant tax avoidance would need to be involved in order for the provisions to be relevant.

3.33.2 TCGA section 190 – Tax recoverable from another group company (Section 190)

Section 190 applies when:

- a chargeable gain has accrued to a company (the taxpayer company);
- the taxpayer company is UK resident when the gain accrues and the gain forms part of its chargeable profits for corporation tax purpose; and
- the whole or part of the corporation tax assessed on the company for the accounting period in which the gain accrued (the relevant accounting period) is unpaid at the end of the period of six months after it became payable.

If a section 190 charge arises and the taxpayer company was a member of a group when the gain accrued ('the relevant date') HMRC can serve notice that the unpaid tax be paid by either the principal company of the group or any other company which, during the 12 months ending with the relevant date, was a member of the group and owned the asset disposed of, or any part of the asset, or in the case where the asset is an interest over another asset, owned either the asset or a part of it. A section 190 charge may also arise in respect of chargeable gains arising on a non-UK resident company with a UK permanent established under sub-section (2)(b).

3.33.3 Secondary Tax Liabilities warranties

a) "There has been no change in the ownership of any company which has been under the control of the Company within the period beginning three years from the date of this Agreement nor has there been any major change in the nature or conduct of the trade or business of any company under the control of the Company during the last three years."

b) "No activities of the trade or business of any company which has been under the control of the Company before the date of this Agreement have ceased or become small or negligible."

c) "During the period beginning three years before the date of this Agreement there have been no transfers of assets of the Company or any company under its control which would fall within CTA 2010 section 710 (*Recovery of unpaid corporation tax*) nor have any arrangements been entered into as referred to under that provision."

d) "The Company has never been involved before the date of this Agreement in any arrangements, nor has any other company which has been under its Control been so involved, whereby corporation tax has been assessed on a company which remained unpaid at any time more than six months after it was assessed such that CTA 2010 section 713 (*Recovery of unpaid corporation tax*) might apply."

e) "There is no unpaid corporation tax relating to a chargeable gain on any Group Member and HMRC have not served notice nor is entitled to serve notice on the Company or any Group Member under TCGA section 190."

f) "The Company [or any member of the Group] cannot become liable for recovery of group relief relating to SDLT under paragraphs 5 and/or 12 FA 2003 Schedule 7."

g) "The Company cannot become liable for a charge to corporation tax arising as a result of a degrouping charge relating to intangible fixed assets under CTA 2009 section 795 (*Recovery of charge from another group company or controlling director*)."

h) "No charge could arise on the Company pursuant to any joint and several liability which may attach to it under VATA section 43 (*Groups of Companies*)."

3.34 Self-assessment

Self-assessment was introduced for companies for accounting periods beginning after 30 June 1999 and replaced the pay-and-file regime. The legislation is contained in FA 1998 Schedule 18

(Schedule 18). Proper self-assessment by a company is an absolute necessity to avoid a claim under a tax indemnity. Whilst this section deals with corporation tax self-assessment, the SDLT regime is also one of self-assessment.

Under self-assessment a corporation has a duty to:

- notify HMRC that it is chargeable to tax if it has not received a notice from HMRC;
- deliver its tax returns to HMRC within the required time limits under Schedule 18 paragraph 14;
- calculate its corporation tax payable for the accounting period in question which in addition to corporation tax arising on chargeable income, gains and trading may include:
  - tax on loans or advances made by a close company to a participators under CTA 2010 section 455 (*Charge to tax in case of loan to participator*);
  - any amount chargeable to tax on profits of any controlled foreign companies under ICTA section 747 (*Imputation of chargeable profits and creditable tax of controlled foreign companies*);
  - supplementary charges if the company operates any ring fence trades (such as oil extraction);
  - cross-border royalties;
- deliver accounts as required under the Companies Act 2006 relating to each accounting period relating to the tax return in question;
- include information relating to any business carried on by the company in partnership during the relevant period;
- keep and retain records sufficient to enable the company to make a correct and complete company tax return; and
- provide relevant information relating to disclosure of any designated tax avoidance schemes.

Interest will arise in respect of tax paid late, and there are a number of penalties which can arise in respect of self-assessment (also set out in **Appendix 1 (Penalties and Errors)** namely:

- a flat-rate penalty (currently £100 if filed within three months of the filling date and £200 in any other case) for non-delivery of the return but increased for successive failures);

- a tax-related penalty for non-delivery, depending on its lateness, at either 10% or 20% of any unpaid tax;
- penalties for an incorrect return;
- penalties for failure to keep records; and
- penalties for failure to produce documents to HMRC when required to do so as provided under statute.

HMRC can amend a return under Schedule 18 paragraph 16 within nine months after a return is delivered, and under Schedule 18 paragraph 24 may issue a notice of enquiry in respect of anything contained in the tax return within 12 months following the statutory filing date or, alternatively, 12 months after filing. After that there are time restrictions on both amending returns and making further enquiries into any such amendments.

HMRC have further powers to make a discovery assessment and a discovery determination under Schedule 18 paragraph 41 if they discover that a company's tax return is incorrect in the following circumstances:

- the error in the tax assessment was brought about carelessly or deliberately by the company, its agent or a partner of the company; or
- after the date on which a notice of enquiry could no longer be made or after their enquiries had been completed, HMRC could not have been reasonable expected based on the information available, to be aware that the tax assessment was incorrect.

Under Schedule 18 paragraph 45, no discovery assessment or discovery determination may be made relating to a mistake in the return which was made in accordance with the practice generally prevailing at the time when it was made. The general time limit for assessment is four years after the end of the accounting period in question under Schedule 18 paragraph 46(1), but in a case involving a loss of tax brought about carelessly by the company it may be made at any time not more than six years after the end of the accounting period to which it relates.[125] An assessment in a case involving a loss of tax brought about deliberately by the

---

[125] Also see also TMA section 36

company, attributable to a failure by the company to comply with an obligation to give notice to HMRC of its chargeability under self-assessment may be made at any time not more than 20 years after the relevant accounting period to which it relates.

Records needed to deliver a correct self assessment return must be preserved by the company for at least six years from the end of the relevant return period under paragraph 21 Schedule 18 and should include:

- details of all receipts and expenses incurred in the course of its activities and supporting documents;
- details of sales and purchases made in the course of its trades involving dealing in goods and supporting documents;
- details of transactions between connected parties for the purposes of the transfer pricing anti-avoidance provisions.

In other circumstances records should be kept for a longer period (including in circumstances when a return has been made late or an enquiry by HMRC have been opened). Under the new penalties regime[126] HMRC emphasise the requirement for maintaining proper records.

As part of the due diligence process in a transaction copies should be asked for of all tax returns for the period of (ideally) six year before completion and the tax lawyer involved in negotiating the tax schedule should ask the accountants conducting the due diligence review to confirm that all returns have been fully and properly completed. The buyer will want disclosures relating to:

- any past amendments to tax returns;
- any penalties and interest charged by HMRC;
- any HMRC enquiries, assessments, and/or determinations;
- details of all claims for tax relief made under self-assessment which will include capital allowances, group relief, and substantial shareholdings exemption.

Aligned to self-assessment is the payment of corporation tax, which must be made no later than nine months from the end of the relevant accounting period[127] other than where the quarterly

---

[126] See **Appendix 12** (Penalties & Errors)

[127] TMA 1970 section 59D

instalment regime applies (in which case payments begin earlier. See paragraph 3.15 (Corporation Tax)).

Warranties specifically relating to self-assessment in the UK are set out as follows, although the principles involved are covered by the Administration and Tax Compliance Warranties (see paragraph 3.5 of this Chapter):

(a) "The Company has properly complied at all times and in all respect with the self-assessment regime under FA 1998 Schedule 18 including its obligations to:

    (i) file company tax returns for all accounting periods ending before and on the Accounts Date together with all accompanying documentation including the relevant accounts;

    (ii) correctly compute corporation tax due for each relevant accounting period, including but not limited to:

- any tax arising on loans or advances made to any Participators in the Company;
- any amount chargeable relating to profits of any Controlled Foreign Companies;
- transactions which fall within the transfer pricing provisions of TIOPA Part 4 (sections 146 to 217);

    (iii) provide full and correct information relating to the Disclosure of Tax Avoidance Schemes regime."

(b) "The Company (including any Associated Companies) is not a 'large' company for the purposes of the Quarterly Instalment Payments regime and has properly paid all corporation tax it has been due to pay no later than nine months after the end of each relevant accounting period ending before and on the Accounts Date."

(c) "The Company, being a large company under the Quarterly Instalment Payments regime, has accurately computed and paid corporation tax as required under that regime, for each relevant accounting period ending before or on the Accounts Date and as at Completion no adjustment will be necessary in respect of payments made before that date."

(d) "The Company has in its possession all records which it is required to keep under to the Self-Assessment regime and such records are sufficient to properly justify the computation by the Company of tax payable for all accounting periods ending up to the Accounts Date."

(e) "There have been no enquiries nor are there outstanding enquiries on the part of HMRC (including any Discovery Assessment and Discovery Determination) in respect tax returns submitted by the Company nor, so far as the Sellers are aware, are any enquiries likely to arise in the future in respect of any Tax Returns submitted by the Company before Completion."

(f) "The Company has not been subject to any penalties or any interest which could arise under the Self-Assessment regime in respect of any period before Completion."

3.35 Stamp Taxes

The United Kingdom stamp taxes regime covers stamp duty, stamp duty reserve tax and stamp duty land tax.

3.35.1 Stamp Duty

As from 10 July 2003 stamp duty has been only chargeable on instruments relating to stock or marketable securities (see FA 2003 section 125(1)). The tax applies to relevant instruments executed in any part of the United Kingdom or, regardless of where executed, to any property in the United Kingdom or to any matter done in the United Kingdom,[128] at a rate of 0.5% of the consideration involved. It is chargeable on instruments, and not on transactions.

Whilst stamp duty currently has a more narrow application than previously, it is nevertheless widely drawn in respect of shares and securities by virtue of the words 'instruments relating to'. Where there is a document under which there is a transfer on sale, whether it is an agreement for sale, a declaration of trust or otherwise where a beneficial interest transfers, stamp duty will be relevant.

Under Stamp Act 1891 section 122(1) stock is defined as including:

---

[128] Stamp Act 1891 section 14(4)

- any share in any stocks or funds transferable by the Registrar of Government Stock;
- any strip (under FA 1942 section 47) of any such stocks or funds; and
- any shares in the stocks or funds of any council, corporation, company or society in the United Kingdom or of any foreign or colonial corporation, company or society.

A marketable security is defined as a security of such a description as to be capable of being sold in any stock market in the United Kingdom.[129] The words 'capable of being' therefore takes the definition outside the narrow ambit of quoted shares to embrace shares which *could be* sold on such stock markets.

Stamp duty had been described as a voluntary tax on instruments and whilst there have been provisions for penalties for inadequate stamping, a more rigorous regime for interest and penalties was introduced on 1 October 1999 for instruments executed on or after that date.[130] Documents which are or were subject to stamp duty but which are unstamped cannot be put forward in civil litigation.[131]

The existence of unstamped documents going back a number of years is a not uncommon phenomenon in transactions. Therefore, in addition to appropriate warranties relating to stamp duty, the tax indemnity should also include protection for any duty interest and penalties arising from documents being liable to stamp duty and executed at any time before completion as well as those requiring stamping after completion.

There are provisions for stamp duty relief in respect of intra-group transfers and reconstructions, under FA 1930 section 42 and FA 1986 sections 75 and 77   Clearance is required under these provisions.

SDLT (see paragraph 3.35.3 below) can be avoided by packaging non-residential UK property into a company ownership. An SDLT charge will be payable on the transfer of the property into the

---

[129] Stamp Act 1891 section 122(1)

[130] Under FA1999 section 109(4) , and Stamp Act 1891 section 15A and 15B

[131] Stamp Act 1891 section 14(4)

company but, thereafter, on transfer of the company stamp duty at the lower rate of 0.5% will apply. Where the property concerned is residential with a value of more than £500,000 and is enveloped by a corporate structure, subject to a number of exceptions, the rate of SDLT will rise to 15% on the transfer and an ATED charge may arise.

3.35.2 Stamp Duty Reserve Tax (SDRT)

Stamp duty reserve tax was introduced in FA 1986 with the principal charge applying where two parties merely agree to transfer chargeable securities for consideration in money or money's worth.[132] The charge (currently at 0.5% of the consideration) does not depend upon a written instrument and therefore covers paperless stock market transactions. It can arise whether the agreement, transfer, issue or appropriation in question is made or effected in the UK or elsewhere and regardless of whether any party is resident or situate in any part of the UK.[133]

Chargeable securities are:

a) stocks, shares or loan capital,

b) interests in, or in dividends or other rights arising out of, stocks, shares or loan capital,

c) rights to allotments of or to subscribe for, or options to acquire, stocks, shares or loan capital, and

d) units under a unit trust scheme.[134]

Chargeable securities do not include securities listed in (a), (b) and (c) above which are issued by a corporation not incorporated in the United Kingdom save where:

- the securities are registered in a register kept in the United Kingdom by or on behalf of the corporate body issuing them; or

- if they are shares paid with shares issued by a UK incorporated company, or

---

[132] FA 1986 section 87(1)

[133] FA 1986 section 86(4)

[134] FA 1986 section 99(3)

THE TAX SCHEDULE

- in respect of securities falling within (b) and (c) above, paragraph (a) or (b) above applies to the stocks, shares or loan capital to which they relate, or
- they are issued by a *Societas Europaea* (SE) and the SE has its registered office in the Kingdom.

If the marketable securities would be subject ordinarily to stamp duty but are exempt they will also be exempt for SDRT purposes. Payment of stamp duty cancels out the requirement to pay SDRT in respect of the same transfer.[135] There are also exemptions for SDRT relating to some intermediaries, clearance services and depositary receipts. SI 1986/1771 (*Stamp Duty Reserve Tax Regulations*) provide for the administration of SDRT. The due date for payment of the tax is ordinarily 14 days following the date of transaction after which interest will start to arise.[136]

3.35.3 Stamp Duty Land Tax (SDLT)

Stamp duty land tax became effective on 1 December 2003 (since when there have been annual and not insignificant changes to the regime), resulting in stamp duty applying to land transactions before that date and SDLT applying from thereon. The statutory provisions are set out in FA 2003 Part 4 (sections 42 to 124 and Schedule 3 to 19).

SDLT is charged in respect of UK land transactions (regardless of the existence of any transfer instrument) involving chargeable consideration and is payable by the purchaser. The rates of SDLT are set out as follows. Residential properties worth over £500,000 and purchased by non-natural persons (corporations, partnerships involving a corporation and any CIS) a 15% SDLT charge applies.

Stamp Duty Land Tax – Residential Property			
Property value	Rate after 4.12.2014 (on portion of value above threshold)	Property value	Rate from 1.4.2016 for second resident owners

---

[135] See FA 1986 sections 88 and 92

[136] SI 1986/1711 regulations 3 and 2

£0 - £115,000	0%	Up to £125,000	3%
£125,001 - £250,000	2%	£125,001 - £250,000	5%
£250,001- £925,0000	5%	£250,001- £925,000	8%
£925,001 - £1,500,000	10%	£925,001 - £1.5m	13%
Over £1.5m	12%	Over £1.5m	15%

Stamp Duty Land Tax – non-residential or mixed use property		
Property value	Charge for 2015-16	On/after 17.3.2016
£0 - £150,000	0%	0%
£150,001 - £250,000	1%	2%
£250,001 - £500,000	3%	
Over £500,000	4%	
Over £250,000		5%

There are exemptions from SDLT,[137] namely:

- transactions in connection with divorce and dissolution of civil partnerships;
- assents and appropriations by personal representatives under a will or involving an intestacy;
- variations of testamentary dispositions;
- transactions where there is no chargeable consideration;
- grants of certain leases by registered social landlords;
- for buyers of new zero-carbon homes in the period from 1 October 2007 to 30 September 2012.[138]

- There are also reliefs available for SDLT, subject to conditions, including the following:
- sale and leaseback arrangements;[139]
- charities relief;[140]

[137] FA 2003 section 49 & Schedule 3
[138] FA 2003 section 58B
[139] FA 2003 section 57A
[140] FA 2003 Schedule 8

- alternative property finance, when land is sold to a financial institutions and leased back[141] or when it is re-sold to the person;[142]
- an incorporation of a limited liability partnership subject to conditions[143];
- transactions between companies which are members of the same group[144] (Group Relief[145]); and
- transfers involved in a reconstruction (Reconstruction Relief).[146]

Group Relief will not be available if there are arrangements in existence at the time of the transfer for there to be a change of control of the buyer but not the seller, or if the consideration or part of the consideration is to be provided or received by a person other than a group company, or if there are arrangements that the seller and the buyer are to cease to be members of the same group.[147] The relief will be withdrawn, essentially, if within three years of the transaction the buyer of the property ceases to be a member of the same group as the seller.[148] The *minutiae* of whether the degrouping arrangements will or will not apply are complex – see FA 2003 Schedule 7 paragraphs 4, 4ZA and 4A.

Reconstruction Relief is available when a company (acquiring company) acquires the whole or part of the undertaking of another company (target company) under a scheme for reconstruction of target company[149] in which case any related land transaction will be exempt from SDLT. In order for the relief to apply the consideration for the acquisition must consist wholly or partly of the issue of non-redeemable shares in the acquiring company to all the shareholders in target company and after the acquisition each

---

[141] FA 2003 section 71A

[142] FA 2003 section 73

[143] FA 2003 section 65

[144] 75% subsidiaries of the other company or both companies are 75% subsidiaries of a third company

[145] FA 2003 Schedule 7 Part 1

[146] FA 2003 Schedule 7 paragraph 7

[147] FA 2003 Schedule 7 paragraph 2

[148] FA 2003 Schedule 7 paragraphs 3 and 4A

[149] FA 2003 Schedule 7 paragraph 7

shareholder of each of the companies is a shareholder of the other and the proportion of shares are the same or nearly the same. The acquisition must be for *bona fide* commercial reasons and not for tax avoidance.

SDLT will be limited to 0.5% in circumstances when an acquiring company acquires the whole or part of the undertaking of the target company (Acquisition Relief)[150] and the following conditions are met:

- the consideration consists wholly or partly of the issue of non-redeemable shares in the acquiring company to the target company or to all or any of target company's shareholders;
- the acquiring company is not associated[151] with another company which is party to arrangements relating to shares of the acquiring company issued in connect with the transfer;
- the undertaking acquired has as its main activity the carrying on of a trade that does not consist wholly or mainly of dealing in UK property; and
- the acquisition is effected for *bona fide* commercial reasons and is not for tax avoidance.

Reconstruction Relief and Acquisition Relief will be withdrawn (subject to specific exceptions) if, within three years of the transaction (or in connection with arrangements made within the three-year period) control of the acquiring company changes and the acquiring company (or an associated company) still holds a chargeable interest in the UK land acquired on the acquisition or reconstruction.[152]

Where relief is withdrawn and SDLT becomes payable and remains unpaid for six months or more, HMRC can require payment from any company that was in the same group as the acquiring company (and above it in the group structure at the time

---

[150] FA 2003 Schedule 7 paragraph 8

[151] Companies are associated if one has control of the other or both are controlled by the same person or persons

[152] FA 2003 Schedule 7 paragraph 9

of the transaction) or from a controlling director of the acquiring company.[153]

3.35.3.1 SDLT anti-avoidance provisions under sections 75A, 75B and 75C FA 2003

These provisions are very broadly drawn, and because there is no requirement for an avoidance motive, it can catch innocent transactions. Section 75A covers any transaction where:

- a seller (V) disposes of a chargeable interest,
- another person (P) acquires the interest or a chargeable interest deriving from it,
- there are a number of scheme transactions, and
- the amount of SDLT payable in respect of the scheme transactions is less than the amount of SDLT which would have been payable on a notional land transaction effecting the acquisition of the seller's chargeable interest by the other person.

FA 2003 section 75A(3) provides that the following may amount to a scheme transaction:

- the acquisition by P of a lease deriving from a freehold owned or formerly owned by V;
- a sub-sale to a third person;
- the grant of a lease to a third person subject to the right to terminate;
- the exercise of a right to terminate a lease or to take some other action;
- an agreement not to exercise a right to terminate a lease or to take some other action; or
- the variation of a right to terminate a lease or to take some other action.

Providing an anti-avoidance warranty which a seller is confident to provide without technically falling within section 75A is likely to be difficult.

3.35.4 SDLT DOTAS

This legislation should be awarded the prize for one of the worst drafted pieces of legislation – it is contained in statutory legislation

---

[153] FA 2003 Schedule 7 paragraph 12

by virtue of Part 7 FA 2004 (sections. 306 to 325). Furthermore, HMRC Guidance is anything but helpful (see HMRC Disclosure of Tax Avoidance Schemes). Essentially, all schemes and arrangements for which the main purpose is to obtain a tax advantage (save for pre-1.4.2010 schemes which were grandfathered) should be reported other than those which fall within one or more of the steps A to F, as follows:

- Step A – the acquisition of a chargeable interest in land by a special purpose vehicle (SPV)

- Step B – any single claim under any of the following reliefs:

  - section 57A (sale and leaseback arrangements);
  - section 58B (relief for new zero-carbon homes);
  - section 58C (relief for new zero-carbon homes: supplemental);
  - section 60 (compulsory purchase facilitating development);
  - section 61 (compliance with planning obligation);
  - section 63 (demutualisation of insurance company);
  - section 64 (demutualisation of building society);
  - section 65 (incorporation of limited liability partnership); section 57A (sale and leaseback arrangements);
  - section 58B (relief for new zero-carbon homes);
  - section 58C (relief for new zero-carbon homes: supplemental);
  - section 60 (compulsory purchase facilitating development);
  - section 61 (compliance with planning obligation);
  - section 63 (demutualisation of insurance company);
  - section 64 (demutualisation of building society);
  - section 65 (incorporation of limited liability partnership);

  - section 66 (transfers involving public bodies);
  - section 67 (transfer in consequence of reorganisation of parliamentary constituencies);
  - section 69 (acquisition by bodies for national purposes);
  - section 71 (certain acquisitions by registered social landlords);
  - section 74 (collective enfranchisement by leaseholders);
  - section 75 (crofting community right to buy);
  - Schedule 6 (disadvantaged areas relief);

- Schedule 6A (relief for certain acquisitions of residential property);
- Schedule 6B (transfers involving multiple dwellings);
- Schedule 7 (group relief and reconstruction acquisition relief);
- Schedule 8 (charities relief);
- Schedule 9 (right to buy, shared ownership leases etc); or
- a single claim to relief under Schedule 61 to Finance Act 2009 (alternative finance investment bonds); or

one or more claims to relief under any one of the following provisions of FA 2003:

- section 71A (alternative property finance: land sold to financial institution and leased to individual);
- section 72 (alternative property finance in Scotland: land sold to financial institution and leased to individual);
- section 72A (alternative property finance in Scotland: land sold to financial institution and individual in common); or
- section 73 (alternative property finance: land sold to financial institution and resold to individual).

- Step C – the sale of shares in a SPC which holds chargeable interest in land, to a person who is not connected to either the SPC or the vendor
- Step D – not electing to waive the exemption from VAT
- Step E – structuring a transaction as a transfer of a going concern for VAT purposes
- Step F – the creation of a partnership to which a property subject to a land transaction.

However, for any arrangement which contains an unlisted step for securing the SDLT there is no exemption from disclosure.

If the target company has been involved in a SDLT avoidance scheme there is likely to be a promoter involved, and documentation setting out the justification for the scheme and the steps to effect the tax advantage should be supplied during due diligence.

3.35.5 Stamp Duty and SDLT Warranties

Due diligence on stamp duties is necessary, particularly in respect of SDLT, in that it may be difficult to determine whether or not the correct amount of duty has been paid under the self-assessment regime. This will depend on whether the duty has been based on the correct amount of chargeable consideration, whether there is documentary evidence of the basis of valuation, and whether delayed charges subsequently arising have been properly dealt with.

Stamp duty and SDLT warranties are set out as follows. They will need tailoring depending on the target's property and share portfolios and whether it is or has been a member of a group:

a) "All stamp duty and stamp duty land tax ("SDLT") arising on conveyance on sale of the Property to the Company has been properly paid and no interest and/or penalty can arise on the Company or in respect of the Property in respect of such stamp taxes."

b) "No Group Company has applied for relief for stamp duty under FA 1930 section 42 ("section 42") in respect of any transfer of property between any associated companies as defined in section 42."

c) "No UK land and property is held in a separate non-trading company, whether incorporated in the UK or elsewhere."

d) "All documents within the possession of the Company or to which they were a party, which were or are subject to stamp duty have been properly stamped and no interest or penalties could arise in respect of such documents."

e) "The Company has properly complied with all obligations and requirements relating to SDLT under FA 2003 and has full and accurate records including all land transaction returns and the basis for the calculation of the chargeable consideration."

f) "The Company has not entered into any contract for a land transaction:

(i) which has not been completed or deemed to have been completed or which has not been substantially performed;

(ii) whereby a chargeable interest for the purposes of SDLT was conveyed to a party who was not a party to the contract, under FA 2003 section 44A (*Contract providing for conveyance to third party*);

(iii) involving an exchange of land whereby FA 2003 section 47 ("*Exchanges*") could apply;

(iv) in respect of which consideration remains contingent, uncertain or unascertained;

(v) involving a connected company whereby the deemed market rule for the purposes of FA 2003 section 53 (*Deemed market value where transaction involves a connected company*) apply; or

(vi) whereby the sale and leaseback provisions under FA 2003 section 57A apply."

g) "There are no outstanding options and rights of pre-emption relating to the Property under FA 2003 section 46."

h) "No Group Company has entered into any arrangement whereby SDLT is exempted or reduced under FA 2003 Schedule 7 (*Group relief and reconstruction and acquisition reliefs*)."

i) "No SDLT could arise on [the Company][any Group Company] from the withdrawal of exemption from or reduction in SDLT arising from any reconstruction under FA 2003 Schedule 7 paragraph 7 or in connection with acquisition relief under FA 2003 Schedule 7 paragraph 8 such withdrawal arising from but not restricted to Completion."

j) "The Company has not been involved in any land transaction in respect of which FA 2003 Schedule 15 (*Partnerships*) is relevant."

k) "The Company has never entered into nor been a party to any scheme or arrangement one of the purposes of which was the avoidance of stamp duty or SDLT or to which FA 2003 section 75A might apply."

l) "The Company has never been required to report any arrangement which would fall within DOTAS under FA 2004 sections 306-325."

3.36 Transfer pricing and non-arm's length transactions

The UK legislation relating to transfer pricing was originally contained in ICTA Schedule 28AA (*Provision not at arm's length*) based on principles set out in article 9 of the OECD's Model Double Tax Convention and now incorporating amendments made to the OECD Transfer Pricing Guidelines for Multinational Enterprises and Tax Administrations, published in July 2010. In 2013 OECD commenced a project to address concerns regarding Base Erosion and Profit Shifting (BEPS) by multi-national enterprise (MNE) groups to minimise their tax burdens and the 2010 Guidelines were amended. UK legislation is now contained in TIOPA 2010 Part 4 (sections 146 to 217) for corporation tax purposes for accounting periods ending on or after 1 April 2010 and for income and capital gains tax purposes for the tax year 2010-11 and subsequent tax years. The fundamental requirement is that tax calculations for any relevant transaction will be based on arm's length principles. Transfer pricing issues will generally relate to large international organisations, groups with overseas activities and in some cases UK companies with overseas branches or agencies.

Transfer pricing issues arise in transactions when the following conditions are met:

- *Condition A*, which applies in a transaction relating to financing arrangements, is that at the time of the transaction or within a six month period thereafter one of the parties was directly or indirectly participating in the management, control or capital of the other party or the same person(s) were directly or indirectly participating in the management control or capital of each of the parties;

- *Condition B*, which applies to a transaction not relating to financing arrangements, is that at the time of the transaction one of the parties was directly or indirectly participating in the management, control or capital of the other or the same person(s) were directly or indirectly participating in the management, control or capital of each of the parties.

Financing arrangements are defined as arrangements made for providing, guaranteeing, or otherwise in connection with any debt, capital or other form of finance.[154] There are separate provisions on transfer pricing for oil transactions, a subject which is outside the scope of this publication.

In order for the transfer pricing provisions to be relevant, the transaction must differ from an arm's length transaction which would have been made between independent enterprises and there must be a potential advantage relating to UK tax to one of the parties. If so, the profits and losses of the potentially advantaged parties must be recalculated on an arm's length basis.

There are exemptions from the basic rules for companies which are dormant[155] and for small and medium-sized enterprises (SME).[156] However, there are exceptions from the SME exemption, namely if the SME elects (irrevocably) that the exemption should not apply, and if the other party to the transaction is a resident of a non-qualifying territory.[157] A non-qualifying territory will be a country other than the United Kingdom or a country in respect of which double taxation arrangements have been made which include a non-discriminating provision, and which either has not been designated as a non-qualifying territory by the Treasury or alternatively the Treasury has designated it as a qualifying territory.[158]

Although transfer pricing issues will apply to members of multinational groups and arise in respect of intra-group transfers of goods, services, finance and IP assets (including transfers between geographical boundaries), the UK legislation has a wide

---

[154] TIOPA 2010 section 148(4)

[155] See TIOPA 2010 section 165

[156] TIOPA 2010 section 166

[157] TIOPA 2010 section 167

[158] TIOPA 2010 section 173

remit and since 2004 can also apply to transfers between UK taxpayers.

The provisions, therefore, can apply in respect of the following circumstances where arm's length principles are not satisfied:

- cross–border transactions between group subsidiaries or involving associated companies;
- transactions involving a company and its controlling shareholder;
- persons acting together in relation to financing arrangements such as providing or guaranteeing any debt, capital or other form of finance;
- transactions characterised as thin capitalisation;
- securitisation structures, finance leasing and debt factoring;
- treasury functions and cash pooling;
- loan relationships involving interest-free or cheap lending, discounts and/or guaranteed debt;
- loans and advances between connected issuing and lending companies;
- transactions with controlled foreign companies.

A company is expected to keep appropriate records to justify that transactions have been on arm's length basis, under general self-assessment principles.

Advance Pricing Agreements (APA)[159] provide for a written agreement between a taxpayer and HMRC relating to any of the following:

- the attribution of income to a branch or agency through which a person, not being a company, has been carrying on or sponsoring a trade in the UK;
- the attribution of income to a permanent establishment through which a company has been carrying on a trade in the UK or is proposing to carry on a trade in the UK;
- the attribution of income to any permanent establishment of a person, wherever situated, through which it has been carrying on on/proposing to carry on any business;

---

[159] TIOPA 2010 sections 218 to 230

- the extent to which income which has arisen/may arise to a person is to be taken to arise outside the UK;
- the tax treatment of any provisions whether before or after the date of the agreement between a person and any associate of that person.[160]

Wide-ranging warranties should elicit relevant disclosures.

3.36.1 Transfer Pricing Warranties

a) **"The Company has at all times effected its business transactions with other parties on an arm's length basis and has never been required to re-compute its profits and/or its losses for tax purposes as required under TIOPA 2010 Part 4 (Transfer Pricing) and has maintained and has in its possession proper records to support this warranty."**

b) **"The Company has never entered into an Advance Pricing Agreement under TIOPA 2010 Part 5 with HMRC or similar arrangement with any other Tax Authority."**

3.37 Value Added Tax

VAT is one of the most important areas for in-depth due diligence. The buyer will want confirmation of the target's compliance history and relationship with its VAT office, assurances about the capabilities of the target's personnel dealing with its VAT affairs, details of its VAT position as at completion, and access to the target's VAT records during the disclosure process. Specific VAT issues arising on a transfer of a business are discussed in **Chapter 5 (Sale and Purchase of a Business)** and issues relating to disclosure of VAT tax avoidance schemes are considered in paragraph 3.18 (Disclosure of Tax Avoidance Schemes).

In relation to the purchase of a company issues requiring confirmation in due diligence via warranties include the following:
- the target company's registration number or details of the VAT group if it is a member of a group;
- details of types of supplies which the target makes, and whether wholly taxable (if so, at what rate) or exempt;

---

[160] TIOPA 2010 section 218

- the target's VAT compliance record including correct operation of VAT, payments and record keeping;
- whether the target operates any special VAT schemes;
- details of any VAT planning including those which require disclosure to HMRC;
- whether the capital goods scheme may be an issue;
- whether an option to tax has been made in respect of the target's land and property;
- whether it is required to register for VAT in another EU territory; and
- whether the target has been involved in any TOGC in the past.

3.37.1 VAT DOTAS

There are separate DOTAS provisions for VAT, with two categories of avoidance schemes which are notifiable to HMRC – namely 10 designated schemes (as set out in SI 2004/1993 Schedule 1 (Schedule 1)) – namely the 'listed' schemes; and any scheme or arrangement involving VAT avoidance involving any of the eight hallmarks ('hallmarked schemes) as set out in SI 2004/1993 (Schedule 2). Exempted from the requirement to notify a listed scheme to HMRC[161] are businesses (either single or part of a VAT group) with an annual turnover of taxable and exempt supplies of less than £600,000 and in respect of any other notifiable scheme, exemption to notify covers businesses with a turnover of less than £10 million. HMRC Notice 700/8 provides full details of the VAT DOTAS provisions including examples of what HMRC consider to fall within or outside the disclosure rules. Due diligence of a transaction where the target has employed schemes or arrangements attempting to reduce VAT should include using the expertise of a VAT specialist.

The ten listed schemes fall within arrangements involving any of the following (as set out in Schedule 1):

---

[161] VATA 1994 Schedule 11 A paragraph 7

Reference Number	
1	The first grant of a major interest in a building
2	A payment handling arrangement
3	Value shifting
4	Leaseback agreement
5	Extended approved period
6	Group third party supplies
7	Exempt education or vocational training by a non-profit making body
8	Taxable education or vocational training by a non-eligible body
9	Cross-border face value vouchers
10	Surrender of a relevant lease

Schedule 1 provides full details of what is covered under the 10 categories as does HMRV Notice 700/8.

The eight hallmarks set out in Schedule 2 are as follows:

1. Provisions associated with schemes:
    - the sharing of a tax advantage with another party to the scheme or with the promoter;
    - a confidentiality condition; and
    - a fee payable to a promoter which is in whole or part contingent on tax savings from the scheme.
2. Provisions included in schemes:
    - a prepayment between connected parties;
    - funding by loan, share subscription or subscription in securities;
    - off-shore loops;
    - property transactions between connected persons; and
    - the issue of face-value vouchers.

3.37.2 VAT Group Issues

If the target is part of a VAT group the main consequences are as follows:

- all inter-group transactions will be disregarded for VAT purposes;

- there will be a single VAT return filed by the representative member of the group;
- supplies made to any group member will be treated as if made to the representative member;
- if a member of the group opts to tax property that option is generally binding on all members of the group;
- each group member will be jointly and severally liable for the VAT debts of all members.

If the target is a holding company, details of all VAT groupings will be needed.

If the target is leaving a VAT group the tax schedule and the completion accounts must make provisions for conduct for removing the target from the VAT group on completion, for VAT group returns relating to the target's supplies to be made by the representative member until termination of the target's group membership, and the outstanding VAT position in respect of the target's supplies in the accounting period in which completion falls.

Set out as follows are comprehensive warranties relating to VAT.

a) **"The Company is a taxable person for the purposes of VAT and is registered for VAT under number [   ], has never been a member of a VAT group and has at all times been compliant with all VAT rules and regulations including (but not limited to) the following:**
  - **registration matters;**
  - **the making of self-supplies;**
  - **registration for supplying electronic services in other EU member states;**
  - **making complete and correct VAT returns and VAT payments within prescribed time limits;**
  - **preserving full documentation and records relating to its VAT affairs for the past six years."**

b) **"The Company is a member of a group for VAT purposes under registration number [ ] ("VAT Group"), in respect of which [ ] is the representative member and it is confirmed that:**

- no group member has opted to tax any property under of VATA Schedule 10 Part 1;
- there are not currently nor will there be at Completion any payments on account relating to VAT required in respect of the Company;
- the representative member has applied for removal of the Company from the VAT Group to be effective at Completion;
- the representative member has at all times been compliant with all VAT rules and regulations in all respects;
- no direction has been made by HMRC under VATA Schedule 9A (*"Anti-avoidance provisions – groups"*) in respect of the VAT Group; and
- there has never been another VAT group within the Group.

c) "The Company is not and has never been registered for VAT in the UK or any other EU territory and has proper records relating to all supplies of goods and services it has made during the past [four] years including in respect of supplies made to and received from other EU member states."

d) "The [Company] [VAT Group] has never been subject to any penalties for failure to take reasonable care or for deliberate understatement of VAT (with or without concealment) nor has the [Company] [VAT Group] been subject to any compliance check from HMRC relating to VAT nor has it been assessed for underpayment of VAT in the past four years."

e) "The [Company] [VAT Group] only makes taxable supplies and does not make nor has ever made exempt supplies for the purposes of VAT and the [Company] [VAT Group] has been entitled at all times to credit for all input tax relating to taxable supplies it has received and has properly and correctly claimed such input tax."

f) "The [Company] [VAT Group] has never operated nor been required to operate any of the following schemes under VATA:

- [second hand margin scheme;]
- [tour operators margin scheme;]
- [retail scheme;]
- [investment gold scheme;]
- cash accounting scheme;
- flat rate scheme;
- annual accounting scheme;
- capital goods scheme."

g) "No assessment or penalty relating to VAT or requirement for security for VAT due has been made or imposed in respect of the [Company] [VAT Group] by HMRC or any other Tax Authority."

h) "The [Company] [VAT Group] has never been involved in any tax planning schemes or arrangements relating to VAT regardless of such scheme or arrangements having a commercial purpose or otherwise."

i) "The [Company] [VAT Group] has never been involved in any scheme or arrangement in respect of any scheme which would require disclosure to HMRC including under FA 2004 Part 7 (*Disclosure of Tax Avoidance Schemes*)."

j) "The [Company] [VAT Group] has never been a party to a transfer of a going concern."

3.37.3 The Capital Goods Scheme (CGS)[162]

These provisions may apply in respect of any acquisition, creation or construction of certain capital assets, being computer equipment costing over £50,000 (exclusive of VAT) and property assets (being land, a building or part of a building, extensions or alterations to a building or a civil engineering work), broadly where the value of the interest is not less than £250,000 (exclusive of VAT). Before 1 January 2011, the value of a capital item was determined by reference to the business-related expenditure only. From 1 January 2011, the value is determined by reference to total expenditure on an asset (both business and non-business expenditure).

---

[162] SI 1995/2518 Part XV regulations 112 to 116 and Notice 706/2/11

The CGS rules can apply for a period of ownership of up to five years in respect of computer equipment and ten years in respect of property assets. The adjustment period is normally ten successive yearly intervals in the case of land and buildings and five successive yearly intervals in the case of computer equipment and leases of land with less than ten years to run at the time it was supplied. Assets to which the CGS rules apply are referred to as capital items.

Before 1 January 2011, only VAT on the business-related expenditure on an asset (i.e. input tax) fell within the CGS. From 1 January 2011, all of the VAT on a capital item (input tax and non-business VAT) falls within the scheme. Under the scheme, where input tax in respect of expenditure on the capital item was initially wholly or partly deductible, and subsequently in one of the intervals forming part of the adjustment period, use for the purposes of making taxable supplies decreases in percentage terms, an adjustment to the initial input tax recovery may be required, with a repayment due to HMRC and so on during each interval until the end of the adjustment period. Likewise, an adjustment or successive adjustments in favour of the taxpayer can arise if a capital item was initially used in making exempt or, in part, non-business supplies and it comes to be used increasingly in making taxable supplies.

Assets acquired solely for resale or wholly used for non-business purposes do not fall within the scheme. Also, so long as the owner of the capital assets has never made exempt supplies or supplies outside the scope of VAT, the provisions should not be relevant.

A buyer of assets under a TOGC or shares in a company will require full records going back ten years or five years as appropriate relating to all capital items, setting out the value, the amount of input tax originally claimed, and full details of adjustments required to be made under the scheme, including on any disposal. The new owner under a TOGC must continue to make the relevant CGS adjustments until the end of the adjustment period.

Warranties specifically relating to CGS issues should always be required:

k) "The [Company] [VAT Group] has always made taxable supplies and has never made exempt supplies for the purposes of VAT and the [Company][VAT Group] has not been required to make any adjustments under the provisions relating to the Capital Goods Scheme."

l) "The [Company] [VAT Group] has made the necessary proper adjustments relating to input tax in respect of all capital items relevant to the capital goods scheme and has full records relating to such capital items which provide accurate details relating to their value and the amount of input tax reclaimed and adjustments to such tax as required under the scheme.

m) "The [Company] [VAT Group] has made no disposals of any capital item which fall within the provisions of the capital goods scheme during the adjustment period, which could have created a net taxable benefit to the Company by virtue of the input tax initially deducted in respect of such item and after taking into account any adjustments under the scheme exceeding the output tax arising on such disposal."

3.38 Value Shifting[163] and Depreciatory Transactions[164]

The types of transactions which might fall within these provisions will essentially represent tax avoidance arrangements within a group of companies, and are unlikely to be admitted to or disclosed in a transaction involving the purchase of a company or group.

The value shifting provisions aim to prevent arrangements whereby value is stripped out of an asset (including shares) and results in a tax-free benefit.[165] They were simplified in FA 2011[166] and now cover arrangements where there is a disposal of shares or securities of another company, their value has been materially reduced, the arrangements do not consist solely of making an

---

[163] TCGA sections 29 to 34

[164] TCGA sections 176 and 177

[165] See also HMRC Capital Gains Tax Manual – CG46800 to CG46922

[166] See TCGA new section 31 1992 for disposals of shares or securities by companies made on or after 19 July 2011

exempt distribution, and the main purpose of the arrangements was to obtain a tax advantage. The relevant asset will be owned by a company which is a member of the same group as the disposing company.

These provisions apply to disposals made on or after 19 July 2011 with the previous provisions applying for disposals made before that date. The provisions can involve intra-group dividends and intra-group asset transfers which take out value in a company's shares and, therefore, any past reconstructions involving the target company should justify related warranties. Examples of arrangements which might fall within the value shifting provisions include an asset transfer within a group at no gain/no loss under TCGA section 171 followed by a revaluation of assets or an intra-group transfer of assets at artificial prices, which could reduce the value of the relevant subsidiary's shares. If the legislative provisions apply to a transaction HMRC can reapportion any gain or loss on the disposal of any asset on a just and reasonable basis. The value shifting rules should not apply if disposals are effected for *bona fide* commercial reasons and do not form part of a tax avoidance arrangement, and in circumstances where allocation of cost has been properly made under accepted accountancy principles.

Depreciatory transactions statutory provisions[167] are aimed at preventing artificial losses on a disposal of shares or securities where value has been extracted from the underlying assets of the company and which is unconnected with genuine commercial transaction.[168] Any intra-group transfer of capital assets at undervalue followed by the disposal of a subsidiary at a price which reflects the depreciatory transaction (namely where the value of the disposed shares have been materially reduced) could fall within the legislation. They also extend to dividend stripping where a company holds at least 10% of the same class of shares in another company, a distribution has been made to the shareholding company with the effect of the distribution being

---

[167] TCGA section 176

[168] See HMRC Capital Gains Tax Manual – CG46500 to46543

that the value of the holding is or has been materially reduced.[169] The distribution will not be treated as a depreciatory transaction if it consists of a payment which is required to be brought into account for the purposes of corporation tax on chargeable gains, in computing a gain or loss accruing to the person making the ultimate disposal.[170] If the transactions are deemed to be depreciatory HMRC can reduce any relevant loss on a just and reasonable basis.

Relevant warranties intended to alert the buyer to transactions which might fall within these anti-avoidance provisions include the following:

a) "There has been no transfer of dividends and/or assets within the Group which could give rise to a tax-free benefit and whereby TCGA sections 30 and 31 ("Value Shifting provisions") might apply, including any such transfers at artificial prices."

b) "The [Company][Group] has not been involved in any arrangements whereby there has been a disposal of shares or securities, and in respect of which their values have been materially reduced for any reason other than due to commercial factors, such that a loss arises on such disposal, including under TCGA section 176 ("Depreciatory transactions within a group") and TCGA section 177 ("Dividend Stripping")."

---

[169] TCGA section 177

[170] TCGA section 177(3)

4 SALE AND PURCHASE OF A COMPANY

4.1 Background issues

An incorporated company is treated under UK law as an independent person, with its own rights and liabilities which are separate from those of its owners.[1] Regardless of a change in its shareholders a company remains a distinct legal entity and its ongoing activities will continue until it is wound up or liquidated. Except for the possibility of a withdrawal of certain tax reliefs if the target company is leaving a group, there should be no immediate changes to a company's tax position as a result of a change of its ownership. However, as the residence of a company can also be determined by the place of its management and control, which can take precedence over its residence in the country of incorporation, a change of shareholders and directors can in some circumstances have a bearing on this issue. This would be a post-completion matter and one purely for the buyer of a company (also see **Chapter 3 (Warranties)** at paragraph 3.32 (Residency Issues)).

Acquiring a UK company involves the acquisition of the legal and beneficial interests in its issued share capital although acquiring control of a company can also be effected, albeit unusually, through the ownership of loan capital and shareholders' agreements, either deliberately or accidentally. The acquisition of a company rather than the acquisition of its underlying business and assets should generally reflect due diligence which confirms there are no significant liabilities of the company (tax and otherwise) including outside the ordinary course of its business. Alternatively, if due diligence uncovers significant liabilities, the purchase price should have been adjusted downwards to reflect them.

The standard form tax indemnity in the UK has been developed for use in transactions where the target is a company or group of companies. **Chapter 10 (The Tax Schedule in the Sale and Purchase of a Company)** covers the separate provisions in detail,

---

[1] *Salomon v Salomon and Company Limited [1897] A.C.22*

including background issues relating to the contents of the tax schedule. This chapter discusses taxation and commercial issues, including the terms of the consideration and other tax and related issues relevant for both the seller and the buyer.

4.2 Issues for the buyer

The immediate tax issue following completion and for the buyer, will be the payment of stamp duty or stamp duty reserve tax, at 0.5% on the purchase price which must be made within 30 days of the completion in most cases. The purchase price together with related expenses will represent the base cost of the acquisition for chargeable gains purposes going forward.

4.2.1 Valuation

4.2.1.1 Trading companies and groups

A trading company is likely to be valued for its future earnings capabilities, with forecasts by the buyer based on a combination of the target company's track record, its ongoing business activities during the due diligence process, possible loss elimination and recovery potential, future cost saving opportunities under the buyer's management, and/or future expectations of the relevant market conditions together with potential for the company to exploit them. If the target is a trading conglomerate the acquisition may be made because the buyer intends to break it up, reflecting its potentially greater value as separate businesses than the market value or purchase price of the group as a whole.

4.2.1.2 Single asset companies

If the target is a single asset company or single purpose company (owning property or IP assets for example) the value of the underlying assets should reflect a combination of market conditions current at the time the heads of terms are entered into and a view on the future earnings potential of the assets in question. Part of the valuation may also reflect potential savings or tax risks associated from its corporate personality. The seller may have packaged assets in a special purchase company for tax purposes including stamp duty land tax savings in the case of a property business. Depending on whether or not the target company has a trading history, a short form tax schedule may be appropriate in these cases (see precedent in **Appendix 2**).

4.2.1.3   *Investment companies*

Investment trust companies are likely to be valued on ratios relating to the underlying asset value – usually it will be based on the discount to asset value, although occasionally investment trusts may trade at a premium to asset value if there is a difficulty in investing directly in the underlying assets. For an industrial conglomerate its valuation may be a mixture of future price/earnings and yields, either for the conglomerate as a whole or for each of the separate divisions.

4.2.2   Hive-downs

Where there are liability issues in the target company significant enough for the buyer to be advised not to acquire the target company, an alternative to acquiring its business and assets is for the seller to pre-package the business, by transferring the trade into a newco which will then be acquired by the buyer (see **Chapter 1** paragraph 1.2.4 discussing a reconstruction under TCGA section 139).

Pre-packaged administrations[2] ('Pre-Packs') may also involve a hive-down into a newco, as may a sale involving a business within a company which is not to be acquired as part of the transaction. Any transfer into a newco (which will then be sold onwards) should be capable of properly representing a transfer of a going concern for VAT purposes (TOGC) and the issues discussed in **Chapter 5 (Sale of a Business)** paragraph 5.5 will be relevant for all the parties (seller, newco and the buyer). Ideally, the buyer should ask for seller TOGC warranties from the seller and confirmation of the issues covered by buyer TOGC warranties as they relate to newco (see **Chapter 5** paragraphs 5.5.10 (a)-(f)). The seller will be expected to provide a full indemnity relating to any pre-hive down tax liabilities which might affect the newco and if the transfer does not represent a TOGC the seller will be required to charge VAT on the individual assets transferred. These provisions should all be included in an adapted standard short form tax schedule (see **Appendix 2**). Due diligence should focus on VAT registration issues (if any) including in respect of any land

---

[2] Pre-packaged administration – discussed further in **Chapter 6 – Special Situations**

and property transferred. The newco will be leaving a chargeable gains tax group and, therefore, specific undertakings relating to group tax issues and degrouping charges will be required (see **Chapter 9 – Group Issues**).

However, under the degrouping rules introduced by FA 2011 Schedule 10, if a degrouping charge arises from a disposal of shares any degrouping charge is added to the consideration received by the seller on disposal under TCGA section 179(3A). While the newco will not have been owned for the required ownership period of 12 months for the purposes of the Substantial Shareholders Exemption (SSE), paragraph 15A, TCGA Schedule 7AC 1992 (inserted by FA 2011) treats the seller as having owned newco for the required period provided the relevant conditions are met (see **Chapter 9**, paragraph 9.8). This extension of the SSE, combined with the new degrouping rules, means that pre-sale hive-down is a more attractive option than previously. However, at the time of this edition going to print there is ongoing HMRC consultation on SSE.

Under the re-written provisions of ICTA section 343 (*Company reconstructions without a change of ownership*), now contained in CTA 2010 Part 22 Chapter 1 (sections 938 to 953),[3] trading losses of a company should be capable of being transferred to newco and on the transfer no balancing allowance or charge will arise in respect of capital allowances under CTA 2010 section 954. The provisions apply where the company ceases to carry on a trade (the 'predecessor') and another company begins to carry it on (the 'successor') and the two companies are under common ownership of at least 75% at any time within one year before the transfer and on or at any time within two years after the transfer. There is no minimum period during which the common ownership tests must be met. However, the trade in question must beneficially belong to the parties[4] and, therefore, a TOGC must be legally effected and newco must take over the trade before any conditional contracts are entered into by the buyer relating to newco. The amount of

---

[3] section 938 to 956

[4] CTA 2010 section 942(8) - see also *Wood Preservation Ltd v Prior 45 TC 112*

trading losses capable of being carried over cannot be greater than any net difference by which the liabilities of the predecessor company at the time of the transfer exceed the value of its assets at that time. The transferred trade will be ring-fenced as a separate trade going forward.

Where part of the consideration price for the target company relates to the availability of trading losses capable of being carried forward (best practice being to quantify them in the tax schedule and any completion accounts), it would be difficult for the buyer to rely on an indemnity if the losses subsequently are not used post completion or if the non-availability is due to post-completion events outside the control of the seller or down to the actions of the buyer. Any indemnity given by the seller should be strictly limited to the quantum of trading losses as agreed by the parties, and to nothing else.

The anti-avoidance provisions in CTA 2010 sections 673 to 676 (*Change in company ownership: Disallowance of trading losses*)[5] disapply the 'carried-forward loss' provisions if, within the period of three years in which the change in ownership occurs, either:

- there is a major change in the nature or conduct of a trade carried on by the company; or
- there is a change of ownership at any time after the scale of the activities in a trade carried on by the company has become small, or negligible, and before any significant revival of the trade.

In these cases the benefit of newco's carried forward trading losses will not be available. A major change in the nature or conduct of a trade is defined as including a major change in the type of property dealt in, or services or facilities provided in the trade, or a major change in customers, outlets or markets of the trade. These provisions apply even if the change is the result of a gradual process which began before the period of the three years.[6]

If the seller is warranting the trading losses of the target company transferred into newco, it will want a carve-out in the tax

---

[5] A rewrite of section 768 ICTA
[6] CTA 2010 section 673 (2) to (4)

indemnity relating to the losses if there is a change in the nature or conduct of the trade following completion. In turn, the buyer will want a specific warranty that nothing has been effected before completion whereby the provisions of CTA 2010 section 673(3) would apply to disallow the trading losses.

4.2.3 Funding the purchase price

Funding may come from the buyer's cash resources, the issue of debentures and/or equity by the buyer to the seller(s), bank borrowings, deferred consideration in cash, shares and securities or both, or a mixture of all these alternatives. If the buyer is a public company, the market will want assurance that the acquisition and the manner of funding will not result in the buyer's earning being diluted (either immediately or in the future), and for privately-held companies its shareholders are likely to have the same expectations. Simply put, so long as the cost of capital and return on the investment in the target company (as measured by its net profits going forward) do not dilute the buyer's net return on capital, its group earnings going forward should not produce reduced returns on shareholders' equity. These principles will equally apply to a purchase of a business.

4.2.4 Post-completion protections

A standard limitation to a tax indemnity should expressly carve out any tax liabilities or loss of tax relief for the target company following its sale which arise in connection with any post-completion restructuring or amalgamation with the buyer's group. The buyer may unwittingly lose tax reliefs such as the availability of trading losses going forward (see paragraph 4.2.2 above, referring to CTA 2010 section 673) and corporation tax relief relating to share schemes under CTA 2009 sections 1001 to 1038 (discussed in **Chapter 7** paragraph 7.2) due to post-completion actions.

If the sellers are to remain with the target company part of the consideration paid may include a post-completion earn-out based on the results of the target company going forward (usually for no more than a two to three year period to avoid any argument that the payment is employment-related). If the payments are 'individualised' – that is there are separate targets for each seller remaining with target – HMRC are likely to argue they are employment-related and should be taxed as income. Equally, any post-completion payment which resembles a 'golden handcuff' (being a payment to ensure an individual stays with the company for a period of time) will be vulnerable in the same way. Earn-outs are discussed in greater depth at paragraph 4.6 below. It should be assumed that any other incentives provided by the buyer to sellers following completion, dependent on them remaining with the company will be taxable as income under ITEPA. Any arrangement to be entered into between the buyer's group and management/shareholders of the target company relating to future incentives and emoluments should be subject to an indemnity provided to the buyer's group by the individuals concerned to cover income tax and NIC liability which might arise as a result of the arrangements. If there is a serious doubt about a payment which is intended to be taxed under the capital gains tax regime but which it is feared might be considered to be taxed as income, a request for a non-statutory clearance from the employing company's tax office should be made, setting out full details of the issues involved and the legal issue about which there is a genuine point of doubt (see **Chapter 1 (Transactional Process)** at paragraph **1.2.10** which discusses non-statutory clearances).

In *Grays Timber Products Ltd v Revenue & Customs Commissioners*[7] the concept of personal rights of a shareholder attaching to shares was discussed, the result being that any benefits arising from personal rights would be taxed as employment income. The facts in this case are important as *Grays Timber* is frequently misconstrued by practitioners when shares with different rights under a company's articles are issued to employee shareholders. A managing director had a shareholding of 6% of the issued share capital of his employer company. He had entered into a written service agreement company as well as a subscription and shareholders' agreement under which he would become entitled to be paid a 'kicker' on the sale of the company which would be in excess of his percentage shareholding – in fact he was paid just over £1.4 million on the sale of the company whereas it would

---

[7] [2010]1 WLR 497, SC.

have been £0.4 million if he had been paid the same price per share pro rata as the other shareholders, for his 6% of the issued capital. The issue in question was whether the difference between these two sums should be taxable as employment income and subject to income tax and national insurance contributions, or whether it should have taxable as a chargeable gain. The Supreme Court rejected the submission that rights attaching to shares might be found in arrangements outside a company's articles – it found that the rights attached to the subscription agreement were personal to the managing director and arose from his employment with the company. As the rights did not attach to the shares, a purchaser obtained no benefit. The shareholder's agreement was classified as a collateral agreement and could not take precedent over the company's articles.

4.3   Taxation issues for the seller

This book focuses on all matters relating to the negotiation of the tax schedule. If acting for a seller (whether an individual or a company), the tax advisor should include in the engagement letter the recommendation that the seller seek specific tax advice regarding the structuring of the consideration including chargeable gains tax issues, and making specific reference to the provisions for entrepreneurs' relief and in the future, investors' relief (if the seller is an individual) and the substantial shareholdings exemption (if the seller is a corporate). If it appears that the advice on which the client is relying is suspect, or there is an obvious disadvantage to the seller in the structuring of the consideration, the tax advisor should include in the engagement letter a strong carve-out of any responsibility relating to these issues, but best practice is always to bring the issue to the attention of the client. It is, as always, advisable to discuss these concerns with the seller early in the course of the transaction but often the tax advisor is instructed only after the heads of terms have been agreed.

4.3.1   Capital gains for individuals

Capital gains tax (CGT) will be payable on any chargeable gains arising in respect of a chargeable asset which accrues to an individual, in the year of assessment during any of which he/she is

UK resident, unless specific exemptions apply.[8] However, a non-UK resident seller could be subject to tax on UK capital gains under the laws of the territory of his or her residence or citizenship. The remainder of this chapter applies to UK CGT arising UK resident sellers. (However a word of warning – the concept of a non-UK domiciled person (deemed or otherwise) and special taxation including in respect of offshore holdings of UK residents, has undergone fundamental change – this book does not consider issues of domicile.)

CGT will be chargeable on the total amount of chargeable gains accruing in the year of assessment after deducting allowable losses accruing in the same year and any brought forward capital losses which were accrued in any previous year of assessment. However, generally if relief against a chargeable loss has been given under the ITA it cannot be given under the TCGA.

4.3.1.1 *Entrepreneurs' Relief*

Entrepreneurs' relief[9] which can reduce the rate of capital gains tax to 10% may be available to individuals and trustees on a disposal of shares in a company. The lifetime limit is £10 million.

The legislation is a re-write of the now withdrawn retirement relief, and therefore it is considered that the case law relating to retirement relief will apply to the same issues for entrepreneurs' relief.

The following conditions must be met if entrepreneurs' relief is to apply to an individual's sale of shares in or securities of a company:

- throughout the period of one year ending with the date of the disposal:
  - the company is the individual's personal company (he or she owns a 5% interest[10]) and is either a trading company or the holding company of a trading group, and
  - the individual is an officer or employee of the company or (if the company is a member of a trading group) of one or

---

[8] TCGA section 2

[9] TCGA sections 169H to 169S

[10] TCGA section 169S(3) – measured by ordinary share capital and voting rights

more companies which are members of the trading group; OR

- the above conditions were met throughout the period of one year ending with the date on which the company ceased to be either:
    - a trading company without continuing to be or becoming a member of a trading group, or
    - a trading group without continuing to be or becoming a trading company,

    AND that date was within the period of three years ending with the date of the disposal.

Several requirements are important to establish and prove through proper documentation, namely whether the company in question was a trading company for at least one year; that the employment requirement is met (evidenced in part by virtue of the shareholder having been paid under PAYE and not through a service company) for at least a year; and that the shares or securities have been held by the shareholder for at least one year and are within the definitions in TCGA section 169S(5).

A trade is defined as 'any venture in the nature of a trade'[11] (the previous ICTA definition referred to every trade, manufacture, adventure or concern in the nature of a trade) and, therefore, will not cover an investment business. Ordinary share capital is defined as *'issued share capital, other than fixed dividend capital with no other rights to share in the company's profits'* and securities are defined as *'including any debentures of the company which are deemed by TCGA section 251(6) to be securities for the purposes of that section'*.[12]

When there is a disposal of trust business assets relating to shares or securities of a trading company the following requirements must be met:

- there must be an individual who is a qualifying beneficiary – i.e. he or she has an interest in possession (otherwise than for a fixed term) in the whole of either:

---

[11] TCGA section 169S(5)

[12] TCGA section 169S(5)

THE TAX SCHEDULE

- the whole of the settled property; or
- a part of the settled property which consists of or includes the settlement business assets disposed of; AND
- throughout a period of one year ending not earlier than three years before the date of the disposal the company is the personal company of the qualifying beneficiary[13] and is either a trading company or the holding company of a trading group AND the qualifying beneficiary is an officer or employee of the company or of one or more companies which are members of the trading group.

The beneficiary therefore must be an officer or employee of the company, and he or she must own at least 5% in his/her own right.

Advising whether or not entrepreneurs' relief will be available requires detailed information on the company and the relief is one which the individual must claim under self-assessment. The interaction between entrepreneurs' relief and the structuring of the consideration through an earn-out is discussed at paragraph 4.6.4 below. The engagement letter for a seller who is an individual should state whether advice is being given on entrepreneurs' relief or alternatively should state that such advice has not been asked for.

4.3.1.2 *Investors Relief*

This new relief applies for newly issued shares to individuals or their spouse or civil partner on or after 17 March 2016 and which have been held for a period of at least three years starting from 6 April 2016 – therefore the first date that relief can be claim will be April 2019. The regime is contained in ss 169VA to 169VR and Schedule 7ZB TGCA.

The rules provide that at the time the shares were issued, none of the shares or securities of the company which issued them were listed on a recognised stock exchange; and the shares were ordinary shares in a trading company or holding company of a trading group and remained so throughout the three year holding period.

---

[13] A 5% interest in the ordinary shares and in the voting control

The definition of trading company or trading group is broadly similar to the entrepreneurs' relief definitions.

Unlike entrepreneurs' relief the investor and any person connected with him or her cannot be an officer or employee of the issuing company or of a connected company during the three year holding period.

A 10% CGT% rate will apply if all the conditions are met and a claim is made, and there will be a lifetime cap of £10 million per individual – this cap is separate from the £10 million cap for CGT relief under entrepreneurs' relief – a generous relief for serial entrepreneurs.

Special provisions are made in circumstances where there is a scheme of reconstruction, a reorganisation where no consideration is given, a reorganisation where consideration is given, and share exchanges. Elections are available to disapply s 127 TCGA under s 169VO, similar to the opt out under s 169Q TCGA where entrepreneurs' relief is available.

There are anti-avoidance provisions whereby disqualification for relief will apply where the investor receives any value, other than insignificant value, from the company at any time in the period of restriction (three years from the date of issue).

4.3.1.3 Inheritance tax

If the shares and securities in the target company represent relevant business property there should be 100% relief from inheritance tax in respect of any transfer (both in life and on death) under business property relief (BPR)[14]. If these provisions apply the disposal will not be brought within a deceased person's estate as a chargeable lifetime transfer for UK IHT purposes.

Relevant business property as it relates to shares and securities is defined[15] as follows:

---

[14] IHTA sections 103 - 114

[15] IHTA sections 105(1)(b), (c) and (cc)

- securities of a company which are unquoted and which (either by themselves or together with other such securities owned by a transferor) gave the transferor control of the company immediately before the transfer;
- any unquoted shares in a company; or
- shares in or securities of a company which are quoted and which (either by themselves or together with other such shares or securities owned by the transferor) gave the transferor control of the company immediately before the transfer.

Control is defined as majority voting control, and can include shares and securities comprised in the estate of a person's spouse or civil partner and/or shares or securities held in a settlement.[16]

Quoted means listed on a recognised stock exchange, and unquoted means not being listed on a recognised stock exchange.[17] (The **Glossary** provides the statutory references as to what HMRC regards as a recognised stock exchange and a recognised investment exchange.)

The shares or securities must be owned by the transferor throughout the two years immediately before the transfer.[18] There are roll-over provisions, whereby the two year ownership requirement is satisfied if the shares or securities replaced property which represented relevant business property, and the transferor owned both sets of property for at least two years falling within the five years immediately before the transfer. Relevant business property also includes assets consisting of a business and land or building, machinery or plant which was used wholly or mainly for the purposes of a business carried on by a company under the control of the transferor or of a business carried on by the transferor[19] so the roll-over provisions should apply when asset-based property is replaced by shares or securities and vice versa, although the relief is restricted to the value of the relevant business property transferred. If the shares are unquoted and are

---

[16] IHTA section 269

[17] IHTA section 105(1ZA)

[18] IHTA section 106

[19] IHTA section 105(1)(a), (d) and (e)

replacement shares under a reorganisation to which TCGA sections 126 to 136 apply, the two year holding period requirement will include the ownership period of the original shares.

4.3.1.4   *Reliefs under EIS, SEIS and SITR*

These reliefs are discussed in depth in **Chapter 8 (Venture Capital Schemes)** – it is unlikely but not impossible that the target may be a SITR investee company in a transaction for which this book is written. There are two main issues for the seller of shares. If the original investment qualified for the relief in question and the shares were held for the minimum time requirement (generally three years after a date of issue) no capital gains will arise on their disposal (CGT relief). If the shares were not held for the required time period, the investor must report to HMRC that a disqualifying event has occurred (namely the sale of the company), part or all of any income tax relief will be clawed back, and CGT will be payable on any gain. If a loss arises on the sale on which income tax relief was claimed, the base cost of the shares will be reduced by the amount of that relief. The second scenario is if the original investment qualified for roll-over relief, and the gain was rolled over into the shares, the original gain will crystallise on their sale and become payable. Alternatively, the crystallised gain can be re-invested into other qualifying shares for relief purposes and the same roll-over relief will apply, available to serial entrepreneurs.

The responsibility for claiming any of the reliefs and reporting disqualifying events is down to the individual claimant under self-assessment and, therefore, it is good practice that any affected seller be advised of this responsibility.

4.3.2   Chargeable gains for companies

Corporation tax rather than capital gains tax will apply in respect of chargeable gains accruing to companies after deducting all allowable losses and any previous allowable losses accruing to the company whilst it was within the charge to corporation tax.[20] Companies are entitled to an indexation allowance to reflect

---

[20] TCGA section 8

inflationary value increases, calculated on the original price paid for the asset and any enhancement expenses during its ownership.

4.3.2.1   *Substantial shareholdings exemption*

The rules on the substantial shareholdings exemption for companies (SSE)[21] are discussed in depth in **Chapter 9 (Group Issues)** at paragraph 9.8 but may well undergo changes following the publication of this edition, following HMRC consultation on the relief.

If the provisions are applicable, any chargeable gains arising from the disposal by a company of a shareholding representing not less than 10% will not be subject to corporation tax. However, any loss on a disposal to which the exemption would apply will not be an allowable loss, by virtue of the general provisions set out in TCGA section 16(2).

Under the SSE regime the investing company (i.e. the seller) must be either a trading company or a member of a trading group for at least 12 months both before the date of disposal and immediately after the disposal.[22] Therefore, under strict interpretation the exemption will not apply where a holding company disposes of its only trading subsidiary, as it will not have a trade following the disposal. However, it would appear that HMRC consider[23] that if the holding company is wound up or dissolved immediately or soon after the disposal, the provisions under paragraph 3(3) of Schedule 7AC can be interpreted as enabling SSE to apply. In such a situation a clearance under CTA 2010 section 748 should be made. This should include the arrangements for the investing company to be wound up.

The investee company must also satisfy the trading requirements before and after the disposal. If there has been an earlier intra-group transfer of the shareholding on a no loss/no gain basis, the pre-transfer period of ownership will be taken into account.[24] There are provisions relating to previous reorganisations,

---

[21] TCGA Schedule 7AC section 192A

[22] TCGA Schedule 7AC paragraph 18(1)

[23] See HMRC Manual CG53165

[24] TCGA Schedule 7AC paragraph 10(1)

reconstructions, demergers and amalgamations which protect the exemption in those situations.[25] There are also special SSE provisions where a disposal involves an insurance company and long-term insurance funds,[26] and arrangements involve repo agreements and stock lending[27] but which are not discussed further in this publication.

A company is defined as one which falls within CA 2006 section 1(1) – a company (other than a limited liability partnership) which is constituted under any other act or a royal charter or letters patent or is formed under the law of a country or territory outside the United Kingdom; a registered industrial and provident society; an incorporated friendly society; and a building society.[28] The SSE, therefore, will not apply where either the investing company or investee companies is a partnership or limited partnership.

4.3.2.2   Inter-action of SSE with the corporate venturing scheme (CVS)

Under the CVS regime (see **Chapter 8 – Venture Capital Schemes)** there were different but generally more exacting requirements for the investee companies, namely they must be small unquoted companies with a UK trade, maximum employee limits and gross asset limitations. In order to be chargeable CVS shares, the shares in the investee company must be chargeable assets for the capital gains tax purposes.[29] However, TCGA section 16(2) does not prevent SSE from applying to CVS shares, by virtue of Schedule 7AC paragraph 32 which provides that the exemptions under the SSE shall be disregarded in determining whether shares are chargeable shares for the purposes of capital gains tax. Therefore, shares which qualified for exemptions under the CVS should also qualify under the SSE provisions.

---

[25] TCGA Schedule 7AC paragraphs 14 & 15

[26] TCGA Schedule 7AC paragraph 17

[27] TCGA Schedule 7AC paragraphs 12 & 13

[28] TCGA section 170(9)

[29] FA 2000 Schedule 15 paragraph 13

4.4 Dealing with Target's Pre-completion Debts

Following changes introduced in 2009, there is no longer a distinction in the treatment of trade and non-trade debts. A release or waiver of a debt is, therefore, taxed under the loan relationship rules.

The following issues may arise in respect of debts due or owed between the target and its seller:

- the release or waiver of a debt could give rise to a loan relationship credit – this will be an issue to be considered by the target's accountants;
- if a person acquires a company subject to a debt, Stamp Act 1891 section 57 (*How conveyance in consideration of a debt, etc, to be charged*) will deem the debt, or any covenant to pay by the transferee, to be part of the consideration and subject to *ad valorem* stamp duty. However, any covenant to pay by the transferor should not fall within the provisions of section 57 – HMRC consider this to be a voluntary disposition.[30] An alternative arrangement could include the buyer procuring that the target company will satisfy the debt immediately after completion, with buyer either lending it the cash or subscribing for further shares in the target company to enable it to repay the debt;
- the benefit of debts of the target company owed to the seller can be assigned by the seller to the buyer for consideration, and stamp duty on the transfer of loan capital will be exempt under FA 1986 section 79(4) so long as the loan falls within the definition in section 78(7) *(The loan capital exemption)* and does not fall within sections 79(5) & (6). Therefore, the terms of the loan cannot include:
  - a right of conversion to shares or other securities or acquisition of shares or securities including loan capital;
  - a right to interest which will be determined by reference to results of a business or to the value of any property;
  - a right to repayment of more than the nominal amount; or
  - a rate of interest above a reasonable commercial return;

---

[30] See SP 6/90

- if the assignment is for less than par and involves corporate bonds, the loan relationship rules are applicable. Any resulting loss should be allowable for the seller as a loan relationship debit, but if it is subsequently repaid back at par the buyer could suffer a loan relationship credit.

4.5 Accounts and Completion Accounts

If no completion accounts are to be prepared, the target company's latest accounts will ordinarily be relied upon by both parties and, under the standard tax indemnity, the seller will be liable for all outstanding tax liabilities of the company before that date other than for liabilities provided for in those accounts. The seller will also be liable for any tax liabilities arising outside the ordinary course of business between the accounts date and the completion date (an 'accounts deal').

An accounts deal is only likely if the accounts date is relatively close to the completion date or the business of the target company is relatively simple. In most cases[31] a working capital statement as at the completion date will be required to ensure that the business has sufficient assets and work-in-progress to cover the current liabilities, which may include VAT and PAYE arising up to the completion date, resulting in effect, in a 'completion accounts' deal.

The main reason for drawing up completion accounts is to provide for either:

- a deferred payment to be made to the seller; or
- a clawback of part of the purchase price, based on the position of some or all of the company's assets and liabilities on the date of completion and which can only be accurately computed following completion.

It would be possible for the consideration to include a deferred payment under an accounts deal including an earn-out, but this is not as common.

The consideration price will have been negotiated, in part based on the due diligence and early disclosures and estimates for the

---

[31] Probably not relevant in a 'fire sale'

target company's trading results and its working capital, net cash position or full balance sheet position as at the completion date. Transactions commonly provide for a pound-for-pound payment from the buyer to the seller by the amount over which the forecast is exceeded and a payment by the seller to the buyer on the same principles if the forecast is not met.

4.6 Structuring the Consideration

The issues discussed below are not restricted to transactions involving the sale and purchase of a company, with paragraphs 4.6.1 and 4.6.3 applying equally for the sale of a business and assets.

4.6.1 Cash consideration

Cash consideration is taxable on the accruals basis, namely on receipt, with capital gains tax for individuals and corporation tax on chargeable gains for companies payable within the statutory time limits as follows:

- an individual is currently required to pay CGT under self-assessment by 31 January in the calendar year following the tax year ending 5 April in which the transaction was effected;[32]
- companies are required to pay corporation tax not later than nine months and one day following the accounting period in which the chargeable gain arose[33].

4.6.2 Delayed consideration

There is no discount on tax for delayed consideration by virtue of TCGA section 48, but if the delayed consideration is not paid an individual can make a claim to recover any overpaid capital gains tax under TMA section 43(1). The time limit for making a claim is four years after the end of the year of assessment to which it relates – hence this should be the limitation period for making a claim under a tax indemnity.

By concession,[34] HMRC will allow a longer period in circumstances where there has been an overpayment of tax due to an error by HMRC and there is no dispute or doubt as to the facts.

---

[32] TMA section 59B

[33] TMA section 59D

For companies the time limit for making claims is also four years from the end of the accounting period to which it relates.[35]

If there is a successful claim for a tax liability by the buyer against the seller under the tax schedule or SPA, the repayment relating to any tax liability is normally capable of being treated as a reduction of the consideration price,[36] in which case the seller will wish to make a claim for overpayment of his or her capital gains tax. However, the four year time limit allowed under TMA section 43(1)/Schedule 18 paragraph 55 rarely fits within the standard six year limitation in most tax schedules, and certainly not within the increasingly common seven year limitation. It is, therefore, entirely reasonable to set the limitation date for the buyer to make a claim against the seller under the tax indemnity to conform to the new four year time limit, and the seller's tax advisor should strongly argue for it. It is the author's experience that often the buyer's tax advisor refuses a request for a four year limitation period automatically without referring the issue to the client, but that most reasonable buyers will agree to it when the issue is explained. It is sometimes necessary for the seller to speak directly with the buyer about this issue.

The time limit for HMRC to make a discovery assessment is also now four years after the end of the accounting period to which it relates under FA 1998 Schedule 18 paragraph 46 for companies. A six year time limit only applies if the company is guilty of careless conduct – therefore the seller's advisor should argue that so long as due diligence has found no such behaviour and there is a relevant warranty, the four year time period should apply.

Under TCGA section 280 if consideration is payable by instalments for a period great then 18 months the taxpayer can apply to HMRC to pay the tax by instalments. However, if the delayed consideration involves contingent consideration (see paragraph 4.6.4 below) tax by instalments is not possible.

---

[34] Concession B41

[35] FA 1998 Schedule 18 paragraph 55

[36] Ordinarily in the UK

4.6.3 Shares and securities as consideration (a share for share exchange)[37]

If there is a reorganisation of share capital under TCGA section 126, whereby new shares or debentures in a new company are allotted, TCGA section 127 provides that the original holding and the new holding will be treated as the same asset acquired as the original shares were acquired. TCGA section 127 also applies, *inter alia*, to reorganisations under TCGA section 135 which covers the following circumstances:

- the new company holds or will hold as a result of the exchange more than 25% of the ordinary share capital of the original company or the greater part of its voting power; or
- the new company issues a new holding in exchange for shares as a result of a general offer made to shareholders of the original company or a class of shareholders and in the first instance:
  - the general offer was made on a condition that if it were satisfied the new company would have control of the original company; or
  - the new company holds or will hold as a result of the exchange the greater part of the voting power of the original company.

The tax effect of a section 135 share exchange is that no chargeable gain is triggered at the time of the exchange in respect of the proportion of original shares which are exchanged for the new shares in the buyer. Any cash consideration received in respect of the original holding will be subject to standard chargeable gains treatment.

Under the first alternative above, 'ordinary shares'[38] means share capital other than capital which give the holders a right to a fixed rate of dividend but which have no other right to share in the profits of the company and, for the purposes of TCGA section 135,

---

[37] TCGA section 135

[38] CTA 2010 section 1119 by virtue of TCGA section 135(4)

units in a unit trust and membership interest in a company which has no share capital.[39]

The provisions require both the issue of shares or debentures (therefore not merely a transfer), and an exchange. If the new shares consist of treasury stock arising from a share buy-back, the transfer out of treasury stock will be treated as an issue of new shares at that time (and not as having been disposed of by the company) by virtue of FA 2003 section 195(8)(b).

Whilst there is no statutory definition of a debenture, TCGA section 251(6) states that a debenture issued by a company on or after 16 March 1993 shall be deemed to be a security as defined in TCGA section 132 (*Equation of converted securities and new holding*) and therefore '*including any loan stock or similar security whether of a government, public or local authority or of any company, and whether secured or unsecured*' if it is issued in exchange for shares in or debentures of another company under TCGA section 135. The roll-over provisions therefore apply to qualifying corporate bonds and non-qualifying corporate bonds (see the **Glossary** for definitions).

If the seller is in a position to claim entrepreneurs' relief in respect of his or her shareholding in the target company, but part of the consideration will consist of shares in the buyer, he or she may wish to make an election under TCGA section 169Q to disapply TCGA section 127 from the share for share exchange – in which case the shareholder may make a claim for entrepreneurs' relief as if the reorganisation involved a disposal of all the original shares. An election must be made on or before the first anniversary of the 31 January following the tax year in which the reorganisation takes place. A reorganisation specifically includes one by virtue of section 135, under TCGA section 169Q(5). Otherwise, part or all of the relief could be lost if the requirements for the relief cannot be satisfied in respect of the new shareholding in the buyer company – namely the 5% holding requirement in an unlisted company as well as the employment requirement. These issues should be discussed with individual sellers for whom entrepreneurs' relief

---

[39] TCGA section 135(4)(a) & (b)

could be available if it is part of the tax advisor's remit in the engagement letter.

When the new investors' relief becomes effective – for disposals made one or after April 2019 –similar advice may be required by individual sellers.

4.6.4 Earn-outs

An earn-out is consideration which is to be paid to the seller following completion of the sale of a company, which will be linked to post-completion results. A key feature is that an earn-out will not be paid unless certain targets are met, which can provide a cash flow benefit to the buyer in funding the purchase price as well as an incentive to the sellers who stay with the target company following completion to ensure that the target achieves certain performance targets. An earn-out is a deferred payment but a deferred payment is not necessarily an earn-out, which must involve unascertainable and contingent consideration. The tax treatment of deferred consideration depends on the nature and terms of future payments, including whether they are ascertainable or unascertainable, or instalment payments.

4.6.4.1 *Ascertainable consideration*

HMRC consider[40] that future payments will be ascertainable if they are known, ascertainable by calculations or ascertainable by making up an account and all of the events which establish the amount have occurred by the date of disposal. This would include specified instalment payments or an amount to be calculated in respect of profits arising for a period ending not later than completion. If the ascertainable amount is contingent upon an event (such as profit exceeding a specified amount) it will be treated in the same way as an ascertainable amount, as the events influencing the future payment take place before completion.

An unascertainable payment will depend on post-completion events, such as results in periods following completion. Most contracts provide a cap on unascertainable deferred payments for commercial reasons, and which will have a bearing on the calculation of stamp duty for the buyer, but which has no bearing

---

[40] HMRC Manual CG 14880

for chargeable gains purposes on whether the amount may be ascertainable.

4.6.4.2 *Instalment payments*

Ascertainable consideration is subject to tax on chargeable gains on the whole amount regardless of some of the payment being deferred (see TCGA section 48 and paragraph 4.6.2 above). Instalment payments are merely deferred payments so long as they are not unascertainable.

4.6.4.3 *TCGA section 138A (Use of earn-out rights for exchange of securities)*

An earn-out right is defined as being a right conferred on a seller which:

- represents part or all of the consideration for the transfer by a seller of shares or debentures in a company ('old securities');
- represents a right to be issued with shares in or debentures of another company ('new securities' and 'new company' respectively);
- the value or quantity of the new securities is unascertainable at the time when the right is conferred; and
- the right cannot be discharged otherwise than by the issue of the new securities under the relevant terms.

If an earn-out satisfies the above strict conditions then the following provisions will apply:

- the earn-out right itself will be treated as a security of the new company and no capital gains tax will arise at completion but will arise at each time the new securities, once issued, are sold;
- the new security cannot be a qualifying corporate bond;
- the definition of new security will extend to any debentures in respect of the right; and
- the issue of share or debentures in respect of the earn-out right will result in its conversion.[41]

These provisions apply automatically, but if a seller wishes to opt out it can elect that the earn-out right is not to be treated as a security.[42] If the seller is a company, the election (which will be

---

[41] TCGA section 138A(2) and (3)

[42] TCGA section 138A(2A)

irrevocable) must be made within the period of two years from the end of the accounting period in which the earn-out right was conferred, and in any other case, on or before the first anniversary of the 31 January next following the year of assessment in which the right was conferred.

In order for the value or quantity of the new securities to be treated as unascertainable:

- the earn-out right must refer to matters relating to the business or assets of the new company or any company within the same group or the company in respect of which the old securities were exchanged or any member in its group; and
- the uncertainty relates to the future business or future assets being included in the business or assets to which they relate.[43]

The value and quantity of the new securities will not be considered to be unascertainable if the transfer of the old securities resulted in a capital gain, and the new securities would be treated as delayed consideration under TCGA section 48.[44]

If the earn-out right includes an alternative merely to choose between shares and debentures in the new company this will not represent unascertainability nor will it interfere with the definition of an earn-out right. Furthermore, merely placing a maximum cap on the earn-out will also not render its value unascertainable.

4.6.4.4   *Marren v Ingles [1980] 2 All ER 95*

As a result of this case TCGA section 138A was enacted. It is often quoted when referring to *'a chose in action'* (being a right to sue), and it is useful to be reminded of its facts, set out as follows:

A taxpayer sold shares for an immediate payment of £750 per share plus the right to receive a sum ('half the profit') which on a flotation was to be one-half of the amount by which the market price of a share would exceed £750. On flotation two years later, the taxpayer received from the buyer the sum of £2,825 per share. The Crown argued that the right to receive 'half the profit' was an asset and that when it matured a capital sum was derived from it. This gave rise to a deemed disposal and, therefore, the taxpayer

---

[43] TCGA section 138A(7)

[44] TCGA section 138A(8)

was chargeable on the gain of £2,825 per share in the year of that deemed disposal. The taxpayer argued that, at the date of the disposal of the shares, a charge to capital gains tax arose based on the cash sum of £750 per share plus the value, on that date, of his contingent right to receive the deferred price, and that no further liability would arise. He argued that the right to receive half the profit was a debt, rather than an asset, and so no chargeable gain could accrue.

The House of Lords held that an 'asset' was defined in the widest terms, to mean all forms of property including a chose in action. Furthermore, it was a separate asset and not simply a deferred part of the price of the shares. Therefore, if the right was an asset any sum derived from that asset was a disposal, notwithstanding that no asset was acquired by the person paying the capital sum. Therefore, the sum received in respect of the taxpayer's right to half the profit represented proceeds on the disposal of an asset and were liable to capital gains tax. The House of Lords further held that a contingent right (which might never be realised) to receive an unascertainable amount of money at an unknown date cannot be considered to be a debt and so there was no debt at the time of the sale of the shares. Whilst there might have been a debt when the contingency arose and the amount of half the profits was ascertained, it was not a debt 'incurred' as required under the legislation. It held that the amount of the debt was derived from the asset (the *chose in action*) and was taxable under the relevant provisions in the legislation. Thus the correct position was that there was an acquisition of an asset, being a chose in action at the time of the sale of the shares, from which a capital sum arose two years later.

Since *Marren & Ingles* was decided its effect on transactions involving earn-outs was circumvented first by extra statutory concession and then by legislation under TCGA section 138A whereby an earn-out meeting the conditions would be treated as part of the original securities and rolled over.

Unless TCGA section 138A applies – the seller can elect under section 138A(2A) for the earn-out right not to be treated as a security of the new company – the earn-out right will require

SALE AND PURCHASE OF A COMPANY

valuation by HMRC as at the date on which it is received by the seller for the sale of the shares in the target company – ordinarily completion. The valuation will be based on the likelihood of the earn-out being paid, its likely quantum, and the 'time value of money' – namely its discounted value reflecting future receipt. Unascertainable future cash payments and new securities to be issued under the terms of the deal will be included in the valuation of the earn-out. It is recommended that an expert in share valuations undertake the negotiations with HMRC on behalf of the seller shortly after completion of any transaction if an election is made under TCGA section 138A(2A).

Entrepreneurs' relief is not available on the disposal of a chose in action. Any seller wishing to apply entrepreneurs' relief in a transaction involving an earn-out could require a different structure for the consideration, which would have a maximum cap on the total payments. This would involve defining the consideration price as the maximum amount payable (to include the consideration payable on completion and total earn-outs). The seller would warrant the post-completion targets of the target company and amounts would be held in escrow relating to the earn-outs. The seller would, therefore, be liable to capital gains tax on the maximum amount of consideration at completion, on which he or she would claim entrepreneurs' relief. Under this structure the limitation period must be set at four years in order for the seller to reclaim any overpaid CGT if the targets are not met and the amounts held in escrow are not all paid. The terms for claims against any escrow amounts should also match this period.

4.6.4.5 *Commercial issues relating to earn-outs*

The High Court case of *Porton Capital Technology Funds and Others v 3M UK Holdings Limited and another [2011] EWHC 2895* is a reminder that any payment of earn-outs will be dependent on a mixture of the buyer's discretion, commercial skill and integrity as well as the underlying commerciality of the target's business. The outcome of this case is a horror story. The sellers were paid initial consideration (primarily representing their outlay on and investment in the target company's development of a diagnostic test used to detect MRSA[45]), and an earn-out payment based on net sales of the target for the calendar year ending just under two years from the date of the agreement – an amount reflecting the anticipated potential of the target company's only product. The projected sales were not realised because the business of the target was terminated at the end of 2008 – whatever the rights and wrong of this case, sellers should be aware such a possibility, either reflecting commercial realities or through deviousness of a buyer, particularly those based in overseas jurisdictions, notably in tax havens. In Porton the judge found in favour of the sellers, as claimants in the dispute, but the victory was pyrrhic in that the damages of just under $1.3 million were well below the amount claimed (being in the region of $56 million) and not much greater than the amount put forward as settlement by the defendants.

Whilst this case involved intellectual property requiring further significant investment and development by the buyer, its lessons could apply to most earn-outs. The buyer agreed to pay an amount based on sales arising from its further investment and development of the product, and the seller was relying on the expertise, integrity of and financial commitment by the buyer.

From a seller's perspective it would be unwise to apportion a high percentage of the total consideration to the earn-out and agree to an earn-out covering more than two (and at most three years) following completion. If the sellers are to remain in control of the target, there should be clear provisions giving the sellers autonomy in managing the business together with proper financial support, and an early payment clause if the employment contracts with the sellers or the subject matter of the business are terminated for any reason. Regardless of whether the sellers stay with the business, there should be provisions for accountants independent of the buyer to audit the performance of the target for the purposes of the earn-out, and comprehensive dispute resolution provisions in the case of disagreement. Any earn-out should be dependent on the business of the target continuing to carry on its business and the sellers should negotiate an early payment of the

---

[45] methicillin-resistant staphylococcus aureus

full earn-out discounted for the time value of money, in the event the target ceases to trade, or winds down its business in a material way. In agreeing to an earn-out the sellers should bear in mind the due diligence it should have carried out on the buyer, including its management capabilities, its financial and marketing strengths, and its track record for developing its acquisitions.

A buyer will not want any failure to pay the earn-out to be challenged as a breach of contract by the sellers. It is, therefore, equally important that the earn-out performance targets are set out clearly and unambiguously and the same for termination and earn-out 'lapsing' provisions and dispute resolutions, including what happens if there is a 'force majeure' incident. Full records relating to the reasons for non-payment of the earn-out should be available to the parties including the independent auditor of the project.

The more specific issues set out in the earn-out conditions, the better it is for the parties. In the case of *Porton Capital Technology Funds*[46] much of the consideration as to the parties' actions rested on what amounted to acting 'diligently' and whether consent was 'unreasonably withheld'. With hindsight more objective criteria would have been preferable.

---

[46] [2011] EWHC 2895

THE TAX SCHEDULE

5 SALE AND PURCHASE OF A BUSINESS

5.1 General Overview

The sale of a business can involve any of the following scenarios:

- a company disposing of all of its business or one of its businesses through the sale of all the assets and goodwill of the business in question;
- the sale by an individual of an unincorporated business;
- the sale of a business by a partnership;
- a transfer of a business through a hive-up or hive-down into a newco as part of a reorganisation or pre-disposal, with the newco sold to a third party.

There will be no tax schedule in these types of transactions, and the limited warranties to be included in the sale and purchase agreement are included in both this chapter and set out in **Appendix 4**.

If the transfer of a business is made to a third party as an arm's length transaction, the standard form tax indemnity is not appropriate as there will be no transfer of the business's tax assets and liabilities. These will remain with the seller in the first three examples above. If a newco is to acquire the assets and business, a short form tax indemnity will be required to cover any tax liability which has arisen in any way since the incorporation of newco or relating to the business after its transfer into newco. In a sale of a business, tax warranties will be limited to matters relating to VAT and PAYE (primarily focusing on tax compliance), and inheritance tax.

A sale of a business is distinct from a sale of a mere group of assets, and will be a question of fact. There is extensive case law considering the differences between the two alternatives and the issue is also important in respect of entrepreneurial relief (discussed in paragraph 5.4.1 below). If there is a sale of assets and not a business then VAT should be charged on the sale of each asset chargeable to VAT. On a sale of a business which represents a transfer of a going concern for VAT purposes (TOGC) the transaction can be ignored for VAT purposes and no VAT should be chargeable.

In the majority of business and asset sale transactions the parties might assume that all conditions for a TOGC are met or they simply do not give it sufficient consideration. Therefore, in the due diligence process there are a number of issues which need to be investigated and which require warranties from both the seller and the buyer. It may not be standard practice for buyers to provide warranties for a TOGC but it is essential that the buyer intends to use the assets transferred in carrying on the same kind of business. The other issues relate to VAT registration (particularly if the assets include land and property) and VAT records.

A business and asset sale will be the preferred disposal route involving insolvency practitioners, who will be unwilling or unable to provide any tax warranties and indemnities for a distressed company. Speedy completion is likely to be a factor with no time for comprehensive due diligence and a buyer will not want exposure to tax liabilities of a company in difficulties. In circumstances where the target has a troubled history with obvious, potential or unknown liabilities (regardless of whether or not an insolvency practitioner is involved) the buyer should purchase the business and assets rather than the shares of the target. Such a decision will ordinarily be agreed at the heads of terms stage, although, if during the due diligence process for a share sale, it is found that the target company's affairs are clearly not in order (tax-related or otherwise) the buyer should renegotiate and insist upon the purchase of the business, being purely for the company's assets.

There are different tax consequences for an owner disposing of a business and assets compared with selling a company and these are discussed below. From the buyer's perspective it is generally the case that it will be more protected from tax issues and liabilities under an asset purchase, but any trading or capital losses of a business ordinarily capable of being carried forward, will be lost on such a transfer.

5.2   Commercial Considerations

It is not the case that a business and asset sale is either more or less complicated than a share sale from a transactional standpoint. Due diligence should be just as rigorous, in that the onus of proving loss and quantum will be the buyer's burden for any claim for breach of warranties, and it will be required to mitigate if it suffers loss. On the other hand, the buyer need not be concerned about acquiring any unknown tax liabilities of the target company. The seller will be required to provide fewer tax warranties than in a share sale, which will be less burdensome, but there will nevertheless be administrative issues relating to VAT and PAYE and there may be tax consequences on the seller arising from such a disposal.

The main commercial issues include the following:

- How will the buyer integrate the business following completion – i.e. through a special purpose vehicle or an established subsidiary – and will any subsequent reorganisation within the buyer's group be required?
- If the business has overseas operations, separate transfer agreements involving different legal jurisdictions will be required.
- What third party approvals are required (both within and outside the UK) if the business is international?
- Are there any minority shareholder issues which might cause difficulties for the transaction?
- Can the business be transferred without interruption?
- If it is not possible to transfer the business without interruption, how quickly can the business be resumed under the buyer's control in order to satisfy the TOGC requirements?
- Are there adequate separate business records and management accounts relating to the business and are they comprehensive and up-to-date?
- Are all contracts which are being transferred assignable and what is the timetable for the assignments?
- What are the alternative arrangements if assignment of any contracts is not possible?
- What provisions are there for change of control in all relevant contracts (both supply side and customer side) and what authorities are required? This is often complex and takes the most time for the corporate lawyers.
- Are the requirements of a TOGC satisfied?

- Will TUPE apply to the transfer in respect of UK employees and what equivalent treatment will apply for employees of the business outside the UK?
- Has the target properly operated PAYE in respect of its workforce and contractors, as evidenced during due diligence and will any change of practice be required following the sale?
- What property issues are there relating to the assignment and/or transfer of licences, leases (including obtaining landlord consents) and/or freeholds and are there elections in place to opt to tax for VAT purposes?
- Will any of the assets represent capital goods under the capital goods scheme?
- Is there agreement as to what amount of consideration should be allocated to each of the assets to be transferred on a fair and equitable basis – discussed further in paragraph 5.2.1.
- SDLT will be chargeable on UK land transferred and in certain types of transfers HMRC may want to apportion some value of goodwill to the chargeable consideration of any 'trade related' properties, and which will be a buyer's issue.[1]

5.2.1   Apportionment of Consideration

Apportionment of the consideration for each of the assets being transferred must be done on the basis of 'fair value' with apportionment on a just and reasonable basis under TCGA section 52(4), for the purpose of calculating:

- any chargeable gains arising on the seller in respect of each of the assets to be transferred;
- SDLT due on any UK land and property to be transferred;
- any balancing allowance or balancing charges on capital assets for the seller;
- capital allowances for the buyer on capital assets acquired.
-

---

[1] See HMRC's Practice Note – *Apportioning the price paid for a business transferred as a going concern* (First published 30 September 2013). Relevant if the business involves pubs, nursing homes, hotels, restaurants, cinemas, petrol stations but also to businesses involving other trades

The parties may agree to enter into a CAA section 198 joint election,[2] under which they must agree a fixed value of the plant and machinery transferred. Apportionment must be quantified and the agreed disposal values cannot be greater than the seller's expenditure incurred in the provision of the assets or the sale price. The election allows the purchaser to claim capital allowances on the assets going forward.

Assets for chargeable gains tax purposes comprise all forms of property including intellectual property, transferrable licences, certain debts (namely a debt on a security under TCGA section 251[3]) and currency other than sterling. In most business and asset sales cash does not transfer nor should any debts other than trade debtors move across. A balance will be need to be struck at completion determining outstanding trade debtors and creditors, payments on account and work-in-progress as at that date and for which some adjustment to the purchase price should be made. Stock in trade, trade debtors and creditors are revenue issues, as is work-in-progress, and while needing a valuation for the purposes of working out the consideration, such valuations should ordinarily be irrelevant for the purposes of chargeable gains.[4]

Goodwill, being an intangible asset under that regime[5] is defined by its accounting meaning under FRS10 as the difference between the consideration payable for a business and the aggregate fair value of its identifiable assets less liabilities (such a figure can be positive or negative). Therefore, in order to arrive at the value of the goodwill the valuation of all other assets transferred must pass the 'fair value' test.

The starting point in determining apportionment of the consideration in the sale of a business will be Section 9 and Section

---

[2] Which will be irrevocable

[3] A security is defined as including any loan stock or similar security issued by a government, local authority or a company and whether secured or unsecured under TCGA section 132(3)(b)

[4] See TCGA section 37(1)– any amount charged to income tax or taken into account as a receipt in computing income or profits or gains of losses of the person making the disposal for the purposes of the Income Tax Acts shall be excluded from the consideration for a disposal of assets

[5] CTA 2009 Part 8 (sections 711 to 906)

19 of FRS 102 under new UK GAAP, for accounting periods starting on or after 1 January 2015, replacing FRS 7, for fair values on acquisition accounting or IFRS 3 under international accounting standards (*Business Combinations*), which apply when one business entity is acquired by another. All the assets and liabilities which exist in the target business at the date of acquisition should be recorded at fair values reflecting their condition at that date. All changes to the acquired assets and liabilities and any gains and losses which arise after the change of control will be reported as part of the post-acquisition financial performance of the buyer. Therefore, the values of the assets to be transferred should have some relationship to their values in the seller's balance sheet, and accounts as at completion if available, or most recent valuations together with adjustments to reflect changes up to completion, to reflect fair value.

Under FRS 102 intangibles other than goodwill may be measured after initial recognition using the cost model or revaluation model. Under the cost model assets are recognised at cost less accumulated amortisation and impairment losses. Under the revaluation model intangibles are measured at fair value at the date of revaluation less subsequent amortisation and impairment losses. Revaluation is only possible when fair value can be determined by reference to an active market for an intangible. Other intangibles and goodwill are considered to have a finite useful life and should be amortised systematically over their life. If it is not possible to make a reliable estimate of the useful life, it should be deemed not to exceed five years.

One of the most significant changes to intangible assets and goodwill is the rate at which they will be amortised under FRS 102. Previously UK GAAP presumed a maximum useful economic life of 20 years, rebuttable if it could be justified that there is a longer life. Subject to conditions, the amortisation of intangible fixed assets and goodwill in the company's accounts may be eligible for corporation tax relief. One of the main aspects of Part 8, CTA 2009 is that intangible fixed assets which are acquired for consideration may be amortised over their useful economic life and a corporation tax deduction claimed for the amortisation. HMRC have issued guidance on FRS 102[6] updated 30 October 2015.

Smaller entities[7] are currently exempt from the FRS unless preparing consolidated statements, in which case they should apply the Financial Reporting Standards for Smaller Entities (FRSSE), a simplified version of the FRS.

Detailed issues relating to a valuation of a business is a specialist subject for accountants experienced in such matters and not within the scope of this book. These accounting issues for a TOGC should be considered at the heads of terms stage, particularly for the buyer going forward.

From the perspective of the seller a major commercial issue will be whether chargeable gains or losses arise on the disposal, which will be dictated by the consideration apportioned to each asset and their base costs. If the apportionment is not done on 'fair and reasonable principles' HMRC may substitute their own figures. From the buyer's perspective the apportionment, in addition to establishing the base cost for the assets going forward, will also determine the amount of SDLT arising in respect of any UK property, and capital allowances available.

5.2.1.1   Trade related properties

Apportioning the price paid for goodwill in a business transferred as a going concern involving trade related property has been the subject of much debate with HMRC, who distinguish between TOGCs where the assets include trade-related properties[8] (such as pubs, hotels, petrol stations, restaurants, care homes and cinemas) and other businesses where there is no reliance on a specific property interest. HMRC consider that if a business carried out from a trade related property is sold as a TOGC the sale price is

---

[6]www.gov.uk/government/publications/accounting-standards-the-uk-tax-implications-of-new-uk-gaap/frs-102-overview-paper

[7] Generally, a company which meets two of the following criteria – having less than 50 employees, turnover less than £5.6 million and gross assets less than £2.8 million so long as it is not a PLC, or the subsidiary of a listed company

[8] See HMRC *Goodwill in Trade Related Properties*
www.gov.uk/government/publications/practice-note-apportioning-the-price-paid-for-a-business-transferred-as-a-going-concern

likely to include some goodwill. HMRC's practice note sets out how their Valuation Office Agency considers the correct allocation of the price paid between goodwill and other assets included in the sale. This will be a major issue for a seller in respect of capital gains tax and for the buyer from an SDLT perspective. Specialist advice should initially be sought by the buyer and communicated to the seller early on in any transaction involving any of the types of business which HMRC list in their practice note. The parties should expect some interest from HMRC as to the justification for apportionment method used.

5.3   Due Diligence

While in a business and asset sale the buyer will have no liabilities relating to the prior tax history of the person (individual or company) selling the asset, it will not have the right for a pound-for-pound payment for any tax liability arising under a breach of warranty against the seller as it would for the same matter covered under a standard indemnity. If the transaction does not allow time for adequate due diligence the buyer should at the very least ensure the following tax issues are investigated before completion:

- the PAYE records for UK employees and any officers are in order and indicate all employment-related payments have been properly made;
- the current employment status of any contractors to the business and of the directors and officers of the company disposing of the business who will transfer with it;
- whether the seller has opted to tax for VAT purposes any UK land and property;
- VAT issues, including whether the supplies made by the business are fully taxable or exempt and what services and supplies involve other EU territories and non EU territories;
- that SDLT has been properly paid and the valuation properly documented, for UK land and property acquired before the completion of the transaction;
- whether assets being transferred fall within the capital goods scheme;
- any tax issues in respect of any transfers of overseas-based businesses and assets including those which are employment-

related, stamp and sales taxes, and reporting and registration requirements.

5.4 Tax Issues

The tax issues arising in a business and asset sale include the following:

- chargeable gains on disposal of the assets:
  - there will be no substantial shareholdings exemption for a corporate seller (SSE only applying on the disposal of shares or an interest in shares in another company);
  - the availability of entrepreneurs' relief for an individual seller or trustee;
  - possible crystallisation of roll-over relief for business assets under TCGA section 152 for the seller;
  - the possibility of using roll-over relief by the buyer;
- SDLT on UK land and property transferred (a buyer's issue for its payment) and withdrawal of SDLT relief for a corporate seller if the disposal is within three years of the relevant relief having been given (see **Chapter 9** paragraph 9.7);
- inheritance tax;
- VAT and whether the transfer will represent a TOGC.

5.4.1 Chargeable gains

From the perspective of shareholders in a company which is selling a business and assets, this can be the least tax efficient method if chargeable gains arise for the company from the disposal. The selling company will be chargeable to corporation tax on any chargeable gains arising at the appropriate corporation tax rate, and there will be a double tax hit on its shareholders through the payment of a dividend or on a distribution on winding up the selling company. However, if the disposal of the business and assets results in capital losses, they can be set off against other profits of the company and/or carried forward.

For the individual seller so long as the lifetime limit has not been used up[9] entrepreneurs' relief should be available to reduce tax payable on any capital gains arising to a 10%. Otherwise capital gains tax for higher rate taxpayers is 20% as from 6 April 2016.

---

[9] £10 million as from 6 April 2011

5.4.1.1 *Entrepreneurs' Relief*[10]

Before the abolition of taper relief in April 2008, which applied to disposals of capital assets by individuals or trustees, a seller could expect to pay 10% CGT on capital gains of an uncapped amount in a high proportion of disposals which represented business assets and shares in qualifying companies (namely any unlisted trading company or a trading company in which the shareholder was an employee or officer) subject to a qualifying period of ownership of two whole years.

A somewhat less complicated regime under entrepreneurs' relief was introduced for qualifying business disposals whereby 10% CGT is charged but capped at a lifetime limit, currently £10 million. Therefore, the relief may be of less use to serial entrepreneurs involved in high value transactions than was taper relief which had no life-time cap. Nevertheless, a tax advisor would be negligent in failing to advise a client selling a business that he or she should take advice as to whether entrepreneurs' relief might be available on such a disposal. While the statutory provisions are reasonably straightforward, a disposal of a business involves scrutiny as to which assets will fall within the regime and which will not. Furthermore, depending on how assets used in a business are owned, some restructuring may be required well in advance of a contemplated sale to get maximum entrepreneurs' relief. This might apply to assets jointly owned and assets held outside a business but used by the business.

The relief, whose statutory provisions are a re-write of the withdrawn retirement relief, applies to the following:

- a material disposal of business assets;
- a disposal of trust business assets; and
- a disposal associated with a relevant material disposal.

A material disposal of business assets is one where an individual sells a business (and not merely a group of assets) or shares in a company as follows:

---

[10] TCGA sections 169H to 169S

- the sale of the whole or part of a business which an individual carries on (either alone or in partnership) throughout the period of one year before the date of disposal;
- the sale of one or more assets (or interest in such assets) in use at the time at which a business ceases to be carried on, such business having been owned by the individual for one year ending on the date of cessation and the disposal is made within the period of three years from the cessation;
- the sale of shares and securities:
  - in a trading company or the holding company of a trading group in which the individual has at least a 5% interest (measured by both ordinary share capital and voting rights) and is an employee or officer (a 'personal company') and which are held for at least one year before the date of disposal; or
  - in a personal trading company as set out above and:
    - the conditions are satisfied for a period of one year ending with the date on which the company ceases to be a trading company, without continuing to be or becoming a member of a trading group; or
    - the company ceases to be a member of a trading group without continuing to be or becoming a trading company and that date is within the period of three years ending with the date of the disposal.

If the disposal is of assets other than shares or securities, the assets must comprise 'relevant business assets', meaning assets including goodwill which are used for the purposes of a business carried on by the individual or a partnership of which the individual is a member, and they are not shares and securities or other assets which are held as investments.

The case law involving interpretation for retirement relief is used as a source by HMRC in its guidance which it considers will, at the very least, be persuasive in any tribunal where entrepreneurs' relief is in issue.

A qualifying disposal of trust business assets is where:

- the assets consist of shares or securities of a company (or an interests in such shares or securities) or are assets used or

previously used, for the purposes of a business and which are part of the settled property (or are interests in such assets);
- there is a 'qualifying beneficiary' being an individual who, under the settlement, has an interest in possession in the whole of the settled property or part of it which include the assets disposed of; and
- if the assets are shares or securities:
  - the company is either a trading company or holding company of a trading group, the beneficiary has a 5% interest and is also an officer or employee of the company;
- if the assets are used for the purposes of a business the business was carried on by the qualifying beneficiary throughout the period of one year ending not earlier than three years before the date of the disposal, and the qualifying beneficiary ceases to carry on the business on the date of the disposal or within the period of three years before that date.

There is a disposal associated with a relevant material disposal if:
- an individual makes a material disposal of business assets which is a disposal of either:
  - the whole or part of his or her interest in partnership assets; or
  - shares in or securities of a company (or interests in such shares or securities); or
- an individual makes a disposal as part of his or her withdrawal from a partnership or by the company; or
- throughout the period of one year ending with the earlier of the date of the material disposal of business assets and the cessation of the business of the partnership or company, the assets disposed of were in use for the purposes of the business.

A business means a trade or profession or vocation conducted on a commercial basis and with a view to the realisation of profits. Because the time periods for holding the assets in question and satisfying the various requirements are rather short it is important that the claimant has good records to prove the periods of ownership and the business and trading requirements. Therefore, good record keeping, including that relating to any closure of a business, is essential.

Entrepreneurs' relief must be claimed by the first anniversary of 31 January following the tax year in which the qualifying business disposal is made.

5.4.1.2 *Roll-Over Relief for business assets under TCGA section 152*

If an individual is carrying on a trade and disposes of assets used for the purpose of the trade, he or she will be entitled to claim roll-over relief if the disposal proceeds or part of the proceeds are re-invested in replacement business assets within the required time period. If a person disposes of old assets and acquires new assets, and the trade in question is carried out not by the individual but by a company which at the time of the disposal and acquisition is his personal company (i.e. he or she has not less than five per cent voting rights), then roll-over relief applies equally to such an individual. The relief applies by the amount of the deferred gain being deducted from the base cost of the replacement asset. On its sale, the gain can be further rolled over into another business asset or will be otherwise crystallised.

The classes of assets must have been used for the purposes of the trade and are as follows:[11]

- goodwill;
- any building or part of a building or any permanent or semi-permanent structure in the nature of a building occupied as well as used only for the purposes of trade (other than a trade dealing in or developing properties or providing services for the occupier of land in which the person carrying on the trade has an estate or interest under TCGA section 156);
- any land occupied and used only for the purposes of the trade subject to the exceptions set out in TCGA section 156 and referred to above;
- fixed plant or machinery which does not form part of a building or of a permanent or semi-permanent structure in the nature of a building;
- ships, aircraft and hovercraft;

---

[11] TCGA section 155

- satellites, space stations and spacecraft including launch vehicles;
- milk quotas, potato quotas and ewe and suckler cow premium quotas;
- payment entitlements under the single payment scheme (income support for farmers);
- fish quotas;
- rights and assets relating to Lloyds membership.

The claimant has a four year period in which the re-investment must be effected, starting with the year before the disposal date and ending on the third anniversary of the disposal date. Good record keeping is therefore essential.

5.4.2 Intangible assets

Intangibles include goodwill and intellectual property such as patents, designs, trademarks and royalty rights, and telecommunications rights. The definition excludes any intangible asset treated as a tangible asset in the company's accounts in respect of which capital allowances were claimed.

If the assets transferred under a business and asset sale include intangibles and the seller or the buyer is a corporate vehicle, the provisions of CTA 2009 Parts 8 and 9[12] will apply for accounting periods ending on or after 11 April 2009 for corporation tax purposes, and for tax years 2009-10 onwards for income tax and CGT purposes.

Prior to 8 July 2015 corporation tax relief was available for companies who wrote off the cost of purchased goodwill and certain customer related intangible assets on the acquisition of a business and assets. HMRC stated that removing the relief brings the UK regime in line with other major economies, reduces distortion and levels the playing field for merger and acquisition transactions as the relief was not generally available to companies who purchase the shares of the target company.

Proper valuation of intangibles and correct apportionment of the consideration price is therefore important in a business and asset sale for both parties (and as discussed in paragraph 5.2.1 above).

---

[12] Sections 711 to 906, and 907 to 931 respectively

5.4.3 Stamp duty and stamp duty land tax

No UK stamp duty should be payable by the buyer on the value of the consideration paid on the transfer of a business, although out of date corporate lawyers often suggest an apportionment of the consideration for each asset set as if stamp duty was still payable on each category.

SDLT, payable by the buyer, will be chargeable on the consideration paid for the transfer of UK commercial property starting at 2% on values between £150,001 and £250,000 and with the top rate of 5% payable on values of more than £250,000.

An appropriate warranty should be provided by the seller relating to stamp duties which might be payable in respect of any of the assets or the business which are outside the UK as follows:

"No stamp duties of any kind (or duties equivalent to stamp duty outside the UK) imposed by any Tax Authority in respect of the Business and Assets will arise and/or will become payable by the Buyer as a result of Completion and there is no relevant outstanding stamp duty."

If a UK property is being transferred, the seller should make a disclosure, preferably with a valuation.

5.4.4 PAYE and employment-related issues

If there is to be continuity of employment for some or all of the employees of the business transferred (and it is essential to ensure that there is no interruption of trading for TOGC purposes), the TUPE Regulations[13] will apply and the buyer will take over the employment contracts of the employees and obligations under any collective agreements with recognised trades unions.

On the assumption that the buyer will wish to retain the goodwill of the transferred employees, it will require full details of the expectations of the workforce relating to anticipated or promised benefits, and of any employment-related incentives. Any option over shares in the seller company which have been granted to employees of the business may be exercisable on its transfer or

---

[13] Transfer of Undertakings (Protection of Employment) Regulations 2006 (SI 2006/246) and the Collective Redundancies and the Transfer of Undertakings (Protection of Employment)(Amendment) Regulations 2014 (SI 2014/16)

alternatively they may lapse, either immediately or at a specified date, as provided for under the relevant rules and agreements. Although this issue will be a contractual issue for the seller, in the interests of the transferred business and the importance for the buyer to maintain the goodwill of the employees, the buyer would be advised to provide replacement incentives if the options lapse on completion and/or the seller does not or cannot honour its commitments. Any taxation arising on pre-completion employment-related income matters will be for the seller but should, nevertheless, be covered by a warranty to reassure the buyer that the seller has considered the issue.

A PAYE liability could become an issue for the buyer in circumstances where transferred employees of the business remain contractually entitled to an employment-related benefit following completion, such as the right to exercise an option over shares in the seller or where there is a bonus payment of some sort from the seller. In these cases, the buyer will want an indemnity from the seller for any tax liability arising from the seller failing to properly account under PAYE when the benefit is provided to its ex-employees.

If PAYE has not been properly administered by the seller, this will cause problems for any transferred employees regardless of whether they self-assess. Problems will also arise if an employer is provided with the wrong tax code for its employees. While any PAYE-related liabilities of the seller should not be capable of being transferred to the buyer on the transfer of the business and assets, the buyer will want details of problems which could affect its new employees in order to assist them in resolving any difficulties with HMRC. Under the due diligence and disclosure process a buyer will, therefore, want assurance relating to the following issues:

- that PAYE has been properly administered in respect of the UK employees of the business as evidenced by PAYE records;
- there are no individuals working for the business who have been treated as self-employed when in fact they were employees (if so it would follow that the buyer must regularise the situation following completion);

- there are no disputes with HMRC or other tax authority relating to PAYE or any equivalent system relating to employment income of the transferred employees of the business;
- there are no special arrangements with HMRC or other tax authorities relating to employees coming to work in the UK or relating to any overseas employment-related contracts including equalisation;
- no person has been granted any rights relating to shares and share options and bonuses by the seller relating to their employment which will expire on the transfer of the business;
- no charge relating to taxation in whatever jurisdiction the employees reside can arise on the transfer of the business or attach in any way to the buyer and the business following the transfer.

The buyer should ask the seller to give the following tax indemnity to cover the issues discussed above:

"The Seller indemnifies the Buyer on an ongoing basis from the date of this Agreement for any Tax Liability which arises in respect of the transfer of any persons under the TUPE Regulations or equivalent legislation outside the United Kingdom and/or in respect of any persons who have been employed or deemed to have been employed or who have received payments in respect of the Business, for services supplied by such individuals before or following Completion, including under PAYE or equivalent legislation in jurisdictions outside the United Kingdom."

The following tax warranties relating to employment-related issues are appropriate in a business and asset sale, although they are no substitute for comprehensive due diligence by the buyer:

a) **"PAYE and all other systems relating to payroll and employment-related taxes and levies relating to the Employees and the Business have been properly administered in all respects and the relevant taxes and payments have been correctly made before and as at today's date, and all relevant records are accurate and up-to-date and** there are no disputes with HMRC or any other Tax Authority in respect of the Business."

b) "There are no individuals who supply services in a personal capacity (whether as an individual or through a corporate entity) to the Business who are not properly classified either as an employee or self-employed such that a liability could arise on the Buyer in respect of the Business due to such incorrect classification."

c) "There are no persons including any of the Employees who have any rights whether under an employment contract or otherwise, relating to bonuses, shares and/or other securities for which he or she would have a right of action against the Buyer or the Business, including in territories other than the United Kingdom or which will be payable, exercised and/or issued following Completion."

d) "There are no special arrangements with HMRC or any other Tax Authority relating to the Employees or any other person coming into the UK to work, or relating to their employment outside the UK including any equalisation arrangements and relating to the Business."

e) "No Tax Liability can or will arise on the Buyer or the Business following Completion, whether in the United Kingdom or any other jurisdiction, and relating to the transfer of the Employees under this Agreement or in any other respect relating to the Employees or any other individual before Completion."

f) "All relevant authorisations required to be obtained have been applied for by the seller and given in respect of the transfer of the working arrangements of the Employees relating to the Business."

5.4.5   Inheritance tax

Issues relating to inheritance tax charges and how they might apply to any sale of shares or assets are discussed in **Chapter 3 (Warranties)** under paragraph 3.22. For the purposes of a sale of a business and assets, the following warranties relating to IHT are standard (even though the likelihood of their being relevant are low) and should be included regardless of whether the seller is a company or an individual:

a) "There is no Inland Revenue charge for unpaid tax as referred to in IHTA section 237 on any of the Assets being transferred under this Agreement which could arise either directly or indirectly."

b) "No person has a limited interest or the power to sell or mortgage, or create a terminable charge on any of the Assets being transferred under this Agreement under IHTA section 212."

5.5   VAT and Transfers as a Going Concern (TOGC)

If a business or part of a business is transferred and the requirements for a TOGC are met, the transfer of the assets of the business will be treated as neither a supply of goods nor a supply of services and, therefore, must be ignored for VAT purposes. The relevant legislation is contained in article 19 of the EU Directive 2006/112/EC, VATA sections 49 and 94(6), and SI 1995/1268 articles 5(1)–(3) and SI 1995/2518 article 5.[14] HMRC's Notice 700/9/08 was replaced with Notice 700/9 in December 2012 and is helpful in that it states HMRCs interpretation and recommendations on TOGCs.

The three major consequences of a TOGC are as follows:

• VAT must not be charged on the consideration paid for the assets – in other words, TOGC treatment is not optional;

• the buyer is treated as the successor to the seller for VAT registration purposes as measured by the turnover of the business before its transfer;

• if VAT is incorrectly charged, the buyer has no entitlement to reclaim from HMRC the VAT it paid for the assets in question. Therefore, if the seller is in distressed circumstances and cannot or refuses to cancel the VAT invoice issued in error and refund the VAT to the buyer, the buyer will be out of pocket for the VAT paid over.

It is important for the buyer to get the TOGC treatment right, as otherwise recovery of input tax will be in issue, and any error will be considered by HMRC to be a matter between the parties. If VAT

---

[14] By virtue of VATA section 5(3)

is wrongly charged and the buyer (wrongly) recovers the input tax, only in exceptional circumstances will HMRC not seek to reclaim it. These are when the purported VAT has been declared and paid to HMRC by the seller and there will be no loss to the Exchequer from allowing the buyer to reclaim the input tax.[15]

Input tax on selling costs on a TOGC can be reclaimed so long as the activities of the business are wholly taxable. If the business is partially exempt then the normal apportionment rules will apply.

5.5.1   Transactional issues relating to a TOGC

Clients should but often don't, understand fully the TOGC rules which require that there is in fact a transfer of an uninterrupted and real business (see paragraph 5.5.3 below). If in doubt VAT should be charged by the seller (with an indemnity in favour of the buyer if HMRC disallows its input tax), or alternatively in a case of real uncertainty and a genuine point of doubt the seller can ask for a ruling from HMRC, specifying why the issue is in real doubt. However, this is not necessarily easy and can lead to delays, both in agreeing the form of asking for such a ruling and waiting for a reply. If the parties wish to put the issue beyond doubt to ensure that the transfer is not a TOGC the transaction can be structured by interposing an intermediary buyer so that the transfer falls outside the TOGC requirements (see paragraph 5.5.3 below).

Under a TOGC there must be consensus between the buyer and the seller regarding the requirements which need to be satisfied, both in respect of the business before completion and activities following completion. This is best documented through clear and unambiguous warranties and/or undertakings provided by both parties to the SPA. In an ideal world, the parties should read HMRC Notice 700/9 before giving the warranties which are set out below at paragraph 5.5.10.

A further pre-completion issue needing consideration early in the transaction (and which is discussed in further detail below in paragraph 5.5.2 below) is whether the buyer is or should be registered for VAT. If a newco is acquiring the business, its

---

[15] See Manual V1-10 – section 3.2

responsibilities to register for VAT will be determined by the turnover of the transferred business, assuming that the buyer does not wish to acquire the business's VAT registration (see paragraph 5.5.2 below). If the turnover is above or likely to be above the VAT threshold requirement the newco must register for VAT or alternatively join the buyer's VAT group.

An additional issue will be whether any of the assets being transferred are capital items for the purposes of the capital goods scheme, in which case the seller must provide the buyer with details of any capital goods scheme adjustments to enable buyer to carry out any future adjustments under the scheme following completion (see **Chapter 3** paragraph 3.37.3 for the background to the capital goods scheme).

5.5.2   VAT registration issues for a TOGC

Where a business or part of a business carried on by a taxable person is transferred to another person as a going concern, for the purpose of determining whether the buyer is liable to be registered for VAT, it is treated as having carried on the business before as well as after the transfer. Therefore, the sales of the business will be included in the buyer's turnover figure.

If the seller is registered for VAT the buyer will be liable to be registered or be registered for VAT on or before the transfer, or, have been accepted for voluntary registration,[16] in order for the TOGC rules to apply to the transfer.[17] If the buyer is not registered or required to be registered for VAT (either because it does not expect the value of the taxable supplies in the next 12 months to be above the deregistration limit or because the seller was not required to be registered but was registered voluntarily at the transfer date) then, unless the buyer has been accepted for voluntary registration, the conditions for the transfer of a TOGC are not met and the sale takes its normal VAT liability. HMRC state[18] that if the seller is not registered because it was trading below the registration limit or was making wholly exempt

---

[16] Notice 700/9 paragraph 2.3.4

[17] SI 1995/1268 paragraph 5(1)(b)(iii)

[18] Notice 700/9 paragraph 2.3.5

supplies, a TOCG is nevertheless possible in both these circumstances. If the transfer of the assets is a relevant supply for VAT registration purposes the unregistered seller will have to register.

The standard de-registration rules may apply to the seller if as a result of the sale of the business, it stops making supplies.

It is not uncommon in transactions that the issue of the parties' VAT registration position is only discussed close to completion, and their tax advisor should bring the issue to the attention of their client at the beginning of the transaction.

5.5.3   Requirements of a TOGC

A TOGC arises in circumstances when a person transfers his business, and the assets of the business are to be used by the transferee in carrying on the same kind of business as that carried on by the transferor, whether or not as part of any existing business.[19]

If the transfer involves only part of a business:
- it must be capable of separate operation; and
- the assets must be intended to be used by the transferee in carrying on the same kind of business as that carried on by the transferor in relation to that part.[20]

Therefore, intention and capability decide whether there can be a TOGC.

HMRC consider[21] that the main conditions are as follows:
- the assets must be sold as part of the transfer of a 'business' as a 'going concern';
- the assets are to be used by the purchaser with the intention of carrying on the same kind of 'business' as the seller (but not necessarily identical);
- where the seller is a taxable person, the purchaser must be a taxable person already or become one as the result of the transfer;

---

[19] SI 1995/1268 paragraph 5(1)(a)

[20] SI 1995/1268 paragraph 5(1)(b)

[21] Notice 700/9 paragraph 1.2

THE TAX SCHEDULE

- in respect of land which would be standard rated if it were supplied, the purchaser must notify HMRC that he has opted to tax the land by the relevant date, and must notify the seller that their option has not been disapplied by the same date;
- where only part of the 'business' is sold it must be capable of operating separately; and
- there must not be a series of immediately consecutive transfers of 'business'.

The business need not be profitable and can be trading under the control of a liquidator, administrative receiver, a trustee in bankruptcy or administrator. If part of a business is transferred it must merely be capable of separate operation and the buyer must intend to use the assets in carrying on the same kind of business as that carried on by the seller. This begs the question as to how HMRC might react if, following the transfer, the original intentions of the transferee are not effected and the assets are used in a different type of business. In any event the documentation for the sale should require an undertaking from the buyer that it will pay any VAT due to the seller if HMRC rules that VAT is due.

HMRC consider that the following transactions do not constitute a TOGC:[22]

- a change in the constitution of a partnership;
- a sale of shares of a company;
- when the buyer does not intend to use the assets transferred in the same type of business activity as carried on before the transfer;
- the seller has not made taxable supplies before completion even though registered for VAT;
- there is a series of immediately consecutive transfers of the business;
- there has been a significant break in the normal trading pattern before or immediately after the transfer.

5.5.4 TOGCs involving land and buildings

There is a two-step process when land or buildings are involved in a transfer of a business and assets – first to establish that the

---

[22] Notice 700/9/paragraph 1.3

general rules of a TOGC apply to the sale of the business concerned, and if so then additional considerations apply to the land and building assets to be transferred. Otherwise, while no VAT will be chargeable on the transfer of the non-land and non-building assets, VAT could apply to the transfer of the land and building. The relevant legislation is contained in SI 1995/1268 articles 5(2) and (2A).

If the seller has opted to tax in respect of the land and buildings under VATA Schedule 10 before completion, or is transferring the fee simple in new and uncompleted buildings or civil engineering works liable to VAT at the standard rate, then the buyer must:

- properly opt to tax before completion (or before any earlier tax point – see discussion of time of supply below);
- notify HMRC before completion (and within the 30 day period beginning with the date of the exercise) of the exercise of the option to tax; and
- undertake to the seller that the option will not be disapplied.

The seller must be satisfied that the buyer's option to tax is in place by the relevant date and it is advisable that it should ask the buyer for evidence, such as a copy of the notification letter. Additionally, the legislation requires that the buyer must notify the seller that the option will not be disapplied by the anti-avoidance provisions in SI 1995/1268 article 5(2B).

If the seller has not opted to tax the land and property being transferred, and the transfer will either be zero-rated or exempt the buyer need not elect to tax the property. This information should be confirmed in writing to the buyer.

The time of supply for VAT purposes will, in all probability, be completion, but if a deposit has been received for the transfer by the seller, depending on the quantum and the rights of the buyer which arise at that time such as access to the property, the date of receipt could be considered to be the tax point for VAT purposes. Therefore, if any deposit is required before completion, if should be held in escrow by a third party (but not by a party acting as agent for the seller) so as not to bring forward the tax point date for VAT purposes.

The following tables supplied by HMRC set out whether a transfer of land and buildings will fall within the TOGC provisions[23] and demonstrate that it is safest, when in doubt, for the buyer to opt to tax the property so long as it does not then disapply the option.

Commercial land or buildings, ordinarily exempt

Has seller opted to tax[24]?	Has buyer opted to tax?	Will the buyer's option to tax be disapplied?	Is it a TOGC?
Yes	Yes	Yes	No
Yes	No	Not applicable	No
Yes	Yes	No	Yes
No	No	Not applicable	Yes
No	Yes	Yes	Yes
No	Yes	No	Yes
Yes but option disapplied	No	Not applicable	Yes

New Buildings (less than three years old), ordinarily standard rated

Has seller opted to tax?	Has buyer opted to tax?	Will the buyer's option to tax be disapplied?	Is it a TOGC?
Yes	Yes	Yes	No
Yes	No	Not applicable	No
Yes	Yes	No	Yes
No	No	Not applicable	No
No	Yes	Yes	No
No	Yes	No	Yes

5.5.5 Property rental business transferred under a TOGC

A property rental business (i.e. a business which receives rental income) may involve nothing more than a property with tenants but HMRC will expect evidence that the transaction is something more than a sale of a building. Explanations of their views are set out in the HMRC VAT Manuals.[25] Examples provided by HMRC

[23] Notice 742A paragraph 11.4

[24] Building over three years old

[25] volume VI-10 paragraph 5.4

of a TOGC involving a property rental business include the following:[26]

- the sale of a freehold with the benefit of an existing lease;
- the assignment of a lease with the benefit of a sub-lease;
- the sale of a building which is let and the sale is effected during a rent-free period;
- the sale of a building in respect of which a lease has been granted but the tenants are not yet in occupation;
- the sale of a freehold to a third party with the benefit of a contractual agreement for a lease but before the lease has been signed;
- the sale of a site by a property developer to a single buyer and:
  - the site is a mixture of let or unlet and/or finished or unfinished properties;
  - the sale would otherwise have been standard rated; and
  - the buyer opts to tax;
- an owner of a number of let freehold properties sells one of them – the sale of a single let or partly let property can be a TOGC;
- a partially-let building which is capable of being a property rental business, so long as the letting constitutes economic activity – i.e. electricity sub-stations or space for advertising hoarding provided that there is a lease in place;
- the purchase of freehold and leasehold property from separate sellers without the interests merging and the lease has not been extinguished, provided that the asset continues to be exploited by the receipt of rent from the tenant.

HMRC regard the following as not being a property rental business:[27]

- a property developer having built the building allows someone to occupy temporarily without any right to occupy after the proposed sale;
- a property developer after building the property is actively marketing it in search of a tenant;

---

[26] Notice 700/9/08 paragraph 6.2

[27] Notice 700/9/08 paragraph 6.3

- the sale of a property whereby a lease is surrendered immediately before the sale; (when a lease is brought to an end the property rental business carried on by the former freeholder has ceased and cannot be transferred);
- the sale of a property freehold to an existing tenant which leases the whole premises; and
- the grant of a lease in respect of a building and the tenant is running a business from the premises; the tenant then sells the assets of his business as a going concern and surrenders the lease to the grantor, who grants the new owner of the business lease in respect of the building.

5.5.6   Assignment of leases

HMRC accept that, if the other conditions are met, the assignment of a lease with the benefit of a sublease can be a TOGC. However, in a surrender if the buyer is the landlord the lease will normally merge with the landlord's existing interest in the land and will cease to exist. HMRC historically took the view that in such circumstances the transaction would not be a TOGC because the landlord would not use the same asset, the lease, in carrying on the business. This policy changed in 2014[28] following the Tribunal decision in *Robinson Family Limited ([2012] UKFTT 360 (TC), TC02046)* which held that the grant of a lease could in some circumstances be a TOGC, and indicated that 'one must look to the substance of the transaction' rather than its form.

HMRC now consider that there is, in principle, no obstacle to the surrender of a lease being a TOGC, subject to all the normal conditions. HMRC state that this will apply where a tenant subletting premises by way of business subsequently surrenders its interest in the property together with the benefit of the subtenants, or where a retailer sells its retailing business to its landlord – in substance the landlord has acquired the tenant's business. They go on to state that this applies equally where the landlord's interest is held via one or more nominees, so that the transaction involves a transfer to the nominee(s) for the landlord's benefit.

---

[28] Revenue & Customs Brief 27/14

5.5.7 Nominee sellers and buyers

If a property is legally held on trust by a nominee who is the seller, paragraph 40 of VATA Schedule 10 deems the beneficial owner to be the seller. Therefore, it is possible for the transaction to be a TOGC. Examples of property held by a nominee include legal title held by four or fewer persons on trust for a partnership or legal title held on trust for an unincorporated association or for a pension fund. However, where the nominee is the buyer, a TOGC is not technically possible because the new beneficial owner will be treated as the person carrying on the business rather than the nominee and the nominee will be treated as the owner of the land. Notice 700/9/08 paragraph 8.1, provides the following concession by HMRC (originally contained in Business Brief 10/96) in circumstances where persons transfer an interest in land to a person who is a nominee for a named beneficial owner (but **not** when there is an undisclosed beneficial owner):

Where the legal title in land is to be held by a nominee for a named beneficial owner, HMRC will, for the purpose of establishing the transfer of a property letting business as a going concern, from 1 June 1996, consider the named beneficial owner of the land and not the nominee acquiring legal title to be the transferee.

The new optional practice allows a person transferring an interest in land to a nominee for a named beneficial owner, with the agreement of that nominee and beneficial owner, to treat the named beneficial owner as the transferee for the purposes of establishing whether there has been a transfer of a going concern. This Business Brief contains an example format that the parties can use to record agreement if they so wish.

The transferor is expected to check the VAT registration and any VAT options made by the beneficial owner. HMRC provide a suggested format of notice of agreement between the parties to such an arrangement as follows, and advises that all parties keep a copy.

5.5.7.1 Notice of Agreement

Address of Property

Name of transferor/vendor (X)

Name of nominee/purchaser (Y)

Future beneficial owner (Z)

X, Y and Z confirm that they have agreed to adopt the optional practice set out in Customs & Excise Business Brief 10/96 in relation to the purchase of the Property under an agreement dated ( ) between X and Y.

Following the transfer of the Property Y will hold the legal title as nominee for Z, the beneficial owner.

Signed for and behalf of X
Signed for and behalf of Y
Signed for and behalf of Z

DATE

5.5.8   VAT records and a TOGC

Before 1 September 2007 it was a requirement under the TOGC provisions that the VAT records must be transferred to the buyer on the transfer. In respect of any TOGC entered into on or after that date the seller must retain the records of the business save where the buyer applies to HMRC for permission to take on the seller's VAT number.

In any event the seller must make available to the buyer the necessary information in order for the buyer to comply with its duties under VATA and this would include information relating to turnover of the business transferred, to enable the buyer to calculate whether or not he/she/it should be VAT registered. If the seller is unhelpful, for any reason, HMRC may disclose to the buyer information it holds on the transferred business, but in such circumstances HMRC will advise the seller of its intention to disclose.

If the buyer applies to HMRC for permission to take on the seller's VAT number the seller is required to transfer the VAT records to the buyer, except where the seller needs to retain the VAT records in which case the seller must apply to HMRC for permission to retain them.

The issue of the VAT records and registration should be provided for in the pre-completion requirements of an asset sale and from the buyer's perspective it should be entitled to be indemnified for any costs arising from the failure of the seller to properly keep the records. However, if the seller is in a distressed state or is likely to deregister for VAT and/or disappear the buyer should apply for permission to retain the VAT records.

The various procedures could be extremely time-consuming, particularly dealing with HMRC, so the issue of VAT records should be raised at the due diligence stage and before negotiating the tax warranties.

5.5.9 VAT groups and TOGC

If a TOGC to an unconnected party involves a member of a VAT group as the seller, the transfer will be deemed to have been made by the representative member of the VAT group.[29] In these circumstances, the representative member should also provide the VAT warranties in the SPA.

If the buyer is a member of a partly exempt VAT group the representative member of the VAT group may have to account for output tax on some of the assets and recover input tax under the partial exemption method – in other words, account for the purchases as a self-supply. However, a self-supply will not be triggered in relation to the following assets acquired under a TOGC:

- any assets which were assets of the previous owner more than three years before the date of the transfer;
- goodwill;
- any assets which are zero-rated or exempt (for example zero-rated or exempt freehold or leasehold interests in land); or
- items which fall within the capital goods scheme.

5.5.10 Seller tax warranties for a TOGC

a) "The Seller is a taxable person for VAT purposes with registration number [   ] and is currently making taxable supplies in respect of the Business."

b) "The Seller is a member of a VAT group with registration number [   ] of which the representative member is [   ] (company registration number [   ]) whose registered address is at [   ]."

---

[29] *Customers and Excise v Kingfisher PLC* QB [1994] STC 63; also see *Manuals V1-10 paragraph 5.4*

c) "The Seller is not and has not been during the past [four] years a member of a VAT group."

d) "The turnover of the Business for VAT purposes during the period of 12 months ending on Completion will be [ ] and the Seller is not and is not required to be registered for VAT."

e) "The Assets have been used to make supplies in carrying on the Business by the Seller since [   ] and as at the date of Completion there were no prior consecutive transfers of the Assets and the Business nor any significant break in the Business's trading before such date."

f) "All VAT and duty payable on import of any of the Assets has been properly paid and accounted for up to and as at the date of this Agreement."

g) "The Assets represent all of the Business being transferred and the Business is capable of continued operation following Completion."

h) "The Assets represent only part of the Business being transferred but are capable of separate operation following Completion."

i) "The Seller has provided copies of all records and returns relating to VAT of the Business for the past [four] year which are accurate and correct as required under VATA."

j) "The Seller undertakes to retain in good order all business records relating to the Assets and the Business for such period as is required under VATA and in any event, not less than [six] years from the date of Completion, and to make available to the Buyer as so requested such information as is necessary for the Buyer to comply with its duties under VATA but if this warranty is breached in any way the Seller agrees to keep the Buyer indemnified in respect of all and any costs it suffers arising from such breach."

k) "The Seller agrees to transfer all business records relating to the Assets and the Business under the relevant VAT legislation in circumstances whereby the Buyer has applied to and been given permission by HMRC to take over the Seller's VAT number, being [   ]. "

l) "The Seller exercised an option to tax under VATA Schedule 10 paragraph 2 in respect of the Property on [   ] and notified HMRC on [ ]. Such option has not been disapplied by HMRC. [A copy of the notification is attached together with HMRC's acknowledgment of receipt]."

m) "None of the Assets or Property transferred represents or shall become a capital item within the Capital Goods Scheme regardless of whether such transfer under this agreement is treated as part of a transfer of a going concern or otherwise."

n) "The transfer of the Property under this agreement will or would fall to be an exempt supply for VAT purposes by virtue of the disapplication of the option to tax under Scheduled 10 VATA paragraph 2(3AA)."

o) "The Seller warrants that the transfer of Property is exempt from VAT under VATA Schedule 9 and that no option to tax has been exercised under VATA Schedule 10 paragraph 2."

p) "The Seller undertakes to refund the Buyer any VAT which may be wrongly charged to and paid by the Buyer in respect of the transfer of the Assets and the Business under this Agreement."

5.5.11 Buyer warranties for a TOGC

a) "The Buyer is registered for VAT under registration number [ ]."

b) The Buyer has applied to be registered for VAT with effect from Completion."

c) "The Buyer intends to continue to use the Assets in the same type of activity as the Business as carried on by the Seller as at Completion and warrants that there shall be no significant break in the trading of the Business immediately after Completion."

d) "The Buyer has notified in writing its option to tax under VATA Schedule 10 paragraph 2 on [   ] and such option shall not be disapplied in respect of the Property."

e) "The Buyer has applied to HMRC to be registered for VAT using the Seller's VAT registration number [   ] and on proper registration and when the Seller has transferred to the Buyer the VAT records relating to the Business, the Buyer undertakes to preserve such records and to permit the Seller reasonable access to any records required under the relevant VAT legislation."

f) "If HMRC confirms in writing that the transfer of the Assets and Business under this Agreement is not a transfer of a going concern, and that accordingly VAT is payable by the Buyer in respect of such transfers, the Buyer agrees to pay the Seller any VAT so payable on receipt from the Seller of a proper VAT invoice together with any relevant interest and penalties."

6 SPECIAL SITUATIONS

6.1 Insolvencies and Administrations

6.1.1 Overview

A brief word to explain the winding up of a company which, in fact, will result in its liquidation for whatever reason. Essentially, the company closes its business and stops employing people; its assets are sold and its creditors are paid, and the remaining assets are distributed to the company's shareholders and, finally, the company is removed from the Companies House register.

An insolvency arises when a company does not have enough assets to cover its liabilities or it is unable to pay its debts as they fall due, and arrangements are entered into relating to the management of the company or its liquidation. Insolvencies are intended to achieve the maximum realisation of the company's assets for its creditors and are primarily dealt with by specialist insolvency practitioners which include administrators, receivers and liquidators.

The term insolvency also covers sequestration, liquidation, administrative receivership, and receivership. A corporate tax advisor involved in the sale and purchase of either a company or business in any insolvency procedure or administration should become familiar with the different processes and related tax issues. The purpose of this chapter is to provide a general background for the procedures which a tax advisor is likely to come across.

Priority payments out of a company's assets in a liquidation are as follows:[1]

1. fixed charge creditors;
2. expenses of the insolvency proceedings;
3. preferential creditors;
4. floating charge creditors;
5. unsecured provable debts;
6. statutory interest;
7. non-provable liabilities; and
8. shareholders.

---

[1] *Re Nortel GmbH* [2014] AC 209

There is a special insolvency regime for banks, created by the Banking Act 2009, but which is not covered in this chapter.

The available insolvency procedures are summarised briefly below:

6.1.1.1 Administrative Receivership

This procedure pre-dates the Enterprise Act 2002 and currently applies only where there is a floating charge over all or substantially all of the assets of a company created before 15 September 2003, although there are some exceptions, with administrative receivership still possible in respect of debentures created after that date in the circumstances set out in IA 1986 sections 72B-72H. An administrative receiver is appointed to manage the affairs of a company by a secured creditor which holds a debenture containing floating charges, or fixed and floating charges, over the whole (or substantially the whole) of a company's assets. Upon the appointment, the floating charge(s) will crystallise (if not previously crystallised). The receiver must treat the business assets covered by the charges in such a way as to recover the money due to the secured creditor. If he or she deems it to be in the best interests of the secured creditor, the business may be allowed to continue to trade.

The company continues to exist after the appointment of the receiver with the directors and officers remaining in their respective positions, although the receiver will have effective control of the company in place of the directors.

6.1.1.2 Creditors' voluntary liquidation ('CVL')

A CVL is a formal process commencing with a special resolution of the shareholders to wind up the company and involves a licensed insolvency practitioner. Once the company is wound up it will be under the control of the creditor. A creditors' meeting will be called so that the creditors of the company may, if they wish, appoint another insolvency practitioner in place of the shareholders' appointee. A liquidation committee may be put in place to which the liquidator will report. Any release of third party debts will not give rise to a taxable credit under CTA 2009 sections 322(2) & (3). A CVL may be involved following the termination of administration.

6.1.1.3   Members' voluntary liquidation ('MVL')

This is a process for winding up the affairs of a solvent company but, counterintuitively, also requires a licensed insolvency practitioner. Initiated by the shareholders, the directors (or a majority of the directors) of a company make a declaration of solvency which states that in the directors' opinion the company will be able to settle its debts in full plus interest within a period not exceeding 12 months of it being placed in liquidation. The declaration must be made within the five weeks immediately preceding the date of the passing of the resolution for winding up. Liquidation takes place when the resolution is passed.

6.1.1.4   Compulsory winding up or liquidation

In this scenario the court will order a compulsory winding up and appoint a liquidator, following the presentation of a petition by the company, its creditors (which can include HMRC), its directors or one or more of the shareholders or by the Secretary of State. Such a winding up may or may not be part of a restructuring of a company or group. Interested parties may apply to the court for the determination of issues arising from the winding-up or agree to, modify or reverse the actions of the liquidator.

6.1.1.5   Provisional liquidation

The court may appoint a provisional liquidator (usually only after the presentation of a petition for a winding up in order) to protect the assets of a company before a winding up order is made. Following that, it usually follows that a permanent liquidator will be appointed.

6.1.1.6   Administration[2]

Administration is primarily intended to provide a means to rescue a company in difficulties and protect it from its creditors taking action, although the administrator will be acting in the interests of all the creditors. An administration may last a short period, during which the company will continue to trade whilst a buyer is sought or the company is reorganised with a view to a sale. Alternatively, the administration may last for a longer period (up to one year,

---

[2] See Insolvency Act 1986 Schedule B1 introduced by the Enterprise Act 2002 coming into effect 15 September 2003

though with the possibility of extension beyond that) while rationalisation may be imposed for the company's longer term rescue. Pre-packaged administrations are discussed below (see paragraph 6.1.4 below).

A company can be put into administration pursuant to court application or by simple notice (and court filing requirements) in certain circumstances. There are different procedures for these alternatives, but the principal statutory aim in all cases is to enable a rescue of the company as a going concern. If that cannot be achieved, the administrator must perform his or her functions with the objective of either providing a better return to creditors as a whole than would be the case in a winding-up, or (if that is not possible) with a view to realising assets in order to make a distribution to one or more secured creditors.

The appointment of an administrator will trigger the end of an accounting period for corporation tax purposes and the beginning of a new accounting period (see CTA 2009 section 10(i)). If a rescue of the company is not possible, the administrator will then organise the sale of the company's assets and/or business to provide a return to the creditors, in accordance with the statutory objectives and the proposals agreed by creditors.

A company in administration does not lose ownership of its property, but control of its property passes to the administrator, who is an officer of the court. In administration a company may continue to trade and will be assessed for corporation tax in the normal way including carry-back of trading losses. As the assets remain in legal and beneficial ownership of the company, any group relationships remain in place during administration. If a subsidiary of a company is in administration, as it will be under the control of the administrator for tax purposes it will not treated as being a member of a group for corporation tax purposes.[3]

Any release of third party debts arranged under an administration should not give rise to a taxable credit under CTA 2009 sections 322(5) & (6).

---

[3] CTA 2010 section 151

6.1.1.7 Scheme of arrangement/Voluntary Arrangement

For an insolvency lawyer a scheme of arrangement is solely that, under what was CA 1985 section 425 (now CA 2006 sections 895 et seq), and is not strictly an insolvency procedure. Therefore, there is no need for a licensed insolvency practitioner.

A company voluntary arrangement under Insolvency Act 1986 Part I is a different procedure with different implementation and procedural requirements. It is capable of implementation without a court hearing but a licensed insolvency practitioner will be involved. Whereas a scheme of arrangement will not be regarded as falling within the ambit of insolvency proceedings under the EC regulation on Insolvency Proceedings 2000, a company voluntary arrangement will.

6.1.1.8 Liquidation

Liquidation results in the liquidator realising the assets of the company and effecting their distribution after costs, to the creditors, with any remaining amounts (should the liquidation prove to be a solvent one) distributed to the company's shareholders. An accounting period will end on the appointment of the liquidator under CTA 2009 section 12 and a new accounting period will begin. Because the company loses beneficial ownership of its assets (which will vest in the liquidator), this results in the company being de-grouped for corporation tax group relief purposes[4] but not for the purposes of chargeable gains groups.[5] Therefore, in respect of chargeable gains for corporation tax purposes, any assets vested in the liquidator (and any acts of the liquidator relating to the assets) will be treated as acts of the company and any acquisitions from or disposals to the liquidator by the company will be disregarded.

It is recognised that failed companies often can give rise to successor or phoenix companies, often involving the same management and/or shareholders buying the assets of the liquidated company for the best price on offer (often very low for a quick sale) and enabling the business in question to continue.

---

[4] CTA 2010 section 141(4)(b)

[5] TCGA section 8(6)

6.1.1.9 Transactional issues

Recommended warranties relating to the issue of insolvency in a standard transaction involving the sale and purchase of a company are set out at paragraph 3.24 in **Chapter 3 (Warranties)**, which enable the buyer to seek assurances that the target company has never been insolvent and does not represent a successor or phoenix company.

6.1.2 Taxation issues during insolvency proceedings

6.1.2.1 Trading losses and profits

If the insolvency practitioner allows the distressed company to continue to trade following insolvency proceedings, its trading losses should continue to be available for set-off in the normal way, but in an insolvent situation this begs the question – what profits are there likely to be for such set-off? The insolvency practitioner's expenses will be treated as incurred wholly and exclusively for the purposes of the company's trade and therefore allowable deductions, and any trading profits will be subject to corporation tax.[6] If the trade ceases, the rules for terminal losses arising in the last 12 months before cessation will apply with entitlement to carry back to the three years before cessation.[7]

6.1.2.2 Accounting periods

Ordinarily, a cessation of trade will result in an accounting period coming to an end.[8] The commencement of a company's liquidation or winding up will also trigger the end of an accounting period and the commencement of a new accounting period of 12 months, beginning on the first day the liquidation and followed by accounting periods each of 12 months until the liquidation is completed.[9]

If a distressed company enters into administration, a new accounting period will begin on the commencement of the administration and end on the day the company comes out of

---

[6] CTA 2010 section 37

[7] CTA 2010 section 39

[8] CTA 2009 section 10(1)(d)

[9] CTA 2009 section 12

administration.[10] Therefore, there will be no intervening 12 month accounting periods.

A post-appointment tax charge, such as tax in respect of a chargeable gain on the sale of an asset with a low base costs, will rank as an expense of the administration and, in most circumstances, will be paid ahead of any distribution to creditors other than fixed charge creditors. Pre-appointment tax liabilities will rank as unsecured creditors. The new accounting period will also ring fence any pre-appointment trading losses. If a receiver is appointed, there are no statutory provisions for changes to the company's accounting period as a result of that appointment. This is one reason why administrative receivership might be more beneficial to a secured creditor than administration or liquidation.

6.1.2.3 *Corporation tax*

Changes to a company's accounting periods may have a bearing on the corporation tax rate for the company. CTA 2010 section 628 provides that corporation tax shall be charged on the profits of a company arising in the winding-up of its final year at the rate of corporation tax fixed or proposed for the previous year.[11] Similar rules apply for companies in administration.[12] No tax will be due on any interest on overpaid tax received in the final accounting period not exceeding £2,000.[13]

6.1.2.4 *Ownership of assets and group issues*

On commencement of winding up beneficial ownership of the company's assets (including its holdings in its subsidiaries) will vest in the liquidator, and thus if a company is a member of a group for corporation tax group relief purposes, this will interfere with group relief arrangements. The commencement of a winding up by a member of a consortium will also have consequences for elections under any consortium relief claim, arising from the change in beneficial ownership of the shares in the consortium member being wound up.

---

[10] CTA 2009 section 10(1)(i) & (j)

[11] CTA 2010 section 628(5)

[12] See CTA 2010 section 626(3)

[13] CTA 2010 section 633

Furthermore, if a holding company enters into liquidation the beneficial ownership of its holdings in its subsidiaries will vest in the insolvency practitioner, and the holding company will fall outside the group for group relief purposes possibly resulting in clawback of group reliefs for SDLT[14] and a degrouping charge under TCGA section 179.

Such vesting does not occur in an administration, although it would become relevant in a failed administration resulting in a liquidation.

Any trading losses of a group company arising before liquidation are eligible for group relief, but group relief will not be allowed in respect of the trading losses of a company already in liquidation. TCGA section 170(11) provides that a commencement of a winding-up of a company does not mean that it leaves a group for chargeable gains purposes at that time. Therefore, transfers on a no gain/no loss basis under TCGA section 171 as well as elections under TCGA section 171A if an asset is disposed to a third party, can be effected before completion of the winding up. However, TCGA section 179 could still apply to a distressed company which had been involved in an intra-group transfer leaving the group by virtue of its insolvency. Substantial shareholding relief may be available so long as all requirements are met (see **Chapter 9 (Group Issues)** paragraph 9.8 for further details of this relief). For disposals after 31 March 2002 TCGA Schedule 7AC paragraphs 2(4) and 16 (*Exemptions for disposals by companies with substantial shareholdings*) provide that assets vested in a liquidator are treated as if they are vested in the company and paragraph 38 disapplies the effect of TCGA section 179. If the substantial shareholdings exemption does not apply, the distressed company and another member within its group can elect to transfer the section 179 charge to the other group member under TCGA section 171A (discussed further in **Chapter 9** at paragraph 9.1).

If a degrouping event arises by virtue of the insolvency procedure within three years of an intra-group transfer of chargeable UK property for which there was SDLT exemption, SDLT will become

---

[14] FA 2003 Schedule 7 paragraph 1(3)

payable. If it is payable by the distressed company but not paid, other members of the group will become liable to pay the charge.[15]

6.1.2.5   VAT[16]

The effect of a company becoming insolvent is that a prescribed accounting period for VAT purposes ends on the day immediately prior to it becoming insolvent, regardless of whether it would normally do so, where the control of a registered person's assets passes to a receiver, liquidator, or person otherwise acting in a representative capacity. A separate VAT return is required in respect of this period. The insolvency practitioner has reporting responsibilities to HMRC on Form VAT 769 (*Notification of Insolvency Details*) and must submit VAT returns and make payments for the period following insolvency. The general rules for VAT deregistration will apply on taxable supplies ceasing to be made, but the process for deregistration will depend on the type of insolvency. If an insolvent business ceases to trade but remains registered, the principal activity will be the sale of assets.

Normal rules for retention of VAT records apply during insolvency and administration procedures (except liquidations, where the liquidator may destroy them one year after the date of dissolution of the company). A concession has been granted to official receivers to allow them on request and with HMRC approval, to destroy VAT records after six months.[17]

An insolvency practitioner will not provide warranties or an indemnity relating to VAT, but he or she is likely to require the buyer to indemnify the seller for any VAT arising on the sale. This may be particularly relevant in the sale of a business, if HMRC consider the sale to be one of merely the assets and not of a business as a TOGC. Issues relating to the sale of a business and TOGCs are discussed in depth in **Chapter 5 (Sale and Purchase of a Business)**.

---

[15] FA 2003 Schedule 7 paragraph 5(2)(b)

[16] See Notice 700/56/06 Insolvencies

[17] Notice 700/56/06 paragraph 19.1

6.1.2.6 New anti-avoidance provisions involving close companies in the Finance (No 2) Bill 2016

Winding up a company need not necessarily merely involve insolvent business, and is often used as a mechanism of returning value to shareholders, for example after the main trading subsidiary has been sold, with the holding company wound up. In such cases capital distributions on a winding up could be treated as a capital receipt for shareholders. A new Targeted Anti-Avoidance Rule (TAAR) will apply to certain company distributions in respect of share capital in a winding up involving phoenix companies, taking effect from 6 April 2016 and which will tax a capital distribution made in the winding-up of a company as income subject to dividend tax rates (rather than taxed as a capital gain), in the following circumstances, involving individual shareholders and close companies:

- If the shareholder or a connected person continues to be involved in the same/similar trade as the wound-up company's trade within two years of the winding-up and the arrangements were to obtain an income tax advantage (aimed at Phoenix companies set up to replace the wound-up company and to carry on its business after the shareholders have taken out retained profits on a tax efficient basis); or

- Profits were retained in the company which were in excess of those required and are not paid out as dividends, and the company is later put into liquidation with the retained profits treated and taxed as capital (referred to as 'moneyboxing').

- Changes have been made to the transactions in securities legislation including the follow:-
    - ITA 2007 section 868 (fundamental change of ownership) considers the overall economic interest rather than simply direct ownership; section 687(2) includes the reserves;
    - s 694 includes an income tax advantage where a distribution could not be paid to the person but could be paid to the person's associate;
    - section 684(1)(c) now considers the purpose of the transaction(s);
    - section 684(2) includes distributions in liquidation and repayments of share capital or premium.

6.1.3   Transactional issues

The sale of a distressed company or a business of a distressed company by an insolvency practitioner is usually done quickly in order to preserve the business as a going concern and get the best return for the creditors. Save for a successful CVA, shareholders have no stake in the business in an insolvency as their share value has disappeared. In circumstances where some part of a group 'goes under', other group members may be affected because their goodwill (amongst other things) may be affected by the insolvency.

Due diligence by the buyer may be, at best, cursory due to the imposed time constraints, but consideration paid for the business may be well below its book value reflecting the element of risk for the buyer. The standard method of disposal is either through the sale of the assets and business (if possible as a TOGC so long as the business has not ceased to trade; or otherwise as a sale of the assets) or by the hive-down of those assets and the business to a newco ('hive-down newco') to preserve any trading losses[18] with the onward sale of hive-down newco to the buyer. In some circumstances the distressed company might be sold in which case the potential liabilities could be considerable for the buyer and which, commercially, may make no commercial sense, even if the purchase price was nominal.

Regardless of how the transaction is structured, it is unlikely that the insolvency practitioner will be able to (or wish to) provide warranties and a tax indemnity, particularly if the buyer is connected with the target company or was part of its previous management. Indeed, the insolvency practitioner may require an indemnity from the buyer for any tax liabilities arising from the transaction in these cases. If the buyer is unconnected with the target company it would be inadvisable for it to acquire the tax history of the company without a robust tax indemnity. Therefore, the buyer is likely to prefer to acquire the assets and the business.

Issues relating to the transfer of a business as a going concern (TOGC) are discussed fully in **Chapter 5 (Sale and Purchase of a**

---

[18] See CTA 2010 section 944

Business) at paragraph 5.5 and the recommended warranties for both the seller and the buyer should ideally be included in the sale and purchase agreement. However, an insolvency practitioner is likely to refuse to provide any seller's warranties other than (perhaps) as to his/her valid appointment. If it is intended that the TOCG provisions are to apply for VAT purposes, both parties should be assured that there has not been an unintentional discontinuance of the trade or business. If the insolvency practitioner is unwilling to provide the relevant warranty (reflecting lack of knowledge) and there is some doubt as to whether there has been a discontinuance of some sort, it would be advisable to structure the transaction so that there is an immediate transfer. In this case, VAT will arise on the sale of the assets. VAT registration issues are discussed in **Chapter 5** at paragraph 5.5.2.

6.1.3.1   Hive-down of assets into newco

By transferring the assets and business to a newco, trading losses can be preserved to be carried forward for offset against subsequent trade profits, with the liabilities remaining with the distressed company so long as the relevant provisions in CTA 2010 for the transfer of a trade are met (see sections 940A to 953 – *Transfer of a Trade without a Change of Ownership*). The conditions are that, on a company ceasing to carry on a trade and another company beginning to carry it on, both an 'ownership test' and a 'tax condition' are met as follows:

- on the transfer or at some time during the two year period beginning immediately after the transfer, a 75% interest in that trade belongs to certain persons; and
- at some time during the year ending immediately before the transfer, a 75% interest in the trade belonged to the same persons; AND
- during the above periods the transferred trade is carried on by companies within the charge to corporation tax or income tax, in respect of the trade.

There is no minimum length of time during the two year period and one year period referred to above in which the trade must be carried on, and it will be a matter of fact whether the trade is carried on. However, the relief for trade losses is subject to CTA

2010 section 945, whereby the 'predecessor' company retains more liabilities than assets. The value of any liabilities which are not transferred in such a transaction cannot be greater than that of both the value of the company's assets immediately before the transfer which are not transferred, and the consideration given for the transferred assets. This test is fundamental as to whether the losses can be carried forward, and any buyer will be vulnerable to the reliability of the seller's valuation of the liabilities and assets, which ideally, therefore, should be agreed between the accounting advisors to both sides if the consideration price is taking into account the availability of any carried forward losses.

There are further anti-avoidance provisions under the change in company ownership provisions of CTA 2010 Part 14 Chapter 1 (sections 672 to 674) where trading losses will be disallowed where there is a change in the ownership of a company and either:

- within any period of three years in which the change in ownership occurs there is a major change in the nature or conduct of a trade carried on by the company; or
- the change in ownership occurs at any time after the scale of the activities in a trade carried on by the company has become small or negligible and before any significant revival of the trade.

The short form warranties and tax schedule would be appropriate in these circumstances if the liquidator is willing to provide them in respect of the newco. However, the availability of any carried forward trading losses will be a matter for the buyer, as it would be unlikely that the liquidator would warrant them or provide an indemnity. If the liquidator provides a warranty or indemnity the buyer should be required to warrant that there will be no major change in the conduct of the trade within three years of the sale of newco.

Immediate tax charges on a hive-down into and sale of newco would be SDLT on a transfer of UK land into the newco, and stamp duty on any transfer of shares into newco, with stamp duty payable by the buyer on the acquisition of the newco.

Following the changes introduced by FA 2011, which extend the substantial shareholdings exemption, pre-sale hive-downs are likely to be much more attractive (see **Chapter 4**, paragraph 4.3.2).

6.1.3.2 *Substantial shareholdings exemption as it applies to insolvencies[19]*

If a group fails the post-disposal trading test because the vendor company is to be wound up or dissolved then the exemption should continue to apply. TCGA Schedule 7AC paragraph 16 provides that although the assets of a company in liquidation vest in the liquidator, for the purposes of establishing whether the substantial shareholdings requirement is met, the company is still treated as the beneficial owner of the assets.

6.1.4 Pre-packaged administration

A 'pre-pack' arrangement is within a formal insolvency procedure and intended to preserve as much of the value of the distressed business in question for its onward sale and enable it to fetch the best price for its creditors. The alternative argument is that a better price for the business could be achieved in a more open public auction.

In a 'pre-pack' (which can be at the direction of secured creditors or in circumstances when the business has no funds to trade), the management of a distressed company, together with its advisors and the advisors of the company's secured creditors, identify potential buyers of the business, structure the disposal of the business appropriately, negotiate the terms with the identified buyer (which in turn must organise the acquisition vehicle and financing) all before the official appointment of the insolvency practitioner (usually an administrator) followed by the immediate sale of the company or business after the appointment of the insolvency practitioner and on the negotiated terms. The proposed insolvency practitioner will be heavily involved in the restructuring and the negotiations with the potential purchaser before his or her appointment in the formal insolvency procedure. In order to arrive at a position for the company to be sold, those involved will have had time to review the company's current tax

---

[19] TCGA Schedule 7AC paragraph 16; also see HMRC Manual CG53076

situation, but speed will be essential. It is unlikely that the buyer will be about to undertake comprehensive due diligence, but essential information should be available from the company and/or the senior lenders if they are driving the transaction.

The buyer in a pre-pack might be an unconnected third party acquiring the company for its business potential, but could be connected with the company's senior lenders or incumbent management. It may involve the managers, directors and/or shareholders of the business acting alone or in tandem with the secured creditors, or acting to give the company a new start as a clean vehicle.

Restructuring for a pre-pack requires specialist tax and accountancy advice from an insolvency expert and, as with every disposal, there will be a number of alternatives. The prime concern will be to avoid unnecessary tax charges on the seller and the target vehicle, such as a degrouping charge (see **Chapter 9** paragraph 9.1.1).

6.2   The Locked Box Mechanism

In a 'locked box' transaction the seller will prepare a set of accounts on which the purchase price of the target company will be decided and negotiated – either under a bidding process or on a 'take-it or leave-it' basis depending on market conditions and the state of the target. The principles behind the 'locked box' mechanism are similar to those for drawing up completion accounts, save that under the locked box procedure the accounts of the target company are drawn up by the seller at a point in time before completion (the 'agreed balance sheet date') and there is no negotiation between the seller and buyer save for the purchase price. There will be no post-completion adjustments to the purchase price for target's working capital and/or cash flow position at completion.

The procedure is considered to offer more certainty and can be more efficient where there is a bidding situation for the target company. The buyer is expected to carry out proper due diligence on the target and the accounts but will take all the risks and rewards of the target's performance following the agreed balance sheet date.

SPECIAL SITUATIONS

The seller will have prepared a balance sheet of the target company (or alternatively full accounts) either using the accounting standards of the target's most recent accounts or sometimes on agreed principles with the buyer. Best practice would be for the accounts to be audited. The purchase price will be determined before completion based on the value of the target as at the agreed balance sheet date and not as at completion. There will be no opportunity for an adjustment to the price following completion save in respect of 'outflows' in the target's business, being cash spent and liabilities arising outside the ordinary course of business between the balance sheet date and completion – often referred to as 'leakages'.

Leakages can either be specifically defined or can be defined as anything other than defined permitted leakages which will be set out in the sale and purchase agreement. These will be negotiated by the parties but should be comprehensive to avoid uncertainty.

Defined leakages are likely to include:
- dividends, distributions and waived shareholders' loans;
- capital expenditure;
- transaction expenses relating to the sale of the target;
- repayment of debt and waiving third party debt other than as agreed;
- expenses and payments made or arising other than in the ordinary course of business;
- interest and penalties relating to tax; and
- any events involving non-arm's length transactions.

Permitted leakages would be expenses and liabilities incurred in the ordinary course of business, which in turn would need a definition.

The principles for determining, after completion, whether there has been any leakage will be provided for in the sale and purchase agreement as will standard 'conduct of claims' provisions, but leakages should be quantifiable within a shorter time frame than it would normally take to draw up and agree completion accounts.

It will be in both parties' interests to complete the transaction in as short a time as possible, following the agreed balance sheet date. The seller will want receipt of the purchase price and the buyer will want control of the target to ensure that trading does not deteriorate in any way. It may be negotiated that either the seller will be entitled to a pound-for-pound payment for the target's net profits arising after the agreed balance sheet date and up to completion (which would defeat the simplicity of the locked box mechanism as the sale and purchase agreement would have to provide for standard provisions for the parties to agree the net profits, and an overpayments/ underpayments clause). More commonly, the buyer will be entitled to all the profits and liabilities of the target as from the agreed balance sheet date.

Under the locked box mechanism, there will be few warranties other than warranties to title, ownership of assets, and possibly relating to employees. No warranties would be required in respect of tax but a tax indemnity would be necessary to cover tax arising in previous accounting periods as a result of errors, interest and penalties. The buyer should satisfy itself as to the tax compliance of the target company during the due diligence and requests for information as with standard transactions. Under the terms of the tax indemnity the buyer would be entitled to make a claim against the seller for any tax liability of the target arising before the agreed balance sheet date save for any provisions for tax in the agreed balance sheet and other limitations as negotiated by the parties.

6.3 Public Listings and Offerings

The security for investors participating in any public offering will be the quality of the due diligence as required by the relevant listing exchange and the information set out in the prospectus and listing documents, and supervised by the nominated advisor (NOMAD) for an AIM listing or in respect of the ISDX growth market, an ISDX corporate advisor; or by the corporate advisor and/or sponsor for a main LSE market listing of the ISDX main board listing. If the company has a track record, past accounts will be published and their accuracy and any verification will be the responsibility of the accountants. Details of the directors, their shareholdings, salaries and options over shares in the company will be given, and the directors may be required to provide a short form tax indemnity to the company to cover tax liabilities arising outside the ordinary course of business and relating to personal

THE TAX SCHEDULE   237 benefits for the directors arising from their actions. Often this is not sought however.

The tax lawyer will need to pay meticulous attention to all details of the company's share and option schemes, both existing schemes and schemes to be put in place following the listing. For past schemes, the tax advisor will be responsible for the due diligence, and will need sight of: the rules of the scheme adopted by the board or the company; the relevant board minutes; copies of option certificates and agreements with the participants; and confirmation of the numbers of shares under options and all details of exercise requirements. A listing may trigger the right or requirement to exercise options or share rights in which case exercise will need to be effected before the listing or subsequently, depending on the terms of the scheme. These issues are discussed in greater depth in **Chapter 7 (Share Schemes)** at paragraph 7.5.

6.4   Partnerships

If a transaction involves the acquisition of an interest in a partnership or a trade from a partnership, ongoing tax liabilities of the underlying trade will continue in the ordinary way in respect of VAT and PAYE relating to that business (and in respect of which pre-completion due diligence is advisable). However, no tax liabilities of the partners (namely tax on the trade's profits) should be capable of attaching to the buyer. The sale and purchase agreement should provide for management accounts to be drawn up as at the completion date in the same way that completion accounts would normally be drawn up, and a working capital statement for the business including credits and debits for VAT and PAYE. Corporation tax will not be an issue.

The standard of due diligence of the business required is the same as in a sale and purchase of a company. The buyer is entitled to reassurance that the partnership is indeed a partnership under general legal principles, or under the relevant legislation, and it would be reasonable to require warranties relating to the following:

• the partnership has always carried on its business with a view to profit between the partners and equally to share in any losses;

- the partnership has never gone into liquidation;
- if UK land and property is involved, that SDLT charges have been properly assessed and paid prior to transfer;
- the partnership is not and never has been an investment LLP or a property investment LLP;
- the partners have properly self-assessed both as a partnership and in respect of their individual partnership interests;
- the management accounts should be fully warranted as being true;
- the partnership has properly complied at all times with the requirements under VAT and PAYE statute, no penalties or interest have arisen in respect of VAT or PAYE and as at the date of completion, payments and reporting requirements will be up to date; and
- no tax liability of the partnership (including penalties and interest) relating to the pre-completion period can arise on the buyers and all such liabilities for the avoidance of doubt will remain the liabilities of the sellers.

HMRC considered that use of limited liability partnerships (LLPs) in certain structures were for anti-avoidance purposes – namely members of an LLP who were engaged on terms similar to employees rather than traditional partners sharing in both the risks and reward – could be taxed as self-employed individuals as partners with resulting benefits for income tax and NIC purposes disguised remuneration through the use of an LLP and the use of partnerships for loss allocation schemes. The new anti-avoidance provisions (referred to a **Salaried Members** rules) took effect from 6 April 2014. They only apply to LLPs formed under the LLP Act and not to general partnerships or limited partnerships nor do they apply to entities outside the UK which are broadly equivalent to UK LLPs under the LLP Act.

The Salaried Member rules are for tax issues only and are independent of employment law.

The rules treat an individual member (M) of an LLP as an employee if three conditions are all met set out as follows:

Condition A – disguised salary

This condition is met if M is to perform services for the LLP and it is reasonable to expect that the amount payable by the LLP will be wholly or substantially 'disguised salary' as follows:

- it is fixed; or
- it is variable but varied without reference to the overall amount of the profits or losses of the LLP; or
- it is not in practice affected by the overall profits or losses of the LLP.

Condition B – Significant influence

This condition is met if the mutual rights and duties of the members and the LLP do not give M significant influence over the affairs of the partnership.

Condition C – Capital contribution

This condition is met if M's contribution to the LLP is less than 25% of the disguised salary and it is reasonable to expect that it will be payable in a relevant tax year in respect of M's performance of services for the partnership.

If all of the above conditions are met then M is a 'salaried member' under the legislation and will be treated as an employee for tax purposes and subject to PAYE and to tax on any benefits in kind.

If the transaction involves the acquisition of the business of an LLP a warranty that the anti-avoidance provisions relating to Salaried Members do not apply is required.

If the transaction involves the transfer of the business and trade of a partnership the warranties relating to a TOGC, as set out in **Chapter 5** paragraph 5.5, should be provided by the parties.

If the buyer is acquiring an interest in the partnership, it should require an undertaking and indemnity that all profits expenses and liabilities arising in respect of the partnership before the acquisition, including SDLT, VAT and PAYE liabilities (particularly secondary NIC in view of forewarned legislative changes affecting LLPs), will be entirely for the account of the original partners. The management accounts should be warranted and the above warranties should be required.

It will be essential that management accounts are drawn up to completion, in order to apportion pre-completion and post-completion trading activities. These should be agreed in the usual way as for completion accounts.

From the seller's perspective, if the partners are to receive consideration shares in the buyer for the sale of their interests in the partnership business, any income derived from the company by a partner is treated as arising from the deemed business representing his interest in the partnership. The partner will be able to carry forward any unrelieved share of partnership losses against income from the company, which would include dividends, remuneration or benefits-in-kind.[20]

---

[20] Notice 700/56/06 paragraph 19.1

THE TAX SCHEDULE

7   SHARE SCHEME ISSUES

7.1   Overview

The parties to a transaction will require comprehensive details of the target company's employee incentive and share purchase schemes and other arrangements whereby the sale of the company is likely to trigger rights and obligations of employees and officers of the company to acquire its shares. If one or both of the parties is/are publicly listed, the Takeover Code will apply to the transaction, and separate offer documents to option-holders will be necessary (discussed below at paragraph 7.5). This is both time-consuming and involved and will need to be provided for in the document production timetable.

Specifically, full details will be required on the following issues:

- the number of shares under option and warrants (both referred to here as options) which will be exercisable on or after completion – necessary to calculate the total purchase price for the target company on the assumption that all option-holders will become shareholders in the target company and parties to the SPA;
- the terms of exercise of all options including:
  - the exercise price;
  - rights or requirements of option-holders to exercise on a change of control of the target and if so the timetable for exercise;
  - whether exercise will be conditional upon performance conditions and whether any condition can or will be waived on a takeover of the target;
  - vesting terms and whether they can or will be waived on a takeover;
  - exercise rights if a compulsory purchase notice under the Companies Act is issued ("squeeze-out" and "sell-out" – see **Appendix 1**);
  - lapsing provisions following a takeover or change of control of target;

- confirmation as to whether or not the option-holder has agreed to pay any secondary NIC which may arise on exercise (see paragraph 7.3 below);
- terms of any arrangements agreed between the target and the option-holders relating to the payment of the aggregate exercise price, and income tax and NIC arising on exercise of the option including any cashless exercise and/or loan arrangements;

- terms of options granted to employees and other persons in jurisdictions outside the UK including relevant statutory regulations which could affect overseas subsidiaries of the target company and overseas option-holders;
- a calculation of corporation tax relief under sections 1001 to 1038 CTA 2009 which could be available on exercise of options and acquisitions of target's shares (*Corporation tax relief*[1]) – (see paragraph 7.2 below);
- likely tax liabilities arising for the target company on exercise of options including secondary NIC (see paragraph 7.3 below); and
- confirmation of whether or not options are capable of remaining outstanding and exercisable following completion.

Due diligence must include confirmation that all employment related securities schemes (ERS) have been correctly registered online, as from 6 April 2014 and that all online filing for issues of options and reportable events have been properly carried out including self-certification for SIPs, CSOPs and SAYEs.

If the target company operates a SIP (see **Appendix 8 – Overview of HMRC-approved employee incentive schemes**) the trustees who hold the various shares on behalf of the participants must act in accordance with the directions of the scheme participants. If the SIP shares have fewer rights than the ordinary shares, the consideration which the SIP participants may receive on a buy-out is likely to be less. In any case, the buyer must make an appropriate offer to the trustees at the same time as the offer is

---

[1] Previously referred to as 'schedule 23 relief' (under FA 2003)

made to ordinary shareholders. This offer should be approved by the non-executive directors of the target company as being fair.

It will be in the interests of both the buyer and the seller for share scheme issues to be identified early in the transaction, to avoid delay in finalising the transaction and to ensure that all contractual and legal obligations of the target company to the option-holders are properly considered. Otherwise the purchase price might need adjustment to reflect the additional and unexpected costs for the target company or the buyer relating to these matters.

The tax advisor acting for the buyer will need copies of the following documents in the due diligence process:

- the rules of the target company's scheme(s) and the relevant board or company resolution adopting them and approving the rules;
- all 'stand-alone' option agreements granted by the target;
- the target's articles of association, which should confirm the board's powers to grant options but which may set limits and/or conditions;
- a comprehensive schedule setting out the following details:
    - all separate categories of options granted and which have not lapsed;
    - the number of shares under outstanding options and the number of issued shares in the target expected at completion excluding option shares;
    - names of option-holders;
    - dates of grant, lapsing dates and exercise prices of all outstanding options;
    - performance conditions and vesting terms of all options;
    - all correspondence and option documentation including certificates and/or agreements, between the target and the option-holders; and
    - all documents filed with HMRC and any overseas taxation authority, and details of any scheme and option reference numbers provided by the tax authorities;
- copies of all company resolutions and board minutes referring to any of the above

- copies of target's accounts which should include details of shares under options, and terms of outstanding option.

Problems relating to share schemes matters are frequently encountered during the due diligence process including the following:

i.   the options were not in fact granted, by virtue of the absence of any option agreements or certificates and board minutes and other written documentation, resulting in the option-holders having no enforceable rights to acquire shares in the target despite undertakings by the board of target company;

ii.   the board of the target exceeded its powers by purporting to grant options over shares in excess of limits previously set, or in excess of the target's authorised share capital, or through the lack of any necessary shareholders' approval as required under the target's articles or company law statute;

iii. statutory requirements for HMRC-approved schemes were not met or were breached resulting in purported options being either void or options lapsing;

iv.   the target company has inadequate documentary evidence available relating to options purported to have been granted, or all relevant documentation is with the option-holders and not with the company;

v.   the absence of change of control provisions in the scheme rules; or

vi.   details of the terms of options granted and the number outstanding as summarised in the target company's latest report and accounts differ from the details set out in the documentation receiving during due diligence;

vii. there are hostile option-holders who may not agree to enter into the SPA following exercise of their options;

viii. not all option-holders are contactable;

ix.   the new disguised remuneration anti-avoidance rules[2] may apply to the scheme in question (discussed below at paragraph 7.8).

---

[2] ITEPA Part 7A

If the target is private and unlisted, its board of directors should be able to remedy the problems set out in paragraphs **i, ii,** and **iv** above by board resolution authorising them to rectify the relevant omissions or errors, either subject to shareholders' consent or not, as the case may be. In order to deal with the discrepancy referred to in paragraph **vi**, the exact position should be confirmed based on the documentation and agreed between the board of the target company, its accountants and the tax advisors to both the seller and the buyer.

Issues arising under paragraph v and **vii** above may be more problematic. If the scheme rules' change of control provisions are inadequate, including failure to provide for early exercise or the absence of lapsing provisions following a change of control of the target, the buyer should seriously consider the ramifications. If the target's option-holders cannot (or refuse to) exercise their options before or following completion, and their rights continue to exist after completion due to the absence of lapsing provisions within strict time limits, on the eventual exercise of the options such option-holders will become minority shareholders in the target when it is a subsidiary of the buyer. Their holdings may have little value and the buyer will be obliged to buy out the group of minority shareholders, or be required to consider their rights going forward if it cannot buy them out.

If paragraphs **iii** or **v** are relevant and the buyer wishes to retain the goodwill of the option-holders, particularly if they are to remain as part of the target company's workforce following completion, the buyer should propose that arrangements be made with the option-holders under which they give up their original rights under the original options over the target company's shares in exchange for new rights. This could involve any of the following:

- a cash payment for the release of the options;
- the grant of a new option over shares in the target company which must be exercised before completion and on the condition that the option-holders accept the offer by the buyer for the target company;

- the grant of a new option over shares in the buyer company, either under an existing scheme or a bespoke scheme set up by the buyer following completion.

In any of these circumstances the buyer might consider renegotiating the purchase price to reflect the unanticipated costs of the new arrangements.

It is preferable that outstanding options be exercised before completion (at least 24 hours would be best) subject to comments on timing relating to corporation tax relief (see paragraph **7.2** below) and that the option-holders become parties to the SPA so that:

- all option-holders will be bought out at completion under the same terms as other shareholders with the consideration to option-holders thus representing part of the buyer's purchase price;
- the issuing of shares on exercise of the options prior to a change of control of the target company falls within the corporation tax relief provisions so that the target company will benefit from a corporation tax deduction. It will be a matter of commercial negotiation as to whether the seller or the buyer receives the benefit of the relief, as it will arise post-completion in respect of a pre-completion event;
- the value of the option-holders' rights are not reduced by virtue of a post-completion exercise in circumstances which would result in them becoming minority shareholders in the target company; and
- the takeover procedures for 'squeeze-outs' of minority shareholders under CA 2006 Part 28 Chapter 3[3] will not apply.

HMRC have set out their view on the valuation of shares in cashless exercise situations involving options[4]. HMRC recognise that in some situations the sale of shares to cover the exercise price payable in respect of the option, and any tax and NIC due, may extend into the day following the exercise – in which case the

---

[3] CA 2006 sections 974 to 978

[4] See HMRC Manual ERSM 220060

THE TAX SCHEDULE

actual sale price achieved may be taken as the market value of the shares at the time of exercise in such situations. Where there are a large number of sales extending over one or two days, the average sale price achieved may be taken as the market value of the shares acquired by each individual employee. This approach may also be adopted where large number of shares vest at the same time under a long term incentive plan not involving options.

7.2 Corporation tax relief – a important negotiating issue

Relief against corporation tax is available where a person acquires shares by reason of his or her employment with the company whose shares are being acquired[5] (employing company) or where such a person has an option and acquires shares on exercise of that option.[6]

The main conditions for the relief on exercise of an employment-related option are as follows:

- the business for the purposes of which the award or grant is made, must be carried on by the employing company which itself is within the charge to UK corporation tax;
- the shares must be ordinary shares, fully paid-up and not redeemable;
- the shares must be either:
  - listed on a recognised stock exchange; or
  - in a company that is not under the control of another company; or
  - in a company which is under the control of another company but that other company's shares are listed on a recognised stock exchange (so long as that other company is not a close company or a company which would be a close company if resident in the UK); and
- the employee option holder is subject to UK income tax under ITEPA in respect of the award.

---

[5] CTA 2009 Part 12 Chapter 2 (sections 1006 to 1013)

[6] CTA 2009 Part 12 Chapter 3 (sections 1014 to 1024)

If all the conditions for the relief apply, the amount of relief for corporation tax purposes will be (except when restricted or convertible shares are involved) the difference between the market value of the shares at the time of the award of the shares (i.e. when the option is exercised) and the amount or value of the consideration given by the recipient in respect of the shares. This rather generous relief will apply as a straight reduction to the pre-tax profits of the company and calculated under self-assessment on the profits of the business in respect of which the award was made. If the award was made for the purposes of more than one business the deduction should be apportioned between them on a just and reasonable basis. The relief is given for the accounting period when the shares are acquired.

The calculation of the corporation tax relief should be relatively straightforward and, therefore, capable of being agreed between the parties to the transaction, once the details of all outstanding options and their exercise prices have been compiled and expectations relating to the target's pre-tax profits following completion have been quantified. It will then be a matter of negotiation, if the issue has not already been considered in principle, as to which party should take the benefit of the relief.

If the target company is not listed or is not under the control of a listed company and is not to be acquired by a listed company, the corporation tax relief will be lost if the options are exercised after a change of control of the target (i.e. normally on completion), because the target will be under the control of the buyer. Therefore, it is important that all options are exercised before completion (in the author's view not later than at least a day before completion or the date the agreement for the acquisition becomes unconditional) and the exercise of those options should be a required pre-completion condition.

If the relevant rules do not provide for pre-completion exercise, they should be amended if possible, before completion to allow for early exercise which results in the availability of the corporation tax relief.[7] The risk with this strategy is that options are exercised but completion does not take place. Such a result can be minimised in most cases by adopting the following procedure:

- the option-holder signs but does not date the notice of exercise, in which case he or she notifies the target company that he or she wishes to exercise the option, accept the terms of the offer and enter into the SPA;

- under a separate power of attorney (which is signed and dated) the option-holder appoints a director as his or her attorney to do all things necessary to accept the offer on behalf of the option-holder including properly dating the notice of exercise prior to completion. A director of the target should be in as good a position as anyone to make a judgment that the deal will complete and to date the exercise notices at least one day before completion, or prior to the agreement becoming unconditional, whichever is relevant. However, the notices on completion in such circumstances must not be backdated – otherwise it would amount to fraud on HMRC.

If the exercise is effected but completion does not take place as anticipated, the option-holders will be required to pay the exercise price and any related tax arising from the exercise, and the target will be required to issue the shares to the option-holders. This potential outcome must be explained to the option holders prior to signing the power of attorney. The option-holders may not have the necessary funds to pay for the shares and any income tax and NIC and if there is no market for the shares, the option-holders may be unable to sell them in order to realise some cash to cover their liabilities. It is for these reasons that notices of exercise often provide that, if completion does not take place, it will be deemed that there was no exercise of the relevant option. In other words, exercise will be conditional upon completion being effected. In the author's view this will put the corporation tax relief in jeopardy, on the basis that HMRC may argue that if exercise is conditional upon completion, exercise could only have been effected on and not

---

[7] If the scheme is HMRC approved, this needs to be discussed beforehand if possible with HMRC to ensure that the change does not jeopardise the tax status of the scheme.

before completion, and therefore co-terminus with a change of control of the target. If exercise takes place, but there is no completion, the company could allow the shares to remain partly paid, in which case a deemed loan could arise under ITEPA section 446Q. Unless the company is a close company, an income tax charge could then arise on the employee shareholder. Nevertheless, this is preferable to the loss of corporation tax relief.

Often, the value of any the corporation tax relief is overlooked at the heads of terms stage and not properly negotiated. Pre-completion exercise of options will be under the control of the seller and unless agreed otherwise, the relief should generally be for the benefit of the seller, as it will arise from a pre-completion event (unless the seller is warranting pre-completion tax reliefs). If the purchase price takes into account the availability of the corporation tax relief for the target, the tax indemnity should protect the buyer if the relief does not become available, except in circumstances when the non-availability is due to a post-completion action of the buyer or absence of profits for the target post-completion. Alternatively, if the seller is to receive the benefit of the relief (say, as deferred consideration at the time it is realised by the target) the seller should be indemnified for its loss due to any actions of the buyer resulting in the loss of the relief (see below).

Which party in the transaction should take the benefit of the relief is often determined by the party with the strongest bargaining position and the quantum of the relief. If acting for the seller who is not to receive the benefit of the relief, at the very least it should be argued that if any claim arises under the tax schedule, it should be capable of being offset against such available corporation tax relief.

The corporation tax relief can be lost as a result of the following post-completion events:
• there is a change in the nature of the business of the target;
• there has been a hive-up of the business of the target;
• the buyer utilises group losses against the target in priority to the corporation tax relief;

- the trade or business of the target ceases; or
- the relief is not claimed under self-assessment within the correct time limits.

The buyer should be made aware of these issues and take care, following completion, not to restructure the target or do anything which could affect the corporation tax relief, regardless of which party to the transaction is to receive the benefit.

Additionally, the timing of the availability of the corporation tax relief for the seller may be an issue – namely the date or dates by which the target actually uses the relief and benefits from reduced corporation tax. It would be reasonable for the buyer to resist paying over to the seller an amount equal to the relief until the target has actually benefited from it. This will be determined by:

- the dates on which the corporation tax relief can be calculated and claimed by the target;
- when, in the target's accounting period, will completion will take place;
- whether the target is making profits, or otherwise when it is likely to become profitable;
- whether the target company makes or will begin to make quarterly payments for corporation tax after completion (thus being able to account for some of the relief earlier than it would do if it was not in the quarterly payment regime);
- the target's rate of corporation tax following completion as part of the buyer's group.

The tax advisors to the seller and buyer should liaise closely with their clients' accountants to agree the procedure for recognising the relief and ensure that the relevant provisions have been incorporated in the tax schedule.

7.3 Tax issues arising in respect of share incentive schemes

No UK income tax charge should arise on an option-holder being granted employment-related securities options.[8] Instead, a charge to income tax and sometimes NIC will arise on the exercise of the

---

[8] ITEPA section 475

option,[9] subject to exceptions for options granted under HMRC-approved option schemes, namely SIPs, SAYE, EMIs and Approved CSOPs (Approved Options).

Income tax arises on the exercise of an unapproved option when the option-holder acquires a beneficial interest in the underlying shares, subject to tax relief if the option-holder pays any secondary NIC arising from the exercise.[10] The tax charge will arise on the difference between the market value of the shares at the date of acquisition less any deductible amounts (mainly secondary NIC which the option-holder has agreed to pay) and the consideration, being the aggregate exercise price.

PAYE must be operated and NIC will arise on the exercise of any unapproved option which has been granted after 27 January 1996 if the shares under option represent readily convertible assets (RCA). The definition of an RCA includes "an asset for which trading arrangements are in existence or are likely to come into existence",[11] so shares of a target company which are about to be acquired are likely to be considered by HMRC to be RCAs. Therefore, the target company (or any subsidiary of the target which is the employer of the option-holder) must make appropriate deductions for income tax and NIC arising on such exercise from (usually) a salary payment made to the option-holder, and pay that amount to HMRC under PAYE rules. If an option was granted before 27 January 1996 but rolled over into a new option after that date, HMRC will require any such PAYE obligations to apply to the new roll-over option.

Income tax liabilities, NIC and PAYE will not arise on the exercise of the following options:

- EMI options (see 7.6.4 below) which were granted at an exercise price which represented market value of the shares under option on the date of grant (market value);

---

[9] ITEPA section 476

[10] ITEPA section 476

[11] ITEPA section 702

- SAYE options (whether or not granted at an exercise price discounted up to 20% of the market value of the underlying shares under the SAYE legislation); and
- Approved CSOPs exercised after the third anniversary of the date of grant (and which, under the legislation, must have an exercise price no less than the market value).

Often rules will provide that the option-holder and the grantor company may enter into arrangements under which the exercise price and any tax liabilities can be deducted from any payments made by the option-holder's employer to the option-holder – such payments are likely to be the individual's salary and bonus – or from proceeds received on a sale of shares following exercise. Procedurally, on the sale of a company in most transactions there is no need for this to be complicated and it should be provided for in the notices of exercise and agreed by the parties to the transaction.

On the basis that the option-holders are to enter into the SPA and accept either cash or shares in the buyer (consideration shares) for their option shares in the target company, there should be some mechanism for the target to be paid the exercise price and any tax liability arising under PAYE to be collected and paid over to HMRC. These amounts can be deducted from any cash proceeds to be received by the option-holders, but if the offer is an all share offer then the option-holders will wish to be able to sell some or all of their consideration shares to realise enough cash to pay off their liabilities (the exercise price and tax and NIC) which will have arisen.

The appropriate wording in the notice of exercise can provide for the option-holder to appoint a director of the target company as his agent to sell sufficient number of consideration shares so as to cover the option-holder's liabilities, and to remit that amount to the relevant employer company in order that it properly discharges its responsibilities under PAYE. If the consideration shares are not readily tradable (the buyer is a private company), the buyer will need to consider offering the option-holders sufficient cash for the exercise liabilities to be covered or alternatively lend them sufficient sums to cover the liabilities (taking into account taxation of employment-related loan issues) or to offer roll-over options (discussed below in paragraph 7.4).

7.4   Roll-over options

If an option-holder receives consideration for the assignment or release of an option, that consideration will be subject to income tax[12] except for any new replacement option provided as part of the consideration. As most option scheme rules provide that options will lapse on any purported assignment, the relevant chargeable event likely to arise in a takeover of a company is when the option-holders are made an offer to release their options either for cash or for a different option with different rights (the roll-over option) or a combination of both. Where a roll-over option is granted it will not be treated as consideration and no income tax charge will arise in respect of its value at that time[13] although any cash or monetary consideration given will be taxable on receipt. The roll-over option will be chargeable to income tax in the same manner as the original option, namely on exercise.

If options are 'under water'[14] at the time an offer is made and the buyer wishes to retain the goodwill of the target's option-holders following completion it should consider offering roll-over options over its shares in consideration of the cancellation of the worthless options. Alternatively, if an issue arises in respect of inadequate change of control provisions in the target's option scheme rules, and the option-holders are not entitled to exercise their options before or on completion so that they are unable to enter into the SPA, it would not be in any party's interest for the option-holders to become minority shareholders in the target on entitlement to exercise options over the target's shares following completion. In these circumstances, the buyer could offer roll-over options on terms that would encourage the option-holders to accept them in consideration for fully releasing their rights under the original option. The 'sweetener' could include a greater value of shares in

[12] ITEPA section 479(5)

[13] ITEPA section 483

[14] When the exercise price is greater than the purchase price under the offer

the buyer company under the roll-over option, relaxed performance conditions, and/or a lower aggregate exercise price. No tax charge will arise in respect of the more attractive option terms at the time of roll-over so long as there is no cash payment for the release of the options in target.

However, if roll-over options are to be offered in respect of SAYE options, Approved CSOP options and EMIs the following conditions will apply:

- the rules of the SAYE scheme and the Approved CSOP scheme must provide for roll-over options[15] on, *inter alia*, a change of control, with the roll-over options equivalent to the old options in all respects, and satisfying the legislative requirements for the relevant type of option;
- the roll-over options must be granted, generally, within six months of the change of control of the company which granted the original option;
- the roll-over options will remain subject to the original scheme in respect of an SAYE scheme and an Approved CSOP scheme, as it had effect immediately before the release of the old options;
- the total market value of the shares subject to the original options immediately before the release and new grant must equal the total market value immediately after the grant of the roll-over options of the shares under option and the aggregate exercise price payable on exercise of the roll-over option must be the same amount which would have been payable on exercise of the original option;
- the requirements relating to eligible employees and qualifying options for the purposes of EMI must be met in respect of roll-over EMI options but the grantor company will not be subject to the gross asset value and employee limits under the EMI legislation.

The roll-over option will stand in the place of the original option for tax purposes.

_____

[15] ITEPA Schedule 3 paragraph 38 and Schedule 4 paragraph 26

7.5 Takeover Code Issues

The amount of attention and time required to provide for the rights of option-holders in a public takeover, and to deal with the terms of an offer which must be made to option-holders should not be underestimated.

Rule 15 of the Takeover Code[16] applies to options by virtue of subsection (e) and, therefore, the offeror (the buyer) is required to make an appropriate offer or proposal to all option-holders as if they were stockholders, in the target company to ensure that their interests are safeguarded. The rule requires equality of treatment.

Rule 15(b) requires that the directors of the target company must obtain competent independent advice on the offer or proposal to option-holders, and the substance of the advice must be made known to the option-holders together with the views of the target's board on the offer or proposal. This can be done either by the advisors to each of the target company and the buyer signing off on the letter to option-holders, or through the letter to option-holders containing a statement from the target's board (normally the independent directors), stating that they have been advised that the offer or proposal being made to all option-holders is fair.

Under Rule 15(c) the offer to option-holders should be dispatched at the same time as the offer document is posted. Often this is not practicable, in which case the rule requires that the Takeover Panel be consulted and the offer be despatched as soon as possible thereafter, with a copy lodged with the Panel. It is good practice for the tax advisor to bring Rule 15(c) to the attention of the corporate advisors and argue for simultaneous mailing of the offer letters.

If the target's option-holders are entitled to exercise their option rights and accept the offer during the course of the offer they should be issued with all relevant documents which are issued to shareholders in the target company and their attention should be drawn to their rights in the documents.

---

[16] Reproduced in **Appendix 1**

The offer to option-holders should not normally be made conditional on any particular level of acceptances.

If there are more than one option scheme adopted by the target it will be necessary to draft separate offer letters for each separate scheme. These letters must mirror the wording in the offer letter to shareholders in all respects relating to the terms of the offer to shareholders, but must also include details of the rights of all option-holders:

- as set out in the rules of the relevant scheme;
- under the relevant legislation if the scheme is an HMRC approved scheme; and
- under any specific terms of the option agreement.

The letters to option-holders must be agreed by all parties to the transactions including the companies' NOMADs.

If a takeover offer has been made under CA 2006 section 974[17], and the buyer has acquired or unconditionally contracted to acquire not less than 90% in value of the shares to which the offer relates and (if voting shares) not less than 90% of the voting rights carried by those shares (90% acceptance), the buyer is entitled to exert its rights to acquire the remaining issued shares in the target company[18]. Alternatively, the holder of any voting shares to which the offer relates who has not accepted the offer is entitled to require the buyer to acquire those shares if, at any time before the end of the period within which the offer can be accepted, the buyer has achieved a 90% acceptance. These statutory provisions will be relevant when options are not, or cannot be, exercised before a change of control of the target in a public takeover.

Following a 90% acceptance the buyer will have a three-month period to give notices for compulsory acquisition of minority shares, beginning with the day after the last day on which the offer can be accepted under CA 2006 section 979[19]. Once these notices are sent out, the buyer will be entitled and bound to acquire the

---

[17] See **Appendix 1** – "Squeeze Out and Sell Outs on Takeover Offers"

[18] CA 2006 section 979

[19] Previously referred to as section 429 notices under CA 1985

outstanding minority interests in the target at the end of six weeks from the date of the notice (see CA 2006 section 981).

Well drafted rules for option schemes should provide that option-holders are entitled to exercise their options within a certain time period following a change of control and that entitlement will lapse after the stated period. If, in a public offer, relevant notices are sent out following a 90% acceptance, additional letters to option-holders will be required, alerting them to an earlier cut-off date for exercise and lapsing.

7.6 Administrative and Reporting Requirements for HMRC-Approved Schemes

Prior to 6 April 2014 all HMRC-approved share and option schemes required approval by HMRC, involving the submission for approval of the rules and relevant documentation. This procedure never applied to EMI schemes. As from 6 April 2014 companies have been required to self certify their approved schemes, and all employment related securities scheme (ERS), including schemes having received HMRC clearance previously as well as EMI schemes, were required to be registered online with HMRC as from that same date. Once registered, HMRC provide a scheme reference number to the employer. If HMRC schemes were not registered by 6 July 2015 the tax advantages will have been lost. There are automatic late filing penalties and penalties for incorrect self-certification. Furthermore, schemes must be self-certified each year. These new requirements fall within the PAYE online requirements.

7.6.1 Approved CSOPs

Prior to April 2014 notification to HMRC's Employee Share Schemes Unit (ESSU) was required in respect of the following:

i.   the proposed takeover or change of control of the target;

ii.   any proposed changes to the rules of the scheme and/or any proposed changes to the terms of any options granted under the scheme (if so, also asking for confirmation that the changes are acceptable and will not result in the options falling outside the criteria for Approved CSOP Options);

iii. terms of any offer under Rule 15; and

iv. terms of any proposed roll-over options to be granted and asking for confirmation that the terms are acceptable under the legislation, and copies of draft correspondence with option-holders had to be sent to HMRC to ensure their approval.

Now under the self-assessment regime an annual return must be filed on or before 8 July in the relevant tax year[20] and which must include details of reportable events, including the take-over of the company.

Once the target comes under the control of another company, except if the new controlling company is listed, the scheme will no longer satisfy the legislative criteria, and therefore the buyer should close the scheme following completion.

7.6.2 SAYE Schemes

The administrator of the SAYE scheme run by the target company should be contacted at the outset of its takeover and that person should be copied in on all draft correspondence relating to the option-holders and the scheme for its approval. The tax advisors and the administrator should agree which option-holders are 'in the money' (i.e. the offer per share is above the exercise price or prices). The administrator will confirm the last payment date to be made by the option-holders out of their salary (determined under the scheme rules) and will be responsible for communicating with the option-holders. The target's payroll or HR department will also need to be involved.

Under the online filing requirements, the annual return must contain the disqualifying events arising from the takeover.

7.6.3 SIPs

The trustees of the SIP and any other party involved in the administration of the plan should be contacted at the same time as other shareholders in the target are informed that a takeover has been agreed, because the trustees are likely to be parties to the SPA acting on behalf of the participants and beneficiaries under the SIP. The tax advisors to the buyer and the seller will want copies of all

---

[20] Schedule 4 ITEPA 2003 paragraph 28B

trust documentation, the SIP rules, copies of the partnership agreements and free share agreements, and full details of the participants and their entitlement under the plan and evidence that the online reporting requirements and PAYE liabilities have been duly complied with. The SIP administrator will need to inform all relevant parties of the last date on which payments may be made into the SIP by participants in respect of the partnership shares.

Under the online filing requirements, the annual return must contain the disqualifying events arising from the takeover.

7.6.4   EMIs

Under the online filing requirements, the annual return must contain the disqualifying events arising from the takeover and/or changes to any terms of the options.

7.7   Partly Paid Shares

A partly paid share is one which is issued for an amount which is less than its full paid up amount – the full paid up value of a share cannot be below its par value.

If the target company has set up a scheme whereby the shares in question are only partly paid by the employee, the provisions of ITEPA Chapter 3C (sections 446Q to 446Z) are likely to apply and the employee with be treated as if he or she was provided with a notional interest free loan, equal to the difference between the market value of the shares (as if fully paid up) at the time of the acquisition less the amount paid for the shares.

Under ITEPA section 175 the employee will be taxed on an amount equivalent to the amount of interest which would have been payable on the notional loan for the tax year in question, at the official rate of interest less any amount of interest actually paid by the employee on the deemed loan for that year. If the company in question is a close company no income tax charge should arise on the deemed loan (see ITEPA section 446(2) and ITA section 383(2) and 392 and 396). It will be important that the partly paid shares are fully paid for before completion, and that the outstanding amount is not merely netted off against the consideration the employee shareholder will receive from the sale of the shares on completion of the transaction. Otherwise, HMRC might consider that the loan has been waived. In which case, income tax could arise on the deemed waiver.

7.8   Disguised Remuneration Rules[21]

These anti-avoidance provisions (which essentially apply for the relevant activities arising on or after 6 April 2011) arise in circumstances where:

- a person (A) is an employee, a former employee or a prospective employee of another person (B); and
- there is a 'relevant arrangement' to which A is a party; and
- it is reasonable to suppose that the relevant arrangement is wholly or partly a means of providing a reward or recognition or loans in connection with A's employment with B (including former or prospective employment); and
- a relevant third person takes a 'relevant step' which it is reasonable to suppose is taken under the relevant arrangement or there is some connection between the relevant arrangement or the relevant step.

The rules are widely drawn and extend to persons linked with A, companies which are members within the same group as B, and with 'relevant third persons' including A or B acting as a trustee or 'any other person'. Therefore, arrangements involving company EBTs can fall within the provisions. Arrangements not involving a relevant third party do not fall within the provisions.

A company (P) will take a 'relevant step' if:

- a sum of money or an asset held by P is earmarked by P with a view that a later relevant step will be taken in relation to the money or asset;
- a sum of money or an assets starts being held by/on behalf of P specifically with a view to a later relevant step being taken in relation to the money or asset;

regardless of the later step having not been worked out and regardless of whether A has a legal right to have the relevant step taken.

---

[21] ITEPA Part 7A (sections 665A to 554Z15)

A relevant step also includes the company (P):

- paying a sum of money to a relevant person or transferring an asset to that person;
- making available a sum of money or assets for use which permits its use as security for a loan to be made to a relevant person or as security for a liability or the performance of an undertaking;
- granting to a relevant person a lease of any premises which is likely to exceed 21 years.

A relevant person means A or a person chosen by A and includes, if P is taking a step on B's behalf or at its direction or request, any other person. References to A include any person linked to A.

If arrangements fall within the provisions and are not excluded (see below) the value of the relevant step will count as employment income of A. The valuation of the relevant step will be the market value of the asset when the step is taken, or if higher, the cost of the relevant step.

The provisions setting out what comprises excluded actions from the relevant actions include (but are not limited to) the following arrangements:

- steps under any HMRC-approved CSOP, SIP or SAYE;
- any registered pension scheme in the UK or pension scheme set up by any other government;
- a loan provided on ordinary commercial terms for which there was no tax avoidance arrangement; and any loan entered into in the ordinary course of P's business;
- a package of benefits which is available to a substantial proportion of B's employees (but in respect of which there are further defined criteria);
- deferred remuneration which is deferred to a vesting date (which is after the award date but not later than five years after the award date), which can be revoked if conditions are not met;
- earmarking shares or money for employee share schemes, made in respect of A's employment with B, on terms:

- whereby the main purpose of which is to defer the receipt of the shares or the money to a vesting date and subject to specified conditions being met before the vesting date;
- where the relevant shares are shares in a trading company or a company controlling a trading company (trading company shares) to be received or paid only if a specified exit event occurs;
- whereby a share option is not exercisable by A before a specified date, and subject to specified conditions being met on or before the vesting date;
- employee car ownership schemes;
- employee pension contributions and other retirement benefits.

7.9   Employee Shareholders and ESS

This special class of employee was established by FA 2013 Schedule 23, and is mentioned in this chapter for completeness. Briefly this regime is as follows:

- an employee can decide to become an employee shareholder in which case his or her company must give, free of charge, shares in that company or its parent company with a minimum value of £2,000 but with no set upper value and with the valuation taking account of any restrictions applying to the shares;
- anyone can apply for or accept an employee shareholder job including existing employees;
- the employer may ask the employee to change his or her employment contract but this is not obligatory for the employee; and
- no income tax and NIC charge arises on the issue of the shares and the first £50,000 of shares received will be free of CGT with a lifetime limit, as from 16 March 2016 of £100,000 exempt CGT.

The following six conditions must be met to become an employee shareholder:

- there must be agreement between both the employee and the company that the individual will be an employee shareholder;

- the employer must give the individual fully paid up shares in the employer's company or employer's parent company at least £2,000;
- the individual must not pay for the shares in any way;
- the employer must give the individual a written statement of the particulars of the status of employee shareholder;
- the individual must get advice from a relevant independent adviser on the terms and effect of the written statement, paid for by the company; and
- the individual cannot accept or agree to an employee shareholder job until 7 days have passed following receipt of the advice.

Set out as follows are the employment rights of an employee shareholder which he or she will retain:
- statutory sick pay
- statutory maternity, paternity and adoption leave and pay
- unfair dismissal rights where they are classed as automatically unfair reasons, where dismissal is based on discriminatory grounds and in relation to health and safety
- minimum notice periods if their employment will be ending (e.g. if an employer is dismissing them)
- time off for emergencies
- collective redundancy consultation
- TUPE
- national minimum wage
- not to have unlawful deductions from wages
- paid annual leave
- rest breaks
- the right not to be treated less favourably for working part time or fixed term
- not to be discriminated against

The rights which an employee shareholder will forego are as follows:
- unfair dismissal rights (apart from the automatically unfair reasons, where dismissal is based on discriminatory grounds and in relation to health and safety);

- rights to statutory redundancy pay;
- the statutory right to request flexible working except in the two week period after a return from parental leave; and
- certain statutory rights to request time off to train.

In addition, an employee shareholder will have to give 16 weeks' notice to their employer if they intend to return early from maternity, extra paternity or adoption leave.

An employer can choose to offer contractual rights that are more generous than those provided for in statute.

A 'written statement' between the company and the employee shareholder must set out what employment rights are to be foregone; whether there are voting rights, dividend rights and/or winding up rights attached to the shares and how the rights of such shares differ from other classes of shares in the company; whether the shares are redeemable and if so, the terms; whether there are any restrictions on the transferability of the shares and what those restrictions are; and whether there are drag-along or tag-along rights, and if so an explanation.

Amendments of the articles of the Company are likely, including terms of transfers and employee shareholders rights on leaving employment. Restrictions on transfer must be explained to the individual. Sale of the shares does not in itself change the employment status of the employee shareholder.

Due diligence will involve confirming that all the statutory requirements have been when ESS have been issued by the target company.

8   VENTURE CAPITAL SCHEMES

Transactions involving the sale or purchase of a company often involve investment under one of the HMRC schemes involving venture capital – all these schemes have been designed to encourage investment by individuals in high risk trading ventures. This chapter provides information on the main technical issues for the investors and the investing companies as an *aide memoire*, to be used as basic reference in any transaction which involves a company which has or will receive venture capital funding. A new venture capital scheme was introduced by the Finance Act 2014 – The Social Investment Tax Relief (SITR) scheme – resulting in there now being four separate schemes designed to encourage investment in small unquoted trading companies with UK-based trades. The Corporate Venturing Scheme (CVS) was closed in 2013 but this chapter includes details for reference purposes.

The four active schemes vary in the detail but have in common strict requirements for the investee (issuing) companies and their trades, the use of the subscription monies, and restrictions to ensure that there are no arrangements aiming to eliminate risk for the investors. The schemes are:

- the **Enterprise Investment Scheme (EIS)** which provides income tax relief for subscribing for shares, capital gains tax relief for gains on share disposals and deferral of capital gains tax on re-investment into EIS shares, available to individuals who invest directly in EIS companies (being smaller high risk companies);
- the **Seed Enterprise Investment Scheme (SEIS)** – a similar relief to that under the EIS, and applicable to shares issued by very early start-up companies and complementing the EIS. The SEIS operates for shares issued on or after 6 April 2012 providing relief to UK tax-paying individuals in the form of an income tax reduction on the subscription amount or £100,000 whichever is greater at a rate of 50%, as well a CGT relief on disposal of SEIS shares. The cumulative investment limit for each company is limited to £150,000. So long as the SEIS company has spent at least 70% of its SEIS subscription monies

it may raise money under EIS or from a VCT but not the reverse – i.e. a company cannot raise SEIS investments if it has issued EIS shares or has received VCT investment;

- the **Social Investment Tax Relief (SITR)** enables individuals to invest in social enterprises either in the form of equity or debt, but otherwise generally reflects reliefs under an EIS and which initially has a five year life span from 6 April 2014 to 5 April 2019;

- the **Venture Capital Trust Scheme (VCT)** which enables individuals to invest indirectly in EIS companies through an investment in a VCT which in turn invests in EIS companies. The investor benefits from a professional manager's investment ability and a wider spread of investment risk, and receives income tax relief on the investment in the VCT, tax relief on any dividends and capital gains tax relief on disposals of the VCT shares;

- the **Corporate Venturing Scheme (CVS)** provided corporation tax relief for companies which invested in EIS-type companies. This scheme was legislated to last for ten years, and came to an end on 31 March 2010. Therefore, the final effective end date for any qualifying investments made was 31 March 2013.

In addition to the above schemes, there are share loss relief provisions for companies and individuals whereby capital losses arising from VC investments can be offset against income ('Share Loss Relief').

The following table provides a snapshot of issues which may arise in a transaction and which will need consideration by the tax advisors.

Transaction	Status of target	Issues
Sale & purchase of a private company	Satisfies EIS,SEIS or SITR requirements	EIS, SEIS or SITR relief for individual investors; Potential investment by VCT
Newco acquires a trade	Newco is potentially an EIS/SEIS/SITR company	As above
Sale of EIS/ SEIS/SITR company	EIS/SEIS company	Possible loss of various investment reliefs – if so, a

		reporting requirement arises; Any CGT deferral relief crystallises
EIS/SEIS buyer offers share for share exchange for target	EIS/SEIS company	Roll-over relief for CGT purposes; Possible withdrawal of EIS/SEIS income tax relief; CGT deferral relief crystallised
Newco raising funds for EIS/ SEIS/SITR company	Newco to set up qualifying business	Prospectus for fundraising; EIS/SEIS/VCT reliefs; Advance clearances; Use of subscription monies within time limits; Compliance certificates post completion

8.1 The Enterprise Investment Scheme

8.1.1 Background

The legislation is contained in ITA Part 5 (sections 156 to 257) and sections 150A, 150B and TCGA Schedule 5B, and applies for EIS shares issued after 5 April 2007 (the current rules). For EIS shares issued between 6 April 2001 and 5 April 2007 the legislation, as set out in ICTA sections 289 to 312, will remain applicable for such shares. For the purposes of this chapter the focus will be on the current rules.

Recent changes to the scheme during the past three years include relaxation of the connected person rules and the definition of shares which qualify for relief. Also, a test was introduced which excludes companies set up for the purpose of accessing relief, acquiring shares in another company and investment in feed-in tariffs businesses (involving installations of 'green' energy technology and selling back electricity to the grid). There is now a disqualifying purposes test for the EIS scheme (as well as for the SEIS, SITR and VCTs).

Generally EIS reliefs for investors can be considerable and therefore the tax advisor in a transaction needs to consider carefully the status of the target company and whether reliefs may be available or alternatively are at risk of being lost as a result of transaction involving the sale and purchase of a company.

Under the EIS, individuals (the 'investor') may claim income tax relief ('EIS relief') on investments made by subscribing for newly-issued ordinary capital in small unquoted UK trading companies (the 'issuing company') as well as capital gains tax relief on disposals of EIS shares ('CGT disposal relief') so long as they have been held, essentially, for at least three years and there have been no disqualifying events during that period. The issuing company must remain within the EIS requirements during the three year period following the share issue – this is a major issue if target company raised EIS capital within three years of its takeover.

There are strict criteria for both the investor (who must have no connection or involvement in the issuing company) and the issuing company, including the use of the subscription monies raised. CGT deferral relief[1] is available for individuals who reinvest the proceeds of realised capital gains on the sale of any capital asset into EIS shares, whereby the rolled over gains will be frozen until the EIS investment is realised and the gain is not re-invested thereafter. (There are also provisions where individuals may subscribe for EIS shares in several companies through an approved EIS investment fund, which will be subject to the same restrictions as apply for direct investments by individuals.[2])

The legislation refers to the 'termination date',[3] which is essentially the last date on which the EIS requirements are required to be met (and after which no relief should be capable of being clawed back). It is defined as either:

- the third anniversary of the issue date of the EIS shares; or
- if the trade of the qualifying business activity of the issuing company has not commenced at the issue date, the third anniversary of the date when the trade commenced.

The definition of a termination date also applies for shares issued between 6 April 2001 and 5 April 2007.

---

[1] See TCGA Schedule 5B

[2] ITA section 251

[3] ITA section 256

There are three periods during which certain restrictions will apply for EIS shares issued after 5 April 2007[4] (referred to as the 'investment periods' in this publication) namely:

- **Period A** – the period beginning with the incorporation of the issuing company or, if the company was incorporated more than two years before the EIS share issue date, two years before the issue date, and ending on the termination date (therefore not greater than five years);

- **Period B** – the period between the EIS issue date and the termination date (a maximum three year period);

- **Period C** – the period beginning 12 months before the EIS issue date and ending on the termination date (essentially a four year period).

8.1.2 Issuing company requirements[5]

The company must satisfy the following requirements in order to be a qualifying company:

- during investment period B it must exist wholly for the purpose of carrying on one or more qualifying trade(s) or, if the company is a parent company, the business of the group must not consist either wholly or substantially of carrying on non-qualifying activities (namely 'excluded activities') ignoring any incidental purposes[6];

- during investment period B the issuing company or its qualifying 90% subsidiary[7] must carry on a qualifying business activity which is conducted on a commercial basis with a view to the realisation of profits and which does not consist wholly or substantially of carrying on any excluded activities – before 6 April 2011 the trade was required to be carried on wholly or mainly in the UK but this requirement was removed for shares issued on or after 6 April 2011;

- at the beginning of investment period B the issuing company

---

[4] ITA section 159

[5] ITA sections 180 to 200

[6] ITA section 181

[7] ITA section 190– primarily determined by holding no less than 90% of the issued share capital and voting rights and entitlement to assets on a winding up

must be unquoted[8] and, therefore, not listed on a recognised stock exchange[9], and there must be no arrangements in place at that time for it to become listed;

- at the beginning of period B the issuing company must meet the financial health requirement, namely it must not 'be in difficulty';
- the issuing company must not, at any time during investment period B, be a 51% subsidiary of another company or be under the control of another company (or of another company and any other person connected with that other company) without being a 51% subsidiary of that other company;[10]
- as from 6 April 2012 the value of the issuing company's gross assets or in the case of a group, its gross assets, must not exceed £15 million immediately before the issue of the EIS shares and must not exceed £16 million immediately after their issue[11] (previously the gross asset thresholds were £7 million and £8 million respectively);
- the number of full-time employees (or equivalent part-time employees) of the issuing company or its group must be less than 250 at the time of the issue of the EIS shares;[12]
- throughout the investment period B all subsidiaries of the issuing company must be qualifying subsidiaries, namely 51% subsidiaries[13] and over which no other person has control;[14] and
- for shares issued on or after 6 April 2011 the company must have a permanent establishment in the UK throughout period B.

Shares may carry a preferential right to dividends providing their amount and the date that they are payable is not dependent on the

---

[8] ITA section 184

[9] See the **Glossary** and the definition of a recognised stock exchanges

[10] ITA section 185

[11] ITA section 186

[12] ITA section 186A

[13] Owning more than 50% of the ordinary share capital – ICTA section 838 by virtue of ITA section 989

[14] ITA section 187

decision of the company, the holder or anyone else, and providing that the dividends are not cumulative.

The excluded activities (identical to those excluded in the SEIS and VCT schemes) are as follows:[15]

- dealing in land, in commodities or futures or in shares, securities or other financial instruments;
- dealing in goods otherwise than in the course of an ordinary trade of wholesale or retail distribution;
- banking, insurance, money-lending, debt-factoring, hire-purchase financing or other financial activities;
- leasing (including letting ships on charter or other assets on hire);
- receiving royalties or licence fees;
- providing legal or accountancy services;
- property development;
- farming or market gardening;
- holding, managing or occupying woodlands, any other forestry activities or timber production;
- shipbuilding;
- producing coal;
- producing steel;
- operating or managing hotels or comparable establishments or managing property used as an hotel or comparable establishment;
- operating or managing nursing homes or residential care homes or managing property used as a nursing home or residential care home;
- providing services or facilities to another person whose business falls within the above activities and the controlling interest in the business is held by a person who also has a controlling interest in the business of the service provider;
- the subsidised generation or export of electricity;
- the subsidised generation of heat or subsidised production of gas or fuel; and
- any activities which are excluded activities under section 199

---

[15] ITA section 192

(provision of services or facilities for another business).

The Finance Act 2012 introduced a disqualifying purpose test, whereby shares will not qualify for EIS relief which are issued:

- subject to arrangements whose main purpose is to generate access to the reliefs,
- in circumstances where either
  - the benefit of the investment is passed to another party to the arrangements; or
  - the business activities would otherwise by carried on by another party.

This provision applies to shares issued on or after 6 April 2012.

A qualifying EIS company can subsequently become a quoted company without the investors losing their EIS relief so long as there were no arrangements to become quoted at the time the shares were issued. AIM and the Special Fund Market on the LSE and the ISDX Growth Market and ISDX Secondary Market on the ICAP Securities & Derivatives Exchange are not considered by HMRC to be recognised stock exchanges at the date of this publication, so companies which are so listed may raise money under the EIS scheme if they satisfy the eligibility criteria.

8.1.3 Investor eligibility for relief[16]

The investor can only subscribe for EIS shares on his or her behalf and must not have had any connection with the issuing company (see paragraph 8.1.4 below regarding 'connection') during the period beginning two years before the investment and ending immediately before the termination date (essentially a five year period) nor can he or she have had any linked loan during period A.[17] A linked loan is simply defined as one which would not have been made or would not have been made on the relevant terms, had the investor not subscribed for the EIS shares.[18] Such terms include the giving of credit and any assignment of a debt from the investor. SP6/98 sets out HMRC guidance relating to loans to

---

[16] ITA section 157

[17] A linked loan to an associate of the investor is also prohibited

[18] ITA section 164

investors involved in any EIS and VCT arrangements. Due diligence if target company raised EIS finance should confirm that there were no linked loans.

If the investor receives value from the issuing company during the investment period the amount of relief will be reduced and is another issue for due diligence. These conditions will also apply to any associate of the investor which is defined as:[19]

- any relative or partner of the investor (relative being a spouse or civil partner, ancestor or lineal descendant, being any child or grandchild etc);
- the trustee(s) of any settlement in relation to which the investor or any relative of him or her (living or dead) is or was a settlor; and
- if the investor has an interest in any shares in a company which are subject to a trust or part of the estate of a deceased person, the trustee(s) of the settlement or personal representative of the deceased.

8.1.4 No connection with the issuing company[20]

The provisions for determining a connection with the issuing company are widely drawn, with an investor being deemed to be connected if he or she or an associate:

- is an employee of the issuing company, any 51% subsidiary of the issuing company or any partner of the issuing company or any of its subsidiaries;
- is a partner of the issuing company or of any 51% subsidiary of the issuing company;
- is a director of the issuing company or of any 51% subsidiary of the issuing company or a company which is a partner of the issuing company or any of its subsidiaries (subject to the exceptions for unpaid directors or business angels and discussed in paragraphs 8.1.5 and 8.1.6 below);
- has an interest (direct or indirect) or is entitled to acquire an interest in the issuing company of more than 30% (save in circumstances where there are only subscriber shares in issue

---

[19] ITA section 253

[20] ITA sections 166 to 171

and the company has not commenced trading) of the following:

- the ordinary share capital of the issuing company or any 51% subsidiary;
- the loan capital and issued share capital of the issuing company or any 51% subsidiary; or
- the voting power of the issuing company or any 51% subsidiary;
- is entitled to acquire on a winding up of the issuing company or any 51% subsidiary (or in any other circumstances) more than 30% of the assets of the company in question which would be available for distribution to its equity holders; or
- has control[21] of the issuing company or any 51% subsidiary of the company.

The Finance Act 2012 brought in an amendment to the concept of 'connected' whereby loan capital will be disregarded for the purposes of the limit on the proportion of a company's capital. These issues should be raised in the tax warranties for confirmation that the requirements of 'no connection' were met.

If the investor is connected or receives a linked loan during the investment period EIS relief will not be available, and will be withdrawn, and no CGT relief would be available on the sale of the EIS shares.[22]

8.1.5 Unpaid directors[23]

So long as a director (alternatively, any associate of an investor who is a director) of the issuing company has not received, or does not/is not entitled to receive, any payments from the company or from any related person (see definition provided below) during the five year period ending on the termination date (an 'unpaid director') he or she will not be considered to be connected with the company and should be entitled to invest in EIS shares and receive EIS reliefs. The following payments made to an unpaid director will be ignored for these purposes:

---

[21] Control – see ITA section 995

[22] TCGA Schedule 5B paragraph 15

[23] ITA section 168

- payments or reimbursement for travelling or other expenses wholly exclusively and necessarily incurred by the individual in the performance of his or her duties as a director;
- interest received representing a reasonable commercial rate of return on money lent to the issuing company or a related person;
- any dividend or other distribution not exceeding a normal return on the investment;
- a payment for the supply of goods not in excess of their market value;
- any rent payment for property occupied by the issuing company or a related person not exceeding a reasonable and commercial rent;
- any necessary and reasonable remuneration paid for services rendered to the issuing company in the course of a trade or profession carried on wholly or partly in the United Kingdom (but not being secretarial or managerial services) and which is taken into account in calculating the profits of the trade or profession for tax purposes.

A 'related person'[24] is any company of which the individual (or his or her associate) is a director and which is a subsidiary or partner of the issuing company or a partner of a subsidiary of the issuing company, and any person connected with any such companies.

8.1.6 Investors becoming paid directors ('Business Angels')[25]

If an investor becomes connected with the investing company by becoming a paid director (or alternatively an associate of an investor becomes a paid director) of the investing company or a subsidiary, or of a company which is a partner of the issuing company, at any time during period A, EIS relief may be available so long as:

- the remuneration in question is reasonable for the services rendered; and
- the investor was issued with the EIS shares at a time when he or

---

[24] ITA section 168(4)

[25] ITA section 169

she had no connection with the issuing company or had never been involved in carrying on the trade, business or profession of the issuing company or its subsidiary (whether on his or her own account, or as a partner, director or employee).

Such an investor will be entitled to make further investments and be capable of receiving relief if he or she makes the investment within three years of having made the first investment.

In the VCM manual, HMRC rather ambiguously state[26] that a director of a company previously carrying on the trade is not regarded as 'having been necessarily involved in carrying on a trade carried on by that company' and that it will be a matter of fact as to whether he or she was involved. The VCM manual refers to the case of *Thomason & Ors v HMRC Commissioners [2010](UKFTT 579)* which established that the test of previous connection and involvement of director should be applied at the time of issue of the shares. In that case, at the time of the share issue the company had no trade so the directors could not have been involved in carrying on the trade of the company previously. The fact the company then went on to acquire a trade that the directors had previously been involved in did not change the eligibility of the shares already issued as the test applies at the time of the share issue. A CAP1 clearance would be in order if this issue arises.

8.1.7   Investor receiving value[27]

If an investor receives value at any time during investment period C either there will be a reduction in the EIS relief if the relief is greater than the amount of the value received (as a percentage of the EIS rate), or the relief will be withdrawn altogether. The provisions do not apply to insignificant amounts of value received, defined as being not more than £1,000.

'Receiving value' is also widely defined and covers the following acts by the issuing company:[28]

---

[26] HMRC manual VCM 11070

[27] ITA section 213

[28] ITA section 216(2)

- any repayment, redemption or repurchase of the investor's shares or securities in the company or making any payment to the investor for giving up any rights relating to the shares or securities on their cancellation;
- any repayment under any arrangements: connected with the acquisition of the EIS shares; of any debt owed to the investor other than a debt which was incurred by the issuing company on or after the issue date of the EIS shares; and in consideration of the extinguishment of a debt incurred before the issue date;
- the making of a payment to an investor for giving up the investor's right to any debt, other than a debt relating to reimbursement for travelling expenses and reasonable remuneration for services of an unpaid director, or for an ordinary trade debt;
- the waiving of any liability of an investor to the issuing company or discharging any liability of the investor to a third person;
- the making of a loan or advance to an investor which has not been repaid in full before the issue of the EIS shares;
- providing a benefit or facility for an investor;
- transferring an asset to an investor for no consideration or for less than market value or acquiring an asset from an investor for more than its market value; or
- the making of any other payment to an investor other than:
  - a payment of a kind mentioned in any of the provisions of ITA section 168(2)(ignoring certain payments made to unpaid directors); or
  - a payment in discharge of an ordinary trade debt.

8.1.8   Qualifying share requirements[29]

The EIS shares must be ordinary shares which do not, during the investment period B, carry any present or future preferential right to dividends or to the company's assets on its winding up, or any present or future right to be redeemed. This reflects changes to the definition of EIS shares in the Finance Act 2012. HMRC consider that a preferential right is one which takes priority over a right

---

[29] ITA section 173

carried by some other shares.[30] In cases where there are two classes of shares such as ordinary shares carrying preferential rights over rights of deferred shares, say, on a winding up, this may not offend the rule against preferential rights as far as HMRC are concerned. In addition, HMRC will not treat shares as having a preferential right in cases where there are two classes of shares in an issuing company and dividends are declared on one class but not the other.

The shares must be subscribed for wholly in cash and fully paid up at the time they are issued. HMRC'S previous advice was that any shares issued during the company registration process (and before a bank account can be opened into which the proceeds would be deposited) would not qualify for relief.[31] HMRC warn in their 2013 guidance[32] that one of the most common reasons for investments failing to qualify for relief under EIS is that shares are issued to investors without the company having received payment for them. They advise that companies and investors should ensure that any shares, on which it is intended EIS relief will be claimed, are not issued during the company registration process but are issued only at a later date when the company is able to receive payment for them.

8.1.9   Annual limits on raising capital

ITA section 173A limits the amount of investments made in the issuing company or any subsidiary (regardless of whether it was a subsidiary of the issuing company at the time of the share issue) to £5 million in any tax year, subscribed for under any risk capital schemes, namely under EIS, SEIS and VCT.

8.1.10 Issuing arrangements and use of the proceeds

The purpose of the share issue must be to raise money for a qualifying business activity all the proceeds must 'employed

---

[30] VCT Manual VCM12030

[31] See HMRC guidance   *An introduction to the Enterprise Investment Scheme – part 1.1* (November 2011)

[32]   https://www.gov.uk/government/publications/the-enterprise-investment-scheme-introduction/enterprise-investment-scheme

wholly for the purposes of a qualifying business activity[33] and be used not later than the second anniversary of the issue date.

The term 'qualifying business activity' means:[34]

- carrying on of a qualifying trade by the issuing company or a qualifying 90% subsidiary on the issue date of the EIS shares;
- preparing to carry on a qualifying trade which the issuing company or any 90% subsidiary intends to carry out wholly or mainly in the United Kingdom and which commences to trade within two years after the issue of the EIS shares;
- carrying on research and development by the issuing company or qualifying 90% subsidiary, which must either be carried on when the EIS shares are issued or be commenced immediately afterwards, and which the company intends should lead to a qualifying trade (R&D).

The Finance Act 2012 amended the definition of qualifying business activity to exclude acquiring existing shares in another company. From 6 April 2012, using the money to acquire shares in another company does not, of itself, count as 'employment' for the purposes of section 179. HMRC state however, if the money is used to acquire shares in a company which after the investment is a 90% qualifying subsidiary, and that subsidiary uses the monies within the appropriate timescale for the purposes of its qualifying activity, then that will be regarded as 'employment' of the monies.[35]

Case law has opined what amounts to preparing to carry on a trade and commencing to trade, and which essentially will be a matter of fact.[36] If a newco is raising money to start up a qualifying trade, it is essential that trading starts within the two year period. Carrying on a trade would include acquiring a trading company

---

[33] ITA section 179(1)

[34] ITA section 179

[35] HMRC 2013 Guidance - Enterprise Investment Scheme

[36] See *Napier v Griffiths [1990] 63 TC 745; Kirk & Randall Ltd v Dunn (1924) STC 663, Birmingham & district Cattle By-Products Co Ltd v IRC (1919) 12 TC 97, Cannop Coal Co Ltd v IRC (1918) 12 TC 31.*

which carries on a qualifying trade or acquiring an existing trade from its owner.

The issuing arrangements must not include any pre-arranged exits,[37] namely arrangements:

- for a subsequent repurchase, exchange or other disposal of the EIS shares or of other shares or securities of the issuing company;
- for the cessation of any trade which is carried on, or may be carried on by the issuing company or by a connected person;
- relating to the disposal of the assets of the issuing company or of a connected person; or
- which have as a main purpose, to provide partial or complete protection for the investors (including by means of insurance, indemnity or guarantee).

8.1.11 EIS income tax relief

This relief takes the form of a reduction in the individual's income tax liability, equal to either tax at the lower rate (20%) on the amount of the subscription or, if that would exceed the taxpayer's liability for the year, whatever amount will reduce his or her income tax liability to nil. EU state aid approval was granted in September 2011 for the increase in the rate of income tax relief from 20% to 30%. The limit on the amount on which relief can be obtained was increased from £500,000 per person per tax year to an annual limit of £1 million[38] applicable for the tax year 2012/13 and thereafter.

The taxpayer can make a claim so long as the trade of the issuing company or its group has been carried on for at least four months and up to the fifth anniversary of the normal self-assessment filing date for the tax year in which the subscription was made.[39] Carry back rules enable an investor to carry back unlimited amounts of EIS relief compared to the previous carry back limits of £25,000. However, the previous annual investment limits will apply to the relevant tax years.

---

[37] ITA section 177

[38] ITA section 158

[39] ITA section 202

EIS relief is taken after any relief for VCT shares and relief on taxable gains on life assurance policies, but any other reliefs and allowance reducing an individual's income tax liability are taken after any EIS relief.

8.1.11.1 *Reduction or withdrawal of EIS relief*

The EIS relief will be reduced if, within the investment period B, the investor disposes of EIS shares by way of an arm's length bargain, with the relief being withdrawn by an amount equal to the EIS rate as a proportion of the consideration received. Any EIS relief given will be withdrawn if, within the investment period B, any of the following events occur:

- the investor disposes of any of the EIS shares not at arm's length;
- there is a change in the share capital of the company such that the qualifying share requirements are no longer met;
- the qualifying company requirements are no longer met, such as loss of independence or by becoming involved in an excluded trade.

There are reporting requirements for both the investor and the issuing company on any of the above events. HMRC have up to six years after the end of the relevant tax year to require the withdrawal or reduction of the relief.[40]

Companies which have raised EIS money are required by law to inform the Small Company Enterprise Centre[41] if they fail to meet any of criteria within 60 days of the event which resulted in the failure.

There are exceptions to the withdrawal of EIS relief where the company is put into liquidation for genuine commercial reasons.

8.1.12 CGT disposal relief[42]

Capital gains on the disposal of EIS shares which qualify for EIS relief and which have been held for three years are exempt for CGT, so long as the income tax relief has not been reduced or

---

[40] ITA section 237

[41] Medvale House, Mote Road, Maidstone Kent ME15 6AF

[42] TCGA section 150A and 150B

withdrawn. If the EIS relief has not been claimed any subsequent disposal of the shares will not qualify for CGT exemption.[43] If a capital loss arises on the sale of EIS shares the base cost will be reduced by the amount of EIS relief[44], with the remaining loss available to offset against capital gains in the tax year when the loss occurs or carried forward in the usual way. The CGT disposal relief will be restricted if the individual does not receive full EIS relief on the subscription of the EIS shares, unless the only reason full income tax relief cannot be given is because the claim reduced the individual's income tax liability to nil. EIS disposal relief will also be restricted if the individual's EIS income tax relief is reduced because the investor has received value from the issuing company; or if the issuing company repays, reduces or repurchases any of its share capital or makes payments for giving up rights to share capital.

8.1.13 CGT deferral relief[45]

Individuals and certain trustees who are UK resident or ordinarily UK resident and who is not regarded as being resident elsewhere can defer capital gains of any amount arising on the sale of any capital assets, by rolling over the gains and re-investing the receipts into EIS shares of an amount equivalent to the chargeable gain, within the period beginning three years before and ending one year after the disposal of the asset. The residency requirements must be met at the time the gain is accrued and at the time of the reinvestment. The time limit for claiming the CGT deferral relief is five years from 31 January following the end of the tax year in which the EIS shares were issued. On the sale of the EIS shares the rolled-over gains will crystallise and become payable, unless there is a new reinvestment of the rolled-over gains into other EIS shares under the legislation.

There are no minimum or maximum amounts for deferral and the investor may be connected with the company. Furthermore, there

---

[43] See HMRC *An Introduction to the Enterprise Investment Scheme* paragraph 1.2.2 (November 2011)

[44] TCGA section 150A(1)

[45] TCGA section 150C and Schedule 5B

is no minimum period during which the EIS shares must be held. However, an individual may not claim both entrepreneurs relief and CGT deferral relief.

8.1.14 Clearance procedure

Before any fundraising, the issuing company should approach HMRC SCEC division for informal advance assurance that the EIS requirements will be met in respect of shares to be issued, the company's trade, and the use of the money to be raised through the share issue. This is done using form EIS(AA) (available on the HMRC website along with guidance[46] which provides the information to be provided in the application and the additional documents which must be attached to it).

The written application[47] should include the following information and documents:

- a copy of the latest available accounts of the company, and of any subsidiary company;
- details of all trading or other activities to be carried on by the company and any subsidiary, and a note of which company or companies will use the money raised;
- the approximate sum the company hopes to raise, and how it will be used;
- confirmation that the company expects to be able to complete the declaration on form EIS1 in due course;
- a copy of the latest draft of any prospectus or similar document to be issued to potential investors;
- an up-to-date copy of the memorandum and articles of association of the company and of any subsidiary, and details of any changes to be made; and
- details of any subscription agreement or other side agreement to be entered into by the shareholders.[48]

The issuing company may be raising more than the permitted EIS maximum of £5 million in which case the application will be in respect of that portion of the fundraising only.

---

[46] www.hmrc.gov.uk/manuals/vcmmanual/VCM14000.htm

[47] See form EIS(AA) (www.hmrc.gov.uk/forms/eis-aa-bw.pdf)

[48] www.hmrc.gov.uk/manuals/vcmmanual/VCM14040.htm

VENTURE CAPITAL SCHEMES

Following the fundraising and issue of the shares and so long as the issuing company has been trading or carrying on the relevant R&D activities for at least four months it can submit form EIS1, which is a statutory declaration by the issuing company confirming its compliance with the relevant requirements. Only after the company has received permission from HMRC via the issue of form EIS2 can the company issue form EIS3 to the relevant investors which enable them to claim income tax relief and CGT deferral relief. A company must submit form EIS1 no later than the second anniversary of the tax year in which the EIS shares were issued or two years after the end of the period of the first four months of trading.

8.1.15 Transactional issues

A number of the following issues may arise in the sale and purchase of a company.

8.1.15.1 The target is an issuing EIS company

- Does the target company satisfy the criteria set out in paragraph 8.1.2 above and will paragraph 8.1.10 requirements be met?
- Do sponsors of the target company fall within any of the criteria relating to potentially eligible investors qualifying for EIS relief (paragraph 8.1.3)?
- Has the annual investment limit (currently £5 million) under paragraph 8.1.9 been exceeded?
- Has an informal clearance been applied for before the EIS issue?

8.1.15.2 The target company is an EIS company being acquired by non-EIS company

- Will EIS relief be withdrawn due to the change of control of the target within three years of the latest issue of EIS shares?

8.1.15.3 Management Buy-outs involving an EIS company

EIS relief will not be available to connected individuals involved in a management buy-out and would only be available for unconnected investors not previously involved in the trade or business.

8.2   Seed Enterprise Investment Scheme

8.2.1   Background

The scheme was introduced by FA 2012 with the legislation contained in ITA 2007 sections 257A to 257HJ for small trading companies carrying on new businesses. The principles of the SEIS scheme are very similar to the EIS scheme, save for the size of the investee company and much smaller limits on investments by subscriber.

The legislation refers to two periods, namely:

- **Period A** – beginning with the date of the company's incorporation and ending immediately before the third anniversary of the date the SEIS shares are issued; and

- **Period B** – the period beginning with the date of the issue of the SEIS shares and ending immediately before the third anniversary of that issue date.

An individual investor who subscribes for shares in a qualifying company and the purpose of the issue and use of the money raised fall within the scheme's requirements, is entitled to income tax relief of 50% up to a maximum of £100,000. CGT relief may be available on disposals of SEIS shares as will CGT deferral relief on investment into SEIS shares. Similar to EIS rules an SEIS investor or an associate of the investor:

- cannot be an employee of the company during period B (but he or she may be a director);
- must not have any linked loan (as for EIS investments);
- the subscription must not involve any tax avoidance;
- cannot have an interest in the company of more than 30% in the company's ordinary share capital, issued share capital or voting power ('substantial interest'); and
- must not be involved in any related investment arrangements, defined as arrangements which provide for another person to subscribe for shares in another company in which the SEIS investor or any other individual who is party to the arrangement, has a substantial interest.

8.2.2 Company requirements

The issuing company[49] must have 25 or fewer full time employees (including directors) and gross assets of no more than £200,000 immediately before the SEIS shares are issued, and must be carrying on or be preparing to carry on a new business. Relief is restricted to a cumulative investment limit of £150,000 for a company.

The issuing company ('qualifying company') must also meet the following criteria:

- it must exist wholly for the purpose of carrying on one or more new qualifying trades during period B, and it must not exist wholly or to a substantial degree in the carrying on of non-qualifying activities;
- it must satisfy the financial health requirement at the beginning of period B – namely the issuing company is not in financial difficulty;
- it must carry on a trade which is commercial, with a view to profit and is not an excluded activity identical to the EIS requirements;
- the qualifying trade must be new – and therefore one which has not been carried on by either the issuing company for longer than two years at the date of the SEIS issue;
- throughout period B the issuing company must have a UK permanent establishment;
- at the beginning of period B the issuing company must be an unquoted company and there must be no arrangements in existence at that time to become quoted;
- it must at no time be a member of a partnership during period A (this applies equally to any 90% subsidiary);
- there must be no arrangements for issuing company to become a subsidiary of another company under an exchange of shares;
- during period A the issuing company must not at any time be under the control of any other company, or under the control of another company and any person connected with that other

---

[49] If the investee company is a parent company, the restrictions will apply to the value of the group's assets

company, and there must be no arrangements at any time in period A whereby the issuing company could fail this test;

- the company must have not received any capital from another risk capital scheme before the SEIS shares are issued.

The SEIS company must provide HMRC with a compliance statement following which it can issue a compliance certificate, which can be issued once one of the following conditions have been met:

- at least 70% of the money raised by the issue has been spent for the purposes of the qualifying business activity for which it was raised; or
- the new qualifying trade which constitutes the qualifying business activity or to which that activity relates has been carried on by the issuing company or a qualifying 90% subsidiary of that company for at least four months.

8.2.3   Withdrawal of SEIS relief

SEIS will be withdrawn or reduced (as indicated) in the following circumstances:

- the investor disposes of any of the SEIS shares before the end of period B other than by way of a bargain at arm's length – if sold at arm's length the relief will be reduced be a formula relating to the original relief;
- the grant by the investor of a binding option whereby the investor is bound to sell the SEIS shares;
- the grant of a put option to the investor whereby the grantor is bound to purchase the SEIS shares from the investor;
- if the investor receives value from the company at any time period A in certain circumstances the relief will be reduced by a formula including the SEIS relief received but excluding receipts of insignificant values as defined in the legislation;
- during period A the SEIS company or any qualifying subsidiary:
  - begins to carry on as its trade, or as part of its trade, a trade which was previously carried on at any time in that period otherwise than by the company or any qualifying subsidiary, or

- acquires the whole, or the greater part, of the assets used for the purposes of a trade previously so carried on, and
- the SEIS investor has an interest amounting in total to more than a half share in the trade (as previously carried on) belonged at any time in period A, and is a person or group of persons to whom such an interest in the trade carried on by the company belongs or has, at any such time, belonged;
- if the SEIS company acquires all of the issued share capital of another company at any time in period A, and the SEIS investor controls or has controlled the SEIS company at any time in period A and at any such time controlled the other company;
- where SEIS relief is found not to have been due.

SEIS relief will not be withdrawn on a share for share exchange, whereby new shares are issued by a newco in respect of and in proportion to the original (old) shares.[50] When the requirements are met SEIS will be carried over.

8.2.4   Transactional Issues

8.2.4.1   The target is an issuing SEIS company

- Does the target company satisfy the SEIS criteria set out in paragraph 8.2.2 above?
- Do sponsors of the target company fall within any of the criteria relating to potentially eligible investors qualifying for SEIS relief?
- Has the annual investment limit (£150,000) been exceeded?

8.2.4.2   The target company is an SEIS company being acquired by non-SEIS company

- Will SEIS relief be withdrawn due to the change of control of the target within three years of the latest issue of SEIS shares?

8.3   Venture Capital Trusts

8.3.1   Background

VCTs are quoted investment trust companies approved by HMRC, which invest eligible shares, namely in unquoted trading companies satisfying a number of criteria but include EIS and SEIS criteria. There are strict reporting requirements for VCTs to ensure

---

[50] ITA section 257HB

that all the investment conditions are met in each of its accounting periods and they are usually audited by accountants who specialise in VCT audits. A VCT will not be subject to corporation tax on chargeable gains on its investments.[51] However, providing advice to VCTs is a specialist subject and not within the remit of this publication.

The re-write of the VCT rules is contained in ITA section 258 to 332, applying to VCT shares issued after 5 April 2006, and which provide for income tax relief on amounts subscribed for in the VCT by individuals ('VCT relief'). Tax relief on dividends received is set out in ITTOIA sections 709 to 712, and exemptions from capital gains tax on VCT investments is set out in TCGA sections 100 and 151A. The regulations relating to conditions and approvals for VCT status (full approval and provisional approval), reporting requirements, and tax reliefs are set out in SI 1995/1979.

VCT shares must be held for a period of at least five years in order for the individual investor to remain eligible for the relief,[52] rather than the three year holding requirements under EIS and SEIS. Deferral of capital gains by reinvestment into VCT shares was repealed by FA 2004 for shares issued after 5 April 2004.

8.3.2 VCT requirements

To be approved as a VCT the company must meet the following criteria[53] in the most recent accounting period, and must continue to meet them in the accounting period for which VCT approval is sought:

- its ordinary share capital must be admitted to trading on a regulated market[54];
- it cannot be a close company;[55]
- its income must be derived wholly or mainly from 'shares' or 'securities' (see definition below);

---

[51] TCGA section 100

[52] ITA section 266(1)(b)

[53] ITA section 274

[54] ITA section 274(2) – applicable on or after 6 April 2011 – regulated market defined under directive 2004/39/EC

[55] ITA section 259(1)(a)

- it has not retained or will not retain more than 15% of the income derived from shares or securities;
- it has no holding in any company, other than another VCT or a company which would qualify as a VCT save for the listing requirement, which represents or will represent more than 15% by value of its investments;
- at least 70% (by value) of its investments has been or will be represented by shares or securities included in qualifying holdings;
- at least 70% (by value) of its qualifying holdings has been or will be holdings in eligible shares; and
- the company has not made and will not make an investment in the relevant period in a company which breaches the permitted investment limits.

8.3.2.1 Definition of a security

A security is defined as including any liability of the VCT relating to a loan (either secured or unsecured) but not loans which require repayment, repurchase or redemption within the period of five years from the making of the loan or the issue of the stock or security; or any stock or security relating to a loan made to the VCT which allow its repayment, repurchase or redemption within that period.[56]

8.3.2.2 Eligible Shares

Eligible shares are ordinary shares which throughout the period of five years beginning on the date on which they are issued, carry no present or future preferential rights to dividends, and have no present or future right to be redeemed.[57]

8.3.2.3 Qualifying holdings by VCT investing companies

The following requirements must be met in respect of the shares and securities first issued to the investing company by the investee company:

- the relevant holding cannot exceed £1 million (the 'maximum qualifying investment').[58] This compares with a limit of £2

---

[56] ITA section 285(2)

[57] ITA section 273(1)

[58] ITA section 287

million which is the total amount of relevant investments made in an issuing company in a year;[59]

- the relevant holding must not include securities relating to a guaranteed loan,[60] defined as arrangements whereby the investing company becomes entitled to receive something from a third party in the event of the failure by any person to comply either with the terms of the loan to which the security relates or the terms of the security;
- the investee company must have a UK permanent establishment and satisfy the financial health requirement at the time of the issue of the relevant holding – namely it is not in difficulty;
- eligible shares must represent at least 10% by value of the totality of the shares or securities of the investee company (including the relevant holding) which are held by the investing company;
- the investee company must carry on a qualifying activity, being a 'qualifying trade' (see below for definition) at all times from the issue of the VCT shares. If the trade has not commenced at the issue date it must be intended to be so carried on, and must commence before the second anniversary of the issue date;
- the investee company must exist wholly in carrying on one or more qualifying trades (meaning a trade which is conducted on a commercial basis with a view to the realisation of profits and which does not consist wholly or substantially in carrying on excluded activities). If the investee company is a parent company the business of the group must not consist wholly or substantially in carrying on non-qualifying activities (being 'excluded activities' – see below) or activities carried on otherwise than in the course of a trade;
- further to the definition of a qualifying trade, this is satisfied if research and development activities are carried on and it is intended that a trade will be derived from the R&D activities which will be a qualifying trade and will be carried on wholly

---

[59] ITA section 173A

[60] ITA section 288

or mainly in the United Kingdom. However, preparing to carry on research and development does not satisfy the requirements of preparing to carry on a qualifying trade;

- the total amount of investments under the EIS, SEIS and VCT schemes made in the investee company in the tax year ending on the issue date must not exceed £5 million;
- the money raised must be employed wholly for the purposes of a qualifying activity within two years of the issue date;
- the qualifying activity must be carried on either by the investee company or a 90% subsidiary;
- the shares, stocks, debentures and other securities of the investee company are unquoted and therefore not marketed to the general public through a listing on a recognised stock exchange or on a designated exchange in a country outside the United Kingdom or dealt in outside the United Kingdom as may be designated by HMRC;[61]
- the investee company must not control (either alone or together with any connected person) any company which is not a 'qualifying subsidiary' (see definition below) and the investee company must not be under the control of another company (or of another company and any other person connected with that other company);
- every subsidiary of the investee company must be a 'qualifying subsidiary', namely a 51% subsidiary of the investee company, and no person other than the investee company or another of its subsidiaries has control of the subsidiary and there are no arrangements where these conditions would cease to be met;
- the gross assets of the investee company (if a single company and not a holding company of a group) must not exceed £15 million immediately before the issue of the VCT shares and must not exceed £16 million immediately after the issue;
- if the investee company is a parent company the value of the group assets must not exceed £15 million immediately before the issue of the VCT shares and must not exceed £16 million immediately afterwards. In measuring the values, any intra-

---

[61] ITA section 295

THE TAX SCHEDULE

group holdings in shares and securities will be ignored;

- the investee company must have fewer than 250 full-time employees at the time the VCT shares are issues, or alternatively part-time equivalent numbers;
- if the investee company has a subsidiary whose business consists wholly or mainly in the holding or managing of land or property deriving its value from land, it must be a qualifying 90% subsidiary.

8.3.2.4   Excluded activities[62]

These are defined as follows (and mirror those for EIS relief):

- dealing in land, in commodities or futures or in shares, securities or other financial instruments;
- dealing in goods otherwise than in the course of an ordinary trade of wholesale or retail distribution;
- banking, insurance, money-lending, debt-factoring, hire-purchase financing or other financial activities;
- leasing (including letting ships on charter or other assets on hire);
- receiving royalties or licence fees;
- providing legal or accountancy services;
- property development;
- farming or market gardening;
- holding, managing or occupying woodlands, any other forestry activities or timber production;
- shipbuilding;
- producing coal;
- producing steel;
- operating or managing hotels or comparable establishments or managing property used as an hotel or comparable establishment;
- operating or managing nursing homes or residential care homes or managing property used as a nursing home or residential care home;
- the subsidised generation or export of electricity;
- the subsidised generation of heat or subsidised production of

---

[62] ITA section 303 to 310

gas or fuel; and

- providing services or facilities carried on by another person when the business falls within the above activities and the controlling interest in the business is held by a person which also has a controlling interest in the business of the service provider.

The Finance Act 2012 brought in a new disqualifying purpose test identical to mirror the same provisions for EIS, whereby shares which are issued subject to arrangements the main purpose of which is to generate access to the reliefs in circumstances where either the benefit of the investment is passed to another party to the arrangements, or the business activities would otherwise be carried on by another party, will be disqualified.

8.3.3   Investor reliefs

8.3.3.1   *Income Tax Relief* [63]

An individual is entitled to claim income tax relief if he or she subscribes on his/her own behalf for newly issued eligible shares in the VCT during a tax year. The issue and subscription must be for genuine commercial reasons and not under tax avoidance arrangements. The investor must be at least 18 years old at the date of issue and the maximum investment must not be more than £200,000 in any tax year. For VCT shares issued before April 2004 the rate of relief was 20%; for shares issued between 6 April 2004 and 5 April 2006 it was 40%; and for shares issued after 5 April 2006 it is 30%.

An investor will be barred from income tax relief if he or she (or an associate) receives a linked loan, (which includes the giving of any credit and the assignment of any debt) at any time during the period beginning either on the incorporation of the VCT or, if later, two years before the issue of the VCT shares and ending on the fifth anniversary of the issue. A linked loan is defined as one which would not have been made or would not have been made

---

[63] ITA sections 261 to 273

on the same terms if the individual has not subscribed for the relevant shares or have not been proposing to do so[64].

For VCT shares which were issued after 5 April 2006 the VCT relief will be lost if the shares are disposed of within five years of their issue on the following basis:[65]

- if the disposal is made otherwise than on an arm's length basis the VCT relief will be withdrawn in its entirety;
- if the disposal is made on an arm's length basis and the VCT relief claimed was greater than 30% of the consideration received for the disposal the relief equal to the 30% will be withdrawn;
- if the VCT relief is equal to or less than 30% of the consideration received it will be withdrawn.

If HMRC approval for a VCT is withdrawn, individuals holding shares at that time on which VCT income tax relief has been obtained will be treated as having disposed of the VCT shares immediately before the date on which the withdrawal takes effect on a non-arm's length basis. The effect will be withdrawal of VCT relief in respect of the tax year in which the relief was originally obtained. It is the individual's obligation to notify HMRC of any event whereby the provisions apply within 60 days of the event coming to his or her attention.

8.3.3.2   CGT Relief [66]

Where there is a gain or loss accruing to an individual investor in VCT shares, and the company was a VCT at the time of acquisition, any disposal will not be treated as either a chargeable gain or an allowable loss. The investor need not have subscribed for the shares but they must be within the maximum annual limits for subscription permitted under the VCT legislation for the years in question when purchased or subscribed for. There is no requirement to hold the shares for five years but if the VCT shares are sold within that time period the VCT relief will be reduced or withdrawn.

---

[64] ITA section 264(3)

[65] ITA section 266

[66] TCGA section 151A

8.3.3.3 *Dividend tax relief*

No income tax will arise on a dividend paid by a VCT in respect of its ordinary shares so long as the VCT requirements were met when the VCT shares were acquired, at the end of the accounting period in which the profits or gains arose in respect of which the dividend was paid and when the dividend was paid. Other requirements are as follows:

- the shareholder must be beneficially entitled to the dividend, and be at least 18 years old;
- when the VCT shares were acquired their maximum value did not exceed £200,000 as measured at the time of acquisition or acquisitions; and
- the VCT shares were acquired for genuine commercial reasons and not for tax avoidance purposes.

8.3.4 Transactional issues

If the transaction involves the acquisition of an EIS or SEIS company by a VCT, the requirements under the legislation must be met and advance assurance from HMRC should be sought. Primarily, these will be issues for the buyer. If the seller is a VCT disposing of an EIS company, an analysis of the effect of the disposal on the VCT reliefs will be required for the seller.

8.4 Social Investment Tax Relief

8.4.1 Background

It may be that there will be few transactions involving SITR in the near term. The SITR was introduced by FA 2014 with effect from 17 July 2014 and for the moment has a five year life span, up to 5 April 2019. It differs from the EIS and the SEIS in that the investment may be by way of shares as well as in debentures.

A social enterprise will be an organisation which helps people and communities, being any of the following:-

- a community interest company;
- a community benefits society[67] which is not a charity;
- a charity;
- an accredited social impact contractor company;[68] or

---

[67] As defined in ITA section 257JB

- any other body prescribed by the Treasury under statutory instrument.

If the social enterprise (**SE**) is neither a charity nor the parent company of a group it must not carry on non-trading activities either in the course of a trade or in the course of preparing to carry on a trade, nor can it carry on excluded activities if they form a substantial part of the trade as a whole.

Investors (being individuals only) are entitled to invest up to a maximum of £1 million per annum with no minimum investment, and income tax relief will be available at a rate of 30% to subscribers under the rules. The investments can be made either in shares or in new qualifying debt instruments. The 'applicable period' of investment will be three years either from the date when the investment is made or from the date the social enterprise is incorporated or established, as the case may be. So long as the investments have SITR income tax relief and are held for three years no tax will arise on capital gains on disposal (the **Investment Period**). Additionally roll over relief on capital gains is available whereby tax can be deferred if capital gain is reinvested into qualifying SE shares and debt. Such a gain must arise during the period from 6April 2014 to 5 April 2019 and the SITR investment must be made in the period one year before and three years are the gain arises.

None of the SITR reliefs will be available if the investor has received relief for the investment under the EIS, the SEIS or the community investment tax relief (CITR)

The requirements of SE shares are as follows:[69]

- they must not carry a right to a return which is a fixed rate; and
- in the event of a winding up of the SE the shares rank after all debts other than the SE debt investments, and the shares do not rank above any other shares in the SE.

---

[68] ITA 2007 section 25JD

[69] ITA section 257L(2) & (3)

A qualifying debt investment means any debentures in the SE where the following conditions are met:[70]

- neither the principal nor an return is charged on any assets;
- the rate of return is not greater than a reasonable commercial rate of return; and
- in the event of the winding up of the SE any sums due in respect of the debt:
  - are subordinated to all other debts of the SE except sums due in the case of other unsecured debentures of the SE which rank equally;
  - rank equally, if there are shares in the SE and they all rank equally among themselves, with amounts due to shareholders; and
  - rank equally, if there are shares in the SE and they do not all rank equally, with amounts due in respect of their shares to the holders of shares that do not rank above any other shares.

There must be no pre-arranged exits requirements and the issuing arrangements for the investment must not include any arrangements with a view to the cessation of any trade or any arrangements for the disposal of assets of the SE. Furthermore there must be no arrangements in existence which could provide partial or complete protection for the investor against what would otherwise be the risks attached to making the investment.

As with EIS and SEIS requirements there are the requirements that there can be no linked loans with the investor or an associate of the investor; there must be no tax avoidance arrangement involving the investment; and the investor must not be:

- an employee of the enterprise or its subsidiary or of its partner;
- a partner or trustee of the SE or its subsidiary; or
- a remunerated director of the SE or a linked company (being a subsidiary, a company which is a partner of the SE or its subsidiary).[71]

---

[70] ITA section 257L(4)

[71] ITA section 257LF

THE TAX SCHEDULE

The value of the assets of the SE organisation (be it a company of group) must not exceed £15 million immediately before the investment is made and not more than £15 million immediately after. The SE cannot be a quoted company and there must be no arrangements to become so. The independence requirements, which must be satisfied over the three year investment period, is that the SI must not be a 51% subsidiary of a company or be under the control of a company and a person connected with the company, without being a 51% subsidiary of the company; and the SI must not be a members of any partnership.

The SE must not have full time employees of more than 500 when the investment is made and it must meet the trading requirements.

The SE must use all money raised from the SE investment within 28 months for the purposes of carrying on the qualifying trade or preparing to carry on the trade which must start within 2 years of the date of the investment. That will not include buying shares or stock in a company although the SE may invest the money raised in a 90% social subsidiary. If the trade is not carried on either by the social enterprise itself or a 90% social subsidiary of the SE the SITR relief will be lost.

The following trades will not qualify under the SITR rules:
- dealing in land, in commodities or futures, in shares, securities or other financial instruments;
- banking, insurance, money-lending, debt-factoring, hire-purchase financing or other financial activities (with the exception of lending money to another social enterprise);
- property development;
- activities in the fishery and aquaculture sector covered by Council Regulation (EC) No 104/2000 of 17 December 1999;
- the primary production of products listed in Annex 1 to the Treaty on the Functioning of the European Union (agricultural products);
- generating or exporting electricity which will attract a feed-in-tariff;
- road freight transport for hire or reward; and

- providing services to another person where that person's trade substantially consist of the above excluded activities.

Some or all of the SITR relief will be withdrawn if at any time during the investment period any of the following occur:

- the investment is disposed of (except to a spouse or civil partner);
- the investor or his/her associate receive 'value' from the SE, or from a person connected with the SE; or
- the SE repays, redeems or repurchases any of its share capital held by another person, but doesn't apply if the other person has had tax relief on their investment which has been withdrawn.

8.5   Corporate Venturing Scheme (CVS)[72]

8.5.1   Background

The scheme became effective on 1 April 2000 and came to an end for qualifying investments on 31 March 2010 and, therefore, the description of the legislation is put in the past tense. The effective end date of the scheme was 31 March 2013 for any investment made just before the end closure of the scheme and, therefore, CVS issues are unlikely to be relevant in a transaction involving an investing company or an investee company before that date, save for investments where the trade had not commenced at the time shares were issued.

Under the scheme certain companies could make a direct investment as minority shareholders in small trading companies and obtain:

- corporation tax relief for the amount subscribed for ('investment relief');
- relief against income for losses on disposal of shares to which investment relief applies; and
- deferral of chargeable gains on the sale of shares, where gains are reinvested in shares to which investment relief applied.[73]

---

[72] FA 2000 Schedule 15

[73] FA 2000 Schedule 15 paragraph 1

There were no UK residency requirements for either the investing or issuing company, although the issuing company's trade was required to be wholly or substantially wholly UK-based.[74]

In order for the investment relief to apply (or not to be withdrawn) the shares in the investee company were required to be held for a three year period, beginning with the date of issue if the trade of the issuing company has commenced. Otherwise, the three year period began with the date on which the trade begins.[75]

Since 19 July 2007 an issuing company was restricted in each tax year to issuing shares not greater than £2 million in total to any VCTs, through EIS investments and under the CVS. This limit applied to any such investments in subsidiaries of the issuing company but does not apply to funds raised by a VCT before 19 July 2007.

The issuing arrangements for the CVS shares could not include arrangements involving a pre-arranged exit. However, HMRC accepted[76] that a company may indicate in advance to potential investors how the directors envisage the shares in the company might eventually be disposed of at a later date.

8.5.2 Qualifying investing company

The investing company was eligible for investment relief subject to the following conditions:

- it must neither hold a material interest in the issuing company, nor control the company (essentially 30%);
- the investment must not be made as part of any arrangements which provide for any other person to subscribe for shares in a related company (a related company being a company in which the investing company has a material interest);
- throughout the qualifying investment period the investing company must exist for the purposes of carrying on one or more non-financial trades (ignoring incidental purposes). This

---

[74] Following the receipt of formal state aid approval from the EU in 2009 relating to the CVS, EIS and VCT schemes, there was a relaxation of the rules relating to the location of the investee companies' qualifying activities, which was provided for in the FA 2010.

[75] FA 2000 Schedule 15 paragraph 3

[76] See HMRC Manuals VCM 12120 and 12130

requirement equally applied to groups of which one of the companies was the investing company.[77] A non-financial trade is defined as a trade carried out on a commercial basis with a view to realising profits and which does not consist wholly or to a substantial degree of carrying on financial activities;

- the CVS shares must be held as chargeable assets by the investing company immediately after issue; and
- there must be no tax avoidance purposes for the investment.

8.5.3   Qualifying issuing company

The requirements which the issuing company must satisfy are as follows:

- it was unquoted at the time the CVS shares were issued and there were no arrangements at that time for any of its shares, debentures or securities to be listed;[78]
- during the qualifying investment period:
  - it was independent;[79]
  - at least 20% of its ordinary share capital was beneficially owned by one or more 'independent individual(s)', namely any individual who throughout the period he or she owned the CVS shares was not a director or employee of the investing company or any company connected with the investing company or a relative of such a director or employee;
  - neither the issuing company nor any of its qualifying subsidiaries could be a member of:
    - a partnership in which the qualifying trade was carried on by the partners (in partnership), and the other partners included at least one other company, and the same person or persons were the beneficial owner(s) of more than 75% of the issued share capital or the ordinary share capital of both the issuing company and at least one of the other partners; or
    - a joint venture in which the qualifying trade was carried

---

[77] FA 2000 Schedule 15 paragraph 10

[78] FA 2000 Schedule 15 paragraph 18

[79] FA 2000 Schedule 15 paragraph 17

on by the issuing company in its capacity as a party to the joint venture, the other parties to the joint venture included at least one other company, and the same person(s) were the beneficial owner(s) or more than 75% of the issued share capital or ordinary share capital of both the issuing company and at least one other party to the joint venture;[80]

- all subsidiaries of the issuing company were 51% subsidiaries and were not under the control of any other person[81] and there were no arrangements whereby this requirement would not be met ('qualifying subsidiaries');[82]
- any subsidiary whose business consists wholly or mainly of holding or managing land or property was a qualifying 90% subsidiary of the issuing company;
- it has to satisfy the trading activities requirement (see paragraph 8.5.4 below); and
- the gross assets of the issuing company must not have been more than £7 million immediately before the issue of the shares and greater than £8 million immediately afterwards, and the issuing company or group must have had fewer than 50 full-time employees (or equivalent part-time employees) at the time of issue.

8.5.4 Trading activities requirements

The trading activities were required to be carried out either by the issuing company or a 90% subsidiary[83] and must exist wholly for the purposes of carrying on one or more qualifying trades (save for incidental purposes). If at the date of issue the issuing company or relevant 90% subsidiary had not begun trading, it was required to do so within two years of the issue date. A qualifying trade is defined as one which is carried on wholly or mainly in the United Kingdom, is conducted on a commercial basis with a view

---

[80] FA 2000 Schedule 15 paragraph 19

[81] Meaning that the affairs of the company are conducted in accordance with the wishes of that person

[82] FA 2000 Schedule 15 paragraphs 20 & 21

[83] Not less than 90% of issued share capital and not less than 90% voting power – see FA 2000 Schedule 15 paragraph 23A

to realising profits and which does not consist wholly or substantially in carrying out excluded activities. R&D activities which are intended to result in a connected qualifying trade are treated as carrying on a qualifying trade, but preparing to carry on R&D activities does not count as preparing to carry on a qualifying trade.

8.5.4.1 Excluded activities[84]

These are identical to the excluded activities for EIS and SEIS companies and VCT, as follows:

- dealing in land, in commodities or futures or in shares, securities or other financial instruments;
- dealing in goods otherwise than in the course of an ordinary trade of wholesale or retail distribution;
- banking, insurance, money-lending, debt-factoring, hire-purchase financing or other financial activities;
- leasing (including letting ships on charter or other assets on hire) or receiving royalties or other licence fees;
- providing legal or accountancy services;
- property development;
- farming or market gardening;
- holding, managing or occupying woodlands, any other forestry activities or timber production;
- shipbuilding;
- producing coal;
- producing steel;
- operating or managing hotels or comparable establishments or managing property used as a hotel or comparable establishment;
- operating or managing nursing homes or residential care homes, or managing property used as a nursing home or residential care home; and
- providing services or facilities for a business carried on by another person where the business consists to a substantial extent of the above excluded activities, and a controlling interest in the business is held by a person who also has a

---

[84] FA 2000 Schedule 15 paragraph 26

controlling interest in the business carried on by the company providing the services or facilities.[85]

8.5.5 Withdrawal of investment relief[86]

If the investment shares were disposed of during the qualifying investment period, the investment relief was withdrawn completely if the disposal fell within one of the following circumstances:

- the disposal was not by way of a bargain made at arm's length for full consideration;
- the disposal was not by way of a distribution in the course of dissolving or winding up of the issuing company;
- the disposal was one falling within TCGA section 24(1);[87] or
- there was a deemed disposal under section 24(2) TCGA under a claim that the value of an asset had become negligible.

If the disposal of the shares during the qualifying investment period was due to any of the above circumstances, and the investment relief was greater than 20% of the proceeds, the relief would be withdrawn by whichever was the smaller of the amount of the investment relief and 20% of the proceeds.

8.5.6 Loss relief

If the investing company incurs an allowable loss on the disposal of CVS shares on which investment relief applied (and which was not withdrawn) it would be entitled to relief so long as the shares were held continuously by the company from the date of issue until disposal, and the disposal fell within any of the kind referred to in paragraph 8.5.5 above. Where loss relief applied, the investing company could make a claim that the loss be set off, for the purposes of corporation tax, against income of the accounting period in which the loss is incurred or, if claimed, of accounting periods ending within the preceding 12 month period.

---

[85] FA 2000 Schedule 15 paragraph 33

[86] FA 2000 Schedule 15 paragraph 46

[87] Disposal where assets lost or destroyed or become of negligible value

8.5.7   Compliance statement and certificate

The issuing company must provide a compliance statement to HMRC which confirms that CVS investment relief requirements were met at the time the CVS shares were issued and have continued to be met at the date of the compliance statement. A statement could not be made until the issuing company had carried on the trade for at least four months and not later than two years after the end of that accounting period. On receiving relevant permission from HMRC the issuing company could issue a compliance certificate to investing companies which stated that the requirements for CVS relief are for the time being met in respect of the CVS shares. Claims by the investing company were made under self-assessment for the accounting period in which the investment was made so long as the investing company has received the compliance certificate from the issuing company.

8.5.8   Transactional issues

If the target company was an issuing company for CVS purposes the buyer should verify that the clearance application was in order and all relevant conditions satisfied. If the target company was an investing company for CVS purposes the main issues will be whether the CVS reliefs were properly applied and that there will be no withdrawal due to its sale during the qualifying investment period.

9   GROUP ISSUES

There are four separate categories of what comprises a group in UK tax legislation. All share the same principle that intra-group transfers can essentially be ignored for tax purposes at the time of transfer, and thereby enable a group to organise its commercial and tax affairs efficiently. The various group relief provisions include anti-avoidance rules.

Where target is leaving a group a number of specific provisions will be required in the tax schedule and there are likely to be issues relating to pre-completion conduct by the seller. If the target is a group, the seller should ensure that it has been compliant with group-related tax legislation, and if the target company is leaving a group due diligence should ensure that no tax charge can attach to it as a result of its acquisition. The standard tax indemnity wording puts the liabilities on the seller for most tax charges which might arise relating to group issues, but the warranties should be drafted so that all group issues are covered to ensure disclosure if relevant.

9.1   Chargeable Gains Groups

A group for chargeable gains purposes is one where there is a principal company which has 75% subsidiaries and any 75% subsidiaries of such subsidiaries and so on, so long as there are no subsidiaries which are not effective 51% subsidiaries of the principal company.[1] A principal company cannot be a 75% subsidiary of another company and a company cannot be a member of more than one chargeable gains group. If a company could be a member of more than one group, there is a series of tests which determine which group it will be a member of, as set out in TCGA section 170(6). There is no requirement that a group company must be UK resident.

A company will be a 75% subsidiary of another corporate body so long as not less than 75% of its ordinary share capital is owned directly or indirectly by that other corporate body.[2] A company

---

[1] TCGA section 170(3)

[2] CTA 2010 section 1154(3) by virtue of TCGA section 170(2)(c)

will be an effective 51% subsidiary (the subsidiary) of the principal company only if the principal company is beneficially entitled to more than 50% of any profits available for distribution to equity holders of the subsidiary and the principal company would be beneficially entitled to more than 50% of any assets of the subsidiary available for distribution to its equity holders on a winding up.[3]

Any transfer of a chargeable capital asset between members of a chargeable gains group will automatically be considered to have been made on a no gain/no loss basis and disregarded for chargeable gains purposes, and any payment made for the transfer will be ignored, under TCGA section 171 (*Transfers within a group: general provisions*) so long as:

- the transferor company is resident in the UK at the time of the disposal, or the asset is a chargeable asset in relation to that company immediately before the disposal; and
- the transferee company is resident in the UK at the time of the disposal, or the asset is a chargeable asset in relation to that company immediately after the transfer.

The no gain/no loss provisions do not apply to the following transactions:[4]

- a disposal of a debt due from the transferee company effected by satisfying the debt or part of it;
- a disposal of redeemable shares in a company on their redemption;
- a disposal by or to an investment trust;
- a disposal by or to a venture capital trust;
- a disposal by or to a qualifying friendly society;
- a disposal to a dual-resident investing company;
- a disposal by or to a company which is, or is a member of, a UK REIT; or
- a disposal by the transferor company in fulfilment of its obligations under an option granted to the transferee at a time when the companies were not members of the same group.

---

[3] TCGA section 170 (7)

[4] TCGA section 171(2)

The commercial effect of these provisions is that intra-group transactions can be ignored for chargeable gains purposes at the time they are effected. However, if the transferee leaves the group within six years of the transfer still owning the transferred asset, any gain or loss on the relevant asset at the time of the intra-group transfer will be chargeable to tax under TCGA section 179 (*Company ceasing to be a member of group*) (discussed at paragraph 9.1.1 below).

If a chargeable gain or loss accrues to a group company, TCGA section 171A provides that that company can, jointly with another company in the chargeable gains group, elect to transfer the gain or loss. The election will have effect if, had the transferor company transferred the asset to the other group company immediately before the actual transfer, the conditions for no gain/no loss treatment in section 171 would have applied. Since 21 July 2009, it is no longer necessary that there is an actual disposal of the capital asset outside the group giving rise to the gain, as was the case previously. The election can be made on or before the second anniversary of the end of the accounting period of the company in which the accrued gain or loss arises. Any payment between the two group companies in connection with a section 171A election is ignored when computing the profits or losses for corporation tax purposes of both parties and cannot be regarded as a distribution, so long as the payment does not exceed the amount of the chargeable gain or allowable loss which is treated under TCGA section 171A as accruing to the group company in accordance with the election. Section 171A allows a group to bring all gains and losses arising from capital assets into one company and an election under section 171A can now be made in respect of a 'degrouping' charge which could arise under TCGA section 179 (see paragraph 9.1.1 below). During due diligence for a transaction involving a group, the parties will want full details of intra-group transfers, and consideration of whether or not section 171A elections should be made prior to completion. Advisors to the seller should make enquiries with target's accountants about this issue.

There are specific rules in TCGA section 173 relating to transfers of assets which were, or become, trading stock within a chargeable gains group. If a capital asset which did not form part of the trading stock of the trade carried on by the transferor company is transferred, the transfer will be treated as having been made on a no gain/no loss basis. If the capital asset is to be used as trading stock by the transferee, the transferee will be treated as having immediately appropriated it at market value for the purposes of its trade. The reverse applies if a company disposes, intra-group, any asset forming part of the trading stock of its trade and the asset is acquired by the transferee company as a capital asset (i.e. not as trading stock). In these situations the transfer will also be treated on a no gain/no loss basis. References to a trade for those purposes mean any trade carried on by a company resident in the UK and any trade carried on in the UK through a permanent establishment by a non-UK resident company. The asset in question must be within the scope of UK corporation tax – otherwise a gain or loss will arise on the transfer of the asset based on its market value at that time.

Warranties set out in paragraph 3.10.2 of **Chapter 3 (Tax Warranties)** cover the above issues for a single company leaving a chargeable gain group, including:

- whether the target company (being a single company) has ever been a member of a chargeable gains group;
- details of chargeable gains grouping issues where the target company is a holding company; and
- details of intra-group transfers.

Paragraph 3.10.2 also provides relevant warranties for circumstances where a group is being acquired.

If the target company or group is capital asset 'heavy' and/or there has been any restructuring, a buyer will want details of all intra-group transfers through disclosure.

9.1.1   TCGA section 179 degrouping charge

Subject to a number of exceptions, a degrouping charge can arise when a company leaves a chargeable gains group if at the time it was holding an asset which had been transferred to it by an earlier transfer to which TCGA section 171 applied. The degrouping charge now falls on the seller company (discussed further below). Before 19 July 2011, the charge fell on the exiting company.

TCGA section 179 applies where there has been an intra-group transfer under TCGA section 171 and the acquiring company ceases to be a group member within a six-year period after the acquisition, in the following circumstances:

- the exiting company was UK resident at the time it acquired the assets or the asset was a chargeable asset immediately after it acquired it; and
- the transferor company was UK resident at the time of the transfer or the asset was a chargeable asset in relation to that company immediately before the transfer.

The degrouping gain is added to the consideration for the disposal of the transferee (the exiting company) by the seller company, or deducted from the consideration if there is a degrouping loss. Any reliefs or exemptions, such as the substantial shareholdings exemption, which would apply to a chargeable gain on the disposal will apply to the degrouping charge. This is a valuable reform, which means that in many cases no charge will arise on a degrouping event provided the conditions for the substantial shareholdings exemption are met. It was previously possible to reallocate a degrouping gain to another group member under TCGA section 179A. This section has now been repealed, but if a gain arises which is not covered by an exemption or relief it can be reallocated under TCGA section 171A.

Degrouping charges in respect of intangible fixed assets to which CTA 2009 Part 8 applies still accrue to the exiting company.

A section 179 degrouping charge will not arise in the following circumstances:

- where a company ceases to be a member of a chargeable gains group as a result of another member of the group ceasing to exist[5] (such as on a liquidation/dissolution of a subsidiary resulting in the parent company no longer being a member of a group);

---

[5] TCGA section 179(1)

- if shares are transferred as part of a transfer or division of a UK business under TCGA section 140A or a transfer or division of a non-UK business under TCGA section 140C whereby a company ceases to be a member of a group and the transferee becomes a member of another group (in such cases, the two groups are treated as if they were the same group);[6]
- where a company ceases to exist as part of the process under TCGA section 140E (a merger leaving assets within the UK tax charge);[7]
- where two or more associated companies cease to be members of a chargeable gains group at the same time;[8]
- certain transfers within a group to an investment trust;[9]
- where a company ceases to be a member of a chargeable gains group by reason only of the principal company becoming a member of another group (but in which case on any exit from the second group within six years of becoming a member of the new group, an exit charge can arise);
- in the case of certain *bona fide* mergers as set out in TCGA section 181.

The standard wording of the tax indemnity will cover any degrouping charge as representing a tax liability arising from a pre-completion event (see paragraph 2.1 of the Long-form Tax Schedule (**Appendix 1**)) but it is preferable for a specific reference to a TCGA section 179 charge to be included if the target is leaving a group or is a group.

9.2 Corporation Tax Groups

9.2.1 Group relief[10]

For group relief purposes, two companies are members of a group if one is the 75% subsidiary of the other or both are 75% subsidiaries of a third company.[11] A company will be a 75%

---

[6] TCGA section 179(1AA)

[7] TCGA section 179(1B) to (1D)

[8] TCGA section 179(2) subject to subsections (2ZA) and (2ZB)

[9] See TCGA section 101A

[10] CTA 2010 Part 5, sections 97 to 188

[11] CTA 2010 section 152

subsidiary of another company so long as not less than 75% of its ordinary share capital is owned directly or indirectly by that other corporation.[12] The parent company must also be beneficially entitled to not less than 75% of any distributable profits to equity holders of the subsidiary company and to 75% of any assets available for distributions to equity holders on a winding up.[13]

These group relief provisions allow trading losses, excess capital allowances, and non-trading deficits on loan relationships, as well as (subject to certain restrictions[14]) allowable qualifying charitable donations, losses from a UK property business, management expenses and non-trading losses on intangible fixed assets, to be surrendered from one company (the surrendering company) to another group member (the claimant company) so long as the losses are eligible for corporation tax relief.[15] The claimant company can make a claim to set off those amounts against its total profits for the corresponding accounting period which matches the surrendering company's accounting period. In this way, a group can manage its corporation tax affairs by transferring losses to other profitable companies within the group. Losses arising from allowable qualifying charitable donations, property business losses, management expenses and non-trading losses on intangible fixed assets can only be surrendered as group relief to the extent that in aggregate they exceed the surrendering company's gross profits for the surrender period.[16] Unused group relief can neither be carried forward nor carried back in the way that unutilised trading losses of a company can be carried forward under CTA 2010 section 45. Therefore, if the target company is leaving a group, the seller will need a full assessment of group relief potential before completion of the sale of target and provisions for group relief planning should be included in the tax schedule.

---

[12] CTA 2010 section 1154 by virtue of CTA 2010 section 151(1)

[13] CTA 2010 section 151

[14] CTA 2010 section 105

[15] CTA 2010 section 99

[16] CTA 2010 section 105

In order for group relief to apply:

- the surrendering company and the claimant company must be members of the same group;[17]
- both companies must be UK related, namely they are either UK-resident or non-UK resident but carrying on a trade in the UK through a permanent establishment.

Losses and other amounts not eligible for corporation tax relief may also be available for group relief if the surrendering company is within a charge to tax under the law of any European Economic Area (EEA) territory and:

- the surrendering company is a 75% subsidiary of the claimant company and the claimant company is UK-resident; or
- both the surrendering company and the claimant company are 75% subsidiaries of a third company which is resident in the UK.

There are also separate rules in the treatment in group relief (but not discussed further in this publication) relating to:

- UK losses of non-UK resident companies;[18]
- surrenders made by non–UK resident companies resident or trading in the EEA;[19]
- limitations on group relief surrendered by certain dual resident companies.[20]

9.2.2 Consortium relief

A company is owned by a consortium if it is not a 75% subsidiary of any company and at least 75% of its ordinary share capital is beneficially owned by other companies each of which beneficially owns at least 5% of that capital.[21] Those shareholding companies which own at least 5% of the share capital are members of the consortium. For a consortium claim for group relief to be made between a surrendering company and a claimant, one of them must be a consortium member and the other must be:

---

[17] CTA 2010 section 152

[18] CTA 2010 section 107

[19] CTA 2010 sections 111 to 128

[20] CTA 2010 section 109

[21] CTA 2010 section 153

- a trading company owned by the consortium and which is not a 75% subsidiary of any company; or
- a trading company
  - which is a 90% subsidiary of a holding company which is owned by the consortium; and
  - which is not a 75% subsidiary of a company other than the holding company; or
- a holding company which is owned by the consortium and which is not a 75% subsidiary of any company.[22]

Both the surrendering company and the claimant company must be UK-resident, or must carry on a trade in the UK through a permanent establishment if not UK-resident. Companies whose trade is dealing in shares are not entitled to consortium relief.

The amount of relief which may be claimed under a consortium claim where the claimant company is a consortium member is limited to the lower of the proportion of the surrendering company's losses corresponding with the claimant consortium member's percentage of:

- the ordinary share capital of the surrendering company which is beneficially owned by the claimant company;
- any profits of the surrendering company available for distribution to equity holders of which the claimant company is beneficially entitled; and
- the assets of the surrendering company available for distribution to shareholders on a winding-up to which the claimant company would be beneficially entitled.[23]

Where the surrendering company is a member of the consortium, the amount which may be set off against the total profits of the claimant company is limited to the relevant fraction of the claimant company's total profits for the relevant period, which will be the lowest of the following percentages of:

---

[22] CTA 2010 section 132 & 133

[23] CTA 2010 sections 143(1) & 144(1)

- the proportion of the ordinary share capital of the claimant company which is beneficially owned by the surrendering company;
- the proportion of any profits available for distribution to equity holders of the claimant company to which the surrendering company is beneficially entitled; and
- the proportion of assets available for distribution to equity holders of the claimant company on a winding-up to which the surrendering company is beneficially entitled.[24]

9.2.2.1 Link companies[25]

A link company is a company which is a member of a consortium and also a member of a group of companies. A group member for the purposes of the link provisions is a company which is a member of the group of which the link company is also a member, but is not itself a member of the consortium of which the link company is a member. Where a link company can make a consortium claim, it may be made by another member of the group. The proportion of the relief will be the same as it would have been if the link company was the claimant company.

9.2.3 Denial of group relief and consortium relief

Group relief will be denied under CTA 2010 sections 154 and 155 if there are arrangements in the accounting period when relief would be normally available but there are arrangements in place which provide that:

- a group member will leave the group and join another group; or
- there is to be a change of control of either the claimant company or the surrendering company but no change of control of the other party to the relief; or
- there is to be a transfer of a trade to a third party.

The denial of consortium relief is similarly applicable where there are arrangements for a change in ownership of the trading company by a different consortium group, or a change in its control, or a transfer of its trade to a third company.

---

[24] CTA 2010 sections 144(2), (3) & (4)

[25] CTA 2010 sections 133, 142 & 145 to 149

These issues will be important before a transaction. HMRC provide the following guidance on whether arrangements in their view might be considered to exist:[26]

- where a shareholder is preparing to dispose of the company, straightforward negotiations for the disposal will not give rise to the existence of arrangements before the point at which an offer is accepted subject to contract or on a similar conditional basis;
- unless there are exceptional features, an offer made to the public at large for shares or a business will not at that stage bring arrangements into existence;
- if a disposal requires the approval of shareholders, operations leading towards disposal will not give rise to the existence of arrangements before that approval is given or until the directors become aware that it will be given;
- if, following negotiations with potential buyers, a shareholder concentrates on a particular potential buyer this will not of itself be regarded as bringing arrangements into existence;
- arrangements might exist if there is an understanding between the parties with the characteristics of an option, such as an offer which might be allowed to remain open for an appreciable period, so that the potential buyer is allowed to choose the moment to enter into a bargain.

The HMRC manuals[27] provide greater detail as to HMRC's treatment of group relief restrictions but any seller intending to claim group relief relating to the target for any pre-completion period may have to restrict its claim to the period before the heads of terms are agreed in writing (referring to the first example above). This could create problems if there is a long delay between that date (heads of terms) and completion.

9.2.4 Claims for group relief

A claim for group relief is made under self-assessment under FA 1998 Schedule 18 part VIII (paragraphs 66 to 77) and may be made after a company has left a group. It is included in the claimant

---

[26] Statement of practice SP 3/93 and ESC C10

[27] See CTM 80175 onwards

company's return for the relevant accounting period, and must state the amount of relief and the name of the surrendering company, which must consent to the surrender in writing to its tax office before or at the time the claim is made. Otherwise, the claim will be ineffective. A consortium claim must include the consent of each consortium member and be accompanied by a copy of the notice of consent to surrender given by each such member in order to be valid. A notice of consent may not be amended but may be withdrawn and replaced with another, by notice to the tax office to which the notice of consent was given.

A claim for relief may be made or withdrawn, usually at any time before the first anniversary of the filing date for the tax return of the claimant company, relating to the accounting period for which the relief is claimed. If any agreement has been made between the seller and the buyer whereby the target will make a claim for relief following completion the tax schedule should provide for consequences if the claim is subsequently withdrawn by the target company without the agreement of the seller – namely the buyer should be liable for the amount of relief not claimed.

If the seller in a transaction intends to claim group relief involving any losses of the target in an accounting period ending before completion, it would be reasonable for the buyer to require that this is done before completion if possible, except when the relevant accounts date is quite close to completion or where the accounts of the claimant and surrendering party have not been drawn up, which is not uncommon. When claiming group relief for the accounting period in which completion falls, the seller may not be able to quantify the relevant amounts to be relieved without full completion accounts for the target, and it may not be possible for the seller's group to make the relevant calculations (namely profits of the claimant company and the losses of the surrendering company) before completion. The tax schedule should, therefore, include post-completion conduct for this issue, with the buyer undertaking to require the target to make the appropriate elections as agreed by the seller and buyer. It should also include terms to deal with the possibility of the relief being refused – this will be an issue for the seller – the buyer should have no liability other than in a case of refusal arising because of obstruction by the target or the buyer. It is advisable that a cap on the group relief claim, which is time limited to allow the claim to be made, is included in the relevant provisions.

9.2.5   Surrender of tax refunds within a group[28]

Where a surrendering company within a group is entitled to a tax refund (being a repayment of corporation tax or income tax or a payment of a tax credit related to any franked investment income received by the company) it may jointly elect with another member of the group (the recipient) that the refund or part of the refund be treated as if the recipient had paid corporation tax for the same period, equal to the amount of the refund. The election must be made before the refund is due and, therefore, it is likely to be a seller's pre-completion issue if the target is leaving a group and the provisions apply.

9.3   Group Payment Arrangements

Under TMA sections 59F to 59H HMRC have discretion to agree to arrangements in which some or all members of a group of companies may pay their corporation tax via a nominated member. A group for the purposes of any group payment arrangements means a company and all its 51% subsidiaries, and all 51% subsidiaries of such subsidiaries and so on. The guidance notes are contained in the HMRC company taxation manual but, essentially, the arrangements will represent a contractual agreement between the companies involved and HMRC. Each participating company will remain liable for its own corporation tax, although the nominated company will be liable to discharge the corporation tax liabilities of all the participating companies. Companies required to pay tax by instalments and companies outside that regime are also entitled to participate.

The nominated company must normally be UK resident, and all the participating companies should have the same accounting period end date as the nominated company. Companies can be in only one payment group. Whilst the nominated company will be

---

[28] CTA 2010 section 963

responsible for the payment of corporation tax of the participating companies, the liability for tax will remain with the participating companies and, therefore, joint and several liability should not be an issue.

A participating company which ceases to be a member of a group must immediately be removed from group payment arrangements, and the nominated company will cease to have any responsibilities relating to that company's tax after that date. If the target company has entered into group payment arrangements the buyer should be given a copy of the agreement with HMRC. Both the buyer and seller should agree the steps required to inform HMRC of a forthcoming change of control of the target group, or that the target company will be leaving a group payment arrangement group. Pre-completion due diligence should determine what amount of tax has been paid on behalf of the target company (assuming that the target is not the nominated company), whether the payment arrangements have been properly applied (and in respect of which the buyer will want an indemnity from the seller), and may involve the buyer having sight of the tax affairs of other members of the seller's group.

Warranties in **Chapter 3** paragraph 3.22 cover these issues, as does paragraph 5 in the Long-form Tax Schedule (**Appendix 1**)(relating to any over-payments or under-payments of corporation tax under the quarterly payments of corporation tax regime, and the target's withdrawal from any group payment arrangements).

9.4   Intangible Assets

CTA 2009 Part 8 (sections 711 to 906) sets out the provisions for intangible fixed assets and CTA 2009 Part 9 (sections 907 to 931) deals with intellectual property: know-how and patents. These provisions were previously contained in FA 2002 Schedule 29-30, and apply to assets acquired or created on or after 1 April 2002.

Under this regime, receipts in respect of intangible fixed assets are recognised in the computation of a company's profit or loss as they accrue,[29] with profits taxed as income and not as capital, and

---

[29] CTA 2009 section 720(1)(a)

losses on disposals and payments being relievable against income. 'Intangible asset' has the same meaning as it has for accounting purposes[30] and includes intellectual property, defined as any patent, trade mark, registered design, copyright or design right and plant breeders' rights.[31] An intangible fixed asset means an intangible asset acquired or created by the company for use on a continuing basis in the course of the company's activities.[32]

CTA 2009 Part 8, Chapters 8 and 9, (sections 764 to 799) set out the legislation for the taxation of intangible assets for groups of companies. Group issues for intangible assets include:

- intra-group transfers;
- roll-over relief which is available on a sale and reinvestment (see CTA 2009 Chapter 7, sections 754 to 763); and
- degrouping issues.

A group is defined as a company and all its 75% subsidiaries and any 75% subsidiaries of such subsidiaries and so on, so long as each subsidiary is an effective 51% subsidiary of the parent company.[33] A company will be a 75% subsidiary of another company so long as not less than 75% of its ordinary share capital is owned directly or indirectly by that other company.[34] An effective 51% subsidiary is a company in respect of which the parent is beneficially entitled to more than 50% of any profits available for distribution to equity holders of the subsidiary and which would be beneficially entitled to more than 50% of any assets of the subsidiary available for distribution to its equity holders on a winding up.[35] The principal company of a group cannot be a 75% subsidiary of another company and a company cannot be a member of more than one group for the purposes of the intangible assets legislation.

---

[30] FRS 102 (replacing FRS10) defines intangible assets as *"non-financial fixed assets that do not have physical substance but are identifiable and are controlled by the entity through custody or legal rights"*

[31] CTA 2009 section 712

[32] CTA 2009 section 713

[33] CTA 2009 sections 765(1) and 766

[34] CTA 2009 section 838

[35] CTA 2009 section 771

A group of companies remains the same group so long as the same company is the principal company. If the principal company becomes a member of another group, the groups will be treated as the same group. Winding up a company other than the principal company is not treated as causing any company to cease to be a member of a group[36] and, therefore, should not result in a degrouping charge.

9.4.1 Intra-group transfers of intangible assets

An intra-group transfer of an intangible fixed asset is tax-neutral, with the original cost of the asset in the hands of the transferor treated as the original cost for the transferee[37] so long as:

- at the time of the transfer both companies are members of the same group;
- immediately before the transfer the asset is a chargeable intangible asset of the transferor; and
- immediately after the transfer the asset is a chargeable intangible asset for the transferee.

A chargeable intangible asset in relation to a company is an asset in respect of which any gain on its realisation by the company would be a chargeable realisation gain, thereby creating a credit which must be brought into account, under the legislative provisions.[38]

9.4.2 Roll-over relief for intangible assets[39]

For roll-over relief purposes two companies in the same group will be treated as the same person if:

- company A sells an intangible fixed asset (the 'original asset') when it is a member of a group;
- company B acquires intangible fixed assets (the other assets) when it is a member of the same group as A at the time of the expenditure (the 'time of expenditure');

---

[36] CTA 2009 section 769

[37] CTA 2009 section 775

[38] CTA 2009 section 741

[39] CTA 2009 section 777

- company B is not a dual-resident investing company within the meaning of CTA 2010 section 109 (*Restriction of losses etc surrenderable by dual residents*) at the time of expenditure;
- immediately after the time of expenditure the other assets are chargeable intangible assets of company B; and
- both company A and company B make a claim for relief.

Normally, the expenditure on the other assets must be incurred in the period beginning 12 months before the date of the sale of the original asset and ending three years after the date of its sale, and the expenditure on the other assets must be capitalised by the company for accounting purposes.[40] However, the roll-over relief will not apply on the expenditure on the other assets if they are acquired from another member of the same group by a tax-neutral transfer.

Roll-over relief will also apply when a company (company A) acquires a controlling interest in another company (company B) and intangible fixed assets (the underlying assets) are held by company B or by other members of company B's group. A joint claim must be made by company A and the companies holding the underlying assets concerned.[41] In these circumstances, the expenditure by company A on the acquisition of the controlling interest in company B is treated as expenditure on acquiring the underlying assets, with the amount of the expenditure taken to be the lower of the tax written-down value of the underlying assets immediately after the acquisition and the consideration given for the acquisition.[42] The underlying assets must be chargeable intangible assets immediately after the acquisition by company A.

Under CTA 2009 section 794, if an election has been made under CTA 2009 section 792 for reallocation of a degrouping (see 9.4.3 below) within a group then the sale of an asset for roll-over relief purposes can be treated as if it had been made by the other member of the group to which the relevant gain is deemed to have accrued.

---

[40] CTA 2009 section 756

[41] CTA 2009 section 778

[42] CTA 2009 section 779

9.4.3 Degrouping[43]

Where there has been an intra-group transfer of a chargeable intangible fixed asset (the relevant asset), if the transferee leaves that group during the period of six years after the date of the transfer and it still holds the relevant asset at that time (or the asset is held by an associated company[44] of the transferee which is also leaving the group) then there is a deemed sale and reacquisition of the relevant asset at market value at the time of the intra-group transfer. The total net credit or debit must be brought into account by the transferee as if it had arisen immediately before the transferee ceased to be a member of the group.

The transferee company can elect, jointly with another company which was a member of the same group before the transferee left, to treat the gain as accruing to that other group company, provided that company is UK resident or carrying on a trade in the UK through a permanent establishment and not exempt from corporation tax because of relief from double taxation e.g. under a treaty.[45]

The degrouping charge will not arise in the following circumstances:

- if the relevant asset is transferred as part of a transfer of business within a European cross-border transfer of business under CTA 2009 section 820;[46]
- the intra-group transfer is between associated companies which cease to be members of a group at the same time;[47]
- a company ceases to be a member of a group because the principal company becomes a member of another group;[48]
- a company ceases to be a member of a group because of an exempt distribution under CTA 2010 section 1076 or 1077, and

---

[43] CTA 2009 section 780

[44] Associated companies being companies which could by themselves form a group of companies (as defined in CTA 2009 section 788(3))

[45] CTA 2009 section 792

[46] CTA 2009 section 781

[47] CTA 2009 section 783

[48] CTA 2009 section 785

so long as there is no chargeable payment within five years of the exempt distribution having been made;[49]

- if a merger is carried out for genuine commercial reasons and not for the avoidance of tax, subject to the conditions set out in CTA 2009 section 789.

Under CTA 2009 section 795 if a company is liable for a degrouping charge and the assessed amount for the relevant accounting period in which the degrouping charge falls to be paid (the payment date) is wholly or partly unpaid at the end of six months following the payment date, HMRC can make an assessment on the principal company of the group and any company which at any time during the period of 12 months before the company leaving the group owned the relevant asset or part of it. HMRC must serve the relevant notice within three years following the date on which the liability to corporation tax for the relevant accounting period is finally determined.[50]

9.4.4 Roll-over relief and the degrouping charge

If a company is treated as having realised an asset as a result of a degrouping charge, the asset which is sold must be a chargeable intangible fixed asset at that time in respect of the transferor, and the expenditure on the new assets must be made within the period beginning 12 months before the date the transferee left the group and ending three years after the date of leaving the group.[51]

9.4.5 Assets excluded from the intangible assets regime[52]

The following types of intangible fixed assets are excluded from the intellectual property provisions:

- those held for non-commercial purposes;
- assets for which capital allowances were previously given (i.e. tangible fixed assets);
- financial assets including loan relationships and derivative contracts, insurance or capital redemption policies or contracts, and rights under a collective investment scheme;

---

[49] CTA 2009 section 787

[50] CTA 2009 section 798

[51] CTA 2009 section 755 amended by section 791

[52] CTA 2010 Part 8 Chapter 10, sections 800 to 816

- shares in a company, rights under a trust and the interest of a partner in a firm;
- assets representing production expenditure on films;
- oil licences;
- sound recordings and master versions of films save in respect of royalties;
- computer software which is treated for accounting purposes as part of the costs of the related hardware, and save in respect of royalties; and
- expenditure on research and development.

Accounting for intangible assets is a specialist subject. Rather than getting bogged down in the specific tax issues, the non-IP expert should think of intangibles as any other assets a company or business will own and require the seller to warrant that they are legally owned by the target company, have been properly accounted for and no post-completion tax liabilities can arise under a degrouping charge. As most companies are likely to have some form of intellectual property, warranties should be provided (see **Chapter 3 (Warranties)** at paragraph 3.25).

9.5   Loan Relationships

The rules dealing with the taxation of loan relationships are set out in Part 5 of the CTA 2009, with chapters 4 to 8 (sections 335 to 379) dealing with group issues. A loan relationship arises when a company stands in the position of a creditor or debtor in respect of a money debt (whether by reference to a security or otherwise) and the debt arises from a transaction for the lending of money.[53] However, this chapter does not cover loan relationships involving companies whose trades are the lending of money.

All profits arising to a company from its loan relationships are chargeable to corporation tax as income. The legislation provides for the application of generally accepted accounting practice (GAAP) in determining the amounts to be brought into account as credits and debits and also makes provisions where accounts do not comply with GAAP. It is fair to say that loan relationships will

---

[53] CTA 2009 section 302

arise in some way in respect of all companies other than dormant companies.

The definition of a group under the loan relationship legislation[54] is the same as under TCGA section 170, namely where there is a principal company which has 75% subsidiaries and any 75% subsidiaries of such subsidiaries (and any 75% subsidiaries below such subsidiaries in the group structure) so long as there are no subsidiaries which are not effective 51% subsidiaries of the principal company[55].

The loan relationship provisions in respect of groups mirror those in:

- TCGA sections 171 and 179 under which intra-group transfers of loans are ignored for tax purposes unless there is a tax avoidance motive[56], and degrouping charges can arise; and
- CTA 2010 section 1086 on chargeable payments in respect of exempt distributions.

9.5.1   Transfers of loans within a group[57]

If there is a transfer or series of transfers of a loan between members of the same group which are within the charge to corporation tax in respect of the loan, and whereby one group company (the transferee) replaces another group company (the transferor) as a party to the loan relationship, subject to the anti-avoidance rules, the transferor will be treated as having made the transfer for consideration of an amount equal to the notional carrying value of the asset or liability in that accounting period and the transferee will be deemed to have acquired the asset or liability for that same amount. The notional carrying value is the value recognised in the accounts of the transferor of the accrued amounts, amounts received in advance or the impairment losses (including provisions for bad or doubtful debts) in respect of the asset or liability transferred immediately before the date when the

---

[54] CTA 2009 section 336(6)

[55] TCGA section 170(3)

[56] CTA 2009 section 347

[57] See CTA 2009 Chapter 4 – sections 335 to 352

transferor ceased to be a party to the loan relationship.[58] The transfer pricing rules (in TIOPA 2010 Part 4 (sections 146 to 217)) do not apply in respect of such transfers.

If the transferee leaves the group within six years after replacing the transferor in the loan relationship (except where there has been a European cross-border transfer of a business, a cross-border merger or an exempt distribution) then the transferee will be treated as having assigned the asset or liability immediately before ceasing to be a member of the relevant group for a deemed fair value consideration and then immediately having reacquired it so long as either of the following circumstances apply:

• a credit would be brought into account by the transferee; or
• there is a creditor relationship and the transferee has a hedging relationship between a derivative contract and the creditor relationship and, because the transferee is leaving the group other than because there is an exempt distribution, a credit is to be brought into account by the transferee in respect of the derivative contract under CTA 2009 Part 7.[59]

9.5.2 Exempt distributions in respect of loan relationships[60]

If a transferee leaves a group because of an exempt distribution, and there is a chargeable payment within five years, the transferee will be deemed to have assigned the asset or liability relating to any transferred loan relationship immediately before the chargeable payment was made for fair value consideration, and immediately reacquired the assets or liability for the same amount. Exempt distributions and demergers are discussed in **Chapter 3 (Warranties)** at paragraph 3.17.

Loan relationships are discussed in general terms in **Chapter 3** (at paragraph 3.27).

---

[58] CTA 2009 section 422(3)

[59] CTA 2009 section 345

[60] CTA 2009 section 346

9.6 Stamp Duty

No stamp duty is payable on a transfer on sale between associated companies on any relevant instrument, so long as relief has been claimed and the instrument has been stamped by HMRC that no duty is payable[61] (stamp duty group relief). Companies are associated if, at the time of transfer, one is the parent of the other or another company is the parent of each of the companies. A company will be the parent of another company if:

- it is the beneficial owner (direct or indirect) of not less than 75% of the ordinary share capital of the subsidiary;
- it is beneficially entitled to not less than 75% of any profits available for distribution to equity holders of the subsidiary; and
- would be beneficially entitled to not less than 75% of any assets of the subsidiary available for distribution to its equity holders on a winding-up.

Ordinary share capital means the issued share capital of a company, other than capital for which the holders have a right to a dividend at a fixed rate but have no other right to share in the profits of the company (referred to as 'body corporate' in the legislation).[62]

There are no rules which specify that stamp duty group relief will be clawed back in certain circumstances, but anti-avoidance provisions under FA 1967 section 27(3) state that the relief will not be given if the transfer was made in connection with arrangements under which:

- the consideration or part of the consideration for the transfer is provided directly or indirectly by a person other than a company which is associated with either the transferor or the transferee (an unconnected person);
- the interest was previously conveyed or transferred by the unconnected person; or

---

[61] FA 1930 section 42 , FA 1995 section 151 (for leases)

[62] FA 1930 section 42(4)

- the transferor and transferee cease to be associated by virtue of the transferor or a third company ceasing to be the transferee's parent.

An application for stamp duty group relief should include confirmation that all provisions are properly satisfied. The onus is on the party making the claim to ensure compliance.

9.7   Stamp Duty Land Tax (SDLT)

The group relief provisions are set out in FA 2003, Schedule 7, Parts 1 and 2 (*Group relief; and reconstruction and acquisition reliefs*). Companies will be members of the same group for SDLT purposes if one is the 75% subsidiary of the other or both are 75% subsidiaries of a third company[63]. A company (company A) will be the 75% subsidiary of another company (company B) if company B:

(a) is the beneficial owner of not less than 75% of the ordinary share capital of company A (either direct or indirect ownership);

(b) is beneficially entitled to not less than 75% of any profits available for distribution to equity holders of company A; and

(c) would be beneficially entitled to not less than 75% of any assets of company A available for distribution to its equity holders on a winding up.

Ordinary share capital means all the company's issued share capital (regardless of what it is called) other than capital for which the holders have a right to a dividend at a fixed rate but no other right to share in the profits of the company. [64]

Any land transaction on which SDLT would arise[65] will be relieved from SDLT if the seller and the buyer are companies which, at the effective date of the transaction, are members of the same group[66], subject to certain provisions as discussed below. The relief must be claimed within 30 days of the effective date of the transaction on

---

[63] FA 2003 Schedule 7 paragraph 1

[64] FA 2003 Schedule 7 paragraph 1(3)

[65] Which only applies to UK land and property

[66] FA 2003 Schedule 7 paragraph 1(1)

the land transaction return[67] and will be based on the market value of the land transaction (because of the deemed market value rule in FA 2003 section 53[68]), regardless of whether consideration has or has not been paid. However, the relief will be withdrawn and SDLT which would have been payable but for the relief will become payable, based on the values and rate applicable on the effective date in specific circumstances, primarily in cases involving degrouping of the buyer within three years of the relevant land transaction (see paragraph 9.7.2 below).

A degrouping charge can be a critical issue for any buyer of either a group of companies (which following completion may undergo restructuring) or of the target company which leaves a group within three years of relief having been given. Due diligence of SDLT matters should require sight of all documents and computations relating to market value of any UK properties transferred intra-group, and not merely the relevant SDLT returns.

9.7.1 Restrictions for SDLT group relief[69]

SDLT group relief will not apply in the following circumstances:

- at the effective date of the land transaction there are arrangements in existence whereby, at that time or some later time, a person has or could obtain control[70] of the buyer but not of the seller (save for any transaction involving an acquisition as part of a scheme of reconstruction falling under FA 1986 section 75 whereby the buyer will be a member of the same group as the acquiring company[71]); or
- the land transaction is effected by, or in connection with, arrangements under which:
  - the consideration or part of the consideration is to be provided or received by a person other than a group

---

[67] Under relief code 12 in the return

[68] In respect of connected companies

[69] FA 2003 Schedule 7 paragraph 2

[70] Within the meaning of CTA 2010 section 1124

[71] Including demutualisation of insurance company under FA 1997 section 96 by virtue of Schedule 7 paragraph 2 (3A)

company (such arrangements are defined in FA 2003 Schedule 7 paragraph 2(3)); or

- the seller and the buyer are to cease to be members of the same group by reason of the buyer ceasing to be a 75% subsidiary of the seller or a third company; or

- the transaction is not effected for *bona fide* commercial reasons or forms part of arrangements, the main purpose or one of the main purposes is the avoidance of liability to stamp duty, income tax, corporation tax, capital gains tax or SDLT.

9.7.2 Withdrawal of SDLT group relief[72]

Anti-avoidance legislation exists whereby SDLT group relief will be withdrawn in the following circumstances:

- the buyer ceases to be a member of the same group as the seller:
  - before the end of the period of three years beginning with the effective date of the transaction; or
  - in connection with arrangements made before the end of that period, *and*
- at the time the buyer ceases to be a member of the same group as the seller (the relevant time), it or a relevant associated company holds a chargeable interest:
  - which was acquired by the buyer under the relevant transaction; or
  - which is derived from a chargeable interest so acquired,

and which has not subsequently been acquired at market value under a chargeable transaction for which group relief was available but was not claimed.

A relevant associated company means a company which is a member of the same group as the buyer immediately before the buyer ceases to be a member of the same group as the seller, and ceases to be a member of the same group as the seller as a result of the buyer leaving the group.

The amount chargeable is the SDLT which would have been chargeable in respect of the transaction but for the group relief, if the chargeable consideration had been market value, and, if the transaction was the grant of a lease at a rent, the rent.

---

[72] FA 2003 Schedule 7 paragraph 3

If a degrouping charge arises on the target company as a completion tax liability, it should be for the seller to pay the SDLT before completion or have it accounted for in a reduced purchase price and the liability paid by target following completion. A land transaction return must be sent to HMRC within 30 days of the date of the withdrawal which will include the unique transaction reference number (UTRN) of the original return on which the relief was claimed, together with the amount of SDLT due. The buyer should be provided with a copy of the new return and evidence of the computation for the SDLT payable. The tax schedule should state in the 'conduct' provisions whether the target, buyer or seller will be responsible for filing the new return and payment of this SDLT charge.

If the company in question does not have proper evidence of the market value of the property, the buyer should include a specific indemnity to cover the expense of agreeing the market value if the SDLT relief is to be clawed back.

The above withdrawal rules will not apply so long as the reason for the buyer leaving the original group is because the seller left that same group and in the following circumstances:[73]

- the buyer ceases to be a member of the same group as the seller by reason of anything done for the purposes of winding up the seller or another company which is above the seller in the group structure; or
- the buyer ceases to be a member of the same group as the seller as a result of an acquisition of shares by another company (the acquiring company) in relation to which stamp duty relief under FA 1986 section 75 applies (reconstruction of a company) and the conditions for relief under that section are met, and the buyer is immediately, after that acquisition, a member of the same group as the acquiring company and the buyer remains a member of that group as at the third anniversary of the effective date of the relevant transaction; or
- the buyer ceases to be a member of the same group as the seller as a result of the transfer of the whole or part of the seller's

---

[73] FA 2003 Schedule 7 paragraph 4(1)

business to another company which involved stamp duty relief for demutualisation of insurance companies and the buyer remains a member of that group as at the third anniversary of the effective date of the relevant transaction.

The anti-avoidance rule in FA 2003 Schedule 7 paragraph 4ZA, while ensuring that a seller can still leave a group without triggering withdrawal of group relief, made it no longer possible to avoid the withdrawal of group relief where, after the seller leaves the group, there is a subsequent change in control of the buyer within three years of the effective date of the group-relieved intra-group transfer, or at any time under or in connection with arrangements made before the end of that period.

Withdrawal of SDLT relief can also arise under paragraph 4A of Schedule 7 in cases involving successive transactions where:

(a) there is a change in the control of the buyer;

(b) that change occurs
  (i) before the end of the period of three years beginning with the effective date of the transaction; or
  (ii) under arrangements made before the end of the period; and

(c) apart from these provisions group relief would not be withdrawn under the previous withdrawal provisions; and

(d) there is a previous transaction whereby:
  (i) SDLT group relief was available under the main provisions or under the provisions for reconstruction and acquisition relief;
  (ii) the effective date of the previous transaction is less than three years before the date where there is a change in the control of the buyer;
  (iii) the chargeable interest acquired under the relevant transaction is the same as or forms part of the chargeable interest acquired under the previous transaction; and
  (iv) since the previous transaction the chargeable interest acquired has not been acquired by any person under a transaction which is not exempt as per paragraph (d)(i) above.

9.7.3   Assignment of exempt lease[74]

If the grant of a lease is exempt from an SDLT charge as a result of group relief then the first assignment of that lease that is not itself exempt from charge under any of certain specified provisions[75] is treated for SDLT purposes as a chargeable transaction comprising the notional grant of a new lease by the assignor (unless the assignee acquires the lease as bare trustee of the assignor).

The grant is treated as being for a term equal to the unexpired term of the actual lease, and on the same terms as those on which the assignee holds that lease after the assignment.

However, this provision does not apply where the relief in question is group relief and is withdrawn as a result of a disqualifying event occurring before the effective date of the assignment of the original lease, since in that situation the exemption given in relation to the original grant of the lease would be the subject of clawback.

9.7.4   Reconstruction and acquisition SDLT reliefs[76]

Whilst not always an intra-group issue, these reliefs may have arisen within target's group prior to the transaction, or alternatively exemptions may apply if a group was involved. Also see paragraph 9.7.6 below for claiming against another group company for withdrawn SDLT relief.

Reconstruction relief applies (and no SDLT is payable subject to the withdrawal of relief provisions) where an acquiring company acquires the whole or part of the business of the target under a scheme for the reconstruction of the target and that acquisition involves UK land and property. The following three conditions must be satisfied:

---

[74] FA 2003 Schedule 17A paragraph 11 as re-enacted in amended form by FA 2004 Schedule 39 Part 2 with effect for transactions with an effective date on or after 22 July 2004.

[75] The specified provisions are:
    (a) section 57A (*sale and leaseback relief*);
    (b) Part 1 or 2 Schedule 7 (*group relief or reconst*ruction or acquisition relief);
    (c) section 66 (transfers involving public bodies);
    (d) Schedule 8 (*charities relief*);
    (e) any such regulations as are mentioned in section 123(3) (regulations reproducing in relation to SDLT the effect of enactments providing for exemption from stamp duty).

[76] FA 2003 Schedule 7 Part 2 paragraphs 7 to 13

- the consideration for the acquisition consists wholly of the issue of non-redeemable shares in the acquiring company to all the shareholders of the target or, alternatively, the consideration consists partly of the issue of non-redeemable shares and the remainder of the consideration consists wholly of the assumption or discharge by the acquiring company of liabilities of the target;
- following the acquisition each shareholder of each of the companies is a shareholder of the other in the same proportion; and
- the acquisition is effected for *bona fide* commercial reasons and not for tax avoidance purposes (tax meaning SDLT, stamp duty, income tax, corporation tax or capital gains tax).

Acquisition relief applies and SDLT is payable at a reduced rate of 0.5% where an acquiring company acquires the whole or part of the business of a company and a land transaction is entered into for the purposes of or in connection with the transfer of the undertaking or part of the undertaking. All the following conditions must be met:

- consideration for the acquisition consists wholly or partly of the issue of non-redeemable shares in the acquiring company to either the company or shareholders in the company;
- if the consideration consists partly of the issue of non-redeemable shares, the rest of the consideration must consist wholly of cash not exceeding 10% of the nominal value of the issued non-redeemable shares or the assumption or discharge by the acquiring company of liabilities of the company or both;
- the acquiring company is not associated[77] with another company which is a party to arrangements with the company, such arrangements relating to shares of the acquiring company issued in connection with the transfer of the business;
- the business acquired has as its main activity the carrying on of a trade that does not consist wholly or mainly of dealing in UK land and chargeable interest;

---

[77] Companies are associated if one has control of the other or both are controlled by the same person or persons.

THE TAX SCHEDULE

- the acquisition is effected for *bona fide* commercial reasons and not for tax avoidance purposes (tax meaning SDLT, stamp duty, income tax, corporation tax, or capital gains tax).

9.7.5   Withdrawal of reconstruction or acquisition relief[78]

These reliefs will be withdrawn and full SDLT will become payable in the following circumstances:

- the control of the acquiring company changes before the end of the period of three years beginning with the effective date of the transaction or under arrangements made before the end of that period; and
- at the time control of the acquiring company changes the acquiring company, or any relevant associated company, holds a chargeable interest in UK land which it acquired under the relevant transaction, and which it did not subsequently acquire at market value, in respect of which reconstruction or acquisition relief was available but not claimed.

The SDLT charge will be the amount chargeable on the market value of the land transaction at the time it was effected. Again, any due diligence relating to this issue should require documentary evidence of the computation of the market value at the date of the intra-group transaction.

The withdrawal rules will not apply[79] when control of the acquiring company changes as a result of:

- a share transaction in connection with divorce;
- a variation of testamentary dispositions;
- an exempt intra-group transfer under FA 1930 section 42 (*Group relief for share transfers* discussed above);
- in circumstances where the control changes as a result of a transfer of shares to another company and stamp duty relief applies under FA 1986 section 77   (*Acquisition of a target company's share capital*); or
- as a result of a loan creditor becoming, or ceasing to be treated as having control of, the company.

---

[78] FA 2003 Schedule 7 paragraphs 9 to 11

[79] FA 2003 Schedule 7 paragraph 10

9.7.6 Recovery of withdrawn SDLT relief from another group company

If the target company is in an SDLT group or is leaving an SDLT group the withdrawal provisions may apply. If SDLT group relief, acquisition relief or reconstruction relief is subsequently withdrawn and has not been paid it can be recovered from:[80]

- any company which at any relevant time was a member of the same SDLT group as the buyer and was above it in the group structure; and
- any person who at any relevant time was a controlling director of the buyer or a company having control of the buyer.

Additionally, if HMRC recover the relief from any of the above-mentioned persons, the recovery will not be allowed as a deduction in computing any income profits or losses for any tax purposes.[81]

Relevant warranties in **Chapter 3** are included in paragraph 3.35.4 and a relevant indemnity is included in the Long Form Tax Schedule in **Appendix 1** at paragraph 2.1.

9.8 Substantial Shareholdings

9.8.1 Background

Any chargeable gain on a disposal by a trading company (the investing company) of a 'substantial shareholding' in another trading company (the investee company) will be exempt from corporation tax, as set out in TCGA Schedule 7AC under the rules in existence at the date of publication (*Substantial Shareholdings Exemption/SSE*). Where the conditions are met, the exemption is automatic. Any loss on a disposal meeting the conditions will not be allowable for the computation of corporation tax by virtue of TCGA section 16(2). The statutory provisions require that the investing company must have held a substantial shareholding in the investee company throughout a 12 month period beginning not more than two years before the disposal date[82]. The SSE is also

---

[80] FA 2003 Schedule 7 paragraphs 5 and 12

[81] FA 2003 Schedule 7 paragraphs 6(6) and 13(6)

[82] TCGA Schedule 7AC paragraph 7

discussed in **Chapter 4 (Sale and Purchase of a Company)** at paragraph 4.3.2.

However, the SSE has been the subject of consultation which closed in August 2016 with five options for possible reform, as follows:-

1. A new wider-ranging exemption
2. Amendment so that only the investee company must meet the 'trading' test
3. Imposition of some other test on the investee company
4. Retention (amended) SSE tests at both investee and investor level
5. Amendment of the definition of substantial shareholding to less than 10%.

A company which is a member of a group is treated as holding shares (any reference to 'shares' in this section includes an interest in shares) held by any other company in the group and as having the same entitlement as the other company to any rights enjoyed by virtue of holding the shares[83] (perhaps better described as a 'look through' situation). A group is defined as any principal company and all its 51% subsidiaries and any 51% subsidiaries of those subsidiaries and so on.[84] A 51% subsidiary is a company of which more than 50% of its ordinary share capital is owned directly or indirectly by another company.[85]

A substantial shareholding is defined as a holding of shares in a company by virtue of which the investing company:

- holds not less than 10% of the company's ordinary share capital;
- is beneficially entitled to not less than 10% of the profits available for distribution to equity holders of the company; and
- would be beneficially entitled on a winding up to not less than 10% of the assets of the company available for distribution to equity holders.

---

[83] TCGA Schedule 7AC paragraph 9

[84] TCGA Schedule 7AC paragraph 26(1)(b) by reference to TCGA section 170(3)(a)

[85] ICTA section 838(1)(a) by virtue of TCGA Schedule 7AC paragraph 26(4)

Certain loan creditors also may be treated as substantial shareholders for these purposes.

9.8.2 Investor and investee SSE requirements

The investing company must be:

- a sole trading company or a member of a qualifying trading group throughout a 'qualifying period' which:
  - begins with the start of the latest 12-month period by reference to which the substantial shareholding requirement is met; and
  - ends with the time of the disposal; and
- a sole trading company or a member of a qualifying trading group immediately after the time of disposal.[86]

The investee company must satisfy the following conditions:

- it was a trading company or the holding company of a trading group or trading sub-group (a 'qualifying company') for the same qualifying period referred to above; and
- it was a qualifying company immediately after the time of the disposal.

A trading company is one carrying on trading activities and whose activities do not include, to a substantial extent, activities other than trading activities[87]. HMRC will generally consider that if the non-trading activities of a company or group are more than 20% of the total that will count as being substantial.[88] In determining whether this 20% limit is breached, the level of turnover, the assets and the amount of management time spent relating to the non-trading activities will be relevant. Therefore, investment income and non-trading assets of both the investing and investee companies will be important issues when determining whether the trading requirements have been met throughout the relevant periods.

---

[86] TCGA Schedule 7AC paragraph 18 – but see paragraph 4.3.2 in **Chapter 4** discussing whether the investing company is not a trading company by virtue of having disposed of its trading subsidiary

[87] TCGA Schedule 7AC paragraph 20

[88] See HMRC manuals CG53072

Trading activities can also mean activities of a company with a view to it acquiring a significant interest in the share capital of another trading company. 'Significant interest' is defined[89] as an interest in the ordinary share capital of another company which would make that company a 51% subsidiary of the acquiring company or which would give the acquiring company a qualifying shareholding in a joint venture company without making the two companies members of the same group. The definition of a 'trading group' is similar to a trading company in that one or more members of the group must carry on trading activities and the activities of the group's members taken together do not include, to a substantial extent, activities other than trading activities.[90]

9.8.3   Joint Venture companies[91]

In determining whether an investing company with a qualifying holding (i.e. 10%) in a joint venture company is a trading company, its holding in the joint venture company shall be disregarded and it shall be treated as carrying on an appropriate proportion of:

- the activities of the joint venture company; or
- where the joint venture company is a holding company, the activities of that company and its 51% subsidiaries.

A joint venture company for the purposes of the substantial shareholdings exemption is a trading company, or the holding company of a trading group or trading sub-group, in which five or fewer persons between them hold 75% or more of the ordinary share capital.

9.8.4   Subsidiary SSE[92]

The substantial shareholdings exemption also applies to disposals of assets relating to shares where the main exemption conditions are met, namely in circumstances in which a gain accrues to a company (company A) on a disposal of an asset related to shares in another company (company B) and:

---

[89] TCGA Schedule 7AC paragraph 20(4)

[90] TCGA Schedule 7AC paragraph 21

[91] TCGA Schedule 7AC paragraph 23

[92] TCGA Schedule 7AC paragraph 2

- immediately before the disposal company A holds shares in company B and any gain accruing to company A on a disposal at that time of those shares in company B would not be a chargeable gain under the principal substantial shareholdings exemption; OR alternatively
- immediately before the disposal, company A does not hold shares or an interest in shares in company B, but is a member of a group and another group member holds shares in company B. If company A, rather than the other group member held the shares, any gain accruing to company A on a disposal of those shares at that time would not be a chargeable gain under the principal substantial shareholdings exemption.

An asset related to shares in a company is defined as:[93]

- an option to acquire or dispose of shares or an interest in shares of that company;
- a security to which rights are attached by virtue of which the holder is or may become entitled to acquire or dispose of:
    - shares or an interest in shares in the company, or
    - an option to acquire or dispose of shares or an interest in the shares, or
    - another security within this definition;
- an option to acquire or dispose of any security referred to above or an interest in any such security;
- an interest in, or option over, any such option or security as referred to above; or
- any interest in or option over any such interest or option as is mentioned if this definition.

9.8.5   Disapplication of the SSE[94]

The SSE exemption will not apply if there are arrangements from which the sole or main benefit would be that any gain on a disposal would not be a chargeable gain under the substantial shareholdings exemption and in which:

- an untaxed gain will accrue to a company (company A) on a disposal of shares in another company (company B); and

---

[93] TCGA Schedule 7AC paragraph 30

[94] TCGA Schedule 7AC paragraphs 5 & 6

- before that gain accrues:
  - company A acquired control of company B or the same person acquired control of both companies; or
  - there was a significant change of trading activities affecting company B at a time when it was controlled by company A or when both companies were controlled by the same person.

A significant change of trading activities affecting company B arises if there is a major change in the nature or conduct of a trade carried on by company B or a 51% subsidiary of company B, or there is a major change in the scale of the activities of a trade carried on by company B or a 51% subsidiary of company B, or company B or a 51% subsidiary of company B begins to carry on a trade.

The exemption also will not apply:
- to disposals made on a no gain/no loss basis or where there would be no chargeable gain under any other enactment;
- to deemed chargeable gains or allowable losses on a disposal in respect of reorganisations, conversions and reconstruction, with the gain or loss held over on an earlier transaction under TCGA section 116(10)(b);[95]
- on a disposal of an asset to which TCGA section 140(4)*(recovery of charge postponed etc.)*applies;[96]
- where there is a disposal of an asset where the substantial shareholdings exemption would normally apply but where its base cost would be affected by a claim for gift relief under TCGA section 165 on an earlier disposal, in which case the held-over gain will accrue to the company at the time of the later disposal.[97]

9.8.6 SSE degrouping issues[98]

If a company leaves a group and would be treated, under TCGA section 179(3), as having sold and immediately reacquired an asset

---

[95] TCGA Schedule 7AC paragraph 34

[96] TCGA Schedule 7AC paragraph 35

[97] TCGA Schedule 7AC paragraph 37

[98] TCGA Schedule 7AC paragraph 38

under the 'degrouping provisions', the degrouping gain is added to the consideration received by the seller, then the substantial shareholdings exemption would apply to the seller's disposal of the company leaving the group, it will also cover the degrouping gain.

The SSE was extended in FA 2011. If a company transfers *assets* (not shares) to a newco, a 12 month ownership period in respect of the shares in newco will be treated as satisfied, provided that those assets have been used as trading assets either by the seller or by another group company. So the SSE can effectively apply to an asset sale as well as a share sale, and this has led to pre-sale hive-downs of assets or business divisions becoming more common.

Warranties relating to the SSE are included in **Chapter 3** at paragraphs 3.10.1(c) and 3.10.3(t).

9.9 VAT Groups[99]

9.9.1 Background

Two or more companies are eligible to be treated as members of a group for VAT purposes if each is established or has a fixed establishment in the UK and:

(a) one of them controls each of the other(s);

(b) one person (whether a corporate or an individual) controls all of them; or

(c) two or more individuals carrying on a business in partnership control all of them.[100]

'Control' is defined as 'empowerment by statute to control that body's activities' or if it is that body's holding company within the meaning of CA 2006 section 1159 and Schedule 6 – namely a company which:

• has the majority of voting rights in the other company;

• is a shareholder or member and has a right to appoint or remove a majority of the board of directors in the other company; or

---

[99] VATA sections 43 & 44 - also discussed in **Chapter 3 (Warranties)** at paragraph 3.37.1

[100] VATA section 43A(1)

- is a shareholder or member and controls alone a majority of the voting rights in the other company.

There are a number of anti-avoidance provisions including those under SI 2004/1931 which prevent partly-exempt buyers of services setting up joint ventures within their VAT group in order to buy in services without incurring irrecoverable VAT. The joint venture companies would, in reality, be run by and for the benefit of third party suppliers who exercise control over them. Under SI 2004/1931, groups which fall within the criteria in the year and are not excepted ('specified bodies') must satisfy both a 'benefits condition' and a 'consolidated accounts condition'.

Group companies must apply to HMRC:
- to be treated as a VAT group;
- for another company to join or leave a group; or
- for an existing group to be no longer treated as a group.

The application must be made by one of the companies or by the person controlling them, and one of the companies must be the representative member of the group. Normally, any granting of group treatment should take effect on the date the application is received by HMRC ('application date') unless HMRC allow an earlier date. HMRC will restrict an earlier registration date up to 30 days before the application date and only if it corresponds to the commencement of the current accounting period of the existing VAT group or any of the companies forming, joining or leaving the VAT group. Therefore, if the commencement of the current accounting period is less than 30 days before the application date, the maximum period of retrospection will be to the beginning of that accounting period. HMRC will grant any date earlier than 30 days before the application date only in exceptional circumstances, namely:
- if HMRC lose the application and are supplied with details of the original application and details of attempts to follow it up; or
- if the delay was caused by inactivity on the part of HMRC (discussed in VAT Notice 700/2/04, paragraphs 2.13 and 2.14).

HMRC have powers to refuse an application or terminate treatment as a member of a VAT group. Refusal must be made within 90 days from the application date:

- if it appears that the bodies are not eligible under the criteria set out in SI 2004/1931;
- if it appears that the bodies are not eligible under the general criteria for group eligibility; or
- for the protection of the revenue.[101]

Additionally, HMRC may give notice for termination of membership of a VAT group for the protection of the revenue.[102]

A group which has been accepted as a VAT group will be treated as a single taxable person for VAT purposes, but a company may not be a member of more than one VAT group at the same time. The effect of membership of a VAT group is that any supply by a group member to another group member is disregarded, and the supply is treated as made by or to the representative member. Any VAT paid or payable by a group member on the acquisition of goods from another EU state or on the importation of goods from outside the EU is also treated as paid or payable by the representative member. All members of a VAT group are jointly and severally liable for any VAT due from the representative member.[103] The representative member must account to HMRC for VAT due on group supplies made to third parties, and file the quarterly VAT return on behalf of the group.

If the target is a group of companies, there may be one or more than one VAT group. Any VAT group will continue following completion save for any changes instigated by the buyer.

Issues relating to deregistration and registration will arise if the target company is leaving a VAT group, as will its liability for VAT matters during its membership of the group. There may be no VAT records relating to intra-group supplies before completion and, therefore, specific information relating to such supplies

---

[101] VATA section 43B(5)

[102] VATA section 43C(2)

[103] VATA section 43

THE TAX SCHEDULE

involving the target company should be requested during the due diligence.

Pre-completion conduct should be agreed requiring notification to HMRC by the seller (or the representative member of the target company's VAT group) that the target will leave the VAT group on completion. The target company must either re-register for VAT as from the completion date or the buyer must apply to have it join a VAT group within the buyer's group. The tax indemnity should also provide that the target and the buyer are both protected for any VAT liability arising due to the target's joint and several liability whilst it was a member of a seller's VAT group. If the VAT period for the target company's VAT group straddles completion, there must be a provision for VAT credits and debits relating to the target's supplies post-completion.

Warranties for group VAT matters and set out in **Chapter 3** at paragraph 3.37.1 and 3.33.3(h).

THE TAX SCHEDULE

10 THE TAX SCHEDULE IN THE SALE AND PURCHASE OF A COMPANY

10.1 Background Issues

A covenant is an agreement or a contract, and a covenant to pay is therefore merely an agreement to pay. An indemnity is more clearly defined, representing compensation for loss incurred. These are the essential words in a tax indemnity.

The purpose of a tax indemnity is to enable the person making a claim for loss suffered[1] to recover a specified amount on a pound-for-pound basis, without the need to prove loss or quantum or to mitigate, as required in any claim for loss arising due to a breach of a warranty. Whilst tax warranties are required as part of the due diligence process, any tax liability which could arise from a breach of the tax warranties is likely to fall within the definition of tax liability for the purposes of a tax indemnity (subject to exceptions discussed in paragraph 10.7 – *Liabilities not covered by the standard tax indemnity*).

Providing a tax indemnity is now standard commercial practice in the sale and purchase of a company in the United Kingdom, and it is usually negotiated and agreed (often almost entirely) between the tax advisors to the buyer and the seller rather than directly between the commercial parties to the transaction. Traditionally there was a separate stand-alone deed containing the tax indemnity and conduct provisions, but it is now equally as common for the provisions to be contained in a separate schedule to the SPA, primarily because it results in there being one less document to sign at completion. Whether there is to be a tax deed or tax schedule, it is best practice for all tax-related matters to be contained only in the one document, including limitations as to quantum and time, and conduct relating to tax claims.

The development of the tax indemnity has resulted in precedents containing indecipherable provisions, usually argued for as representing market practice. A valid question throughout the

---

[1] Usually the buyer in a transaction

negotiations, and on agreeing the final terms, is whether the provisions are sufficiently clear and unambiguous to prevent or resolve a future dispute. The tax indemnity is ordinarily intended to protect the buyer from tax liabilities arising from the seller's past actions which were not discovered during due diligence, and in respect of which the tax authorities may yet make a tax assessment on the target company within the statutory time limits. The buyer will want a quick solution to the issue, looking to the tax schedule for the necessary steps to make a claim against the seller. The seller will, in turn, expect unambiguous provisions in the tax schedule as to what its obligations and rights are, relating to any such claim.

Whilst the bargaining position of the parties to a transaction may determine the ability of the tax advisors to argue successfully for the best position for their respective clients, the more important issue will be what the commercially-agreed principles are. There is no reason why the tax advisor for the stronger party should be entitled to stray beyond this remit. During the negotiation process, it is not unknown that one side (usually the seller) is asked to agree to a provision which might be unworkable, unfair or uncommercial, or merely too wide-ranging. First and foremost, the parties should expect the final agreed document to provide certainty as to when past tax liabilities of the target company will cease to be the liability of the seller and when the buyer's protection under the tax schedule ceases.

10.2 Drafting Principles

The approach in this book is to pare down the provisions in the standard tax schedule to avoid ambiguity and provide a clear basic framework which the parties to the negotiation can then adapt for specific issues arising in the transaction in question.

The main principle behind a standard tax indemnity is generally agreed to be that a buyer will wish to be compensated for any unexpected tax liability of the target company, which has not been taken into account in the consideration price, and which arises in respect of any period before the change of its ownership. A buyer is likely to have negotiated the consideration price on, amongst other things, representations by the seller relating to the tax position of the target either as at the most recent accounts date or (as is becoming more common) up to completion. The buyer will need to know whether there is sufficient working capital to pay for tax liabilities for the period up to completion, and it will be a matter of negotiation whether those tax liabilities will relate to PAYE and VAT only or will include corporation tax.

The seller is entitled to certainty as to what will comprise a valid claim, the time period during which it will remain liable under the tax indemnity, any cap on the quantum, and the seller's right to dispute with HMRC any tax assessment relating to the claim. Additionally, it should be protected from any tax liability which could arise from a post-completion action of the buyer or the target company or any post-completion event, save in the limited circumstances where it has been specifically provided for. Such liabilities could arise under the employment-related securities regime, withdrawal of SDLT group relief and other degrouping reliefs, and certain capital allowances charges relating to the pre-completion period. It is unlikely to have been knowingly and commercially agreed between the buyer and seller that the seller should provide wide-ranging indemnities which are intended to capture unknown and unexpected tax liabilities which may befall the target company in the future, but merely have an incidental connection with the pre-completion period. At the heart of any transaction involving the acquisition of a company is the necessity for the buyer to carry out careful due diligence, and for the seller to disclose properly against the relevant warranties, both of which are intended to reduce the possibility of unexpected liabilities arising.

10.3 Short Form or Long Form Tax Schedule?

This book provides both a short form tax schedule together with short form tax warranties ('short form') as well as a long form tax schedule ('long form'). The long form tax warranties must be adapted to reflect the activities, trade and business of the target company and should not be included in their entirety without any thought as to whether they are relevant to the transaction.

The short form tax schedule is suitable in a transaction:

- when the target is a new company or has a limited track record;
- where the consideration price is modest or nominal;
- when there is limited time for negotiating the SPA;
- in a public offering when the directors are expected only to provide a general indemnity against any wrongdoing by them and by which they personally benefited (discussed further in **Chapter 6 (Special Situations)** at paragraph 6.3); and
- where the target has been loss-making and the losses are not being warranted by the seller.

However, subject to further provisions covering specific issues relating to the commercial transaction, the short form indemnity together with longer form tax warranties should be appropriate in most transactions. Certainly, in some jurisdictions, including the USA, the standard tax indemnity can be a mere paragraph and there may be few if any provisions for conduct of a claim.

Unfortunately, it has become the norm in most company sales for the long form tax schedule to be too wide ranging, and drafted to cover obscure situations, resulting in its negotiation becoming protracted and expensive. The long form in this publication attempts to reduce the provisions to fit in with the principles of the short form tax schedule, whilst providing more detail for specific issues relevant to the target and which may concern the tax advisors.

10.4 Tax Liabilities

UK companies are required to pay a number of different UK taxes in a variety of contexts:

- corporation tax on profits of the business and chargeable gains, and income tax on interest income;
- stamp duty and stamp duty reserve tax (SDRT) involving the acquisition of shares and securities;
- stamp duty land tax (SDLT) on acquisitions of chargeable interests in UK land;
- employer's national insurance contributions (NIC);
- local taxes such as business rates;
- excise duty;

- VAT on goods and services received which is not capable of being claimed back; and
- special taxes as may be relevant such as landfill tax, tonnage tax and aggregate levies tax.

The standard definition of tax should include all of the above as well as related interest and penalties imposed by a taxation authority. (*A word of warning* – in a 2012 case[2] the judge ignored the inclusion of interest in the definition of Tax which was payable by HMRC on a tax refund to the target company, on the grounds that the parties did not intend such a payment to include earned interest.)

Against this background companies are entitled to claim reliefs against various expenses and activities which will reduce or delay their tax bill, including:

- capital allowances;
- roll-over relief for chargeable gains;
- corporation tax relief relating to employment-related securities and options under CTA 2009 sections 1001 to 1038 (previously contained in FA 2003 Schedule 23);
- group reliefs relating to corporation tax, chargeable gains, stamp duty, stamp duty land tax, intellectual property, and VAT;
- R&D expenditure;
- loss reliefs.

The payable amount of corporation tax in respect of any tax year will reflect the various reliefs claimed or which apply automatically, and with future revisions potentially available from the ability to carry back reliefs, including trading losses.

Because businesses act as tax collectors on behalf of HMRC in respect of VAT, employees' income tax and NIC under PAYE, tax due under the construction industry scheme ('CIS'), and withholding tax on certain payments, failure to deduct and account properly for the relevant tax to HMRC will result in the liability in question and related interest and penalties eventually

---

[2] *Teesside Power Holdings Limited v Electrabel International Holdings BV & GDF International SAS* [2012] EWHC 33

falling on the business. It is for these reasons that the seller should carry out a review of its tax affairs before entering into negotiations to sell the target company, and that particular due diligence needs to be carried out by the buyer on the expertise of the tax functions within the target company. If doubts arise, the tax indemnity should specifically refer to issues which give the buyer concern as well as provisions for resolving any uncertainty.

10.4.1 Actual and deemed tax liabilities

An actual tax liability arises when a company must make a payment to a tax authority for whatever reason, including under self-assessment for corporation tax, the operation of PAYE, any withholding tax regime, SDLT and under VAT. Where a tax relief claimed proves not to be not allowable for whatever reason or is clawed back (such as a degrouping charge arising due to completion and the target leaving a group), or there has been a calculation error, an immediate actual tax liability is likely to arise.

A 'tax asset' is any of the following (and a deemed tax liability will be the loss of or reduction in such tax assets without necessarily an immediate actual tax liability arising):

- the target company has losses and/or management expenses to carry forward or back to set off against tax arising, thereby reducing an actual tax bill;
- allowable reliefs as prescribed under statute which reduce the amount of profits subject to tax;
- the target has a right to a repayment of tax from a taxation authority or the right to set off an amount against another tax.

10.4.2 Arguing the treatment of tax assets

There are three issues relating to the treatment of tax assets and related tax liabilities in the tax indemnity, namely:

- whether there are in fact any such assets inherent in the target company at the time of completion;
- whether the seller is willing to warrant their availability after completion; and
- whether the availability of any tax assets has been taken into account in the consideration price.

In the author's view, if tax assets have not been taken into account when negotiating the consideration price then the seller should not under any circumstances warrant them. Thus, in this scenario, if the tax asset becomes unavailable in the future the seller should not be liable for their loss. Furthermore, if the heads of terms are silent on this issue, and there are to be no completion accounts, it should be assumed that the seller is not warranting any tax assets or, alternatively, there are in fact no tax assets. Therefore, as a starting point references to 'deemed tax liabilities' should not be included in the definition of tax unless the heads of terms refers to them. If completion accounts are to be prepared which are to include any tax assets, there must be specific reference to them and they should be quantified in the completion accounts schedule. As both parties will be agreeing their quantum, there should be little room for a later dispute.

10.4.3 Tax repayments

The target company may have a right to a repayment from a tax authority (often included in the definition as a tax asset) which could arise when there has been a previous overpayment of tax from, say, an incorrect self-assessment, a mistake of law, success by a party (not necessarily the target) in litigation with a tax authority which establishes a new tax treatment, and/or change in practice by a tax authority. If, before completion, the target is entitled or is expected to be entitled, to a repayment of tax, it would be commercial for the seller to be paid for the benefit in the negotiation of the consideration price. In which case, any loss or reduction of such a tax asset will be the seller's liability. However, if an unexpected repayment of tax arises for the target company after completion in respect of a pre-completion period, unless there are particular provisions for its treatment in the tax schedule, it will be a windfall benefit for the buyer unless it has been negotiated otherwise. Providing for the treatment of tax repayments is discussed further in paragraph **10.9** below.

10.5 An Accounts Deal

In an accounts deal there will be no completion accounts, and the point of reference for quantifying the target company's tax liabilities and tax assets will be the target company's accounts for the last accounting period before completion. The seller will be warranting these accounts in the ordinary way but, under the standard limitation it will be protected for any tax liability provided for in those accounts. The limitations should, therefore, extend to accounts warranties.

The standard wording for the limitations in an accounts deal provides for, in addition to any tax provisions in the accounts, any tax arising in the ordinary course of business between the accounts date and the completion date (or alternatively from the accounts date onwards). This leaves the buyer able to claim under the general tax indemnity for any tax liabilities arising outside the ordinary course of business between the accounts date and the completion date. However, if the accounts in question are unaudited, they may not provide either a profit and loss statement or for any tax liabilities and tax assets, in which case the seller will be completely unprotected under the tax indemnity. Therefore, it is absolutely essential that the seller's tax advisor be given the relevant information from its client regarding what the accounts provide for. If they do not provide for tax, the reference in the limitations should be to those tax liabilities as used in the company's tax computations for the tax returns for the period ending on the accounts date. Any actual tax liability arising in respect of an earlier period, however, will fall within the tax indemnity. Proper due diligence by the buyer of target's accounts and tax return is essential in these circumstances.

In an accounts deal, it is standard that any tax liability arising in the ordinary course of business following the accounts date will not be the seller's liability, implying that any tax liabilities arising outside the ordinary course of business following the accounts date up to completion will be a seller's liability. The preferred alternative is to specify both these issues in the indemnity. This begs the question as to what tax liabilities arise in the ordinary course of business and what arise outside the ordinary course of business. Both the short form and long form tax schedules in this publication contain reference to the ordinary course of business as being the business and trade of the company as carried on at the completion date (see paragraph 3 in both) with the long form also setting out, for the avoidance of doubt, what shall not amount to the ordinary course of business. This paragraph should be extended to cover issues of concern arising during the due diligence.

The buyer will have no confirmation of the target company's outstanding tax liabilities before completion, save for the information provided during due diligence and disclosures. Tax warranties in an accounts deal must, therefore, be more specific regarding the target company's tax position as close as possible to the completion date, and in the negotiations the seller should be required to forecast outstanding tax liabilities and cash resources available to discharge them following completion.

10.6 A Completion Accounts Deal

Under a completion accounts deal, draft accounts are drawn up, usually for the period beginning on the day following the last accounts date and ending on the completion date, based on the accounting principles used in the target company's last accounts. It is standard to have a separate completion accounts schedule which sets out which party initially prepares them, the time limits for the preparation, the rights and requirements of the other party to agree them or alternatively raise objections, and a dispute mechanism. Whilst it is not usual for the tax advisors to negotiate the completion accounts provisions, they should be aware of whether or not they are to provide for tax liabilities and tax assets, and to ensure there are no conflicts with the provisions in the tax schedule. If the draft completion accounts appended to the completion accounts schedule do not provide for a specific reference to the target's tax liabilities and tax assets, the seller will not be protected properly for any tax liabilities of the target company which arise during that period. It is unlikely that the target company will have no tax liabilities at completion – at the very least there are likely to be obligations under VAT and PAYE.

Completion accounts can be drawn up on a number of different principles, from merely agreeing the position of the target company's working capital, cash position and balance sheet as at the completion date, to requiring full profit and loss and balance sheet statements for the period ending on the completion date.

Normally, there are provisions in the SPA for an adjustment to the consideration price based on the actual completion accounts' net asset position versus its estimated net asset position as projected before completion.

If the purpose of the completion accounts is to draw up only the working capital or net cash position of the target at completion, the tax liabilities are likely to be limited to the position for VAT and PAYE, in which case there may not be provisions for corporation tax for the relevant period. If this is the case, the seller could find itself liable for pre-completion corporation tax which was not due to be paid before completion. Commercially, this would not be fair in that the buyer will have the benefit of the profits to which the tax related (assuming the profits are to be left in the target) and the tax will have arisen in the course of its business. If the completion accounts provide a full balance sheet and profit and loss account, any tax assets will be relevant in computing the corporation tax payable for the period ending on the completion date. These should also be specified in the completion schedule and not merely netted off.

10.7 The Seller's Indemnity

The indemnity should be made by the seller to the buyer and likewise, any payment to be made pursuant to a claim under the indemnity must be made to the buyer and not to the target company. This is to ensure that the target company is not subject to chargeable gains on any payment made to it,[3] and so that the payment will be deemed to be a reduction in the purchase price of the target company for both parties.[4] In the absence of a cap on any payment under the indemnity, if the tax liability payment is greater than the purchase price (which is possible in transactions involving low consideration for a target with large tax liabilities) HMRC could look to tax the amount received by the buyer which is in excess of the purchase price as a capital sum arising from the chose in action, being a right to sue. The standard gross up clause

---

[3] Under the case *Zim Properties* and discussed at paragraph 10.17 in this chapter

[4] Whilst this is the standard treatment in the UK under D33 it may not be the case if a party is in a non-UK jurisdiction

(discussed in paragraph **10.16** below) is intended to protect the buyer from any such tax charge which might arise on a payment under the tax indemnity.

The tax indemnity contained in the short form tax schedule is sufficient protection for the buyer, save for specific liabilities which may arise after completion and which are connected with a pre-completion event. The extension of the basic indemnity to cover specific issues which are, in any event, covered under the basic indemnity is best practice. It can be helpful in setting out areas of concern of the buyer so that there is no doubt about the future liability. It is useful if the itemised events cover the tax issues which come to light during the due diligence, so these potential liabilities are brought to the seller's attention.

The so-called 'combined events' clause is not included in the pro-forma tax schedule precedents in this publication, due to its vague, indeterminate, and possibly unenforceable nature. In the author's view, it provides little if any protection for the buyer. If the event which triggers the tax liability is not pre-completion then the post-completion event which triggers the tax liability (obviously pre-completion) should be identified. A standard wording in many tax indemnity precedents, as set out below, should not be accepted by either party:

> "a reference to an Event occurring on or before Completion includes a series of Events the first of which was an Event occurring on or before Completion or which commenced on or before Completion."

Even less clear, and also not to be agreed to, is the following provision:

> "a series of Events the first of which occurred before Completion [in the ordinary course of business] and the second which occurred after Completion [outside the ordinary course of business]."

The above definitions which are commonly seen in standard precedents[5] beg the question which tax liabilities are they intended to cover. The better course is to set out specific tax liabilities which

---

[5] Both are drawn from documents often seen by the author while working on transactions for clients.

will not be covered under the main indemnity, in that they will arise after completion but will be only related to pre-completion issues and events and are not clearly within the general indemnity.

Set out below are provisions which cover possible issues which the buyer may wish to be included in the tax indemnity:

- withdrawal of any pre-completion tax relief as a result of completion including, for the avoidance of doubt:
  - SDLT under sections FA 2003 Schedule 7;
  - TCGA section 179;
- CTA 2009 section 780 (*Deemed realisation and reacquisition at market value*) of intangible fixed assets;
- any income tax and NIC liability arising after completion in respect of any securities issued and securities options granted before completion.

10.8 Limitations

The limitations are arguably the most important provisions within the tax schedule, providing certainty for the parties as to which tax liabilities remain with the target company following completion, and which are not the liability of the seller. Whilst the tax indemnity in the short form tax schedule extends to only one paragraph, the limitations provisions should be as comprehensive as in the long form schedule, as any pre-completion tax liability not provided for in the limitations will fall on the seller. The limitations should reflect the commercial deal negotiated between the buyer and seller.

The notes to the limitations contained in the long form tax schedule should be read in conjunction with this paragraph. Every transaction is different and it is difficult to state what is standard for arrangements between the commercial parties relating to a target's tax liabilities and assets. Therefore, if the heads of terms do not cover the following points they need to be answered before the tax schedule is drafted.

- Accounts/Completion Accounts:
  - What are the tax assets and the tax liabilities which need to be provided for?

- Will the provisions include corporation tax payable in respect of the business up to the accounts date or the completion date?
- Are any exceptional tax items to be included?
- If it is an accounts deal, have the tax computations been filed or at the very least prepared – if not what are the arrangements for their preparations and filing?
- What disclosures have been made against the accounts warranties – if there are any are they to be included or excluded under the tax indemnity?
- What tax liabilities for the pre-completion period have been paid and what will remain unpaid as at completion (see the note to the limitation in paragraph 3.1(b) of the tax schedules)?

- Has it been agreed that any change in tax law or treatment by a tax authority which is announced after completion but which would have an effect on the provisions relating to tax in the accounts or completion accounts, will be a valid limitation protecting the seller?
- What arrangements relating to the target's tax affairs have been entered into by the target company before completion including claims, surrenders, disclaimers, elections, notices and consents?
- Will a pre-completion dividend be paid and, if so, when?
- Are any post-acquisition acts by the target or the buyer being planned such as hiving up any of the target company's business?
- Is the target within the quarterly payment instalment regime and what effective rate of tax is it paying?
- Where in the target company's VAT reporting account will completion fall, and which party will have conduct following completion for any period straddling completion?
- Which party will have conduct of the target company's PAYE responsibilities for the tax month in which completion falls?
- What will be the cut-off date for the seller to make a claim to revise its chargeable gains on sale of the sale shares if it needs to make a payment under a valid claim under the tax schedule? Ideally for the seller, the time limit for the buyer to make a

claim against the seller should be identical, but this is often not negotiated by the commercial parties and, therefore, an issue for debate between the tax advisors. If there is a possibility that the seller could be liable for a claim, but in respect of which it could not make a reclaim for chargeable gains tax previously paid or accounted for and the tax advisor does not bring this possibility to the attention of the seller, this could amount to negligence on the part of the tax advisor, in the view of the author.

10.9 De Minimis and Maximum Caps

The standard position most often taken is that any claim under the tax indemnity should not be subject to a *de minimis,* under the principle that the buyer is entitled to be covered on a pound-for-pound basis for any tax claim. The area where tax claims may arise is in respect of PAYE. HMRC PAYE investigations can be frequent and expose past errors, which can be quite expensive to resolve with interest and penalties to pay.

It is common for a cap on all claims to be equal to the purchase price, possibly on the basis that it would be futile to pursue the seller for amounts in excess of the consideration it received. However, these are commercial issues and a buyer is entitled to argue, in principle, that if the seller has provided warranties which state that no unexpected tax liabilities will arise following completion why should it also ask for caps on any tax liability claim.

10.10 Third Party Recovery

If the SPA provides for third party recovery then it is often argued that it is reasonable for the tax schedule to provide the same. Third party recovery is likely to be relevant in respect of (but not limited to) employment-related issues, recovery from persons previously connected with the target such as past directors, and also in respect of recovering overpaid tax from a tax authority. If any overpayment includes interest, the parties should agree whether the buyer or seller takes the benefit.[6]

If a claim has been made by the buyer and the target company is entitled to recover that amount from a third party, then standard third party provisions allow the seller to require the buyer and the target to seek enforcement against that third party, subject to being fully indemnified by reasonable costs and expenses. The buyer should not automatically agree to this, in view of the nuisance factor for the target company, particularly if successful recovery is not a foregone conclusion. If the third party recovery right is granted, then the buyer should have discretion to reasonably refuse to assist in any recovery in the following circumstances:

- it could cause bad faith;
- the amount is below a *de minimis* cap;
- it might interfere with its commercial relationships; or
- it is not clear cut that rights to recovery from another party are that strong.

However, in a contractual dispute, the judge's finding on what amounts to reasonableness may appear arbitrary to the losing party.

The second set of circumstances where a seller might wish to argue for third party recovery rights is where taxpayers (including the target company) are entitled to claim back from a taxing authority overpaid tax for previous years due to, say, a change of practice or as required under law, and the right to repayment arises after completion but relates wholly to the pre-completion period. The seller should be able to take advantage of the repayment made to the target company subject to time limits. Alternatively, any amount due from the seller under a successful claim should be offset against receipts (actual or potential) from a tax authority. If litigation is ongoing at the time of the negotiations of the transaction, whereby it is considered that the target company might benefit from a litigator's success against the tax

---

[6] See *Teesside Power Holdings Limited v Electrabel International Holdings BV & GDF International SAS [2012] EWHC 33* - where the judge did not accept that an intention to include interest could be inferred from a tax deed provision to enable the sellers to benefit from any tax repayments received by the buyers

authorities, the seller's tax advisor should make provisions for its client to benefit from a successful outcome of the litigation in question and the right to claim back overpaid tax. If, on the balance of probabilities, success is likely the seller could argue for a cash sum from the buyer once the target company receives the repayment or, at the very least, that the maximum cap be reduced to reflect the benefit which the target company will eventually receive.

10.11 Overprovisions

The overprovisions clause has become almost standard in tax schedules but, in the author's view, generally it should not be accepted by the buyer. The principle behind the clause is that if, after completion it is found that the target company has fewer tax liabilities than previously quantified and provided for in the completion accounts, its value will be greater and the seller should be entitled to some benefit from the lower than estimated liabilities. Standard drafting for overprovisions allows the seller to request the auditors of the target company to review the provisions for taxation in the accounts or completion accounts and if there has been an overprovision, that amount can be set off against any payment due from the seller by a claim under the tax schedule. This principle assumes that the purchase price has been based solely on the target's last accounts which is often not the case (see **Chapter 1 (The Transactional Process)** at paragraph 1.6 which discusses alternatives as to why the buyer wants to acquire the target, and what the purchase price will be based on). Standard drafting also provides the buyer with the right to ask for reconfirmation of the tax provisions from the auditors of the first review. However, such provisions are certainly not appropriate when the transaction involves drawing up completion accounts which are to provide fully for tax liabilities of the target company. Standard drafting for the completion accounts schedule requires that either the seller or the buyer prepare the first draft of the completion accounts based on standard accounting principles consistent with those used by the target company for drawing up the accounts, and with both parties agreeing the computation. Additionally, the completion accounts schedule will contain a disputes mechanism clause. If there is also an overprovisions clause in the tax schedule this will cut into the integrity of the completion accounts mechanism, which is intended to be final.

If, on the other hand, there are to be no completion accounts the parties will be relying on the accounts, which will have been prepared and warranted by the seller, who in turn will be hard-pressed to argue for the need for an overprovisions clause to protect it against incorrect calculations and which would also cut across the purpose of the accounts warranties. If the accounts do not specify tax liabilities, an overprovisions clause would serve no purpose whatsoever because there would be nothing for it to apply against.

If the buyer agrees to the inclusion of an overprovisions clause it should be restricted in time (in the author's view two years at most) and quantum (see paragraph 8 in the Long Form Tax Schedule in **Appendix 1**).

10.12 Reliefs and Savings

Relief and savings provisions have become standard, and the author also questions their automatic inclusion in so many transactions. In effect, they provide that if a tax liability arises and a claim is made by the buyer against the seller, the amount of the claim should be reduced by any amount of savings in tax which arise from the payment of tax liability in question. This is not without complications. The amount under a claim will be paid to the buyer (as recompense for having paid too much for the acquisition and effectively for breach of a warranty) but the tax liability in question will have been paid by the target company reducing its cash flow and net profits. However, some tax liabilities such as secondary NIC, SDLT, and unrecoverable input VAT, which are revenue expenses, will result in lower pre-tax profits on which lower corporation tax will be due from the target company – so that the net effect on the target may be less than the actual tax liability. The argument under the relief and savings provisions is that any amount of lower corporation tax should come off the amount claimed by the buyer under the tax indemnity. However, the target company *has* suffered a cash outflow when it pays the tax liability and, despite a reduction in corporation tax relating to any higher revenue expenses, it is likely that the target company's net profits position will be lower due to the unexpected tax liability. Quantifying any tax offset and the cash flow effect on the target company for each and every claim under the tax schedule would be onerous and time-consuming for both the buyer and the target company.

If the buyer agrees to include a reliefs and savings provision, it needs to be tightly-worded to cover only actual and identifiable savings in the corporation tax of the target company and to take into account the cash flow effect, subject to a *de minimis* amount, and both the auditors' costs and the management time of the target company and the buyer being paid for by the seller. (See paragraph 9 (Relief and Savings) in the Long Form Tax Schedule in **Appendix 1**.)

10.13 Mitigation and/or Shared Pre-completion Tax Reliefs

Once a buyer has control of the target it should not be under any obligations to mitigate a pre-completion tax liability of the target company as it will want to organise the group's affairs going forward as it wishes. Only if it has been agreed as a commercial issue should the buyer be obliged to require the target company to use pre-completion tax reliefs to mitigate any pre-completion tax liability for the benefit of the seller. An example would be group relief claims but if so, the specific arrangements should be set out in a specific clause and not under a general mitigation clause.

In some circumstances the parties may agree to share available pre-completion tax reliefs such as corporation tax relief for share option and share schemes (contained in CTA 2009 sections 1001 to 1038) (see further discussion in **Chapter 1 (The Transactional Process)** paragraph 1.9.1). Alternatively, it could be agreed that the seller can offset a claim against some or all available pre-completion tax reliefs.

If the target is leaving a group it may be agreed that it will surrender either profits or losses available for surrender in respect of the pre-completion period to another member of the group, in which case provisions should be included to require the buyer and the target company to do all things necessary to effect the surrender, failing which the buyer's indemnity will be triggered (see paragraph 10.14 below). However, the wording of the provisions for post-completion conduct involving pre-completion group relief needs to be comprehensive, reflecting the exact agreement the parties came to including setting out the amounts to surrendered and claimed. In *Drachs Investment No. 3 Limited v Brightsea UK Limited* [2011] EWHC 1306 conduct for the target company's tax affairs pre-completion was given to the seller's agent, Deloittes. As a result Deloittes organised the claims for group relief, essentially, so as to take the benefit of an underprovision in the completion balance sheet. Litigation was expensive and could presumably have been avoided if the tax schedule had been explicit and quantified the maximum amounts of group relief. The case is required reading for tax advisors involved in transactions where pre-completion group relief provisions arise.

10.14 Buyer's Indemnity

It is becoming standard for the buyer to provide an indemnity to the seller for any tax liability in respect of a charge which could arise under the anti-avoidance provisions involving a change of ownership (previously ICTA sections 767AA and 767B and now contained in CTA 2010 sections 706 to 718). In the opinion of the author it is virtually impossible for these provisions to apply in any arm's length transaction which has no tax avoidance purpose. In order to apply, there needs to be an intention that corporation tax is not paid by the target company following the change of ownership and which would thereby involve the seller in some way. However, the seller's advisor may argue that if the provisions cannot apply the buyer should have no problem providing the indemnity.

If the target is leaving a group, it may be reasonable for the buyer to provide an indemnity relating to any tax liability arising from the withdrawal or amendments to any quantified pre-completion tax relief claimed by the seller or the seller's group before completion as well as an indemnity relating to any migration or change of residence of the target company following completion resulting in a tax liability of the target company. The pro-forma tax schedule in this publication also includes in the buyer's indemnity any tax liability for which the target company or the buyer has been put in funds but is not paid to the tax authority following completion.

Any buyer's indemnity should be subject to strict financial limitations and time limits, a gross up clause and specific conduct terms but these provisions should not necessarily be identical to those which apply to the seller's indemnity.

The taxation of a payment from a buyer to a seller representing a loss suffered by a disallowance of group relief should be capable of representing an increase in the consideration price for a UK seller and a reduction in the acquisition price for the buyer. The gross up clause should be worded to include tax payable by the seller less any CGT or corporation tax reliefs, together with interest and penalties imposed by HMRC. The situation may be different if the seller is not UK resident or incorporated.

10.15 Conduct Provisions

There are four major issues relating to conduct, three of which must be provided for in the tax schedule:

(a) preparation of pre-completion accounts and related tax returns (if not already prepared and filed by the target company);

(b) preparation of the completion accounts (if any);

(c) preparation of the straddle period returns for VAT and PAYE; and

(d) conduct of any tax claim under the tax schedule.

10.15.1 Pre-completion tax issues

As the seller will be liable in most transactions for any tax liability which arises before the completion there is no justification for the buyer to have automatic rights to prepare any pre-completion accounts and tax returns, particularly when the buyer will have less knowledge of the target company's tax affairs than the seller. The target will be required to submit them to HMRC under self-assessment, and so there must be adequate provisions for the target company's assistance in their preparation and filing post-completion. As costs relating to the preparation of tax returns would normally be allowable revenue expenditure for the target company, it would follow that they should be the target company's expense rather than the seller's expense, save where there are interest and penalties for late or incorrect filing. If completion accounts are prepared, it would be standard that these expenses are included as costs shared by the parties.

There could be circumstances where the buyer might insist on conduct, including if the target is late in filing its self assessment returns, or due diligence has disclosed late payments by the target company or significant problems within the target company including its administration functions. In these circumstances, the buyer is unlikely to absolve the seller from any tax liability arising in respect of errors in those returns, and there should be provisions for the seller and the seller's agents to agree the computations and returns and that the seller's liabilities under the tax indemnity remain in place in the normal way.

If the buyer insists upon having rights to amend the pre-completion tax returns and accounts, it would be unfair that the seller be liable for any tax liabilities arising in respect of that pre-completion period which arise because of those returns which are incorrect as a result of the amendment. Rather than provide the buyer with such a right, it is more straightforward that the buyer's sole rights to comment on the draft accounts would only arise in respect of obvious error, resulting in the seller becoming fully liable for any errors, with the buyer retaining rights to sue under the indemnity.

If the target company's tax personnel are to stay with the target company and prepare the pre-completion returns on behalf of the seller(s) it would be preferable that the target company's accountants act as agent for the seller(s) to review them – otherwise a conflict could arise.

10.15.2 Completion Accounts

These should be dealt with in a separate schedule in the SPA, and will require input from the tax advisors. Often negotiated and finalised on the eve of completion, they are absolutely central to protecting the positions of both the buyer and seller relating to the cut-off for transferring the tax liabilities of the target company. Most importantly as previously discussed, they must provide specific references (including quantum) to all tax assets and tax liabilities of the target company as at the completion date and not merely a net figure for tax liabilities. They should also contain full provisions for conduct in their compilation, rights of the other party to make amends, and detailed dispute mechanisms including time limits for resolution. Paragraph 10.11 above discusses the issue of 'overprovisions' and how they would conflict with completion accounts.

10.15.3 Straddle period tax returns

Client instructions will be needed as to which party will be preparing the returns for PAYE and VAT covering the period in which completion falls, as the filing will most likely be required following completion. The assumption would normally be that the buyer would wish this conduct with rights of the seller to make amendments. If completion accounts are to be prepared, it would be standard for the party preparing the initial draft to have conduct for the straddle period returns as well. If there are completion accounts, both parties should be properly protected by the provisions for tax liabilities and the straddle period returns may not have a bearing on the seller's liability under the tax indemnity, always assuming that the completion account will provide for VAT and PAYE tax issues as at the completion date.

If the transaction is an accounts deal, the seller should not be liable for tax arising in the ordinary course of business between the accounts date and the completion date. This will cover VAT and PAYE liabilities properly arising and will, therefore, include the straddle period accounts. Therefore, it would be proper for the buyer to prepare them.

10.15.4 Conduct of Claims and Tax Disputes

The claims provisions will be triggered in a number of circumstances, and should be covered in the definition of what amounts to a 'tax assessment' including any of the following:

- the target company or the buyer is alerted to an incorrect assessment to tax for the target under past self-assessment

returns relating to the pre-completion period – this may come from a party external to the target company/buyer or internally;
- HMRC open a discovery assessment on the target company or issues a notice of enquiry;
- HMRC issue a notice of assessment under FA 1998 Schedule 18 paragraph 47(1);
- the target company receives a claim for tax in respect of a connected party relating to the pre-completion period; or
- there is a withdrawal of tax relief or a previous tax charge relating to the pre-completion period is crystallised following completion, which results in a tax liability which falls within the tax indemnity.

The buyer should be required to give written notice to the seller of any likelihood of an unexpected pre-completion tax liability together with available details, promptly, on the issue coming to its attention and, failing any response from the seller within a stipulated time period (relatively short), that notice will be treated as final and the tax liability automatically belongs to the seller.

The notice of claim should include details of the liability, reference to the provision within the tax schedule under which the seller is liable, and the last date on which the seller is entitled to ask the buyer to instruct the target company to dispute the claim. The seller's right to make an appeal should be subject to indemnifying the buyer and the target company and putting them in funds for any estimated costs (including interest and penalties) arising from the dispute. It should be set out in the tax schedule as to whether costs for management time should be included as a valid cost.

The conduct of claims provisions are sometimes the most disputed during the tax schedule's negotiation, with the seller's tax advisor arguing for the unlimited right of the seller to dispute any tax assessment and to have unfettered conduct in the matter, and the buyer wanting limits on the seller's rights. However, the target company must be the party to seek a resolution with the tax authority. This is partially effected under the following provisions:
- the seller to confirm in writing within a specified period that it wishes the target company to dispute the tax assessment;

- the seller to fully indemnify the buyer and target company for costs and expenses of disputing the claim;
- an opinion from tax counsel if a dispute may result in litigation with a tax authority;
- all correspondence with the tax authorities drafted by the seller to be agreed by the buyer, agreement not to be unreasonably withheld[7]
- restrictions on the seller being entitled to dispute a claim if:
  - there is alleged fraud or deliberate carelessness relating to the tax assessment;
  - it would materially prejudice the activities of the target company or the buyer or their relationship with a tax authority;
  - any time limit within the tax statute to make an appeal has passed.

10.16 Gross-up and Withholdings

It is standard for the tax schedule to provide that any payments by the seller to the buyer in the transaction made under the tax schedule and the SPA be free of tax and any withholding, but if that tax arises on a payment or withholding is required, then the payee must gross up the payment to include the tax and/or withheld amount. This could be an issue if a tax authority was to impose a tax charge on the payment (as discussed in paragraph **10.7**) or if a jurisdiction outside the United Kingdom is involved, or there is a change of law and/or practice by a tax authority. It should be a requirement that the buyer provides the seller with the relevant authority that the payment will be subject to tax or withholding, which is provided for in paragraph 12.2 of the Long Form Tax Schedule (**Appendix 1**) and paragraph 7 of the Short Form Tax Schedule (**Appendix 2**).

10.17 Zim Properties[8]

This case is important in that it is likely to apply if a payment is made under the tax indemnity directly to the target company. The

---

[7] Although what amounts to reasonable and unreasonable can be a source of dispute in itself

[8] *Zim Properties Limited v Procter (Inspector of Taxes)* [1985] STC 90

taxpayer company (Zim) bought as investments some properties which, 13 years later, were damaged by fire. It entered into a contract in July 1973 to sell three properties to another company for £175,000 with completion to take place one year later. Completion did not take place because Zim had lost the original conveyance to one of the properties. The buyer sued Zim for the return of the deposit paid on the exchange of contracts and Zim issued a writ against its solicitors for damages for negligence. It was agreed that its solicitors had known when drafting the contract that Zim did not have the relevant conveyance. Zim argued that the solicitors failed to advise that the loss of the conveyance would create difficulties and that the contract should have been drafted differently. The damages claimed by Zim comprised £100,000, representing the difference between the sale price of £175,000 and the value of the properties at the date of the intended but unsuccessful completion, and £4,138.46 which was to represent interest on a loan which Zim obtained as a result of the non-availability of the sale proceeds, for use in its business. The parties to the litigation came to an agreement in which the solicitors' insurers made a payment of £69,000 to Zim (£60,000 being paid on 4 February 1976 and £9,000 paid on 23 April 1976).

It was argued by the Revenue that Zim's right of action against the solicitor was an asset and that the £60,000 payment derived from that asset or, alternatively, the payment was 'derived' from the asset consisting of Zim's right under its contract with the solicitor. Either way, tax was payable on the whole of the £60,000 as, in effect, pure capital gain. Zim argued that the £60,000 was derived from the three properties and, therefore, it was entitled to a deduction in computing its capital gain for its expenditure on the acquisition of the properties. Alternatively, it argued that there was no 'asset' of Zim within the meaning of the legislation from which the £60,000 could have been 'derived' and therefore no tax at all would be payable.

It was held that the claim was an asset for capital gains purposes, based on *O'Brien (Inspector of Taxes) v Benson's Hosiery (Holdings)*

Ltd[9] which held that contractual rights were an asset for capital gains tax purposes because they were something that could be turned to account – and that the £69,000 derived from the right held by Zim, namely a right to sue. Therefore, it followed that the capital sum of £69,000 was not derived from the properties and therefore its receipt could not be treated as part disposal of the properties. Furthermore, the acquisition of the chose in action, being the time when the contract was entered into by the parties, was not by way of a bargain made at arm's length and therefore it was deemed to have been acquired for consideration equal to its market value.

---

[9] *O'Brien (Inspector of Taxes) v Benson's Hosiery (Holdings) Ltd* [1979] STC 735, [1980] AC562

Appendix 1.   LONG FORM TAX SCHEDULE

Part A

1.   Definitions and Interpretation

1.1 In this Schedule [   ] the following words and expressions shall have the following meanings:

"Accounts"	the [audited] [unaudited] [consolidated] balance sheet and profit and loss accounts of the Company [and the Subsidiaries] for the period ending [ ] (**"Accounts Date"**);
"Associated Company"	a company which is associated with another company for the purposes of CTA 2010 section 25, namely when one of the two has control of the other or both are under the control of the same person;
"ATED"	annual tax on enveloped dwellings
"Auditors"	the Company's auditors for the time being and acting as experts and not as arbitrators;
"Business Day"	any day during which banks in the United Kingdom are not open for business with members of the public;
"Buyer's Tax Relief"	any Tax Relief of the Company which arises in respect of an Event following Completion and is unconnected with any pre-Completion period and any Tax Relief of the Buyer and the Buyer's Group other than any Tax Relief of the Company;
"CAA"	the Capital Allowances Act 2001;
"CIS"	the Construction Industry Scheme under FA 2004 Part 3 Chapter 3 (sections 57 to 77) and SI 2005/2045;
"Claim"	a claim made by the Buyer under this Schedule [ ] and whereby each and every Claim shall be a single set of legal proceedings for the purpose of ESC D33;
[**"Completion Accounts"**	the completion accounts as defined in this Agreement;]
'**Consideration Price'**	as defined in the SPA;
"CT Instalment Regulations"	means Corporation Tax (Instalment Payment) Regulations SI 1998/3175;
"Deemed Tax Liability"	a tax liability as defined in paragraphs 1.3(a) to 1.3(c) of this Schedule [ ]; **[see note 1]**
"Degrouping Charge"	a charge to Tax arising when a company leaves a group and relating to withdrawal of intra-group Tax

	Relief - see TCGA section 179; CTA 2009 sections 780 & 795; CTA 2009 sections 344 to 346; TCGA Schedule 7AC paragraph 38; and FA 2003 Schedule 7 paragraphs 3 & 9; [CTA 2009 section 344 to 352];
"Discovery Assessment"	an assessment made by HMRC under FA 1998 Schedule 18 paragraph 41(1);
"Discovery Determination"	a determination as referred to in FA 1998 paragraph 41(2);
"Dividend"	any dividend or distribution for the purposes of Taxation including under CTA 2010 section 1000;
"DOTAS"	the disclosure of tax avoidance schemes regime as set out in FA 2004 sections 306 to 319
"ESC"	Extra-Statutory Concession of HMRC
"Employment Income"	employment income as defined under ITEPA section 7;
"Event"	shall have its ordinary meaning and including without limitation any transaction (including Completion), receipt or payment of a Dividend or distribution; any acquisition or disposal; any transfer or payment; the receipt or making of a loan or an advance; the death of a person; a change of residence; and ceasing to be a member of a group (however defined) for the purposes of any Tax;
"FA"	followed by a number means the Finance Act of that year;
"GAAR"	the general anti-avoidance rules under FA 2013 sections 205 to 215;
"Group"	means the Company and its Subsidiaries and **"Group Company"** shall mean any of them;
["Group Payment Arrangements"	means arrangements entered into under TMA sections 59F to 59H involving the Company and other Group Companies;]
"Group Relief"	defined in CTA 2010 section 97(2) and relating to amounts eligible for relief from corporation tax and which may be surrendered or claimed under CTA 2010 sections 98 to 128;
["Group Relief Claims"	a claim for Group Relief to be made by the Company (as surrendering/claimant company) and [ ](as claimant/surrendering company for [£ /nil payment];]
"HMRC"	Her Majesty's Revenue & Customs;

"ICTA"	the Income and Corporation Taxes Act 1988;
"IHTA"	the Inheritance Tax Act 1994;
"ITA"	the Income Tax Act 2007;
"ITEPA"	the Income Tax (Earnings and Pensions) Act 2003;
"ITTOIA"	the Income Tax (Trading and other Income) Act 2005;
"NIC"	national insurance contributions;
"Notice of Assessment"	a notice of assessment to Tax as referred to in FA 1998 Schedule 18 paragraph 47(1);
"Notice of Claim"	a notice of claim under paragraph 6.1 of this Schedule [ ] and in the form provided in Appendix [1] attached hereto
"Notice of Enquiry"	a notice referred to in FA 1998 Schedule 18 paragraph 24;
"Ordinary Course of Business"	shall be the business carried on by the Company as at Completion, being [ ];
"PAYE"	the pay-as-you-earn system of collecting and accounting for income tax and NIC whereby an employer deducts amounts from employees' wages and salaries on their behalf as provided for under ITEPA sections 682 to 712 and SI 2003/2686 (Income Tax (Pay As You Earn) Regulations) including under the 'real time' regime;
"Relevant Territory"	a country or territory other than the United Kingdom including a country or territory where the Company is or may be subject to Tax under any relevant Tax Statutes;
["Reorganisation"	the series of transactions entered into on [ ] by the Company whereby [ ];]
"Roll-over Relief"	roll-over of tax payable under TCGA section 152;
"SDLT"	stamp duty land tax under the provisions of FA 2003;
"SDRT"	stamp duty reserve tax charged where there is an agreement between two people to transfer chargeable securities for consideration in money or money's worth under the provisions of FA 1986 sections 86 to 114;
"Secondary Tax Liability"	a liability to Tax which falls on a party as a result of the failure of a connected person (including another member of a group in which the company was or is a member) to pay a Tax Liability, including liabilities arising under CTA 2010 sections 706 to 718; TCGA section 190; FA 2003 Schedule 7 paragraph 12 and

	[joint and several liability for VAT if a member of a VAT group];
"Self-Assessment"	the system for assessing Taxation by persons under FA 1998 Schedule 18;
"Stamp Duty"	duty imposed under the Stamp Act 1891 and which applies to instruments relating to stock or marketable securities by virtue of FA 2003 section 125;
"Taxation/Tax"	any tax, charge, duty, impost, levy or withholding imposed by a Tax Authority including, without limitation, income tax, corporation tax, capital gains tax, inheritance tax, Stamp Duty, SDLT, the ATED, SDRT, NIC, VAT, excise duties, landfill tax, local rates, and aggregate levy, and any related penalty, fine, surcharge and/or interest;[1]
"Tax Assessment"	any claim, demand, query, notice and/or assessment relating to a Tax Liability originating from a Tax Authority or any Tax Liability or increased Tax Liability arising under Self Assessment;
"Tax Authority"	any authority or body whether in the United Kingdom or elsewhere which has authority to impose Tax under relevant statutory authority, including HMRC;
"Tax Claim"	any claim made by a Tax Authority against the Company;
"Tax Indemnity"	the indemnity set out in paragraph 2 in this Schedule;
"Tax Liability"	means an actual liability to pay Taxation [and any Deemed Tax Liability] **[see note 1]**;
"Tax Relief"	any relief against the payment of Taxation and including in respect of any losses of a capital or revenue nature, allowances, exemptions, set-off, credits and reliefs available in computing any Taxation under any Tax Statutes;
"Tax Return"	a return, assessment, form and/or other document relating to chargeability to and/or payment of Taxation made by a person to a Tax Authority including in respect of but not limited to Self-Assessment, PAYE, VAT, CIS, and SDLT or equivalent in any Relevant Territory;
"Tax Statute"	any statute, regulation and other order which

[1] See *Teeside Power Holding Limited v Electrabel International Holdings BV & GDF International SAS (2012) EWHC 33*

	provides the source and authority for Tax Authorities to impose Taxation;
"Tax Warranties"	the warranties set out in part B of this Schedule [ ];
"TCGA"	the Taxation of Chargeable Gains Act 1992;
"TIOPA 2010"	Taxation (International and Other Provisions) Act 2010
"TMA"	the Taxes Management Act 1970;
"VAT"	value added tax under VATA;
"VATA"	the Value Added Tax Act 1994.

1.2   For the avoidance of doubt, this Schedule [ ] forms part of this Agreement and all words and expressions defined in this Agreement apply to this Schedule [ ] except where expressly defined herein, but where a conflict arises relating to Taxation the provisions in this Schedule [ ] shall prevail.

1.3   A Tax Liability includes not only a requirement to make an actual payment of Taxation but also:

(a)   the loss of any Tax Relief which was available to the Company on or before Completion and taken into account when computing and reducing any provision for Taxation of the Company, and whereby such relief was capable of being set off against:

(i)   past, current or future income profit or gains of the Company; or

(ii) any Tax Liability of the Company;

(b)   the loss of a right to repayment of Taxation to the Company from a Tax Authority, such right having been available to the Company on or before Completion being [£…..];[2]

(c)   the use of a Buyer's Tax Relief against a Tax Liability of the Company arising in respect of any income, profits or gains earned, accrued or received on or before Completion and in circumstances where the Buyer would have been entitled to make a Claim against the Seller(s) in respect of such Tax Liability save for the use of the Buyer's Tax Relief.

---

[2] Best practice is to refer to the amount of any repayment

1.4 The amount that is to be treated as a Tax Liability falling within paragraphs 1.3(a), 1.3(b) and 1.3(c) above (in each case a "**Deemed Tax Liability**") shall be determined as follows:

(a) a Deemed Tax Liability which falls within paragraph 1.3(a) shall be [the amount of Tax Relief so lost and no longer available] [£   ];

(b) a Deemed Tax Liability which falls within paragraph 1.3(b) shall be [the amount of the repayment right so lost] [£   ];

(c) a Deemed Tax Liability which falls within paragraph1.3(c) shall be the amount of the Tax Liability which has been set-off by the Buyer's Tax Relief.

Note 1: Although the provisions for the treatment of a Deemed Tax Liability set out in paragraphs 1.3(a) and (b) above are common in most Tax Schedules they should only be included where it has been agreed that the Seller is guaranteeing the availability of the Tax Relief or Taxation repayments and quantum has been agreed. Furthermore a Deemed Tax Liability will only be pertinent if any Tax Liability under paragraphs 1.3 (a) or (b) exists. In the event that such Tax Liabilities are relevant and quantum has been agreed, best practice is to include the exact amounts. Alternatively, if there are to be Completion Accounts which include recognising such Tax assets, and which will be recognised in the Consideration price, these provisions in the Tax Schedule will be relevant. Otherwise, unless target is being acquired purely for its trading losses and other Tax Reliefs and the Consideration has been negotiated on those amounts, it would be unwise for the Seller to indemnify the Buyer for any Deemed Tax Liabilities. If target is or has recently been loss making or there are built-up Tax Reliefs, take instructions as to which party should take the benefit going forward and ensure that provisions for any such Tax Liabilities in the Completion Accounts conform with the commercial deal.

Alternatively, the deal may provide that a Claim may be set off against Tax Reliefs of target available at Completion, either completely or partially, and in which case the definitions above

should remain and the Limitations should include any Claim which falls within the agreed amount of those Tax Reliefs.

1.5   Any reference to profits being earned, accrued or received shall include any profits deemed for Taxation purposes to have been earned, accrued or received.

1.6   Words and expressions not otherwise defined in this Schedule [   ] and/or in this Agreement but which are defined or used in a Tax Statute shall have the same meaning as they have in such legislation.

2.   Indemnity

2.1   Subject to the provisions of this Schedule [   ] the Seller(s) [jointly and severally] fully indemnify/ies the Buyer **[see Note 2]** and covenant(s) with the Buyer to pay to the Buyer an amount equal to any Tax Liability which falls on the Company which arises by reference to any income profits or gains earned, received or accrued on or before Completion or in respect of any Event which occurred or deemed to occur or was effected on or before Completion including in respect of the following liabilities:

Note 2: Ensure that the indemnity is paid to the Buyer and not to target, so that the transaction will fall within the requirements of ESC D33 and not within the principles of Zim Properties (discussed more fully in Chapter 10 (The Tax Schedule in the Sale and Purchase of a Company), paragraph 10.17). If Zim applies any indemnity payment is likely to be subject to capital gains for the recipient, in which case the Seller will be required to gross-up the payment to include the tax affect (see paragraph 12 – Gross-Up provisions). In other words, the risk will be with the Seller. However the definition of Claim defines each such Claim to be a single set of legal proceedings, to ensure that HMRC changes to ESC D33 with effect from 27 December 2014 which exempts £500,000 only for each set of legal proceedings don't apply.

(a)   SDLT arising by reference to any United Kingdom land transaction involving the Company on or before Completion;

(b)   [any Degrouping Charge arising as a result of

Completion][3];

(c) [any Secondary Tax Liability arising in respect of a pre-Completion Event and which falls to be paid by the Company at any time][4];

(d) any securities and securities options as defined in ITEPA Part 7 Chapters 1 to 5 granted by [the Company] [a Group Company] before Completion and regardless of whether the Tax Liability arises before or after Completion;

(e) any breach of any Tax Warranty;

Note 3: Sub-paragraph (3) will cover any Tax Liability which could arise after Completion, say, on the sale of an asset when a balancing charge arises or when a previous tax charge is crystallised and so long as the relevant warranties have been provided – if a disclosure has been made, say, in respect of roll-over relief or balancing charges check what the parties have agreed in respect of any future liability. Often the buyer's advisor will refuse to accept such a provision.

(f) [*any issues provided for in the post-Completion conduct clause*];

(g) [TMA sections 109B to 109F and arising as a result of the cessation of residence in the United Kingdom of a company which is at, or has been before Completion, or is at any time within twelve months after the date of Completion a member of the same group as the Company;]

(h) [the Reorganisation];

Note 4: Regardless of whether any reorganisation has received HMRC approval under the legislation always include this as a specific indemnity as such approvals are very limited, confirming only that HMRC are satisfied the transaction was not for tax avoidance purposes.

(i) [the requirement of the Company to repay any part of any payment it has received for Group Relief or arising from the withdrawal of consent to surrender losses to

---

[3] Relevant only if the Company has been part of a group

[4] Relevant only if the Company has been part of a group

the Company for which the Company was a claimant under Group Relief under an agreement or arrangement entered before Completion;]

Note 5: This will only be relevant if target is leaving a group and payments for Group Relief have been in issue.

(j) [any apportion of profits of a controlled foreign company to the Company under ICTA section 752 (*apportionment of chargeable profits and creditable tax*) for accounting periods beginning before 1 January 2013;]

(k) a payment or deemed payment by the Company constituted as a chargeable payment connected with exempt distributions under CTA 2010 section 1086 made before Completion;

(l) [any liability arising on the Company solely due to it having been a member of the Seller's Group before Completion and regardless of whether such liability arises before or after Completion;]

Note 6: This covers secondary tax liabilities – if acting for the Seller require references to statutory provisions – either in the definitions or set out separately in this paragraph.

(m) [CTA 2010 sections 710 or 713, or TCGA section 190 relating to corporation tax assessed on the Company in respect of any period before Completion;]

(n) any waiver, forgiveness or treatment of any debt on or before Completion owed to the Company or alternatively owed to another company within a group of which the Company was a member before Completion;

(o) increased corporation tax not previously provided for due to the existence of an Associated Company at any time before Completion;

(p) the making, release or writing off of loans or advances by the Company before Completion giving rise to a liability under CTA 2010 sections 455 to 464 (*charges to tax in connection with loans by a participator in close company*);

(q) the anti-avoidance provisions by reference to CTA

2010 sections 731 to 751 (*Transactions in securities*) subject to clause 4.1(c) below; and

(r) IHTA sections 94 and 202 (*charge on participators/Close Company provisions*).

2.2 The Tax Indemnity contained in paragraph 2.1 above shall cover all costs and expenses on a full indemnity basis reasonably incurred by the Buyer and/or the Company in connection with or arising out of any successful Claim.

Note 7: The Seller will not wish to be responsible for open-ended costs arising from a fishing expedition brought by the Buyer or target – hence the reasonable requirement (if acting for the Seller) for a Claim to be successful before the Buyer can claim costs. If the Buyer considers that a pre-Completion Tax Liability has arisen it must start the process for making a Claim according to the relevant provisions under paragraph 6 (Conduct of Claims and Tax Disputes). An additional issue will be whether the management time of the Buyer and target should be included in the definition of 'costs reasonably incurred' which the Seller is advised to specifically carve out.

3. **Limitations**

Note 8: The Limitations clause is the most important protection for both the Buyer and the Seller as it should specify all Tax Liabilities which will stay with target as commercially agreed between the parties, with any other Tax Liabilities falling within the Indemnity for the account of the Seller. If the Completion Accounts only provide for working capital (in which case Taxation provisions may only include debits and credits for VAT and PAYE payments and nothing for corporation tax, for example) the Limitations clause should include other taxes (usually including corporation tax) arising from the trading activities of target but not due to be paid before Completion.

General

3.1 The Tax Indemnity shall not apply to a Tax Liability of the Company to the extent that:

(a) a specific provision or reserve in respect of that provision was made in the [Completion] Accounts ([not being] [including] a provision or reserve for deferred Taxation)] [or referred to in the [Completion] Accounts notes]

Note 9: Regardless of which party you are acting for, require details of what Tax Liabilities will be provided for in the Completion Accounts or have been specifically provided for in the Accounts – if the Accounts are abbreviated or have no specific provisions (which is common) request details of all Tax liabilities at the Accounts Date and refer to them in an appendix to the tax schedule or the SPA.

(b) it was paid on or before Completion but not taken into account in the [Completion] Accounts;

Note 10: This situation could arise, for example, if target has made a quarterly payment for corporation tax before Completion but the Completion Accounts only provide for working capital tax liabilities, or simply if a payment for Tax has inadvertently not been included in the Completion Accounts workings or the Accounts.

(c) the provision or reserve in respect thereof was made in the [Completion] Accounts and is insufficient or such Tax Liability arises, only by reason of an increase in rates of Taxation or as a result of any change in the law or withdrawal or any regulation or published practice of a Tax Authority made after Completion with retrospective effect;

(d) [it can be offset or partially and is so offset against an Available Tax Relief (as defined in this Agreement) under the provisions of paragraph 10 (**"Mitigation"**) below;]

Note 11: Include only in circumstances where this has been commercially agreed.

(e) it arises or relates solely due to transactions by the Company in the ordinary course of its business after the Accounts Date so long as it does not represent interest or penalties relating to any Tax;

Note 12: If there are no Completion Accounts it is essential for the Seller that this limitation is included.

(f) [it has arisen solely due to a voluntary act outside the Ordinary Course of Business of the Company effected by the Buyer or the Company following Completion other than any act in fulfilment of a legally binding commitment entered into by the Company on or before Completion or an action carried out with the [written] approval of the Seller(s) and which the Buyer ought reasonably to be aware could give rise to a Claim;]

Note 13: Rather than provide such a potentially wide ranging limitation the Buyer should require specific examples of what voluntarily acts could result in a pre-Completion Tax Liability and only then agree to them by reference in the limitation.

(g) it arises from the failure of the Buyer to do something and/or remedy a situation (or to procure that the Company so does or remedies) which came to the knowledge of the Buyer before Completion and in respect of which the Buyer knew [or ought reasonably to have known] it was obliged to so do or remedy and/or in respect of which the parties to this Agreement agreed that the Buyer would so do or remedy following Completion;

Note 14: This is intended to cover any Taxation issue which came to light during the Due Diligence and which is required under tax Statute or by a Tax Authority to be remedied. Whether or not the Tax Liability will relate purely to interest and penalties or include the underlying liability Tax will depend on whether the Consideration has been calculated to take it into account.

(h) it would not have arisen but for a change after Completion in the accounting reference date or change in accounting policies or practices used in the Accounts save in the event such change was required under any Tax Statute in effect before Completion;

(i) it arises as a result of a cessation of trading by the Company or a change in the nature of its trade after Completion;

Note 15: The Buyer should ensure that as a result of any restructuring involving target following Completion, these provisions cannot apply - otherwise they will prevent a legitimate claim from being made under the Tax Indemnity.

(j)   it arises under a Claim made by the Buyer after [*the fourth anniversary of the date of Completion*] **[see Appendix [6] – Time Limits for assessments & Claims]**;

(k)   the Tax Liability arises solely in respect of income profits or gains of the Company arising or deemed to have arisen before Completion and remaining with the Company at Completion and which were not provided for in the Completion Accounts;

Note 16: This is intended to cover any pre-Completion windfall profits discovered following Completion so long as they were not dissipated some way such as through the payment of a pre-Completion distribution. If there are no Completion Accounts this issue is covered in paragraph 3.1(e) for tax arising in the ordinary course of business but not in respect of windfall profits.

(l)   it has been made good to the Company or the Company or the Buyer has otherwise been compensated, at no expense to the Buyer or the Company;

Note 17: This ensures no double recovery which might arise such as in respect of an unpaid pre-Completion employment related tax which has been made good by the employee following Completion.

(m)   [it would not have arisen but for the failure to the Buyer to comply with its obligations under paragraph 6 [ ] of this Schedule [ ];]

Note 18: If acting for the Buyer restrict this limitation to penalties and interest arising from any such failures save in the event paragraph 6 includes specific obligations on the Buyer.

(n)   it arises from a disclaimer by the Company after Completion of capital allowances, Tax Relief and/or Group Relief available and claimed by the Company before Completion in respect of any relevant period ended on or before [Accounts Date] [Completion] save for any such disclaimer agreed between the Buyer and the Seller(s) to be so made;

(o)   [it would not have arisen but for a failure by the

Company to make any claim, election, surrender or disclaimer or give any notice or consent or do any other thing after Completion, of which the making or giving or doing was taken into account in computing the provision for Taxation in the [Completion] Accounts;]

Note 19: Save in circumstances where completion occurs fairly close to the Accounts Date, this is likely to be relevant only if there are Completion Accounts as it will have been the responsibility of target to make the relevant claims, etc. provided in the Accounts.

(p) [it arises in connection with an insufficient instalment payment made by the Company under the CT Instalment Regulations where such instalment payment would not have arisen but for the profits earned by the Company after Completion proving to be greater than the profits expected by the Company at the date of the relevant instalment payment made before Completion;]

Note 21: Only relevant if target has been paying corporation Tax under the instalment regime.

(q) it arises solely as a consequence of a claim, election, surrender or disclaimer relating to Taxation and made after Completion by the Company or the Buyer other than a claim, election, surrender or disclaimer made or given (or agreed to be made or given) in computing the provisions for Taxation, Tax Reliefs, Group Relief and/or reserves relating to Taxation in the [Completion] Accounts; or

(r) it has been specifically provided for in determining the Consideration including in respect of which there is a post-Completion adjustment to the Consideration Price;

(s) it is in respect of any supplemental penalty, charge, interest or default surcharge arising due to a delay or default of the Buyer or the Company after Completion in paying an amount to a Tax Authority where such amount has been recovered from the Seller(s) under a Claim or provided for in the [Completion] Accounts.

3.2 For the purposes of this paragraph 3, none of the following shall be regarded as occurring in the Ordinary Course of Business (but without limitation to the definition of that expression):

(a) any payment of a Dividend (including a deemed distribution);

(b) a change in the nature of the trade or business of the Company;

(c) any transaction effected otherwise than at arm's length principles;

(d) the Company ceasing, or being deemed to cease, to be a member of any group of companies or associated with any other company for any Taxation purpose;

(e) any event which represents tax avoidance or forms part of a scheme, the sole or main purpose of which is the avoidance of tax;

(f) the disposal of any capital asset;

(g) any transaction or series of transactions entered into for the [sole] purpose of reducing any Tax Liability of the Company;

(h) the creation, cancellation or reorganisation of any share or loan capital of the Company;

(i) the failure by the Company to deduct or account for any Taxation in respect of any Event which gives rise to any fine, penalty, surcharge, interest or other imposition relating to Taxation;

(j) [*any other issues coming to light under the due diligence*].

3.3 The limitations set out in paragraph 3.1 above (**"Limitations"**) shall not apply in the event a Claim in respect of a Tax Liability which relates to or arises as a result of [obvious] fraud [and/or was brought about deliberately or carelessly] on the part of the Seller(s) or the Company [in which case any limitations arising under any relevant Tax Statute shall apply to the time limit of making a Claim].

Note 22: A Buyer may object to any limitation in respect of fraud but a Seller would be hard pressed to insist on a qualification if a relevant warranty has been provided.

Maximum [and Minimum] cap on Seller(s)' liability

Note 23: It is generally not advisable for a minimum cap be provided for a Claim under the Tax Schedule, on the principle that the Buyer is acquiring target for Consideration on the basis that all pre-Completion Tax Liabilities have been provided for. The provision of the more common maximum cap is based on the principle that the Buyer should not profit from receipt of an amount greater than the purchase price paid for target.

3.4   [The maximum aggregate liability of the Seller(s) under this Schedule [ ] shall be £[   ].]

Note 24: This may be provided in a global figure in the body of the Agreement in which case include a cross reference in the Tax Schedule.

3.5   [The Seller(s) shall not be liable in respect of any Claim unless such Claim together with the aggregate of claims by the Buyer under this Agreement and any other Claims under this Schedule [ ] amounts in aggregate to a sum in excess of £[ ] whereupon the full amount of all Tax Claims shall be recoverable.]

Note 25: The Buyer should reject this provision, under the same principles for rejecting any *de minimis* limitation, although it will be a commercial decision for the parties.

3.6   The Seller(s) shall not be liable under this Schedule [ ] for any Tax Liability to the extent that the Seller(s) has/have fully satisfied a liability elsewhere under this Agreement in respect of any breach of Warranty, representation or undertaking which relates to the same amount of Tax Liability arising in respect of the same Event.

Time Limits for making Claims

3.7   Subject to the provisions in paragraph 3.3 no Claim shall be made unless it is notified in writing to the Seller(s) in the manner provided for in this Agreement and within [*four years*] of the Completion Date [save in the event the subject matter of the Claim is one whereby HMRC may under

Statute make an assessment outside that time limit of [*four*] years in which case the time limits for the Buyer to make a Claim shall be that as set out under such Statute].

4. **[Buyer's Indemnity]**

Note 26: It is becoming more common for a Seller to require an indemnity from the Buyer in respect of a charge which could hypothetically arise on the Seller under CTA 2010 sections 706 to 718 (previously ICTA 767A, 767AA and 767B) and discussed in Chapter 3 (Warranties) – these anti-avoidance provisions are unlikely to apply in an arm's length commercial transaction and if target has never been a member of a group then this paragraph can be dispensed with.

4.1 The Buyer covenants with the Seller(s) to pay to the Seller(s) an amount equal to any of the following:

(a) [any Tax Liability of the Seller(s) or any member of the Seller's Group which arises as a result of the reduction or disallowance after Completion of Group Relief previously surrendered by the Company before Completion and relating to an accounting period ended on or before Completion as a result of the Company withdrawing its consent to such Group Relief; or]

Note 27: This is the counterpart to the Tax Indemnity referred to in paragraph 2.1(i) above and will only be relevant if target is leaving a group.

(b) any Tax Liability which falls to be paid by the Seller(s) [or any member of the Seller's Group] in respect of a Claim or otherwise which:

(i) arises due to the activities of the trade or business of the Company ceasing or becoming negligible following Completion;

(ii) is due to the migration or change in residence of the Company following Completion (including by virtue of a change in its control and management) and which may arise under TMA section 109E; and/or

(iii) relates to any Event income profits or gains [occurring in the Ordinary Course of Business of the Company] in respect of a period before Completion for which the Seller is not liable under the terms of this Schedule [   ] and falls to be paid by the Company following Completion but remains unpaid such that the Seller or member of the Seller's Group become liable;

(c) [any Tax Liability arising under CTA 2010 sections 731 to 751 (*cancellation of corporation tax advantage from certain transactions in securities*) in respect of Consideration received under this Agreement to the extent that such a liability would not have arisen but for the payment of an abnormal amount by way of dividend by the Company following Completion];

(d) all costs and expenses on a full indemnity basis reasonably incurred by the Seller(s) in connection with or arising out of any successful action taken in respect of this paragraph 4.

Note 28: This provision should mirror paragraph 2.2.

4.2 Any payment made by the Buyer under this paragraph shall be subject to the same provisions as set out in paragraph 12 (Gross Up Clause) but references to Buyer shall mean Seller and vice versa.

4.3 No claim shall be capable of being made by the Seller(s) against the Buyer under this paragraph 4:

(a) after the relevant date contained in any relevant Tax Statute under which the Seller(s) becomes liable; or

(b) in the event paragraph 4.2(a) does not apply following the [*fourth*] anniversary of the Completion Date

AND which exceeds [£ *amount*].

Note 29: It would be unwise for the Buyer to provide an uncapped indemnity to the Seller but it would be equally unfair to the Seller(s) not to be covered by the amount they might be liable for, in the unlikely event the above circumstances apply due to the Buyer's conduct.

4.4 Where the Buyer becomes liable to make any payment under paragraph 4.1 the due date for the making of that payment should be the later of the date on which the Tax

Liability is due to the Tax Authority demanding the same and seven days after written demand therefore by the Seller(s) to the Buyer.

4.5   Where the Buyer fails to make a payment in satisfaction of a liability under paragraph 4.1 the liability of the Buyer shall be increased to include interest on such liability from the date on which the Buyer becomes liable to the date of payment at a rate of [four] per cent above the base rate from time to time of [Barclays] Bank plc compounded monthly (such interest to accrue after as well as before judgment).

Note 30: Check the interest clause in the body of the Agreement and ensure it corresponds with paragraph 11.2 of this Schedule and this provision.

5.   **Pre-Completion Taxation Issues**

Note 31: Take instructions on these points early in the transaction and ensure there is no a conflict with the provisions agreed for any Completion Accounts.

5.1   The Seller(s) and the Buyer agree that:

(a)   for all of the Company's accounting periods ended on or before Completion ("**Pre-Completion Accounting Periods**") the Seller(s) shall at the Company's expense but with full co-operation of the Company and the Buyer:

(i)   have sole conduct of, properly and promptly within the required time limits set by Tax Statutes, preparing the accounts relating to the Pre-Completion Accounting Period (**"Pre-Completion Accounts"**) and for the submission of the Tax Returns of the Company (including, but not limited to, the preparation of all relevant correspondence and claims) ("**Pre-Completion Tax Returns**") to the relevant Tax Authority;

(ii)   be provided with such necessary information and assistance and access to all documents and records of the Company as it/they may require to prepare properly the Pre-Completion Accounts and the

Pre-Completion Tax Returns;

(iii) be entitled to require the Buyer to procure that the Company properly makes any claims for any available Tax Reliefs in respect of all and any Pre-Completion Tax Returns as required by the Seller(s) [including the Group Relief Claim];

(iv) be entitled to require the Company to execute all documents required for the proper filing with the Tax Authorities of the Pre-Completion Tax Returns, save in the case of manifest error in which case the Buyer shall inform the Seller(s) promptly of any concern of such error in which case such error shall be properly rectified by the Company;

Note 32: These provisions are necessary if pre-Completion accounts have not been prepared and/or pre-Completion Tax returns have not been filed before Completion which is usually the case. As the Sellers will be liable for any related Tax Liability, it is only correct that they be entitled to have full conduct. As target must file the returns, the Seller(s) will require its full co-operation and it should only be in the case of manifest error that the Buyer should be entitled to comment on the return. If the Buyer's tax advisor does not agree to this then the Seller should refuse to provide a Tax Indemnity in respect of those accounts. If target is leaving a group and there is to be a claim for group relief made by the group involving target, full details should be included in the definition for 'Group Relief Claim' including quantum. If there is no exact quantum available, there should be reference to a capped amount, and a side letter setting out the procedure for the sellers agreeing the amount of relief within a specific time frame.

(b) for the accounting period in which Completion falls (**"Straddle Period"**) and subject to the provisions of paragraph 5.2 below:

(i) the [Buyer][Seller(s)] shall at the Company's expense have sole conduct of preparing, within the relevant time periods required under Tax Statute, and submitting to the relevant Tax Authorities the accounts of the Company and all returns relating to Taxation arising in respect of the Straddle Period (**"Straddle Period Tax Returns"**);

(ii) the [Seller(s)][Buyer] shall assist the [Buyer][Seller(s)] and the Company in the preparation of the Straddle Period Tax Returns so far as he/they is/are able relating to the period before Completion;

Note 33: Client instructions are needed as to which party is to have conduct for the straddle period but it would be usual for the Buyer to have full conduct with the Seller have the right of comment. If there are Completion Accounts both parties should be properly protected by provisions for Taxation and the Straddle Period Returns will have no bearing on the Seller(s) liability under the Tax Schedule. If there are to be no Completion Accounts the Seller will normally be liable only for Tax Liabilities arising outside the ordinary course of business between the Accounts Date and Completion and therefore the Seller(s) would, in most circumstances, want the right to consider the accounts and tax returns to agree any Tax Liabilities which would fall on them.

(c) the [Seller(s)] [Buyer] shall at the expense of [the Company] have the sole conduct of preparing returns relating to PAYE and VAT of the Company for the relevant period in which Completion falls.

5.2 Under paragraphs 5.1(b) and 5.1(c) above, before any submission to the relevant Tax Authority the [Seller(s)][Buyer] shall first submit draft accounts, tax computations and draft correspondence relating to the preparation of the Straddle Period Tax Returns and the PAYE and VAT Returns to the [Buyer] [Seller(s)] who may make such reasonable representation as it/they think(s) fit and provided such representations are made promptly and in any event within [14] Business Days of such submission the [Seller(s)] [Buyer] shall take account of any such reasonable representations and accordingly amend such.

5.3 Further to paragraph 5.2 above in the event a dispute arises and agreement cannot be reached between the Buyer and the Seller(s) regarding the Straddle Period Returns and the

VAT and PAYE Returns the Auditors shall be asked to make a ruling in respect of any dispute, which shall be binding on the parties.

5.4   The Buyer shall procure that the Company will not amend, withdraw or disclaim any elections or claims previously made by or on behalf of the Company in respect of the Pre-Completion Accounting Periods and the Buyer shall procure that the Company shall not carry back losses from accounting periods ending after Completion in circumstances where such carry back will interfere with such elections or claims.

5.5   [The Seller acknowledges that the Company shall cease to be entitled to be a member of the Group Payment Arrangements on Completion and that it has informed HMRC of the Company's withdrawal from such arrangements.]

5.6   [The Seller and the Buyer acknowledge that the Company will cease to be a member of VAT Group No [ ] on Completion and that the Seller has so notified HMRC of this issue.]

6.   Conduct of Claims and Tax Disputes

6.1   If the Buyer or the Company becomes aware of a Tax Assessment on the Company or a potential Tax Claim which may give rise to a Claim against the Seller(s) under this Schedule [ ], the Buyer shall [as soon as reasonably practicable but not as a condition precedent to any Claim under this Agreement] [immediately] give or procure that the Company gives to the Seller(s) written notice of such assessment or claim, with relevant details which the Buyer and the Company are reasonably able to provide, including the amount of any Tax Liability of the Company and the latest date for payment (**"Notice of Claim"**) and [save as provided for in this paragraph 6] the Seller(s) shall reimburse the Buyer the amount of such liability within the time limits set out in the Notice of Claim which shall be under the provisions of paragraph 11 below.

6.2 Each and every Notice of Claim shall be treated as initiating a single set of legal proceedings[5].

6.3 If the Notice of Claim relates to any Pre-Completion Tax Returns the Seller(s) shall have the right to require the Company to respond to such Tax Assessment or Tax Claim and to answer any related queries by the relevant Tax Authority as it/they direct(s) (subject always to the provisions set out in paragraphs 6.4 to 6.7 below).

Note 34: If the Seller(s) prepared the Tax Returns and are liable for any Tax Assessment they should have the right to investigate and appeal. However, they can only instruct target to liaise with the Tax Authority and the Seller should never be granted unfettered right to conduct the appeal.

6.4 Under paragraphs 6.1 and 6.3 above but subject to paragraphs 6.5 to 6.6 below, on the Seller receiving a Notice of Claim (and so long as such Notice of Claim does not relate to a Discovery Assessment relating to deliberate behaviour by the Seller as referred to in FA 1998 Schedule 18 paragraph 46 in which case the Buyer and the Company shall be entitled to deal fully with the Tax Assessment in question), the Buyer shall procure that the Company will afford the Seller(s) all reasonable facilities and opportunities to investigate the relevant matter which is the subject of the Notice of Claim including access to records and take such action as the Seller(s) may reasonably request to properly dispute, avoid, resist, appeal against or compromise the Tax Assessment or Tax Claim (**"Appeal"**) **PROVIDED THAT**:

(a) the Buyer or Company shall not be obliged to appeal against any Tax Assessment raised on the Company if, having provided to the Seller(s) the Notice of Claim, the Buyer has not within [15] Business Days thereafter received instructions in writing from the Seller(s) to make such Appeal;

(b) if the Appeal relates to litigating the matter with a Tax

---

[5] This provisions reflects changes to HMRC treatment of ESC D33, whereby an exempt amount is capped at £500,000 for each single set of proceedings

Authority counsel nominated by the Buyer and of at least ten years call and experience in Taxation matters (**"Tax Counsel"**) opines in writing that the matter is likely to succeed on the balance of probabilities;

(c) the Seller(s) shall not be entitled to request the Buyer and/or the Company to take any action under this paragraph 6 in respect of any Tax Assessment or Tax Claim if it is alleged that either the Seller(s) or the Company whilst it was under the control of the Seller(s), committed acts or omissions which may constitute fraud or deliberate tax evasion;

(d) neither the Company nor the Buyer shall be required to take action which in the opinion of the Buyer's directors interferes with the normal course of the business of the Company and/or which is likely to materially prejudice the business of the Company and/or its relationship with the relevant Tax Authority, but in which case the Buyer shall set out in writing to the Seller(s) the detailed basis for such opinion;

(e) the Seller(s) fully indemnifies and secures the Buyer and the Company to their reasonable satisfaction against the liability in question and all costs and expenses (including, without limitation, interest, fines, penalties and interest on overdue Taxation) which may be incurred in respect of making the Appeal; and

(f) all communications written or otherwise relating to the matter which are to be transmitted to the Taxation Authorities shall be drafted by the Seller(s) and submitted for approval by the Buyer, the Company and their agents and shall be transmitted by the Company following approval (and in the absence of specific approval within [21] Business Days of such submission such approval shall be deemed to have been given).

6.5   The Company and/or the Buyer (as the case may be) shall be at liberty without reference to the Seller(s) to instruct the Company to admit, compromise, settle, discharge or otherwise deal with any Tax Assessment or Tax Claim after the earliest of:

(a) [oral instructions confirmed in writing or] the service of a notice in writing on the Buyer and/or the Company by any of the Seller(s) to the effect that it/they consider the matter should not be resisted;

(b) where paragraph 6.4(b) applies receipt of notification in writing from Tax Counsel that the Appeal is on the balance of probabilities likely to fail;

(c) the expiry of a period of [ten] Business Days following a service of written notice by the Buyer and/or the Company on the Seller(s) [or any of them] requiring the Seller(s) to clarify the terms of any request to make an Appeal under paragraph 6.4 and during such period no such clarification has been received by the Buyer and/or the Company; and

(d) the expiration of any period prescribed by applicable legislation for the making of an appeal against either the Tax Assessment or Tax Claim in question or the related decision of any court or tribunal.

6.6   Neither the Buyer nor the Company shall be obliged to take any action in respect of an Appeal, the effect of which in the opinion of the Auditors will, or is reasonably likely, to increase the amount of Taxation payable by the Company [and/or the Buyer] in respect of accounting periods ending after the Accounts Date beyond what it would have been liable but for the taking of such action nor shall either party be obliged to take any action under this paragraph 6 the effect of which in the opinion of the Auditors is reasonably likely to prejudice the ability of the Company and/or the Buyer to order its affairs in such a way as to properly minimise its liability to Taxation in respect of any later accounting periods.

6.7   The Seller(s) shall be bound to accept for the purposes of this Schedule [ ] any admission, compromise, settlement or discharge of any Tax Assessment and Tax Claim and the outcome of any related proceedings made or arrived at in accordance with the provisions of this paragraph 6.

Note 35: The Buyer should have the stronger rights in respect of any tax disputes with the Tax Authorities and it should only be in exceptional circumstances that the Seller should be entitled to require target to litigate a Tax issue.

7. Recovery From Other Persons

7.1 In the event a Claim arises on the Seller(s) and the Company is contractually entitled to recover from another person (**"Third Party"**) any sum in respect of the Tax Liability which is the subject of the Claim, the Buyer shall procure that the Seller(s) is/are notified of such entitlement and, if so requested by the Seller(s) the Buyer may at its entire discretion take appropriate steps to enforce such recovery from the Third Party **PROVIDED THAT**:

(a) the Seller(s) fully indemnifies and secures the Buyer and the Company to their reasonable satisfaction against the liability in question and all costs and expenses which may be incurred in taking such steps;

(b) enforcement of such recovery would not be against the best interests of the Company and/or the Buyer and its Group.

7.2 Under paragraph 7.1 above any amount so recovered by the Buyer from the Third Party shall be offset against the Seller's liability under the Claim or in the event the Seller(s) has/have made a payment in respect of the Claim, the Buyer shall account to the Seller(s) for whichever is the lesser of:

(a) any sum so recovered by the Buyer from the Third Party; and

(b) the amount paid by the Seller(s) to the Buyer under the Claim.

Note 36: It is fair that the Buyer should have total discretion to recover from a third party under the principle that target was acquired on the basis of the truthfulness of the Sellers' Tax Warranties. A likely scenario is if target has wrongly administered PAYE before Completion and after Completion target remains entitled to collect any underpayment of income tax and/or NIC from a director or employee. In such a case, the

Buyer may not wish to disturb the goodwill of its workforce by enforcing payment from the individual and would wish to simply recover from the Seller(s) under the Tax Indemnity.

8.   [Overprovisions]

Note 37: These provisions should be included only in certain circumstances and preferably at the discretion of the Buyer. They are NOT appropriate if there are Completion Accounts which make full provisions for the Tax Liabilities of target and which should have a disputes and amendment mechanism. This issue is discussed in Chapter 10 (The Tax Schedule in the Sale and Purchase of a Company) at paragraph 10.11.

A Seller would be hard pressed to argue for an overprovisions clause in respect of any accounts which it has prepared and warranted to be true and accurate. If there are no provisions for Tax Liabilities in the Accounts an Overprovision clause is clearly not appropriate. Otherwise if the Buyer is minded to agree to the provisions they should strictly be limited in time and quantum in order to deter the Seller from seeking to apply them. If acting for the Buyer it is advisable not to include paragraph 8.1(b) below.

8.1   Subject to paragraph 8.2 below if the Seller(s) request (at its/their expense) the Buyer to instruct the Auditors to consider whether the provisions for Taxation in the Accounts have proved to be an overprovision (**"Overprovision"**) and the Buyer at its entire discretion agrees to instruct, and the Auditors certify that there has been an Overprovision other than an Overprovision which is attributable to the effect of a change after the Completion Date in rates of Taxation or in any accounting practices or policies or an accounting date with retrospective effect) (**"Certification"**) the Overprovision shall be dealt with as follows:

(a)   it shall first be set off against any payment then due from the Seller(s) under a Claim; and

(b)   [to the extent that there is no such Claim and set-off or there is an excess after such set-off under sub-paragraph 8.1(a) above, a refund shall be made to the Seller(s) of any previous payment or payments made by the Seller(s) under a previous Claim and not previously refunded under any other circumstances, up to the amount of the lesser of the Overprovision and such excess; and]

(c) in the event any excess referred to in sub-paragraph 8.1[(a)][(b)] above is not exhausted, the remainder of the excess shall be carried forward and set off against any future payment or payments which become due from the Seller(s) under a Claim.

8.2   Any request by the Seller(s) under paragraph 8.1 must be made and the Auditors must consider and if relevant make a Certification not later than the [*second anniversary*] of the Completion Date after which the Seller's rights to make such a request shall expire.

8.3   Any amount of Overprovision referred to in paragraph 8.1 shall be limited to [£   ].

8.4   In the event the Auditors consider that there has been no Overprovision their consideration shall be final.

8.5   If within a period of six months following the making of a Certification paragraph 8.4 above does not apply, the Buyer may (at the Seller's expense) request the Auditors to review such Certification in the light of any relevant issues relating to Taxation which have become known since such Certification, and to confirm whether such Certification remains correct or requires amendment.

8.6   If a request has been made by the Buyer under paragraph 8.5, and the Auditors confirm that the Certification should be amended:

(a) in the event there is an amended Overprovision, that amended Overprovision shall be substituted for the purposes of paragraph 8.1 and such adjusting payment (if any) as may be required by virtue of the above-mentioned substitution shall be made as soon as practicable by the Seller(s) or (as the case may be) to the Seller(s);

(b) if the Auditors confirm there is no Overprovision the Seller(s) shall forthwith reimburse the Buyer for any amount so set-off or paid to the Seller(s) under the provisions of paragraph 8.1 above.

9.   **[Reliefs and Savings]**

Note 38: Often tax schedules include a 'Reliefs and Savings' provision whereby if a Tax Liability arises and a Claim is made, that Claim can be effectively reduced by any amount of savings in Tax which arises directly from the Tax Liability in question. An example would be if target has to pay for a previous underpayment of secondary NIC which on payment by target to the Tax Authorities, it would become an allowable trading expense for the accounting period in question, which in turn would result in a lower corporation tax charge for target. In essence, a provision covering this would result in Claims being netted off, with the Buyer receiving a reduced payment for the Tax Liability in question, with target liable to pay the Tax Liability and its after tax income for the relevant period reflecting the net position accordingly. Target's net earnings will inevitably be less than the earnings warranted by the Seller if it is an Accounts deal or expected under the Completion Accounts mechanism, and the Buyer will be acquiring an asset which is worth less than agreed at Completion. The concept is, therefore, fundamentally flawed from the perspective of any buyer and ignores the importance of the truthfulness of the tax warranties and disclosure requirements. It also begs the question of 'Why should the onus be on the Buyer to calculate any savings when a Claim arises?'

A savings provision cuts into the principle of a 'pound for pound' indemnity and a Seller could invoke the clause in respect of each and every Tax Liability which results in a Claim, causing a real nuisance for the Buyer and target. If a Buyer is mindful to agree to such a provision, the provision needs to be tightly worded to cover only actual and identifiable savings in corporation Tax of target. Any savings provision should be subject to a *de minimis* amount and both the Auditors costs and management time of target and Buyer should be included to deter frivolous claims by the Seller. The Buyer could also require that the netting off should not result in target's net income figure for the relevant period being less than warranted in the Accounts or calculated in the Completion Account, but it is difficult to think of when the provision could be invoked.

9.1   In the event a Claim has been made and the Buyer has been put in funds by the Seller(s) for the full amount payable under the Tax Indemnity and under the provisions of this Schedule [ ], and the Seller(s) have received written advice from the Auditors that the Company will receive an actual saving in respect of its corporation Tax as a result of the Tax Liability in question (**"Savings"**) the Seller shall be entitled to forward such advice to the Buyer and to the Company and request that an amount equal to the Savings be set off against any future Claim made against it **PROVIDED THAT**:

(a) the Auditors confirm that such a Savings has been effected and so long as the amount of savings is not less than [£XXX] net of costs referred to below in sub-paragraph (b);

(b) the Seller has fully indemnified and secured both the Buyer and the Company for all their costs and expenses relating to their actions necessary to consider the advice received by the Seller referred to above, as well as the related costs and expenses of the Auditors.

10.   Mitigation

Buyer's Mitigation

Note 39: The concept of the Buyer being required to mitigate if a pre-Completion Tax Liability and Claim arise is fundamentally flawed from a commercial perspective and should only be agreed to in specific circumstances. Once the Buyer has control of target it will not wish to be under an obligation to take action for the benefit of the Seller in the event a Claim arises. If it has been commercially agreed to share any pre-Completion Tax Reliefs or, alternatively, the Seller is not warranting any Tax Reliefs, and if the Seller can offset a Claim against any pre-Completion Tax Reliefs there should be a provision to require the Buyer to ensure that target uses the relevant available Relief in a timely fashion. The limitation in paragraph 3.1(d) cross-refers to this.

An example of a definition of a 'shared' Tax Relief is provided as follows which should quantify the amount of the Relief and the latest date on which it can be used:

"Available Tax Relief" means [trading losses of the Company as at [Completion][the Accounts Date] up to but not greater than [£], [Corporation Tax Relief of £[...] arising under the provisions of CTA 2010 sections 1011 to 1038 but only to the extent that such relies became available before [date]."

10.1   The Buyer shall procure that the Company:

(a)   shall use the Available Tax Relief as soon as it is able to under the relevant Tax Statute [and in any event before [ ]];

(b)   at the Seller(s) expense, delivers to the Seller(s) a certificate from the Auditors confirming that:

(i)   all such Available Tax Reliefs have been so used; or

(ii)   such Available Tax Reliefs are no longer available and/or that the Company is unable to so use them.

10.2   Within [14] Business Days of the Auditors confirming the use of the Available Tax Reliefs under paragraph 10.1(b)(i) the Buyer shall confirm to the Seller that [   ]% of such relief shall be available to be offset against any Claim which may arise under this Schedule [ ].

10.3   In the event paragraph 10.1(b)(ii) is relevant the Seller(s) shall have no further rights and the Buyer shall have no further obligations under this paragraph 10.

[Seller(s) Mitigation using Group Relief]

Note 40: This is relevant only if target is leaving a group in respect of which Group Relief is available for the pre-Completion period and the parties have agreed that the Seller's group shall be entitled to make use of it. Best practice is to include as much detail relating to the amount of relief to be surrendered and claimed including quantum.

10.4   The Buyer shall ensure that the Company surrenders to any member of the Seller's Group as elected by the Seller [£][the maximum amount] of trading losses of the Company being [£], and which are available immediately prior to Completion and that the Company shall provide its written consent to HMRC as required under self-assessment for the relevant Tax Return for the relevant accounting period in which Completion falls and does all things necessary to ensure that such claim for Group Relief for the benefit of the Seller's Group is effected for no consideration and not withdrawn at a later date.

11.   Payments

11.1   Payments by the Seller(s) under this Schedule [ ] shall be made on the later of the following:

    (a) if the payment under a Claim involves an actual payment of Taxation the later of:

        (i) five Business Days before the last day on which the Taxation must be paid by the Company to the relevant Tax Authority without incurring interest or penalty; and

        (ii) five Business Days following receipt by the Seller(s) of a Notice of Claim as referred to under paragraph 6.1 above;

    (b) [if the payment under a Claim relates to a Deemed Tax Liability:

        (i) which involves the denial or loss of a right to repayment of Taxation or credit for Taxation, the date on which such Taxation would otherwise have been repaid or credited in accordance with the relevant Taxation legislation, or, if earlier where the repayment or credit was dependent upon the making of an application or the satisfaction of some other condition, the earliest date upon which the application could have been made or the conditions satisfied; or

(ii) which involves the denial or loss or setting off in whole or in part of any Tax Relief, the date on which the Taxation saved thereby would otherwise have become fully due and payable to the relevant Tax Authority in accordance with the relevant Taxation legislation; or

(iii) in any case other than as referred to in paragraphs 11.1(b)(i) and (ii) above, the date falling five Business Days after a Notice of Claim;]

(c) in the cases of the costs and expenses referred to in paragraph 2.2, five Business Days after the date on which the Buyer or the Company produces receipts invoices or other proof of such costs and expenses to the Seller(s).

11.2   **Interest**

If any amount due to be paid by a party under this Schedule is not made by the due date under paragraph 11.1 above ("**Due Date**") the Seller(s) shall pay to the Buyer interest on such amount not paid at the rate of [   ]   per cent per annum above the Base Rate for lending of [Barclays] Bank Plc from the Due Date until the date of actual payment compounded at 91 day intervals subject to any other agreement between the Buyer and the Seller(s) relating thereto.

Note 41: The rate of interest should be sufficiently high so as to incentivise the Seller(s) to make the relevant payment and not incur extra costs.

12.   **Gross Up Clause**

Note 42: In the United Kingdom, so long as Extra Statutory Concession D33 ("ESC D33") applies and its conditions are satisfied (including amounts paid under a Claim being made to the Buyer and not to target), no capital gains tax should arise on the Buyer on sums paid up to £500,000 for each set of legal proceedings. However, if either ESC D33 becomes no longer recognised by HMRC (which is unlikely in view of the 2014 consultation and likely enshrinement of the concession in legislation), or the circumstances of the Tax Indemnity and the payments do not fall within its conditions, the Seller is entitled to be informed as a matter of priority. Therefore, paragraph 12.2 has been drafted as a positive obligation on the Buyer to confirm that no tax will arise on the payment under the Claim.

12.1   All sums payable under this Schedule including under or related to a Claim shall be paid, insofar as is lawful, free and clear of all deductions and withholdings but in the event that a deduction or withholding is lawfully required to be made the claimant shall provide to the payer the details of the requirements to make such deduction or withholding (including the relevant Tax Statute and/or any legal argument) and pay such greater sum which, after such deduction or withholding, results in a net payment to the Buyer equal to the amount due under this Schedule [ ].

12.2   In respect of a Claim the Buyer shall confirm to the Seller(s) in the Notice of Claim if any sum payable by the Seller(s) to the Buyer under a Claim is subject to Taxation (including reference to the relevant Tax Statue and any legal argument), and in the event such Taxation arises the Buyer shall provide details of the Tax computation in the Notice of Claim and the Seller(s) shall pay to the Buyer such additional sum as will after such Taxation leave the Buyer with the same amount as the Buyer would have received in the absence of such Taxation.

13.   Miscellaneous

13.1   Any payment by the Seller(s) to the Buyer under this Schedule [   ] shall be treated pound-for-pound as a reduction in the Consideration paid for the Shares under this Agreement.

13.2   [Unless where specifically provided for in this Agreement nothing in this Schedule [   ] shall confer or be deemed to confer on any person a right to enforce any terms under this Schedule under the provisions of the Contracts (Rights of Third Parties) Act 1999.]

Note 43: Only include this provision if the Schedule is in the form of a deed or if the body of SPA does not include this provision.

Part B

Tax Warranties

Appendix 1 of Schedule [ ]

NOTICE OF CLAIM

[Recorded] [Special] Delivery

To: **for the attention of [   ]**
                [the Seller(s)]

Date: **[ ]**

UNDER an agreement entered into between the [**Buyer**] and the [**Seller**] on [**date**] relating to the acquisition of the entire share capital of [**the Company**] (**"Agreement"**) **THIS NOTICE OF CLAIM IS MADE** pursuant to paragraph 6 of Schedule [ ] of the Agreement (**"Schedule [ ]"**). Definitions in Schedule [ ] shall apply for the purposes of this Notice of Claim.

1.   Under paragraph 6.1 of Schedule [ ] we give notice that it has come to our attention that [*confirm whether a Tax Assessment or Tax Claim has arisen on the Company*] with the Tax Liability in question amounting to [£   ].

2.   The details as provided to us at the date of this Notice of Claim relating to the [Tax Assessment] [Tax Claim] are as follows:

      [*set out available details including the quantification*]

3.   If you wish to Appeal this [Assessment] [Claim] please reply at the very latest by [*15 Business Days from the date of the Notice of Claim*] and forward to us [£   ] which represents an estimated amount of the costs of [the Company] to assist in the Appeal and your agreement in writing to fully indemnify us on an ongoing basis and under paragraph 6.4 of Schedule [ ].

4.   If you do not respond to this Notice of Claim by [*15 Business Days*] your rights to make such an Appeal shall cease.

5.   In any event please forward to us an amount of [£   ] representing the Tax Liability by:
      (a) [*date*] and under paragraph 11 of Schedule[ ] if you do not wish to Appeal the [*Assessment*] [*Claim*]; or

    (b) [*15 Business Days from the date of the Notice of Claim*] if you wish to Appeal the [*Assessment*] [*Appeal*].

6.   For the avoidance of doubt the provisions of Schedule [ ] shall apply fully to the subject matter of this Notice of Claim and your rights to make an Appeal and all related matters.

7.   Please return a copy of this letter duly signed and dated for my attention as soon as possible but in any event no later than [*15 Business Days*].

[*Company Secretary/Finance Director*]

[Buyer]

[*Address*]

Copy Letter

We confirm receipt of your letter dated [date] and give notice to **[Buyer]** that [*under paragraph 3 that we wish to make an Appeal and accordingly we attach a cheque for [£   ] and indemnify you fully for all costs and expenses arising from the Appeal as well as the Tax Liability in question*] [*we do not wish to make an Appeal. Accordingly we shall forward you an amount representing the Tax Liability by [date] as set out in your letter*].

[The Seller(s)]

[Address]

Date:..............................

APPENDIX 1

THE TAX SCHEDULE

Appendix 2.   SHORT FORM TAX SCHEDULE
Part A

Tax Schedule

1.   Definitions and Interpretation

1.1   In this Schedule [   ] the following words and expressions shall have the following meanings:

"Accounts"	the [audited] [unaudited] [consolidated] balance sheet and profit and loss accounts of the Company [and the Subsidiaries] for the period ending [ ] ("Accounts Date");
"Business Day"	any day during which banks in the United Kingdom are open for business with members of the public;
"Claim"	a claim made by the Buyer under this Schedule [ ] and whereby each and every Claim shall be a single set of legal proceedings for the purpose of ESC D33;
["Completion Accounts"	the completion accounts as defined in this Agreement;]
"Discovery Assessment"	an assessment made by HMRC under FA 1998 Schedule 18 paragraph 41(1);
"DOTAS"	the disclosure of tax avoidance schemes regime set out in FA 2004 sections 306 to 319;
"Event"	shall have its ordinary meaning and including without limitation any transaction (including Completion), receipt or payment of a dividend or distribution; any acquisition or disposal, transfer or payment; the receipt or making of a loan or advance; the death of a person; a change of residence; and ceasing to be a member of a group (however defined) for the purposes of any Tax;
"FA"	followed by a number means the Finance Act of that year;
"GAAR"	the general anti-avoidance rules under FA 2013 sections 205 to 215;
"HMRC"	Her Majesty's Revenue & Customs;
"ICTA"	the Income and Corporation Taxes Act 1988;
"Notice of Enquiry"	a notice referred to in FA 1998 Schedule 18 paragraph 24;
"PAYE"	the pay-as-you-earn system of accounting for income

	tax and NIC whereby an employer deducts amounts from employees' wages and salaries on their behalf under ITEPA sections 682 to 712 and SI 2003/2686 (Income Tax (Pay As You Earn) Regulations) including under the 'real time' regime;
"SDLT"	a Tax chargeable on the acquisition of a chargeable interest in UK land under FA 2003 sections 43 to 217;
"Secondary Tax Liability"	means a liability to Tax which falls on a party as a result of the failure of a connected person (including another member of a group in which the Company was or is a member) to pay a Tax Liability, including such liabilities arising under CTA 2010 sections 706 to 718, TCGA section 190, FA 2003 Schedule 7 paragraph 12, and [joint and several liability for VAT if a member of a VAT group];
"Tax"	any tax, charge, duty, impost, levy or withholding imposed by a Tax Authority or under statutory authority and any related penalty, fine, surcharge and/or interest;
"Tax Assessment"	any claim, demand, query, notice and/or assessment relating to a Tax Liability originating from a Tax Authority or any Tax Liability or increased Tax Liability arising under self assessment;
"Tax Authority"	any authority or body whether in the United Kingdom or elsewhere which has authority to impose Tax under relevant statutory authority including HMRC;
"Tax Indemnity"	the indemnity set out in paragraph 2 below;
"Tax Liability"	means a liability to Tax including but not limited to the requirement to make a payment of tax, the loss of Tax Relief, and including any Secondary Tax Liability and related interest and penalties;
["Tax Relief"	means any relief against the payment of Taxation and including any losses of a capital or revenue nature, allowances, exemptions, set-off and/or credits available in computing any Taxation, namely [£];]
"Tax Statute"	any statute, regulation and other orders which provide the source and authority for Tax Authorities to impose Taxation;
"Tax Warranties"	the warranties set out in part B of this Schedule [ ];

1.2   For the avoidance of doubt, this Schedule [ ] forms part of this Agreement and all words and expressions defined in this Agreement apply to this Schedule [ ] except where expressly defined herein, but where a conflict arises relating to Taxation the provisions in this Schedule [ ] shall prevail.

2.   Tax Indemnity

Subject to the provisions in this Schedule [ ] the Seller(s) [jointly and severally] full indemnifies(y) the Buyer and covenant(s) with the Buyer to pay to the Buyer an amount equal to any Tax Liability which falls on the Company which arises by reference to any income profits or gains earned, received or accrued by the Company on or before Completion in respect of any Event which occurred or was deemed to occur or was effected on or before Completion as well as all costs and expenses reasonably incurred by the Buyer in connection with a [successful] Claim under this [Agreement][Schedule].

3.   Limitations

3.1   The Tax Indemnity shall not apply to a Tax Liability of the Company to the extent that:

(a) a [specific] provision or reserve was made for it in the [Completion] Accounts; or

(b) such liability to Tax arises only by reason of any increase in rates of Taxation or as a result of any change in the law or withdrawal of any regulation or published practice of a Taxation Authority made after Completion with retrospective effect; or

(c) it arose in the ordinary course of business of the Company after the Accounts Date;

(d) it would not have arisen but for a voluntary act effected by the Buyer or the Company after Completion; or

(e) it would not have arisen but for a change after Completion in the accounting reference date or change in accounting policies or practices used in the Accounts; or

(f) it relates to a Claim which was made by the Buyer after the [fourth] anniversary of the Accounts Date.

3.2   The maximum aggregate liability of the Seller(s) under the Tax Indemnity shall be £[   ].

3.3   The Buyer agrees with the Seller(s) that the Seller(s) shall not be liable under this Schedule [ ] to the extent that the Seller(s) has/have fully satisfied a liability elsewhere under the Agreement in respect of any breach of Warranty, representation or undertaking which relates to the same amount of Tax Liability arising in respect of the same Event.

4.   Buyer's Indemnity

The Buyer covenants with the Seller(s) to pay to the Seller(s) an amount equal to any Tax Liability which falls to be paid by the Seller(s) under the Tax Indemnity which arises due to the activities of the trade or business of the Company ceasing or becoming negligible following Completion and the reasonable costs and expenses of the Seller(s) arising in connection with taking any action under this paragraph 4 so long as such amount is not greater than [£].

5.   Conduct of Claims

5.1   If the Buyer or the Company becomes aware of a Tax Assessment on the Company or a potential Tax Claim which may give rise to a Claim against the Seller(s) under this Schedule [ ], the Buyer shall immediately give written notice with full relevant details to the Seller(s) (**"Notice of Claim"**) and save as provided for in this paragraph 5 the Seller(s) shall reimburse the Buyer for the amount of the liability which is the subject of the Notice of Claim within the time limits set out in the Notice of Claim and under paragraph 6 below.

5.2   Subject always to the provisions set out in paragraphs 5.3 to 5.5 below on receiving a Notice of Claim the Seller(s) shall have a right to deal with any Tax Assessment as referred to in paragraph 5.1 above and give instructions to the Company to answer any queries by the relevant Tax Authority, so long as that Notice of Claim does not relate to a Discovery Assessment relating to a loss of tax brought about by deliberate behaviour of the Company (as referred to in FA 1998 Schedule 18 paragraph 46) in which case the Buyer and the Company shall be entitled to deal fully with the Tax Assessment.

5.3 Under paragraph 5.2 above the Buyer will procure that the Company will afford the Seller(s) all reasonable facilities and opportunities to investigate matters relating to the Tax Assessment and take such action as the Seller(s) may reasonably request to dispute, avoid, resist, appeal against or compromise the Tax Assessment (**"Appeal"**) provided that:

(a) the Buyer or the Company shall not be obliged to assist in an Appeal relating to any Tax Assessment if, having provided to the Seller(s) the Notice of Claim, the Buyer has not in the following [15] Business Days received instructions in writing from the Seller(s) to make such Appeal;

(b) the Seller(s) shall not be entitled to request the Buyer and/or the Company to take any action under this paragraph 5 in respect of any Appeal if it is alleged that either the Seller(s) or the Company while it was under the control of the Seller(s), committed acts or omissions which may constitute fraud or deliberate tax evasion;

(c) the Seller(s) fully indemnifies(y) and secure(s) the Buyer and the Company to their reasonable satisfaction against all losses, costs, damages and expenses (including, without limitation, interest, fines, penalties and interest on overdue Taxation) which may be incurred in respect of the Appeal.

5.4 The Company and/or the Buyer (as the case may be) shall be at liberty without reference to the Seller(s) to admit, compromise, settle, discharge or otherwise deal with any Tax Assessment after the earliest of:

(a) the service of a notice in writing on the Buyer and/or the Company by [any of] the Seller(s) to the effect that [it] [they] consider(s) the matter should no longer be resisted;

(b) the expiry of a period of [ten] Business Days following the service of a notice by the Buyer and/or the Company (as the case may be) on the Seller(s) requiring the Seller(s) to clarify or explain the terms of any request to make an Appeal under paragraph 5.3 above and during such period no such clarification or explanation has been received by the Buyer and/or the Company; and

(c) the expiration of any period prescribed by the applicable Tax Statute for the making of an appeal against either the Tax Assessment in question.

5.5   Neither the Buyer nor the Company shall be obliged to take any action under paragraph 5.3 above, the effect of which is likely to increase the amount of Taxation payable by the Company and/or the Buyer in respect of accounting periods ending after the Accounts Date beyond what it would have been liable for but for the taking of such action nor shall either of the Company or the Buyer be obliged to take action under this paragraph 5 the effect of which is likely to prejudice the ability of the Company and/or the Buyer to order their affairs in such a way as to properly minimise their respective liability to Tax in respect of such later accounting periods.

6.   Payments

6.1   Payments due under this Schedule [ ] shall be made as follows:

(a) If the payment under a Claim involves an actual payment of Tax the due date shall be the later of:

(i.) five Business Days before the date on which the Tax must be paid by the Company to the relevant Tax Authority without incurring any interest or penalty; and

(ii.) five Business Days following receipt by the Seller(s) of the Notice of Claim;

(b) [in respect of a liability to make a payment in respect of the loss of a Tax Relief available to the Company at Completion, the due date for payment shall be the later of:

(i.) five Business Days following the date on which such Tax Relief became unusable; and

(ii.) five Business Days following receipt by the Seller(s) of the relevant Notice of Claim;]

(c) in respect of costs and expenses relating to the Claim the due date for payment shall be five Business Days after the date on which the Buyer or the Company produces receipts invoices or other relevant proof of payment to the Seller(s);

(d) if a payment is due to the Seller(s) from the Buyer under paragraph 4 above the provisions of paragraphs 6.1(a) and (c) above shall apply save that provisions which refer to the Company and/or the Buyer shall apply to the Seller(s) and vice versa.

6.2 **Interest**

If any amount due to be paid by a party to this Schedule is not paid by the due date under paragraph 6.1 above ("**Due Date**") the payer shall pay to the payee interest on the unpaid amount at the rate of [4] per cent per annum above the Base Rate for lending of [Barclays] Bank Plc from the Due Date until the date of actual payment compounded at 91 day intervals.

7. **Gross Up Clause**

7.1 All sums payable under this Schedule [ ] shall be paid legally free and clear of all deductions and withholdings but if a deduction or withholding is legally required to be made the payer shall pay the payee the sum which after such deduction or withholding results in a net payment to the payee equal to the amount due under this Schedule [ ].

7.2 If any sum payable under this Schedule [ ] is subject to Tax in the hands of the payee then the payer shall pay to the payee such additional sum as will after such Tax leave the payee with the same sum as the payee would have received in the absence of such Tax.

8. **Miscellaneous**

Any payment by the Seller(s) under this Schedule [ ] shall be treated pound-for-pound as a reduction in the consideration paid for the Shares sold under this Agreement and any payment by the Buyer to the Seller under paragraph 4 above shall be treated as a reduction in such consideration.

Part B

Short Form Tax Warranties

1. Administration

1.1 The Company has properly complied with all requirements and obligations relating to its liabilities to Tax under all Tax Statutes and as required under the Companies Acts [since incorporation] [during the last four years].

1.2 All Tax returns filed by the Company [since incorporation] [during the past four years] were true and accurate in all material respects (including computations relating to claims for Tax Relief), have not been nor [so far as the Seller is aware] are likely to be the subject of any Tax Assessment.

1.3 All Tax Liabilities of the Company as at Completion will have been correctly and duly paid and no related outstanding fines, penalties and/or surcharges have arisen nor will arise on or after Completion.

1.4 The Accounts which have been prepared on a consistent basis under generally accepted accounting principles, fully and accurately provide for all and any Tax Liabilities of the Company as at the Accounts Date as required under any Tax Statute[s] and include full provisions for contingent and/or deferred Tax[es] at such a date.

1.5 Since the Accounts Date no Tax Liability of the Company has arisen other than in the Ordinary Course of Business of the Company.

2. Anti-Avoidance and Disclosure

2.1 The Company has never been involved in any arrangement or arrangements which included a pre-conceived or pre-ordained series of transactions which had no commercial purpose other than for the [avoidance][evasion] of Tax including any reportable under DOTAS and/or which could fall within the GAAR.

2.2 The Company has included in its [self-assessment] Tax returns the relevant reference number for all notifiable arrangements under the DOTAS regime it has been involved in.

2.3 The Company has never been involved in any arrangements which if they had been effected after 1 August 2004 could have represented notifiable arrangements under the DOTAS regime.

3. **Associated Companies**

3.1 The Company is not [and has not in the last [four] years been] controlled by any person or persons who also control other companies which as a result are associated with the Company so that the Company was or is not entitled to the small profits rate of tax for corporation tax purposes.

4. **Capital Allowances**

4.1 [The Company has made no claims relating to capital allowances [statutorily][under the Capital Allowances Act 2001]] OR

4.2 [The Company did not own at the Accounts Date any asset, in respect of the capital expenditure on which the Company was entitled to claim allowances under the Capital Allowances Act 2001, whose book value as shown in the Accounts, exceeds the residue of qualifying expenditure or written down value attributable to such asset for the purposes of the Capital Allowances Act 2001.]

5. **Chargeable Gains**

5.1 No capital assets owned by the Company as at the date of this Agreement have been acquired whereby roll-over relief under TCGA sections 152 to 158 (*Replacement of business assets*) has been claimed and there are no capital assets of the Company in respect of which a charge to Tax could crystallise at any time under such provisions.

5.2 The Company had no capital losses available to be carried forward as at the Accounts Date nor will it have at Completion.

5.3 The Company has never transferred any of its assets otherwise than by way of a bargain made at arm's length nor have the provisions of TCGA section 125 (*Shares in close company transferring assets at an undervalue*) been applicable.

6. Close Companies

6.1 The Company has made no loans or advances to, nor has it been assigned any debt in respect of, any shareholder or director, including under CTA 2010 section 455 (*Charge to tax in case of loans to participators*) for which the Company could or did become liable to Tax.

6.2 The Company has not at any time [in the last [four] years] released, written off or waived any loans it has made to any individual.

7. Corporation Tax

7.1 The Company has never received a Notice of Enquiry, nor has any Tax Authority (including HMRC) amended any Tax return nor opened a Notice of Enquiry nor made a Discovery Assessment relating to any corporation tax self-assessment return of the Company.

8. Employment-related issues

8.1 All salaries wages fees and benefits in money or money's worth paid by the Company at any time to employees, officers or directors of the Company under ITEPA section 62 have been made subject to deduction of income tax and employees' NIC and the Company has at all times properly complied with all the requirements in respect of the PAYE provisions (and similar provisions outside the United Kingdom), including the proper deduction of income tax and other charges on all payments made to persons who supply services to the Company.

9. Stamp Taxes

9.1 All documents within the possession of the Company or to which the Company is or was a party, which were or are chargeable to stamp duty have been properly stamped and no interest or penalties could arise in respect of such documents.

9.2 The Company has properly complied with all its obligations and requirements relating to SDLT under FA 2003 and has in its possession full and accurate relevant records including all land transaction returns for the last [four] years of assessment.

10. VAT

10.1 The Company is a taxable person for the purposes of VAT and is registered for VAT under number [   ] and has [during the last [four] years of assessment] complied with all relevant VAT rules and regulations.

10.2 The Company is not nor has it ever been registered for VAT nor has it ever been required to be registered for VAT and it has proper records relating to its supplies of goods and services for the last four years including in respect of supplies made to and received from other EU member states.

10.3 [The Company has never been a member of a VAT group.]

10.4 [The Company is a member of a group for VAT purposes under registration number [ ] ("**VAT Group**") and in respect of which [ ] is the representative member and it is confirmed that:-

(a) no group member has exercised an option to tax in respect of any property;

(b) there are not currently nor will there be at Completion any payments on account relating to VAT in respect of the Company;

(c) the representative member will apply for deregistration of the Company from the VAT Group to be effective at Completion;

(d) the representative member has at all times been compliant with all relevant VAT rules and regulations in all respects;

(e) no direction has been made by HMRC under VATA Schedule 9A (*Anti-avoidance provisions – groups*) in respect of the VAT Group;

the Group has never been required to deregister as a VAT group.]

Appendix 3. LONG FORM TAX WARRANTIES FOR THE SALE OF A COMPANY

When inserting the relevant tax warranties into either the long form or the short form tax schedule, any capitalised words will need defining in paragraph 1.1 of the schedule.

1. Accounts, Tax Computations and Payments

a) "The Accounts which have been prepared on a basis consistent with previous accounts and under generally accepted accounting principles fully and accurately provide for all Tax Liabilities of the Company as at the Accounts Date including full provisions for contingent and/or Deferred Tax at such a date."

b) "Since the Accounts Date no Tax Liability of the Company has arisen other than in the ordinary course of business of the Company."

c) "The Company is not a large company for the purposes of the Corporation Tax (Instalment Payments) Regulations 1998 ("SI 1998/3175") and has correctly made payment of its corporation tax arising in the accounting period ending on the Accounts Date under TMA section 59D."

2. Administration and Tax Compliance

a) "The Company has complied with all requirements and obligations relating to its liabilities to tax under all Tax Statutes and as required under the Companies Acts [since incorporation] [during the past four years] [at all times] including but not limited to:

  (i) proper preparation and submission of the Accounts of the Company to the relevant Tax Authorities;

  (ii) proper filing of all Tax Returns, notices, computations, assessments (including self-assessment), amendments, registrations and de-registrations together with relevant correspondence with the relevant Tax Authorities;

  (iii) timely and correct remittances of Tax by the Company to the relevant Tax Authorities;

  (iv) proper maintenance of all records and correspondence relating to the Company's tax affairs (including Tax

Returns) as required, including for the avoidance of doubt relevant documentation relating to the computation for Taxation of the Company."

b) "All Tax Returns including any amended Tax Returns filed by the Company [since incorporation] [during the past four years] were true and accurate in all [material] respects (including computations relating to claims for Relief), have not been and [so far as the seller is aware] are not likely to be the subject of any enquiry or investigation or dispute with any Tax Authority."

c) "All disclosures and statements provided to any Tax Authorities relating to the Company's Tax affairs were complete, true and accurate in all respects."

d) "No arrangements have been entered into by the Company with any Tax Authority for the postponement or reduction of, or any dispensation relating to, the payment of any Tax by the Company and the Company has not at any time benefited from any Relief relating to its Tax affairs for which it is not entitled under Tax Statute."

e) "All Tax Liabilities of the Company as at Completion will have been correctly and duly paid and no outstanding fines, penalties and/or surcharges have arisen before nor will arise as at Completion."

f) "There are no ongoing proceedings with any Tax Authority involving the Company including any which could adversely affect the Seller's ability to enter into this Agreement."

3. Advance Corporation Tax (ACT)

"There is neither unrelieved surplus ACT nor any shadow ACT for the Company or any Group Company as at the date of this Agreement."

4. Anti-avoidance

"The Company has never been involved in any arrangement or arrangements which included a pre-conceived or pre-ordained series of transactions, which had no commercial purpose other than tax [avoidance] [evasion] including any reportable under DOTAS and/or which could fall within the GAAR and/or the TAAR."

5. Associated Companies

a) "There are no, nor have there been any, companies which are under the control of the same person or persons which control the Company such that the Company was not entitled to the small profits rate of tax for corporation tax purposes."

b) "There have been no circumstances when the Company relied on ESC C9 relating to control of the company by associated persons ("Associated Companies")."

6. Capital Allowances

a) "The Company has made no claims under self assessment relating to capital allowances during the past [four] years, including in respect of the following:
   (i)   plant and machinery;
   (ii)   industrial buildings;
   (iii)   [business premises renovation;]
   (iv)   [agricultural buildings;]
   (v)   [flat conversions;]
   (vi)   [mineral extraction;]
   (vii)   [research and development;]
   (viii)   know-how;
   (ix)   patents;
   (x)   [dredging;]
   (xi)   [assured tenancies.]"

b) "The Company has always made claims for capital allowances under self-assessment using the maximum available relief under the relevant Tax Statutes in each of the past [four] years and there are no unutilised capital allowances as at the date of this Agreement nor will there be at the Completion Date."

c) "Neither a balancing allowance nor a balancing charge in respect of capital allowances would arise on the Company on the disposal of a capital asset or discontinuance of a qualifying activity as at the date of this Agreement."[1]

---

[1] This could be rejected by the seller as being onerous if it has a large asset base. If so and there is concern by the buyer about potential future balancing charges, a tax indemnity should be included in the tax schedule referring to any capital allowance balancing charge arising on the sale of an asset following completion, but it would need to carve out any capital allowances claimed following the buyer's purchase of the target company

d) "All available capital allowance claims made by the Company have been made correctly under self-assessment and under the relevant legislation and records have been maintained relating to such claims (including but not restricted to records kept as required under Self-Assessment) which provide full and accurate information including the dates when the relevant capital expenditure was incurred."

e) "The Company has only one plant and machinery pool."

f) "The Company has never participated or been involved in arrangements relating to capital allowances which could be perceived as tax avoidance."

g) "The Company has never been involved in financial transactions involving capital allowances including those involving finance leases or operating leases."

7. Chargeable Gains

a) "The Company is not and never has been, nor has been deemed to be part of a group for Tax purposes including in respect of chargeable gains."

b) "No capital assets owned by the Company as at the date of this Agreement have been acquired whereby roll-over relief under TCGA sections 152 to 158 (*Replacement of business assets*) has been claimed and there are no capital assets of the Company in respect of which a charge to tax could crystallise at any time under those provisions."

c) "The Company has properly assessed chargeable gains and losses for corporation tax purposes on all disposals of any of its capital assets, and has in its possession all records relating to all disposals of capital assets including all relevant computations and assessments including the basis for any valuation and relevant for Substantial Shareholdings exemption."

d) "The Company has never been involved in any reorganisation and/or reconstruction including under sections 135 TCGA (*Exchange of securities for those in another company*), 136 TCGA (*Scheme of reconstruction involving issue of securities*), or 139 TCGA (*Reconstruction involving transfer of business*)."

e) ["HMRC have never issued any notices to the Company under section 184I TCGA relating to avoidance arrangements involving losses under TCGA section 184G (*Avoidance involving losses: schemes converting income to capital*) and 184H TCGA (*Avoidance involving losses: schemes securing deductions*)."[2]]

f) "The Company had no capital losses available to be carried forward as at the Accounts Date nor will it have at Completion."

g) ["The Company has never transferred any of its assets other than by way of a bargain made at arm's length nor have the provisions of TCGA section 125 (*"Shares in close company transferring assets at an undervalue"*) been applicable."][3]

h) "The Company has never received a capital distribution from a connected party whereby a chargeable gain will have accrued and in respect of which it could be subject to unpaid corporation tax of the connected party under section 189 TCGA (*Capital distribution of chargeable gains recovery from the shareholder*)."

i) "The Company has never been nor deemed to be a member of any group other than the Group nor a member of more than one group of companies, however defined."

j) "The Company has never been involved in any transfer of capital assets on a no gain/no loss basis under TCGA section 171 (*Transfers within a group*) nor has it been a party to any elections under TCGA section 171A (*Election to reallocate gain or loss to another member of the group*);

k) "The Company has neither acquired nor disposed of an asset whilst being a member of the Group whereby TCGA section 173 (*Transfers within a group: trading stock*) could apply."

l) "The Company has not been a party to any claim for roll-over relief under TCGA sections 152 to 158 whilst being a member of the Group and whereby TCGA section 175 (*Replacement of business assets by members of a group*) would apply."

---

[2] Include only if there is an indication during due diligence that it might be relevant

[3] Do not include if the target company is clearly not a close company

m) "No charge to tax is capable of arising on the Company under TCGA section 179 (*Company ceasing to be member of group: post-appointed day cases*) at any time including on Completion."

n) "The Company has neither received nor paid any consideration for a transfer of any capital asset from or to any member of the Group."

o) "There have been no transfers of capital assets within the Group on a no gain/no loss basis under TCGA section 171 (*Transfers within a group*) nor have any Group Members made any election under TCGA section 171A (*Election to reallocate gain or loss to another member of the group*);

p) "There have been no transfers within the Group whereby TCGA section 173 (*Transfers within a group: trading stock*) could apply."

q) "There have been no claims for roll-over relief under TCGA sections 152 to 158 whereby TCGA section 175 (*Replacement of business assets by members of a group*) would apply."

r) "No charge to tax is capable of arising on any Group Member under TCGA section 179 (*Company ceasing to be member of group: post-appointed day cases*) at any time including on Completion."

s) "There have been no payments made between Group Companies for any transfer of any capital asset from or to any member of the Group."

t) "There have been no disposals by the Company whereby exemption from chargeable gains arose under the Substantial Shareholding regime nor in respect of which paragraph 38 TCGA Schedule 7AC (*Degrouping*) could apply."

8. Clearances

a) "The Company has never submitted an application to any Tax Authority during the past [four] years whether required under statute or otherwise, whereby the Tax Authority was required or able to provide a ruling, clearance, guidance and/or opinion relating to any transaction, arrangements or schemes effected or entered into by the Company."

b) "There have been no transactions or arrangements entered into by the Company for which a clearance application could or should have been made to a Tax Authority but which was not made by the Company including any transaction having an EU dimension."

9. Close Companies

a) "The Company has made no loans or advances to, or been assigned any debt in respect of, any shareholder or director, or employee benefit trust including but not limited to under CTA 2010 section 455 (*Charge to tax in case of loans to participators*) in respect of which the Company could or did become liable to a corporation tax charge."

b) "The Company has not at any time released or written off or waived any loans it has made to any person."

c) "The Company has properly accounted for corporation tax purposes under self-assessment all loans and deemed loans it has made to participators, shareholders and directors under CTA 2010 section 455 (*Charge to tax in case of loans to participators*) and all tax and other liabilities arising on the Company have been properly accounted for within the required time period."

d) "The Company has provided no benefit in connection with any shareholder or director or a participator (as defined under CTA 2010 section 454) which would not be allowable as a trading expenses for the purposes of corporation tax such benefit to include the provisions of living accommodation, of entertainment, of domestic services, and/or the use of company assets."

e) "All benefits provided by the Company to any employee, director, shareholder and persons associated to such persons under CTA 2010 section 1064 (*Distribution to include certain expenses of close companies*) which would be treated as a distribution, have been properly accounted for under self-assessment [and the Company is fully indemnified by such persons in respect of any income tax arising from the provisions of such benefits]."

f) "The Company has at no time been a close investment-holding company as defined under CTA 2010 section 34 and has at all times existed wholly or mainly for the purposes of carrying on its trade of [   ] on a commercial basis."

g) "There have been no transfers made by the Company other than on an arm's length basis and for commercial purpose and the Company has never made nor could be deemed to have made a transfer of value whereby apportionment to the participators was required under IHTA section 94 (*Charge on participators*) and no charge to tax has arisen or could arise on the Company under section 202(1) IHTA (*Close companies*)."

h) "The Company has properly assessed for all transfers of value under which tax has arisen on the Company under IHTA section 202."

i) "There have been no alterations to the share capital and the loan capital of the Company."

10. The Construction Industry Scheme (CIS)

a) "The Company has never spent more than £1 million on average annually in any three year period on construction or building work."

b) "The Company has never been required to operate under any of the provisions of the Construction Industry Scheme at any time and has at no time been a contractor or sub-contractor as defined under such scheme."

c) "The Company has at all times properly operated under the provisions within the Construction Industry Scheme including making proper and appropriate deductions for income tax from payments it has made to sub-contractors as required and has never been subject to any penalties under the scheme."

11. Controlled Foreign Companies (CFC)

a) "The Company has at no time held an interest (either directly or indirectly) in another company which is resident outside the United Kingdom which could fall within the definition of a Controlled Foreign Company and whereby profits of such non-UK resident company should have been or were apportioned to the Company."

b) "The Company has at no time entered into a transaction or a series of transactions with any other company which is or could be considered to be a Controlled Foreign Company other than on an arm's length basis and has proper and appropriate records which can justify this warranty."

c) "The Company has properly reported under self-assessment its interests in companies resident outside the United Kingdom which are Controlled Foreign Companies."

d) "The Company has never asked for clearance from HMRC nor has it done so in respect of any other Tax Authority relating to its transactions with companies resident outside the United Kingdom in which the Company has an interest."

12. Corporation Tax

a) "The Company has never received a Notice of Enquiry, nor has any Tax Authority (including HMRC) amended any tax return or made a Revenue determination relating to any corporation tax return which has been filed by the Company."

b) "All copies of correspondence and evidence of communications between the Company and Tax Authorities relating to the corporation tax affairs of the Company have been properly maintained and the Company has in its possession all tax records as recommended by HMRC in its guidance and under relevant statutory requirements."

c) "The Company is not, nor has been a member of a group for corporation tax purposes, nor of a consortium."

d) "The Company has never been within the quarterly instalment payment regime."

13. Deferred tax

"There are no deferred taxes which would become payable by the Company in the future and required to be accounted for under Section 28 FRS 102 or any equivalent accounting standard reference."

14. Demergers and Exempt Distributions

"The Company has never been involved in a demerger and/or an exempt distribution as provided for in CTA 2010 sections 1073 to 1099."

15. Disclosure of Tax Avoidance Schemes (DOTAS)

a) "The Company has never been involved in any scheme or arrangement which might fall within any provisions requiring reporting of the details of such scheme or arrangement to HMRC or any other Tax Authority, including the disclosure requirements in FA 2004 sections 306 – 319 ("Notifiable Arrangements") including (but not limited to) such schemes or arrangements in respect of the following:

(i) income tax, capital gains tax and/or corporation tax;
(ii) national insurance contributions;
(iii) stamp duty land tax;
(iv) ATED;
(v) VAT;
(vi) IHT;
(vii) financial products including but not limited to shares and securities.

b) "As far as the Sellers are aware there is no reason why HMRC would be entitled to enquire into any arrangement entered into by the Company which could be a Notifiable Arrangement including where a penalty might arise under TMA section 98C (*Notification under Part 7 of Finance Act 2004*)."

c) "The Company has included under self-assessment the relevant reference number relating to all Notifiable Arrangements it has been involved in."

16. Distributions and Dividends

a) "The Company has made no distributions as set out in CTA 2010 section 1000(1), save for dividends other than a capital dividend."

b) "The Company has made the proper returns within the required period relating to all non-qualifying dividends it has made under CTA 2010 section 1101."

17. Dormant Companies

a) "There are no, nor have there ever been, any dormant companies within the Group."

b) "Those subsidiaries within the Group classified as being dormant have at all times been dormant and never carried on any activities, including but not limited to trading activities, such that an adjustment to the Company's taxation could be required by any Tax Authority."

18. Employment-Related Tax Issues

a) "All salaries wages fees and benefits in money or money's worth paid by the Company at any time to employees and officers and directors of the Company under ITEPA section 62 have been made subject to deduction of income tax and employees' NIC and the Company has at all times properly complied with all the provisions in respect of the PAYE provisions and similar provisions outside the United Kingdom, including the proper deduction of income tax and other charges on all payments made to persons who supply services to the Company."

b) "The Company has never had a PAYE audit by HMRC or any other Tax Authority relating to PAYE or equivalent system operating outside the United Kingdom to which the Company and any of its Subsidiaries are subject."

c) "The Company has comprehensive and accurate records properly compiled during the past [four] years relating to payments it has made or deemed to have made including emoluments and benefits provided to all its employees and officers and directors and such records will be up to date as at Completion."

d) "The Company has never claimed for dispensations relating to income tax payable on particular expenses payments or benefits of any directors and/or employees under ITEPA section 65 ("*Dispensations*")."

e) "The Company has full documentation relating to all dispensations under ITEPA section 65 ("*Dispensations*") applied for and all such applications were properly made and given by HMRC and so far as the Sellers are aware there is no reason for HMRC to withdraw such Dispensations."

f) "The Company has no employees nor any directors or officers who are not UK resident, or who are non-UK domiciled or who might be considered to have dual residency."

g) "The Company has never entered into any arrangements with any Tax Authority relating to employees coming to or leaving the United Kingdom for work purposes including tax-equalisation arrangements."

h) "The Company has no employees, officers or directors based outside the United Kingdom with whom special arrangements have been entered into relating to reduction in income tax, and there are no arrangements relating to payments to employees officers or directors wherever-based whereby payments are made involving offshore jurisdictions including under dual employment contracts."

i) "The Company has at no time employed agency workers to which ITEPA section 688 (*"Agency Workers"*) could apply."

j) "The Company has never been involved in arrangements involving agents and agency workers whereby ITEPA sections 44 to 47 could apply (*"Agency workers provisions"*)."

k) "The Company has at no time been involved in arrangements involving intermediaries (either as a client or as an intermediary) whereby ITEPA sections 48 to 61 (*"Workers under arrangements made by intermediaries"*) could apply."

l) "The Company is not a managed service company nor is it a managed service company provider for the purposes of ITEPA section 61A to 61J (*"Managed Service Companies"*)."

m) "The Company [and its Subsidiaries] has [have] never granted options over its shares or issued shares at any time to any of its employees officers or directors or to their associates nor have there been any transfers of Shares by other persons to such persons."

n) "The Company has agreed in writing with Shares Valuation HMRC the market value of any Shares including ESS which it has issued to its employees officers and directors and their associates and all information supplied by the Company to HMRC in respect of such agreement was accurate and true in all respects."

o) "The Company has never issued shares to employees under the provisions of Finance Act 2013 Schedule 23 (Employer Shareholder Shares/ESS)."

p) "There are no outstanding options over the Company's shares nor will any rights arise whereby a person shall be entitled to acquire shares in the Company on Completion or at any time after Completion and there are no circumstances whereby following Completion a charge to income tax and/or NIC could arise in respect of such shares held by any person or in respect of such options and rights."

q) "The Company has not at any time participated in any scheme or arrangement one of the purposes of which was to avoid or reduce the payment of income tax and/or NIC."

r) "No payments have been made by the Company relating to termination of employment under ITEPA section 401 (*Payments connected with termination of a person's employment*)."

s) "Payments made in respect of termination of employment under ITEPA section 401 have received clearance from HMRC and such payments have been made after the proper deduction of income tax and no liability to NIC can arise in respect of such payments."

t) "The Company has never provided loans to any employee officer and/or director of the Company or to any of their associates."

u) "The Company has never provided any employment-related loans which would be regarded as taxable cheap loans under ITEPA Part 2 Chapter 7 (*Applications of provisions to agency workers*) and no employment-related loans have ever been released or written off."

v) "All payments made by the Company relating to or in connection with (including deemed payments and benefits of any kind) to employees officers and directors were and remain properly allowable as a trading expense and deductible in calculating the profits of the Company."

19. Group Issues

a) "The Company is not and never has been a member of a group for any tax purposes whatsoever."

b) "The Company has never claimed or been involved in a claim for group relief referred to in CTA 2010 section 97(2) (including consortium claims and surrenders); has never been involved in group payment arrangements to which the provisions of TMA section 59F may apply; and has never been involved in a surrender of a tax under CTA 2010 section 963."

20. Inheritance Tax

a) "There is no Inland Revenue charge for unpaid tax as referred to in IHTA section 237 (*Imposition of Charge*) on [any assets of the Company] [on the assets being transferred][on the Shares] which could arise either directly or indirectly."

b) "No person has a limited interest nor has any person the power to sell or mortgage, or create a terminable charge on [any of the assets of the Company] [on any of the assets being transferred] [on the Shares] under IHTA section 212 (*Power to raise tax*)."

c) "The Company, being a close company under IHTA section 202 (*Close Company*), has made no transfer of value whereby a tax charge could arise on a participator in the Company under IHTA section 94 (*Charge on participators*)."

21. Insolvency Issues

a) "The Company has at all times had sufficient assets to pay its debts and has never entered into arrangements, either voluntary or involuntary, formal or informal, involving its liquidation or winding up, it being put into administration, the appointment of an administrative receiver, receiver or liquidator, or entering into a scheme of arrangement."

b) "The Company has never sought, nor should have sought, at any time protection from its creditors nor has it ever been involved in insolvency arrangements involving its business or the business of another person."

22. Intellectual Property

a) "The legal situs of the IP Assets is the United Kingdom and all related rights are recognised and protected under UK law and are owned absolutely by the Seller."

b) "The IP Assets were acquired or created by the Company after 1 April 2002 and fall within the definition of 'intangible fixed assets' in CTA 2009 section 711(2)."

c) "None of the IP Assets were created or acquired on or before 1 April 2002."

d) "None of the IP Assets have been acquired or disposed of since the Accounts Date."

e) "Since the Accounts Date no circumstances have arisen as a result of which any IP Assets will need to be revalued."

f) "The Company has not made any election under CTA 2009 section 730 to write down the cost of an intangible fixed asset for tax purposes at a fixed rate."

g) "The Company has not made any claim for roll-over relief under CTA 2009 section 757 in respect of any IP Asset."

h) "The IP Assets are held for the purpose of a trade and none are held for non-commercial purposes."

i) "All receipts received by the Company in respect of the IP Assets have been taxed as income and not as capital."

j) "No payments have been made to any employee of the Company in respect of the IP Assets, the right to receive such a payment being under Patents Act 1977 section 40."

k) "All appropriate withholdings and tax deductions required to be made in respect of payments made by the Company relating to the IP Assets have been made and have been properly accounted for to HMRC."

l) "No IP asset has been transferred to or by the Company on a no gain/no loss basis in a case where the Company and the other company (being either the transferor or the transferee) are members of the same group under CTA 2009 section 775."

m) "The execution or completion of this agreement [or any other Event since the Accounts Date] will not result in any IP Asset being deemed to have been disposed of and re-acquired by the Company under section 780 CTA (*Deemed realisation and reacquisition at market value*) or CTA 2009 section 785 (*Principal company becoming member of another group*)."

n) "The Company has not made any claim to postpone a charge on transfer of a trade under CTA 2009 section 827 (*Claims to postpone charge on transfer*)."

o) "No reallocation of a degrouping charge relating to IP assets has been made within the Group as referred to under CTA 2009 section 792 (*Reallocation of charge within group)*."

p) "The Company has not entered into any tax avoidance arrangements, the main object or one of the main objects of which was to enable the Company to obtain a debit to which it would not otherwise be entitled or to avoid having to bring a credit into account or to reduce the amount of any such credit."

23. Land and Property Issues

For a trading or holding company without property:

"The Company has no property business, either in the United Kingdom or outside the United Kingdom, and as defined in CTA 2009 sections 204 to 206."

Or, if the target has a property business:

a)   "The Company has had a UK property business as defined in CTA 2009 section 205 since incorporation but has never been involved in an overseas property business as defined in CTA 2009 section 206."

b)   "The Company has at all times properly accounted for the profits of its property business and including for the avoidance of doubt under CTA 2009 sections 210 and 214."

c)   "The provisions of CTA 2009 Part 4 Chapter 4 (*Profits of property businesses: Lease Premiums etc*) are not and have not been relevant in respect of the Company's property business."

24. Loan Relationships

a)   "The Company has properly accounted for all loan relationships as defined in CTA 2009 section 302   to which it has been a party."

b)   "The Company has never been a party to a creditor relationship for the purposes of a trade."

c)   "The Company has not entered into any arrangements relating to loans with a participator (referred to in CTA 2010 sections 455, 459, and 460) nor any arrangements set out in CTA 2010 sections 464A and 464C."

d)   "No Group Company has ever been a party to an intra-group transfer of a loan or a reorganisation to which CTA 2009 Part 5 Chapter 4   (section 335 to 347 – *Continuity of treatment on transfers within groups or on reorganisations*) could apply."

e)   "The Company has never been a party to a scheme or arrangement involving any loan relationship for the purpose of tax avoidance including for the avoidance of doubt arrangements to which CTA 2009 section 440 to 455A   (*Tax Avoidance*) could apply."

f) "The Company has never been involved in a relationship which would fall within the definition of a 'connected companies relationship' as defined under CTA 2009 section 348(2) nor where CTA 2009 Part 5 Chapters 5, 6 and 8 could apply."

25. National Insurance Contributions (NICs)

a) "The Company has at all times abided by its legal obligations as an employer in relation to the collection, payment and reporting of NIC to the relevant Tax Authorities, and it has full documentation relating to all such matters in its possession, and no liabilities relating to NIC applicable to any period before Completion will arise on or after Completion including in respect of securities issued and/or securities options granted before or on Completion."

b) "The Company has never made payments to third parties or deemed payments of employment earnings on which NIC could arise nor has it been required to pay Class 1A and/or Class 1B contributions."

c) "The Company has at all times deducted and made the appropriate payments in respect of NIC on all payments made to its directors and office holders, including non-executive directors providing services under a letter of engagement and shadow directors."

d) "There are no employees of the Company who have worked outside the United Kingdom who have been subject to NIC."

e) "The Company has had no involvement in any scheme or arrangement designed to reduce or avoid the payment of or obligations in respect of NIC including any which require reporting under the DOTAS regime."

f) "So far as the Sellers are aware the Company has never entered into any arrangements which could fall within the provisions of the Disguised Remuneration Rules under ITEPA sections 554A to 554AZ21."

26. PAYE

a) "The Company has at all times correctly operated the PAYE system, all payroll records of the Company have at all times been properly maintained and are in proper order, all year end returns have been correctly made, all deductions required to be taken from payments and benefits made and provided to employees, officers and directors (full-time, part-time, executive, non-executive and shadow directors) have been properly effected, and the Company is currently up to date with all its obligations under the PAYE provisions."

b) "As at Completion the Company will have no outstanding liabilities relating to the PAYE nor will any such liabilities arise after Completion which relate to any period before Completion."

c) "HMRC have never been required to make a determination of unpaid tax in respect of the Company under Regulation 80 SI 2003/2682 (*Income Tax (Pay As You Earn) Regulations 2003*)."

d) "The Company has never had a PAYE inspection by HMRC."

e) "The Company has never operated the quarterly payment regime under Regulation 70 SI 2003/2682 (*Income tax Pay as you earn) Regulations 2003*)."

27. Penalties Regime

a) "The Company has always taken reasonable care when dealing with HMRC and its tax affairs, and has never been guilty or accused by HMRC, of negligent or fraudulent or careless behaviour relating to such affairs and the Company has never concealed any error it was responsible for to HMRC nor suffered any penalty relating thereto."

b) "The Company has set up and has in place proper systems and procedures (including accounting systems) which cover all applicable taxes and their proper computation, and has all records providing confirmation that the Company has properly considered the proper tax treatment arising in respect of its affairs and has sought and followed advice from tax professionals."

c) "There are no issues relating to Taxation which have come to the attention of the Company and/or its officers and directors in respect of which a voluntary disclosure should have been but was not made to HMRC or any other Tax Authority, or in respect of which consultation with HMRC would have been appropriate."

28. Research and Development (R&D)

a) "No Group Company has made a claim for relief of any sort relating to expenditure on research and development as defined in CTA 2010 section 1138 nor under CTA 2010 Part 8A (*Patent Box Regime*)."

b) "The Company is a small or medium-sized companies as referred to in CTA 2009 section 1119, and has maintained full records relating to claims made for corporation tax relief for qualifying expenditure on research and development and all such claims have been properly made under section 87 and CTA 2009 Part 13 (sections 1039 to 1142)."

29. Residency issues

a) "The Company has always been resident in the United Kingdom by virtue of its incorporation and its effective management and control has always been situate in the United Kingdom and it has never been deemed to be dual resident for Taxation purposes by virtue of any tax treaty or otherwise."

b) "There are no shareholders of the Company which Control the Company (either alone or together with Connected Parties) [so far as the Seller is aware] which are resident outside the United Kingdom."

30. Secondary Tax Liabilities

a) "There has been no change in the ownership of any company which has been under the control of the Company within the period beginning three years from the date of this Agreement nor has there been any major change in the nature or conduct of the trade or business of any company under the control of the Company during the last three years."

b) "No activities of the trade or business of any company which has been under the control of the Company before the date of this Agreement have ceased or become small or negligible."

c) "During the period beginning three years before the date of this Agreement there have been no transfers of assets of the Company or any company under its control which would fall within CTA 2010 section 710 (*Recovery of unpaid corporation tax*) nor have any arrangements been entered into as referred to under that provision."

d) "The Company has never been involved before the date of this Agreement in any arrangements, nor has any other company which has been under its Control been so involved, whereby corporation tax has been assessed on a company which remained unpaid at any time more than six months after it was assessed such that CTA 2010 section 713 (*Recovery of unpaid corporation tax*) might apply."

e) "There is no unpaid corporation tax relating to a chargeable gain on any Group Member and HMRC have not served notice nor is entitled to serve notice on the Company or any Group Member under TCGA section 190."

f) "The Company [or any member of the Group] cannot become liable for recovery of group relief relating to SDLT under paragraphs 5 and/or 12 FA 2003 Schedule 7."

g) "The Company cannot become liable for a charge to corporation tax arising as a result of a degrouping charge relating to intangible fixed assets under CTA 2009 section 795 (*Recovery of charge from another group company or controlling director*)."

h) "No charge could arise on the Company pursuant to any joint and several liability which may attach to it under VATA section 43 (*Groups of Companies*)."

31. Self-assessment

(a) "The Company has properly complied at all times and in all respect with the self-assessment regime under FA 1998 Schedule 18 including its obligations to:

  (i) file company tax returns for all accounting periods ending before and on the Accounts Date together with all accompanying documentation including the relevant accounts;

  (ii) correctly compute corporation tax due for each relevant accounting period, including but not limited to:

  • any tax arising on loans or advances made to any Participators in the Company;

  • any amount chargeable relating to profits of any Controlled Foreign Companies;

- transactions which fall within the transfer pricing provisions of TIOPA Part 4 (sections 146 to 217);

(iii) provide full and correct information relating to the Disclosure of Tax Avoidance Schemes regime."

(b) "The Company (including any Associated Companies) is not a 'large' company for the purposes of the Quarterly Instalment Payments regime and has properly paid all corporation tax it has been due to pay no later than nine months after the end of each relevant accounting period ending before and on the Accounts Date."

(c) "The Company, being a large company under the Quarterly Instalment Payments regime, has accurately computed and paid corporation tax as required under that regime, for each relevant accounting period ending before or on the Accounts Date and as at Completion no adjustment will be necessary in respect of payments made before that date."

(d) "The Company has in its possession all records which it is required to keep under to the Self-Assessment regime and such records are sufficient to properly justify the computation by the Company of tax payable for all accounting periods ending up to the Accounts Date."

(e) "There have been no enquiries nor are there outstanding enquiries on the part of HMRC (including any Discovery Assessment and Discovery Determination) in respect tax returns submitted by the Company nor, so far as the Sellers are aware, are any enquiries likely to arise in the future in respect of any Tax Returns submitted by the Company before Completion."

(f) "The Company has not been subject to any penalties or any interest which could arise under the Self-Assessment regime in respect of any period before Completion."

32. Stamp Duty Land Tax (SDLT)

a) "All stamp duty and stamp duty land tax ("SDLT") arising on conveyance on sale of the Property to the Company has been properly paid and no interest and/or penalty can arise on the

Company or in respect of the Property in respect of such stamp taxes."

b) "No Group Company has applied for relief for Stamp Duty under FA 1930 section 42 ("section 42") in respect of any transfer of property between any associated companies as defined in section 42."

c) "No UK land and property is held in a separate non-trading company, whether incorporated in the UK or elsewhere."

d) "All documents within the possession of the Company or to which they were a party, which were or are subject to Stamp Duty have been properly stamped and no interest or penalties could arise in respect of such documents."

e) "The Company has properly complied with all obligations and requirements relating to SDLT under FA 2003 and has full and accurate records including all land transaction returns and the basis for the calculation of the chargeable consideration."

f) "The Company has not entered into any contract for a land transaction:
   (i) which has not been completed or deemed to have been completed or which has not been substantially performed;
   (ii) whereby a chargeable interest for the purposes of SDLT was conveyed to a party who was not a party to the contract, under FA 2003 section 44A (*Contract providing for conveyance to third party*);
   (iii) involving an exchange of land whereby FA 2003 section 47 ("*Exchanges*") could apply;
   (iv) in respect of which consideration remains contingent, uncertain or unascertained;
   (v) involving a connected company whereby the deemed market rule for the purposes of FA 2003 section 53 (*Deemed market value where transaction involves a connected company*) apply; or
   (vii) whereby the sale and leaseback provisions under FA 2003 section 57A apply."

g) "There are no outstanding options and rights of pre-emption relating to the Property under FA 2003 section 46."

h) "No Group Company has entered into any arrangement whereby SDLT is exempted or reduced under FA 2003

Schedule 7 (*Group relief and reconstruction and acquisition reliefs*)."

i) "No SDLT could arise on [the Company][any Group Company] from the withdrawal of exemption from or reduction in SDLT arising from any reconstruction under FA 2003 Schedule 7 paragraph 7 or in connection with acquisition relief under FA 2003 Schedule 7 paragraph 8 such withdrawal arising from but not restricted to Completion."

j) "The Company has not been involved in any land transaction in respect of which FA 2003 Schedule 15 (*Partnerships*) is relevant."

k) "The Company has never entered into nor been a party to any scheme or arrangement one of the purposes of which was the avoidance of Stamp Duty or SDLT or to which FA 2003 section 75A might apply."

l) "The Company has never been required to report any arrangement which would fall within DOTAS under FA 2004 sections 306 – 325."

33. Transfer Pricing

a) "The Company has at all times effected its business transactions with other parties on an arm's length basis and has never been required to re-compute its profits and/or its losses for tax purposes as required under TIOPA 2010 Part 4 (Transfer Pricing) and has maintained and has in its possession proper records to support this warranty."

b) "The Company has never entered into an Advance Pricing Agreement under TIOPA 2010 Part 5 with HMRC or similar arrangement with any other Tax Authority."

34. Value Added Tax

a) "The Company is a taxable person for the purposes of VAT and is registered for VAT under number [   ], has never been a member of a VAT group and has at all times been compliant with all VAT rules and regulations including (but not limited to) the following:
  • registration matters;
  • the making of self-supplies;

- registration for supplying electronic services in other EU member states;
- making complete and correct VAT returns and VAT payments within prescribed time limits;
- preserving full documentation and records relating to its VAT affairs for the past six years."

b) "The Company is a member of a group for VAT purposes under registration number [ ] ("VAT Group"), in respect of which [ ] is the representative member and it is confirmed that:

- no group member has opted to tax any property under of VATA Schedule 10 Part 1;
- there are not currently nor will there be at Completion any payments on account relating to VAT required in respect of the Company;
- the representative member has applied for removal of the Company from the VAT Group to be effective at Completion;
- the representative member has at all times been compliant with all VAT rules and regulations in all respects;
- no direction has been made by HMRC under VATA Schedule 9A (*"Anti-avoidance provisions – groups"*) in respect of the VAT Group; and
- there has never been another VAT group within the Group.

c) "The Company is not and has never been registered for VAT in the UK or any other EU territory and has proper records relating to all supplies of goods and services it has made during the past [four] years including in respect of supplies made to and received from other EU member states."

d) "The [Company] [VAT Group] has never been subject to any penalties for failure to take reasonable care or for deliberate understatement of VAT (with or without concealment) nor has the [Company] [VAT Group] been subject to any compliance check from HMRC relating to VAT nor has it been assessed for underpayment of VAT in the past four years."

e) "The [Company] [VAT Group] only makes taxable supplies and does not make nor has ever made exempt supplies for the purposes of VAT and the [Company] [VAT Group] has been entitled at all times to credit for all input tax relating to taxable supplies it has received and has properly and correctly claimed such input tax."

f) "The [Company] [VAT Group] has never operated nor been required to operate any of the following schemes under VATA:

- [second hand margin scheme;]
- [tour operators margin scheme;]
- [retail scheme;]
- [investment gold scheme;]
- cash accounting scheme;
- flat rate scheme;
- annual accounting scheme;
- Capital Goods Scheme."

g) "No assessment or penalty relating to VAT or requirement for security for VAT due has been made or imposed in respect of the [Company] [VAT Group] by HMRC or any other Tax Authority."

h) "The [Company] [VAT Group] has never been involved in any tax planning schemes or arrangements relating to VAT regardless of such scheme or arrangements having a commercial purpose or otherwise."

i) "The [Company] [VAT Group] has never been involved in any scheme or arrangement in respect of any scheme which would require disclosure to HMRC including under FA 2004 Part 7 (*Disclosure of Tax Avoidance Schemes*)."

j) "The [Company] [VAT Group] has never been a party to a transfer of a going concern."

k) "The [Company] [VAT Group] has always made taxable supplies and has never made exempt supplies for the purposes of VAT and the [Company][VAT Group] has not been required to make any adjustments under the provisions relating to the Capital Goods Scheme."

l) "The [Company] [VAT Group] has made the necessary proper adjustments relating to input tax in respect of all capital items relevant to the Capital Goods Scheme and has full records relating to such capital items which provide accurate details relating to their value and the amount of input tax reclaimed and adjustments to such tax as required under the scheme.

m) "The [Company] [VAT Group] has made no disposals of any capital item which fall within the provisions of the capital goods scheme during the adjustment period, which could have created a net taxable benefit to the Company by virtue of the input tax initially deducted in respect of such item and after taking into account any adjustments under the scheme exceeding the output tax arising on such disposal."

35. Value Shifting and Depreciatory Transactions

a) "There has been no transfer of dividends and/or assets within the Group which could give rise to a tax-free benefit and whereby TCGA sections 30 and 31 ("Value Shifting provisions") might apply, including any such transfers at artificial prices."

b) "The [Company][Group] has not been involved in any arrangements whereby there has been a disposal of shares or securities, and in respect of which their values have been materially reduced for any reason other than due to commercial factors, such that a loss arises on such disposal, including under TCGA section 176 ("Depreciatory transactions within a group") and TCGA section 177 ("Dividend Stripping")."

Appendix 4. TAX WARRANTIES FOR THE SALE OF A BUSINESS

1. Stamp duty and stamp duty land tax

"No stamp duties of any kind (or duties equivalent to stamp duty outside the UK) imposed by any Tax Authority in respect of the Business and Assets will arise and/or will become payable by the Buyer as a result of Completion and there is no relevant outstanding stamp duty."

2. PAYE and employment-related issues

a) "PAYE and all other systems relating to payroll and employment-related taxes and levies relating to the Employees and the Business have been properly administered in all respects and the relevant taxes and payments have been correctly made before and as at today's date, and all relevant records are accurate and up-to-date and there are no disputes with HMRC or any other Tax Authority in respect of the Business."

b) "There are no individuals who supply services in a personal capacity (whether as an individual or through a corporate entity) to the Business who are not properly classified either as an employee or self-employed such that a liability could arise on the Buyer in respect of the Business due to such incorrect classification."

c) "There are no persons including any of the Employees who have any rights whether under an employment contract or otherwise, relating to bonuses, shares and/or other securities for which he or she would have a right of action against the Buyer or the Business, including in territories other than the United Kingdom or which will be payable, exercised and/or issued following Completion."

d) "There are no special arrangements with HMRC or any other Tax Authority relating to the Employees or any other person coming into the UK to work, or relating to their employment outside the UK including any equalisation arrangements and relating to the Business."

e) "No Tax Liability can or will arise on the Buyer or the Business following Completion, whether in the United Kingdom or any other jurisdiction, and relating to the transfer of the Employees under this Agreement or in any other respect relating to the Employees or any other individual before Completion."

f) "All relevant authorisations required to be obtained have been applied for by the seller and given in respect of the transfer of the working arrangements of the Employees relating to the Business."

3. Inheritance tax

a) "There is no Inland Revenue charge for unpaid tax as referred to in IHTA section 237 on any of the Assets being transferred under this Agreement which could arise either directly or indirectly."

b) "No person has a limited interest or the power to sell or mortgage, or create a terminable charge on any of the Assets being transferred under this Agreement under IHTA section 212."

4. Seller tax warranties for a TOGC

a) "The Seller is a taxable person for VAT purposes with registration number [   ] and is currently making taxable supplies in respect of the Business."

b) "The Seller is a member of a VAT group with registration number [   ] of which the representative member is [   ] (company registration number [   ]) whose registered address is at [   ]."

c) "The Seller is not and has not been during the past [four] years a member of a VAT group."

d) "The turnover of the Business for VAT purposes during the period of 12 months ending on Completion will be [ ] and the Seller is not and is not required to be registered for VAT."

e) "The Assets have been used to make supplies in carrying on the Business by the Seller since [   ] and as at the date of Completion there were no prior consecutive transfers of the Assets and the Business nor any significant break in the Business's trading before such date."

f) "All VAT and duty payable on import of any of the Assets has been properly paid and accounted for up to and as at the date of this Agreement."

g) "The Assets represent all of the Business being transferred and the Business is capable of continued operation following Completion."

h) "The Assets represent only part of the Business being transferred but are capable of separate operation following Completion."

i) "The Seller has provided copies of all records and returns relating to VAT of the Business for the past [four] year which are accurate and correct as required under VATA."

j) "The Seller undertakes to retain in good order all business records relating to the Assets and the Business for such period as is required under VATA and in any event, not less than [six] years from the date of Completion, and to make available to the Buyer as so requested such information as is necessary for the Buyer to comply with its duties under VATA but if this warranty is breached in any way the Seller agrees to keep the Buyer indemnified in respect of all and any costs it suffers arising from such breach."

k) "The Seller agrees to transfer all business records relating to the Assets and the Business under the relevant VAT legislation in circumstances whereby the Buyer has applied to and been given permission by HMRC to take over the Seller's VAT number, being [   ]."

l) "The Seller exercised an option to tax under VATA Schedule 10 paragraph 2 in respect of the Property on [   ] and notified HMRC on [ ]. Such option has not been disapplied by HMRC. [A copy of the notification is attached together with HMRC's acknowledgment of receipt]."

m) "None of the Assets or Property transferred represents or shall become a capital item within the Capital Goods Scheme regardless of whether such transfer under this agreement is treated as part of a transfer of a going concern or otherwise."

n) "The transfer of the Property under this agreement will or would fall to be an exempt supply for VAT purposes by virtue of the disapplication of the option to tax under Scheduled 10 VATA paragraph 2(3AA)."

o) "The Seller warrants that the transfer of Property is exempt from VAT under VATA Schedule 9 and that no option to tax has been exercised under VATA Schedule 10 paragraph 2."

p) "The Seller undertakes to refund the Buyer any VAT which may be wrongly charged to and paid by the Buyer in respect of the transfer of the Assets and the Business under this Agreement."

5. Buyer warranties for a TOGC

a) "The Buyer is registered for VAT under registration number [   ]."

b) The Buyer has applied to be registered for VAT with effect from Completion."

c) "The Buyer intends to continue to use the Assets in the same type of activity as the Business as carried on by the Seller as at Completion and warrants that there shall be no significant break in the trading of the Business immediately after Completion."

d) "The Buyer has notified in writing its option to tax under VATA Schedule 10 paragraph 2 on [   ] and such option shall not be disapplied in respect of the Property."

e) "The Buyer has applied to HMRC to be registered for VAT using the Seller's VAT registration number [   ] and on proper registration and when the Seller has transferred to the Buyer the VAT records relating to the Business, the Buyer undertakes to preserve such records and to permit the Seller reasonable access to any records required under the relevant VAT legislation."

f) "If HMRC confirms in writing that the transfer of the Assets and Business under this Agreement is not a transfer of a going concern, and that accordingly VAT is payable by the Buyer in respect of such transfers, the Buyer agrees to pay the Seller any VAT so payable on receipt from the Seller of a proper VAT invoice together with any relevant interest and penalties."

Appendix 5.   HMRC   INFORMATION   & INSPECTION POWERS[1]

HMRC powers, taxpayer's rights, requirements & penalties	FA 2008 Schedule 36 reference	Comments
HMRC power requiring a taxpayer to provide information or produce a document	Para 1	• Must be given by written notice ('taxpayer notice') • Must be reasonably required by HMRC officer to check the taxpayer's tax position
HMRC power requiring a third party to provide information or produce a document	Para 2(1)	• Must be given by written notice ('third party notice') • Must be reasonably required for HMRC officer to check a known person's tax position
Third party notice required to name the taxpayer	Paras 2(2) & 3	• Tribunal can disapply this requirement if satisfied that HMRC have reasonable grounds for believing that naming the taxpayer may seriously prejudice the assessment/collection of tax • Third party notice to be given only with the agreement of the taxpayer (in which case it must receive a copy) or tribunal approval
HMRC power requiring a person to provide information or documents of a person(s) whose identity is not known	Para 5	• Must be by notice ('paragraph 5 notice') • Must be reasonably required by HMRC to check the UK tax position of the person(s) • Needs tribunal agreement • Does not cover foreign tax and VAT
HMRC power requiring a person to provide information about another person whose identity can be ascertained, subject to four conditions being met	Para 5A	• Information is reasonably required to check a person's tax position • The person's identity is not known to HMRC but they hold info by which the identity can be ascertained • HMRC reasonably believe the other person can ascertain the tax payer's identity from HMRC's info and in the course of his/her business • Taxpayer's identity can't be ascertained by other means
All 'information notices'	Para 6	• Note the word *may* and not *must*

[1] FA 2008 Schedule 36

HMRC powers, taxpayer's rights, requirements & penalties	FA 2008 Schedule 36 reference	Comments
(namely a taxpayer notice, third party notice and paragraph 5 or 5A notice) may specify information or documents required		• Information notice must state that tribunal approval has been given if that is the case • Tribunal decision for the issue of any notice (see above) is final
Information notice should provide reasonable period during which information/ documents to be supplied	Para 7	Venue to be agreed between person and HMRC unless HMRC specify (which must be reasonable)
Production of documents required under an information notice	Para 8	May be a copy unless the notice requires the original
HMRC powers to enter business premises to inspect premises, and business assets and business documents on the premises	Para 10	• Must be reasonably required to check that person's tax position • No power to inspect premises which are used solely as a dwelling
HMRC powers to enter business premises of an 'involved third party' to inspect premises, business assets and business documents	Para 10A	• Inspection is reasonably required by HMRC for the purpose of checking the position of any person or class of persons as regards a relevant tax and whether or not the identity of that person is known • Cannot inspect part of the premises used solely as a dwelling
Involved third parties	Para 61A Schedule	• HMRC approved bodies for payroll giving and donations to charity • Individual investment plan managers • Child trust fund account providers • Lloyds syndicate agents • Any person involved in the insurance industry • An accountable person for SDRT purposes • Responsible person re an oil field • A person involved in aggregate exploitation • A person involved in land fill disposal
HMRC power to enter & inspect premises and inspect goods &	Paras 11 & 12	• HMRC must have reason to believe that the premises are used in connection with the supply of taxable goods, acquisition

HMRC powers, taxpayer's rights, requirements & penalties	FA 2008 Schedule 36 reference	Comments
documents in connection with taxable supplies		of goods from another EU state or in connection with a fiscal warehouse • Inspection at a time agreed to by occupier of the premises or at any reasonable time either on seven days notice or with HMRC officer agreement (involving written notice) • Premises not to include those used solely as a dwelling
HMRC powers to inspect premises for valuation purposes	Paras 12A & 12B	• Must be reasonably required to determine a person's income tax or corporation tax • May enter premises to value or determine the character of the premises if required to check any person's position re CGT, chargeable gains for corporation tax, IHT, SDLT or SDRT • The time of inspection is agreed by premises occupier/person who control premises or alternatively tribunal has approved the inspection
HMRC power to take copies or to remove documents	Paras 15 & 16	• Removal must be at a reasonable time and retained for a reasonable period and must appear to HMRC officer to be necessary
Restriction on HMRC powers relating to information notices	Paras 19, 20 & 23	• Relating to the conduct of an appeal; • Journalistic material under s 13 PACE • Personal records under PACE • Documents more than six years before notice date unless notice is given by HMRC officer • Legally privileged information

Restrictions on HMRC re taxpayer notice to check a self-assessment return	Para 21	• If it relates to return for income tax and CGT or corporation tax UNLESS:
		  ○ an enquiry is ongoing OR
		  ○ HMRC reasonably suspects an incorrect assessment OR
		  ○ notice has been given to check any other taxes OR
		  ○ notice has been given that the purpose is to check deductions or repayments of tax or withholding of income under PAYE regs

HMRC powers, taxpayer's rights, requirements & penalties	FA 2008 Schedule 36 reference	Comments
Change of ownership of companies – para 21 does not apply	Para 36	• Circumstances involve the change of ownership of a company and recovery of unpaid corporation tax under CTA 2010 s 710 or 713 applies (the seller may become liable); also restrictions re giving taxpayer notice won't apply
Notices following Non-resident CGT returns – no taxpayer notice allowed unless three conditions met	Para 21ZA	• A notice of enquiry has been given under TMA s 12ZM or the taxpayers has made a claim • HMRC believe that an amount is payable on account under TMA s 12ZE or payment is insufficient • An information notice has been given to taxpayer
No notice following SDLT return allowed unless three conditions met	Para 21A	• To check the SDLT position UNLESS: • a notice of enquiry is open re the return or a claim has been made OR • HMRC have reason to suspect underassessment of SDLT or excessive SDLT relief OR • the notice is given to check that person's position regarding other taxes
No notice to be given following ATED return to check the amount of tax in the return unless three conditions met	Para 21B	• unless an enquiry has not been completed or HMRC suspect ATED was incorrectly assessed or underpaid or is required to assess another tax
A notice cannot cover privileged communications between legal advisers and clients	Paras 23 to 26	• Auditors and tax advisors cannot be required to supply information/ documents subject to exceptions including paragraph 5 notice asking for identity information

Taxpayer right to appeal a notice	Paras 29 to 32	• Cannot appeal against:
		  o information/documents which are statutory records OR
		  o a tribunal approved notice
		• Must be given within 30 days of the notice date
		• The tribunal may confirm, set aside or vary the information notice
		• Tribunal decision is final

Penalties	Paras 39 to 51	• Failure to comply/deliberate obstruction - £300 and further penalties up to £60 for

HMRC powers, taxpayer's rights, requirements & penalties	FA 2008 Schedule 36 reference	Comments
		each subsequent day • Careless/deliberate inaccuracy/failure to inform HMRC - up to £3,000 & a penalty for each inaccuracy • The taxpayer may claim reasonable excuse to HMRC or on appeal to the tribunal
Concealing documents following information notice	Paras 53 to 55	• Concealment, destruction or disposal of documents required under a notice approved by the tribunal is an offence, liable on summary conviction to fine/ up to two years imprisonment/or both

THE TAX SCHEDULE

Appendix 6. TIME LIMITS FOR ASSESSMENTS & CLAIMS AND RELATED MATTERS

Matter	Stat Ref.	Time limits	
		HMRC	**Taxpayer**
Re individuals & trustees			
Notice to HMRC by individual of liability to income tax or CGT	TMA s7(1)		Within six months from end of the tax year
Ordinary time limit to assess income tax/CGT relating to individual taxpayers	TMA s34	At any time not more than four years after the end of the year of assessment to which it relates	
Assessment of a loss of income tax/CGT re individuals due to carelessness	TMA s36(1)	At any time not more than six years after the end of the year of assessment	
Assessment of loss of income tax/CGT brought about • Deliberately • Failure of taxpayer to give notice under TMA s7 • DOTAS failures under FA 2004 ss 309, 310 or 313	TMA s36(1A)	At any time not more than 20 years after the year of assessment	
Amendment of personal or trustee tax return by taxpayer	TMA s9ZA		Not more than 12 months after the filing date (being generally 31 January)
Correction of personal or trustee tax return by HMRC	TMA s9ZB	Not more than nine months after date the return was delivered or after an amendment was made by the taxpayer under TMA s9ZA	
Non-resident CGT returns (NRCGT)	TMA s12ZB(1)		Taxpayer must file a return within 30 days after completion of disposal
HMRC to correct NRCGT return	TMA s12ZB(1)	HMRC has nine months from date of	

Matter	Stat Ref.	Time limits	
		HMRC	Taxpayer
		return delivery to make corrections	
HMRC to give notice of enquiry for NRCGT return	TMA s12ZM	up to the end of the period of 12 months after the day on which the return was delivered on/before 31 January; or if the return was delivered after the annual filing date, up to and including the quarter day next following the first anniversary of the day on which the return was delivered	
HMRC to enquire into a personal or trustee tax return (notice of enquiry)	TMA s9A	• Within 12 months of delivery date if filed before the filing date • Up to/including the first quarter day following the first anniversary of filing date if return filed after filing date • Up to/including the first quarter day following first • anniversary of any amendment date	
Requirements to retain records by individuals, trustees and partnerships • For trade, profession or business	TMA s12B		• Fifth anniversary of 31 January next following year of assessment or (as the

Matter	Stat Ref.	Time limits	
		HMRC	**Taxpayer**
Otherwise			case may be) the sixth anniversary • First anniversary of 31 January next following year of assessment
Claims for relief in respect of income tax or capital gains tax	TMA s43		Not later than four years after the end of the year of assessment to which it relates; HMRC concession B41 will allow claims outside the statutory time period if it was HMRC error and there is no dispute of the facts
Recovery of overpaid income tax/CGT paid to a taxpayer	TMA s30	Entitled to recover as if it was unpaid tax; assessment not to be made out of time under TMA s34 (i.e. four years) subject to TMA s29	
For corporations			
Company to give notice to HMRC that it is chargeable to tax	FA 1998 Sch 18 Para 2		Within 12 months from the end of the accounting period
Company requirement to deliver a company tax return following receipt of HMRC Notice	FA 1998 Sch 18 Paras 3 & 14		Must be delivered not later than the filing date namely whichever is latest: • 12 months from the end of the return period • if period of accounts is not longer than 18 months, 12 month from the end of that period • if account period is longer than 18 months, 30 months from the beginning of

Matter	Stat Ref.	Time limits	
		HMRC	**Taxpayer**
			that period • three months from the date on which HMRC notice was served
Amendment of Correction of company return	FA 1998 Sch 18 Paras 15 & 16	Not later than nine months after date the return was delivered or after the date the company made an amendment	Not later than 12 months after the filing date
Notice of enquiry into a company tax return	FA 1998 Sch 18 Para 24	• Up to 12 months from the day on which the return was delivered • If company is a member of a group up to 12 months from filing date • If return was filed late, notice of enquiry can be given any time up to/including 31 Jan, 30 Apr, 31 Jul or 31 Oct next following the first anniversary of the day the return was delivered	
General time limits for company assessments	FA 1998 Sch 18 Para 46(1)	Not more than four years after the end of the accounting period to which it relates	
General time limit for making claims for relief under any provision of the Corporation Tax Acts	FA 1998 Sch 18 Para 55		Within four years from the end of the account period to which it relates
General time limit for assessment of a loss of tax brought about carelessly by the company	FA 1998 Sch 18 Para 46(2)	At any time not more than six years after the end of the accounting period to which it relates	

Matter	Stat Ref.	Time limits	
		HMRC	**Taxpayer**
A loss of tax brought about by the company/related person • Deliberately or • carelessly or • failure to comply with DOTAS under ss 309, 310 & 212	FA 1998 Sch 18 Para 46(2A)	Not more than 20 years after the end of the accounting period to which it relates	
Making a claim for relief for overpaid tax by a company	FA 1998 Sch 18 Para 51B		May not be made more than four years after the end of the relevant accounting period
Recovery of excessive repayments	FA 1998 Sch 18 Para 53		Within the general four year period if made before the end of the accounting period following the year it was made or, if later, before the end of three months beginning with the date HMRC completed its enquiry
Determination & Assessments – becomes exercisable if the company does not deliver a company tax return on the ascertainable filing date OR the later of 18 months from the period end in the notice or three months from the day the notice was served	FA 1998 Sch 18 Para 36	A determination must be made within three years after the day on which the power becomes exercisable	
A company's duty to preserve records	FA 1998 Sch 18 Para 21		Standard period is until the sixth anniversary of the end of the period of the return
Claims for group relief (either made or withdrawn)	FA 1998 Sch 18 Para 74		The later of • First anniversary of filing date for the claimant company's tax return for the period for which the claim is made

Matter	Stat Ref.	Time limits	
		HMRC	Taxpayer
			• 30 days after any enquiry is completed • 30 days after notice of an HMRC amendment to a return under an enquiry • 30 days after the date on which an appeal is finally determined • At any later time allowed by HMRC
Claims for capital allowances by a company (made amended or withdrawn)	FA 1998 Sch 18 Para 82		As above under FA 1998 Sch 18 paragraph 74 (for group relief)
Claims for R&D tax reliefs by a company (made amended or withdrawn)	FA 1998 Sch 18 Para 83E		At any time up to the first anniversary of the filing date for the company tax return for the accounting period for which the claim is made or at any later date allowed by HMRC

Appendix 7.   HMRC CLEARANCES

TRANSACTION	DETAILS	HMRC ADVANCE CLEARANCE	HMRC CLEARANCE PROCEDURE
Chargeable payments connected with exempt distributions – **advance clearance under CTA 2010 section 1091**	Following a demerger & exempt distribution a chargeable payment made within five years could be subject to tax – advance clearance prior to the payment that there are no anti-avoidance purposes	Must be made prior to the chargeable payment	HMRC Clearance & Counteraction team[1]; return to local HMRC inspector
Company migration TMA sections 109B to 109F; SP 2/90	Companies intending to become non- UK resident must give notice to HMRC and make arrangements to pay all tax due before the migration date	Mandatory but Treasury consent no longer necessary; See also CT Manual 34195	HMRC Business International[2]
Controlled foreign companies ICTA sections 747 – 756 to 31.12.2012; for a/c periods from 1.1.2013 TIOPA 9A See HMRC INTM 214130 onwards	Clearance procedure to provide certainty regarding the application of the CFC legislation	Voluntary	CTIS Business International CFC Team[3]
Demergers CTA 2010 section 1091 advance clearance for distributions involving a demerger in respect of CTA 2010 section 1077	Transfer of a trade and the issue of shares by the transferee to the members of the transferor – clearance that the issue of shares in the newco to shareholders in transferor company is an exempt distributions; Advance clearance under TCGA section 138 should be made for a direct	Not mandatory but clearance cannot be given retrospectively	HMRC Clearance & Counteraction team[4]

[1] CTIS Clearance SO483 Newcastle, NE98 1ZZ

[2] Foreign Profits Team, 100 Parliament Street, London SW1 2BQ

[3] Foreign Profits Team Registry (CFC Clearance), 100 Parliament Street London SW1 2BQ

[4] CTISA Clearance SO528 PO Box 194, Bootle, L69 9AA

TRANSACTION	DETAILS	HMRC ADVANCE CLEARANCE	HMRC CLEARANCE PROCEDURE
	demerger and an indirect demerger if they fall within the rules of a reorganisation as a scheme of reconstruction		
Earn-out rights TCGA section 138A(4A)	An election to disapply automatic treatment under section 138A, namely '*Marren & Ingles*' earn-out right	Election required within time periods under section 138A(5)	HMRC inspector
Exempt distribution CTA 2010 section 1091	Advance clearance that a distribution can be treated as an exempt distribution under CTA 2010 sections 1077 to 1080	Not mandatory but a return required	HMRC Clearance & Counteraction team; return to local inspector
EIS , SEIS & VCT	Informal advance assurance that the shares to be issued will qualify for EIS, SEIS and VCT purposes	Not mandatory	Small Company Enterprise Centre[5]
EIS reorganisation ITA section 247(1)(f) requiring clearance under TCGA section 138(2)	Clearance required prior to the issue of new shares that exchange is for genuine commercial reasons and not for tax avoidance - continuity of EIS relief should apply to new shares	Clearance mandatory and prior to issue of the new shares	HMRC Clearance & Counteraction team
Reconstruction involving transfer of a business TCGA section 139	Confirmation that the anti-avoidance provisions under TCGA section 139(5) will not prevent TCGA section 139 from applying on a proposed company reconstruction or amalgamation involving a transfer of a business	Not mandatory but clearance cannot be given retrospectively	HMRC Clearance & Counteraction team
Roll-over relief under TCGA section 162	Arises on a TOGC by an individual to a company under TCGA section 162	Election is mandatory for the provisions	HMRC Inspector

---

[5] Local Compliance Small Company Enterprise Centre Administration Team,, SO777 PO Box, 3900 Glasgow G70 6AA

TRANSACTION	DETAILS	HMRC ADVANCE CLEARANCE	HMRC CLEARANCE PROCEDURE
(incorporation Relief) – election under TCGA section 162A for the relief not to apply	when the person does not want CG to roll into the shares	to apply	
Roll-over relief on a cross-border transfer involving intangible fixed assets CTA 2009 section 827	A UK resident company carrying on a trade outside the UK through a permanent establishment transferred is wholly/partly in exchange for securities by the transferee and for a genuine commercial transaction requirement	It is mandatory to make the claim before the transfer	HMRC Clearance & Counteraction team
Purchase of own shares by unquoted trading company CTA section 1044 2010; CTA 2010 section 1046 SP 2/82	Payment made for redemption, repayment or purchase by unquoted trading company of its own shares not to be treated as a distribution	Not mandatory but return under CTA 2010 section 1046 within 60 days is mandatory	HMRC Clearance & Counteraction team ; return sent to local inspector
Share exchanges; Scheme of reconstruction involving issue of securities TCGA section 138	Clearance that anti-avoidance provisions under section 137 will not prevent share exchanges under TCGA section 135 or 136 from applying to the proposed arrangements and which therefore will be tax-neutral	Not mandatory but retrospective approval not possible	HMRC Clearance & Counteraction team
Stamp duty – company reconstructions & acquisition reliefs FA 1986 sections 75 & 77	Relief from stamp duty where a company acquires a business of another company under a scheme of reconstruction; relief from stamp duty involving the acquisition of another	Mandatory	HMRC Birmingham Stamp Office[6]

---

[6] 9th Floor, City Centre House, 30 Union Street, Birmingham B2 4AR

TRANSACTION	DETAILS	HMRC ADVANCE CLEARANCE	HMRC CLEARANCE PROCEDURE
	company's share capital under a scheme of reconstruction and mirrored by the shareholdings		
Stamp duty relief FA 1930 section 42	Where a beneficial interest in shares or securities is transferred between two associated companies	Mandatory adjudication for the relief to apply	HMRC Birmingham Stamp Office[7]
Stamp duty land tax group relief FA 2003 Schedule 7 Part 1	Intra-group transfers of UK land so long as there is no 'degrouping' within three years	Mandatory claim for the relief to apply	Filing the SDLT return
Stamp duty land tax reconstruction & acquisition reliefs FA 2003 Schedule 7 Part 2	SDLT relief available when there is a transfer of an undertaking wholly or partially for the issue of shares	Mandatory claim for the relief to apply	Filing the SDLT return
Transaction in land - assignments for profit of lease granted at undervalue under CTA 2009 section 222	An application under CTA 2009 section 237 to an HMRC inspector for a certification of a statement of accuracy relating to whether there has been a receipt and if so the amount, for the purposes of CTA 2009 section 222	Not mandatory	HMRC inspector
Transaction in land – gains obtained from land disposals in some circumstances under CTA 2010 section 819 & ITA 756	In circumstances where there is a speculative purchase or a development designed to realise a gain on disposal and a gain has arisen – confirmation under CTA 2010 section 831 that CTA 2010 section 819 does not apply and under ITA section 770 that ITA section 756 does not apply	Not mandatory – applicant provides HMRC with written particulars showing how the gain has arisen or would arise; see also BIM 60300	HMRC inspector

---

TRANSACTION	DETAILS	HMRC ADVANCE CLEARANCE	HMRC CLEARANCE PROCEDURE
Transactions in securities ITA section 701 & CTA 2010 section 748	Confirmation that provisions cancelling tax advantages obtained from certain transactions in securities will not apply	Not mandatory	HMRC Clearance & Counteraction team
Transfer of business or trade involving intangible assets CTA 2009 section 831	Confirmation that transfers of intangible assets will be tax-neutral in a company reconstruction, a transfer of UK trade between companies resident in different EU member states; a transfer of assets to non-resident companies, and a transfer of a non-UK trade	Not mandatory but will not be granted retrospectively	HMRC Clearance & Counteraction team
Transfer or division of UK business between EU member states TCGA sections 140A and 140B	Confirmation that anti-avoidance provisions will not apply to prevent no gains/no loss treatment for CGT purposes from applying	Not mandatory	HMRC Clearance & Counteraction team
Transfer by UK company of a non-UK trade to a company in another EU member state TCGA sections 140C and 140D	Confirmation that anti-avoidance provisions will not apply in respect of any allowable losses of the transferor on the transfer to be set off against chargeable gains	Not mandatory	HMRC Clearance & Counteraction team
Transfer Pricing (Advance Pricing agreements)	Advanced Pricing Agreements programme since 1999 to assist businesses in identifying solutions for complex transfer pricing issues.	Not mandatory	CTIS Business International[8]

---

[8] CTIS Business International, East Spur, Euston Tower, 286 Euston Road London NW1 3UH

THE TAX SCHEDULE

Appendix 8. OVERVIEW OF HMRC APPROVED EMPLOYEE INCENTIVE SCHEMES

8.1. Approved Share Incentive Plans ("SIPs")[1]

SIPs were introduced in July 2000 – under the scheme an employer company may grant shares to employees who are UK resident taxpayers, subject to certain maximum values in each tax year and in respect of which the employee is not liable to income tax on the value of his or her beneficial interest in the company, at the time of the award or acquisition. The purpose of any SIP must be to provide employees who are UK resident taxpayers with a continuing stake the company.

 The shares must form part of the ordinary share capital of:
- the company, or the company controlling that company; or
- a company which either is or has control of a company which is a member of a consortium owning either the company or the controlling company.

A company can award to each scheme participant 'free shares' (that is, without payment) with an initial market value of up to £3,600 in any tax year; the scheme can provide for participants, in addition, to acquire 'partnership shares' worth the lower of £1,800 per tax year or 10% of his or her total salary (deductions to be taken from the gross salary); and a participant buying partnership shares may be granted, without payment, 'matching shares' (which are of the same class with the same rights as the partnership shares) by the company on a ratio of up to two free shares for every partnership share bought (thus representing an annual maximum of £3,600 in value). Finally, any participant who receives cash dividends on free, partnership or matching shares may reinvest the dividends to buy 'dividend shares' at the trustees' discretion. The dividend shares must be of the same class and carry the same rights as the shares in respect of which the dividend is paid, and not be subject to any provision for forfeiture.

A SIP need not include all four types of share awards. Nevertheless, if a plan provides for the maximum amount any

---

[1] ITEPA section 488 & Schedule 2

participant could be entitled to on an annual basis, grants could be worth £9,000 p.a. excluding dividend shares equating to some £27,000 on a three year time frame. This compares very favourable to the maximum Approved CSOP option entitlement.

Taxation issues

No income tax or NIC will arise on the award of the free, matching or partnership shares to a participant or on the acquisition of dividend shares on behalf of the employee,[2] nor will there be a tax charge on the sale of free, matching or partnership shares which are held for five years or in the case of dividend shares, for three years.[3] Otherwise, a capital receipt will be treated as employment income in the tax year of disposal.

If the shares cease to be subject to the SIP for whatever reason during the five year period following acquisition, an employment income charge can arise depending on the period in which the shares were subject to the SIP, as set out in the table below, unless the participant leaves employment as a 'good leaver' (due to an injury or disability, redundancy, a transfer of employment under TUPE, retirement, death, or the company or part of the business for which the participant works is sold).[4]

The table below[5] sets out what income tax and NIC a participant has to pay for his or her SIP shares if they fall outside the SIP requirements unless he or she is a good leaver:

Type of share	Participant acquires the shares	Participant takes shares from the SIP during the first three years	Participant takes shares from the SIP during years 3 to 5	Participant takes shares from the SIP after five years
Free shares and matching shares	No income tax or NIC to pay on the value of the shares	Income tax payable on the market value of the shares when taken out of the SIP	Income tax payable on the lower of the market value of the shares at the time acquired and the market value when taken out of the SIP	No income tax or NIC to pay
Partnership shares	No income tax or NIC to pay on the money used to buy the shares; deductions taken from gross salary	Income tax payable on the market value of the shares when taken out of the SIP	Income tax payable on the lower of the pay used to buy the shares and the market value of the shares when taken out of the SIP	No income tax or NIC to pay
Dividend shares	No income tax or NIC to pay on dividends used to buy dividend shares	Dividends used to buy shares are taxed as a dividend in the year when the shares are taken out of the SIP	No income tax or NIC to pay	No income tax or NIC to pay

The company setting up the SIP must notify HMRC and self-certify by notice that the plan meets the legislative criteria – referred to as a Schedule 2 SIP – and thereafter make an annual return by 6 July in each year as required under ITEPA Schedule 2 paragraph 81B.

The company setting up the SIP will be allowed a deduction in computing its taxable profits for the costs of setting up the scheme. Deductions are also available for any contributions the company makes towards the trustees' costs in running the plan and any payment to the trustees to buy a block of shares in the company on behalf of the employees, subject to certain conditions.[6] Companies are allowed a deduction against their profits for the costs of awarding free or matching shares, equal to the market value of the shares when acquired by the trustees. Deductions may be withdrawn in respect of contributions a company makes for the acquisition of shares if either less than 30% of the acquired shares have been awarded before the end of the five year period beginning with the date of acquisition or, if not all the acquired shares have been awarded, before the end of 10 years.

Corporation tax relief is also available when an employee acquires shares which are employment-related securities and certain conditions are met, under CTA 2009 sections 1001 to 1038.

SIP shares can be transferred directly into an ISA, free from CGT, so long as the transfer is effected within 90 days of leaving the SIP. In addition, SIP shares can be transferred directly into a stakeholder or personal pension within the same 90 day period, subject to the rules of the pension scheme allowing for this.

Eligibility and other requirements

The legislation requires that a SIP is open to all employees of a company who are UK resident so long as the participant (together with his or her associates) do not have a 'material interest'[7] in the company, namely more than 25% of the ordinary share capital or, where the company is a close company, an entitlement to receive more than 25% of the assets on a winding up. The company has the discretion to set eligibility hurdles based on qualifying periods of service[8] which primarily limit any such conditions to 18 months, and it can allow non-UK resident employees to participate. The rules of the SIP must not include terms which are neither essential nor reasonably incidental, and they must be approved by HMRC. They must not allow preferential treatment for directors and there can be no discrimination against lower paid employees in a group plan.

---

[6] CTA 2009 sections 983 to 998

[7] ITEPA Schedule 2 paragraph 20

[8] ITEPA Schedule 2 paragraph 16

Participants must be able to withdraw from the partnership share agreement and be repaid any partnership share money. They must also be entitled to withdraw partnership shares from the SIP, but if they are taken out within three years of the award, the participant may lose the matching shares which were awarded with them. The free, matching and dividend shares cannot be taken out of the SIP within the first three years or up to five years in respect of the free and matching shares if the company provides for this in the SIP rules. If a participant leaves his or her employment the partnership shares must come out of the SIP, and the rules can provide for the free and matching shares to be forfeited if a participant leaves within three years after the grant of the awards.

The shares awarded under a SIP must be ordinary shares, fully paid up and not redeemable and must be any of the following:

- shares of a class listed on a recognised stock exchange;
- shares in a company which is not under the control of another company (other than a listed company);
- shares in a company which is subject to an employee ownership trust; or
- shares in a company which is under the control of a listed company.

The employer is entitled to impose certain conditions on the shares such as limited or no voting rights and certain forfeiture events.

The company operating a SIP cannot be a service company (namely a company which substantially provides the services of persons employed by it)[9] or under the control of a service company.

Administrative issues

Due to the requirements of setting up and administering a trust which satisfies the legislative criteria, and the cost of administering a SIP (which might be done in-house by the employer company but is more commonly done by a bank or third party trustee) a SIP may not be attractive for companies unless there is a workforce of sufficient size to justify the administrative expenses, which can be high. In order for the tax advantages to apply to a SIP the scheme

---

[9] ITEPA Schedule 2 paragraph 29

must satisfy the legislative rules – there is no longer an approval procedure involving HMRC before being put into operation – instead the company must self-certify.

So long as all the necessary conditions are met the employer company can claim relief against corporation tax for the costs of setting up a SIP and will not be liable for employer's NIC on shares awarded to or purchased by the participants.

If at any time there is an alteration to a key feature of the SIP or the plant trust this must be reported on the annual return with a declaration that the alteration has not caused the requirements of Schedule 2 not to be met.

The trust set up to hold the SIP shares must be constituted by a trust deed which complies with ITEPA Schedule 2 and subject to UK law, and the trustees must act at all times in the best interests of the beneficiaries of the trust. The trustees are required to deal with the disposals and rights of the shares held under the SIP as directed by the participants and will be liable to income tax on dividends and other distributions they receive in connection with shares held under the SIP if they have not been appropriated to employees, at the tax rate applicable to trusts. Trustees are also obliged to keep records for PAYE purposes and have responsibilities to meet PAYE obligations. On the winding up of the trust the trustees will be responsible for the final divestment of the trust property, including any money held and for the transfer of shares it holds, to the beneficiaries.

The company operating the SIP must file returns[10] to HMRC after the end of each tax year and the trustees are required to file a self assessment trust return for each tax year.

On a takeover the trustees must act in accordance with the directions of the participants holding shares in the company under the SIP. If an offer is agreed the trustees will receive the consideration on behalf of the participants and must pay this over as soon as practicable.

---

[10] Form 39

THE TAX SCHEDULE

8.2. Schedule 4 Company Share Option Plans ("CSOPs")[11]

Schedule 4 CSOPs were introduced in 1984, whereby options to acquire shares may be granted to certain employees at the company's discretion with tax benefits on acquisition. The legislative requirements are generally less flexible than EMI schemes but CSOPs are not restricted to small trading companies. The overall entitlement to receive tax-enhanced awards is limited to an aggregate market value of shares under option of £30,000 per employee, excluding options which have been exercised. This means that employees may be offered CSOPs every three year up to £30,000 in value. The company adopting an CSOP has no statutory limits over how many options it might issue and their overall value.

Taxation issues

No income tax or NIC will arise on the grant of an option under an CSOP. The rules must provide that the exercise price is not less than the market value of the shares under option on the date of grant, the options must not be transferable; and subject to other legislative provisions being satisfied in respect of the scheme, so long as exercise is three or more years after the date of grant, no income tax or NIC will arise on exercise of a CSOP option.

If the rules allow for exercise within three years of any grant due to participants leaving employment of the company due to injury, disability, redundancy or retirement, or a transfer of employment under TUPE or in the event the employer company leaves the scheme group ('good leavers') the income tax relief will apply so long as exercise is within six months of the date of leaving. However, if exercise takes place within three years of grant for other reasons, such as leaving employment or the takeover of the company or any other change of control event, the income tax relief will not be available. CGT will apply in the normal way on the subsequent disposal of the shares acquired on exercise of the option with the acquisition cost plus any amount of income tax charged at exercise, being treated as the base cost.

---

[11] ITEPA sections 521 to 526 and Schedule 4

The costs incurred in setting up an CSOP will be allowable as a deductible expense for corporation tax purposes, for the period of account in which the expenditure is incurred. In addition, corporation tax relief is available on the acquisition of the shares on exercise of the option if certain conditions are met.[12] So long as the shares are neither restricted nor convertible the amount of relief is the difference between their market value on acquisition less the total amount of consideration given for the shares (see below for shares criteria).

Eligibility and other requirements

Only qualifying employees are eligible to be granted options under an CSOP, being either an employee of the company who is not also a director of the company or of a constituent company, or a full-time director. Participants must have no material interest in the company if it is a close company at the date of grant or within the preceding 12 months. A material interest is defined[13] as beneficial ownership of or the ability to control directly or indirectly more than 30% of the ordinary share capital of the company or possession or entitlement to acquire such rights which would, on the winding up of the company, provide an entitlement to receive more than 30% of the assets available for distribution among the participators. Furthermore, a participant will lose tax relief if he or she exercises options at any time if she or he has, or has within the preceding 12 months had, a material interest in a close company whose shares may be acquired on the exercise of the option or which has control of the company.

Shares under option must be fully paid up and cannot be redeemable. They should not be subject to restrictions other than restrictions attaching to all shares of the same class or restrictions imposed by the company's articles, with a limited exception for shares held by employees which are required to be disposed of, or offered for sale, on ceasing to be employed by the company.

Eligible shares must form part of the ordinary share capital of the scheme organiser, a company which controls the scheme organiser

---

[12] CTA 2009 sections 1001 to 1013

[13] ITEPA Schedule 4 paragraph 10 and 11

or a company which either is, or has control of, a company which is a member of a consortium owning either the scheme organiser or a company controlling the scheme organiser. The eligible shares must be:

- shares of a class listed on a recognised stock exchange;
- shares in a company which is not under the control of another company; or
- shares in a company which is subject to an employee-ownership trust.

An individual may not receive tax relief if granted share options which would at the time of grant cause the aggregate market value of the shares under option to exceed £30,000.

Administrative issues

As from 6 April 2014 companies must self-certify by notice to HMRC that the scheme satisfies the provisions of Schedule 4 and thereafter must submit online the annual return to HMRC.[14]

8.3.   Enterprise Management Incentives (EMIs)[15]

EMIs are tax-advantaged share options which may be granted by small companies which satisfy certain trading criteria, to full-time employees and directors, so long as the purpose of the grant is for commercial reasons and in order to recruit or retain an employee, and not part of a tax avoidance scheme or arrangement. EMI options may be granted under a formal scheme or individually to the eligible employees but must be by way of a written agreement. Notice of a grant of an EMI must be provided to HMRC within 82 days after its grant – otherwise it will not be a qualifying EMI. The notice must contain a declaration that all the Schedule 5 requirements are satisfied and the participant must make a declaration that he or she satisfies the working time requirements. In addition, the company must file electronically an annual return with HMRC.

Taxation issues

---

[14] ITEPA Schedule 4 paras 28A and 28B

[15] ITEPA sections 417 to 548 & Schedule 5

No income tax or NIC is charged on the grant of an EMI option. So long as there are no disqualifying events and the exercise price is the market value of the shares under option at the date of grant (as agreed with HMRC share valuations), no income tax or NIC charge will arise on exercise. If the exercise price is less than market value at the date of grant ("a discounted option") there will be an income tax charge on exercise on the element of the discount to market value, as well as NIC payable if the shares are readily convertible assets[16] (RCA). A share will be considered to be an RCA, *inter alia*, if it is capable of being traded.

On exercise of an EMI option when the shares are retained and before any disposal, if there are restrictions or conditions attached to shares, an income tax charge could arise when the restrictions and conditions are lifted. On disposal of the shares, if they are unrestricted or subject to a section 431 election to ignore restrictions, any taxable gain will be subject to capital gains tax. Only if an EMI option is exercised within 40 days of a disqualifying event are the tax advantages preserved for the option-holder.

Corporation tax relief should be available on the exercise of an EMI option when shares are acquired under CTA 2009 sections 1001 to 1013.

Eligibility and other requirements

The company or parent of a group of companies wishing to issue EMI options must be a 'qualifying company' under ITEPA Schedule 5 paragraph 8 and:

- cannot have gross assets which exceed £30 million;
- must be independent;
- must have fewer than 250 full-time employees (or equivalent part-time employees);
- may not be a 51% subsidiary of another company nor under the control of another company;
- has a UK permanent establishment;[17]

---

[16] defined in ITEPA section 702

[17] See ITEPA section 14A

- must carry on a qualifying trade, namely one conducted on a commercial basis with a view to the realisation of profits, and the trade does not consist, either wholly or substantially, in the carrying on of excluded activities. Excluded activities are defined as follows:
  - dealing in land, commodities or futures, or in shares, securities or other financial instruments;
  - dealing in goods otherwise than in an ordinary course of wholesale or retail distribution;
  - banking, insurance, money-lending, debt-factoring, hire-purchase financing or other financial activities;
  - leasing, including letting ships on charter or other assets on hire;
  - receiving royalties or license fees;
  - providing legal or accountancy services;
  - property development;
  - farming or market gardening;
  - holding, managing or occupying woodlands, or other forestry activities or timber production;
  - shipbuilding;
  - producing coal;
  - producing steel;
  - operating or managing hotels or comparable establishments, or managing property used as a hotel or comparable establishment;
  - operating or managing nursing homes or residential care homes, or managing property used as a nursing home or residential care home.

There are also exclusions in respect of companies which are service providers to other businesses.

An EMI option may be granted over shares in a company to any individual who is an employee of that company or of a 51% qualifying subsidiary of that company or a 90% holding in a property management subsidiary of that company, and who satisfies the working time criteria, namely:

- his or her committed working time averages at least 25 hours a week or if less, 75% of the employee's total working time; and

- he or she does not have a material interest in the company (that is, more than 30% of the ordinary share capital of the company, or an entitlement to more than 30% of the assets, if it is a close company).

An employee may not hold unexercised qualifying EMI options which are over shares with a total market value at the time of grant(s) of more than £250,000. In calculating that limit, any options under an HMRC CSOP are included. Once an employee has been granted EMI options with a total market value of £250,000 any further EMI options granted within a three year period cannot qualify under the EMI provisions but rules of the scheme can provide that they be treated as unapproved options.

The total value of shares in respect of which unexercised EMI options exist must not exceed £3 million at any time. The market value of an EMI option is the unrestricted market value of the shares under option at the date of grant of the EMI option.

EMI options can only be granted over shares which form part of the ordinary share capital of the company, are fully paid up, and are not redeemable. The EMI option must be granted under a written agreement between the company and the employee.

If any of the qualifying conditions fail to be satisfied at any time, a disqualifying event will be deemed to have occurred, and the beneficial tax treatment accorded to an EMI option will no longer apply after 40 days following the event. The following is an outline of the main disqualifying events:

- the employee ceases to satisfy the commitment to working time;
- the company loses its independence;
- the company no longer meets the trading activities requirement;
- the option-holder ceases to be an eligible employee;
- there are changes to the terms of the EMI options;
- a CSOP option is granted which takes the option-holder over the individual £250,000 EMI limit;
- there is an alteration to the company's share capital.

Administrative issues

The EMI scheme is the most generous HMRC-approved employment incentive option scheme to date in terms of the maximum amount of a single award able to be granted to an employee but it is limited to small trading companies. The statutory requirements are also the most flexible of the four HMRC approved schemes with no prior HMRC approval for rules or EMI agreements required. However, there is a requirement that the employer notifies the HMRC within 92 days of the grant of an EMI option, following which HMRC may enquire into the grant at any time within 12 months beginning with the end of the 92 day period. If a notice of enquiry is not given the EMI option can be taken to meet the statutory requirements at the end of the 12 month period. The scheme organiser is required to file an annual return relating the EMI scheme.[18]

It is advisable to agree with HMRC the market value of shares as at the date of grant.

8.4.   Schedule 3 SAYE Option Schemes[19]

The SAYE option scheme, also called a savings-related or save-as-you-earn scheme, was introduced in 1980 and represents the first employee incentive scheme in which all employees and full-time directors were entitled to participate. It has two aspects:

(a) share options are granted over shares in the company at an exercise price of not manifestly less than 80% of the market value of the shares; and

(b) the participant enters into a special certified savings contract (a certified SAYE savings arrangement) which, after regular saving out of salary over either three, five or (until 23 July 2013) seven years,[20] will provide the funds for the acquisition of the shares on exercise of the option ('linked savings arrangements').

The exercise period is aligned with the date when repayments under the savings scheme become due. The contractual savings schemes are operated by building societies, banks and authorised

---

[18] Form 40

[19] ITEPA sections 516 to 519 & Schedule 3

[20] Withdrawn on the recommendation of the Office of Tax Simplification (OTS)

European savings institutions. As from 23 July 2013 options granted from that date must be held for a three or five year period and if at the time of exercise the options are under water (the exercise price is greater than the market value) the participant may keep the cash (together with interest earned and any bonus) and allow the option lapse.

Taxation issues

No income tax arises when the options are granted, and so long as exercise of the option is after three years following the date of grant no tax or NIC will arise on exercise. The participant must agree to make a fixed regular monthly sum of between £10 and £250 over a fixed three year or five year period, which will normally be deducted from his or her after-tax salary. The costs a company incurs in setting up an SAYE scheme should be allowable as a deduction in computing its profits for corporation tax purposes, normally for the period of account in which the expenditure is incurred. The exercise price of an SAYE option may be granted at a discount of up to 20% of market value of the shares under option.

If a participant is paid a bonus and interest from the savings contract rather than receiving shares on the exercise of an SAYE option no income tax will be payable on that bonus and interest.

A company may deduct set-up costs for an SAYE against corporation tax relief[21] in addition to claiming relief against corporation tax when participants exercise their options and acquire the shares, subject to conditions.[22]

Eligibility and other requirements

The 'all-employee' nature of the scheme requires that all employees and any full-time director of the company offering the shares, who have been an employee or full time director of the scheme organiser or group member, at all times during a qualifying period of not more than five years, and their earnings from employment or the office are general earnings under ITEPA section 15 (earnings for the year when an employee is UK

---

[21] CTA 2009 sections 999 and 1000

[22] CTA 2009 sections 1001 to 1038

THE TAX SCHEDULE

resident), are entitled to participate. The scheme must ensure that no individual is eligible to participate if he or she has, or has had within the 12 months ending with that date a material interest (being 25% of the ordinary share capital or assets) in a close company whose shares may be acquired on exercise of the options or which has control of a company whose shares may be acquired as a result of exercising options under the scheme. The rules of the scheme are allowed to require participants to meet a qualifying period of employment so long as it is not more than five years. The terms of participation must be on similar terms for all participants and there must be no preferential treatment of directors and senior employees.

The shares under option must form part of the ordinary share capital of the company must be fully paid up and must not redeemable. The company can be:

- the scheme organiser;
- a company which has control of the scheme organiser; or
- a company which either is, or has control of, a company which is a member of a consortium owning either the scheme organiser or a company having control of the scheme organiser.

In addition, the shares under option must be:

- shares of a class listed on a recognised stock exchange; or
- shares in a company which is not under the control of another company.

The shares must not be subject to any restrictions other than those attaching to all shares of the same class or restrictions imposed by the relevant articles, *inter alia*, requiring all shares held by directors or employees to be sold on cessation of employment.

Under the certified SAYE savings arrangements the participant's contributions must, as nearly as possible, equal the aggregate option price for the maximum number of shares capable of being acquired on exercise of the option subject to a minimum of £10 per month or maximum savings of £500 per month.[23] The scheme may also provide for a bonus to be paid, but that provision must be stated at the date of grant of the option.

---

[23] ITEPA Schedule 3 paragraph 25

Options must not be capable of being exercised before the bonus date or later than six months after that date. However, the scheme rules must allow early exercise within six months of cessation of employment due to injury, disability, redundancy or retirement. The scheme rules may permit early exercise within six months following a take-over, a winding up or the employer company leaving the group, and may provide for early exercise for any other reason so long as the option has been held for more than three years.

The savings contract must provide for savings to be made over a three year or five year period requiring either 36 or 60 monthly contributions in total. For a five year contract if the savings are left for a further two years, a larger bonus will be available to the participant for options granted before 23 July 2013 only. The rates of bonus are reviewed each year and posted on HM Treasury's website. Simple interest will apply for early leavers who leave an SAYE scheme between the first and third anniversaries for a three year savings contract, and between the first and fifth anniversaries for a five year savings contract. No interest will be payable if repayment is taken before the first anniversary.

If a participant ceases to meet the employment requirements he or she can arrange with the savings body to continue to make monthly payment on the savings contract.

Administrative issues

As from 6 April 2014 companies have been required to self-certify that their SAYE schemes satisfy the legislative requirements and they must file annual returns online. However, the rules relating to certified savings arrangements must be approved by HMRC.[24] Before the savings contracts are entered into by the participant and the savings body, the savings body will want assurance from the company organiser that the SAYE scheme satisfies the requirements of ITEPA Schedule 3. The monthly savings will be paid to the savings body and is usually deducted from the participant's salary. Therefore the employer's payroll department

---

[24] ITTOIA section 705

and the savings body need to liaise closely during the operation of the scheme.

The legislative requirements must be met at both the date of grant and exercise of the SAYE options. If the rules are amended at any time these must be reported on the annual return.

Appendix 9.   EIS OVERVIEW CHECKLIST[1]

	Confirmation
1. Qualifying Company issuing EIS Shares	
1.1. It is not listed on a recognised stock exchange or a designated exchange in a country outside the UK (i.e. it is "unquoted") and there are no arrangements for it to become quoted[2].	
1.2. The Company exists wholly for the purposes of carrying on one or more Qualifying Business Activity (*see paragraph* 8 *below*); OR the Company is the parent of a trading group which satisfies the trading requirement (*see paragraph* 7 *below)*, essentially for at least a three year period from the date of issue of the EIS shares ("qualifying period").	
1.3. A trading group must have one or more Qualifying Subsidiaries and not more than 20% of the group's business comprises an Excluded Activity (*see paragraph 9 below*) and activities carried on otherwise than in the course of a trade.	
1.4. The Company is not under the Control[*] of another company or under the Control of another company and any person connected with that company, and there are no arrangements for the Company to come under the Control of another company during the qualifying period.	
1.5. A Qualifying Business Activity must be carried on by the Company or by a Qualifying 90% Subsidiary (*see paragraph 6 below*).	
1.6. The company must have a permanent establishment in the UK.	
1.7. The issuing company must meet the financial health requirement – meaning that it is not in difficulty – at the time of issue of the EIS shares.	
1.8. The Gross Assets Test is satisfied (*see paragraph 3 below*).	
1.9. The Employee Restrictions test is satisfied (*see paragraph 4*).	
2. Eligible Shares for EIS Purposes ("EIS Shares")	
2.1. The Shares are:	
a) new ordinary shares, fully paid up and issued for *bona fide* commercial reasons and not for tax avoidance; and	

---

[1] ITA sections 156 to 259; see also **Chapter 8** of this book for further specific details

[2] AIM, the Specialist Fund Market (SFM) and the ISDX Growth Market, are not recognised stock exchanges for tax purposes at the time of writing and shares traded in the High Growth Segment of the LSE are not considered to be 'listed' by HMRC;

[*] Control – ITA section 995, except for sections 185(1)(a), 199(3)(a) and (b), 232(3) and 243(4) in which 'control' is read in accordance with CTA 2010 sections 450 and 451.

b) subscribed for wholly in cash by the investor.

2.2. The shares carry no present or future:
  a) preferential rights to dividends;
  b) preferential rights for the Company's assets on a winding up; or
  c) right to be redeemed.

2.3. Not more than £5 million may be raised by the issue of EIS shares annually by the issuing company.

2.4. The shares are issued to raise money in a Qualifying Business Activity (*see paragraph 8 below*).

2.5. The provisions of *paragraph 11* below are satisfied (**"Use of Proceeds"**).

2.6. There are no pre-arranged exits and no tax avoidance arrangements.

3. Gross Assets Test

3.1. The gross assets of the Company or Trading Group must not exceed £15 million immediately before the issue of the EIS Shares and £16 million immediately after the issue.

4. Employee Restrictions

4.1. The Company or Group must have less than 250 full-time employees (which include directors) or equivalent part-time employees at the time of issue of the EIS Shares.

5. Qualifying Subsidiaries

5.1. The subsidiary is a 51% subsidiary (more than 50% of the ordinary share capital is directly/indirectly owned by the Company) and no-one other than the Company or another of its subsidiaries can Control it (other than a property managing subsidiary – *see paragraph 5.2 below*).

5.2. A property managing subsidiary whose business is wholly or mainly holding or managing land must be a Qualifying 90% Subsidiary of the Company.

6. Qualifying 90% Subsidiary

6.1. The holding company:
  a) owns at least 90% of its issued share capital;
  b) owns at least 90% of its voting power;
  c) will receive at least 90% of its assets on winding-up;
  d) has beneficial entitlement to at least 90% of profits available for distribution; AND
  e) no other person has control of the subsidiary and no arrangements are in place whereby the above conditions will cease to be met.

7. Trading Activities

7.1. Single Company – it exists wholly for the purpose of carrying on one or more Qualifying Business Activity (*see paragraph 8 below*).

7.2. Parent Company – all of its subsidiaries are Qualifying Subsidiaries; and the activities of the Trading Group companies taken together do not consist, wholly or substantially, in carrying on Excluded Activities (*see paragraph 9 below*).

8. Qualifying Business Activities[3]

8.1. The Company or Qualifying 90% Subsidiary must carry on a 'qualifying trade' and be conducted substantially on a commercial basis with a view to realising profits.

8.2. Not more than 20% of the trade is involved in carrying on Excluded Activities (*see paragraph 9 below*).

8.3. The trade must begin within two years of the issue of the EIS Shares, either by the issuing Company or any Qualifying 90% Subsidiary.

8.4. The activity cannot be that of acquiring existing shares in another company.

8.5. The activity cannot comprise receipt of feed-in tariffs (FiTs) or similar subsidies.

9. Excluded Activities[4]

9.1. Dealing in land commodities or futures or in shares, securities or other financial instruments;

9.2. Dealing in goods otherwise than in the course of an ordinary trade of wholesale or retail distribution;

9.3. Banking, insurance, money-lending, debt-factoring, hire-purchase financing or other financial activities;

9.4. Leasing, including letting ships on charter;

9.5. Receiving royalties or licence fees;

9.6. Shipbuilding;

9.7. Producing coal;

9.8. Producing steel;

9.9. Providing legal or accountancy services;

9.10. Property development;

9.11. Farming or market gardening;

9.12. Holding, managing or occupying woodlands, any other

---

[3] See **Chapter 3** paragraph 3.31 for special rules including R & D provisions

[4] See ITA sections 192 to 199 for detailed provisions

forestry activities or timber production;

9.13. Activities (other than R&D) carried on otherwise than in the course of a trade;

9.14. Operating or managing hotels, guest houses or hostels in which the trading company has an interest or which occupies it under licence;

9.15. Operating or managing nursing homes or residential care homes, in which the trading company has an interest in which it occupies;

9.16. The subsidised generation or export of electricity; and

9.17. Providing services to another company where the other company's trade consists to a substantial extent of Excluded Activities carried on by another person which consists to a substantial extent in carrying on excluded activities as set out in the above sub-paragraphs.

10. Disqualifying purpose test[5]

The shares must not be issued subject to arrangements whose main purpose is to generate access to the EIS reliefs in circumstances where either the benefit of the investment is passed to another party to the arrangements, or the business activities would otherwise be carried on by another party.

11. Use of Proceeds

11.1. All of the money raised by the EIS issue is employed wholly for the qualifying business activity by the end of the two year period beginning with the issue.

11.2. Employing money on acquiring share in a company does not in itself amount to employing the money for the purposes of a qualifying business activity[6].

12. Qualifying Investor

12.1. He/she must have no connection with the issuing company for a period starting two years before the issue of the EIS shares up to the end of the qualifying holding period, with 'connection meaning:

a) being an employee, director or partner[7];

b) having a 30% or more interest in the company (shares and voting power);

c) having any 'linked loan';

d) having a 'tax avoidance' motive in acquiring the EIS shares;

---

[5] ITA section 178A

[6] ITA section 175(1A)

[7] See **Chapter 8** paragraph 8.1.6 for exceptions for 'business angels'

12.2. The maximum annual subscription in EIS shares is £1 million.	
12.3. The investor must make a claim for EIS relief after the receipt of a compliance certificate from the Company.	

Appendix 10. SEIS OVERVIEW CHECKLIST[1]

	Confirmation
1. Qualifying Company[2] issuing SEIS Shares	
1.1. Throughout the three years beginning with the issue of the shares:	
a) It exists wholly for the purpose of carrying on one or more new qualifying trades (see paragraph below) or the company is a parent company and the business of the group does not consist wholly or to a substantial part in carrying on non-qualifying activities, namely excluded activities (*see paragraph 8.2 below*) or activities apart from R&D carried on otherwise than in the course of a trade;[3]	
b) The relevant new qualifying trade, any relevant preparation work and any relevant research and development must be carried on by the issuing company or a qualifying 90% of that company and not by any other person;[4]	
c) It must have a permanent establishment in the UK.[5]	
1.2. At the date of issuing the SEIS shares, the issuing company must not be in 'difficulty' (the *financial health requirement*).[6]	
1.3. At the date of issuing the SEIS shares, it must be unquoted and there must be no arrangements in existence for it to cease to be unquoted or to become a subsidiary of another company on an exchange of shares and there are arrangements for the other company to cease to be unquoted.[7]	
1.4. During the three year period beginning with the incorporation date of the company:	
a) the issuing company must not at any time control any company which is not a qualifying subsidiary nor can there be any arrangements whereby the issuing company fails this requirement; and the issuing company must not at any time be under the control of	

---

[1] ITA sections 257A to 257HJ

[2] ITA sections 257D to 257DN

[3] ITA section 257DA

[4] ITA section 257DC

[5] ITA section 25DD

[6] ITA section 257DE

[7] ITA section 257DF

any other company (whether on its own or together with any person connected with it); and[8]

b) neither the issuing company nor any qualifying 90% subsidiary may be a member of a partnership.[9]

1.5. The Gross Assets Test is satisfied (*see paragraph* 3 *below*).

1.6. The number of Employees requirement test is satisfied (*see paragraph* 4).

1.7. The issuing company has received no EIS or VCT investment on or before the date the SEIS shares are issued[10] and the amount raised through the SEIS must not exceed £150,000[11] during any three year period.

2. The Shares requirement[12]

2.1. The relevant shares are ordinary shares which do not at any time during the three years starting with their issue carry:

a) any present or future preferential right to dividends

b) any present or future preferential right to a company's assets on its winding up, or

c) any present or future right to be redeemed.

2.2. The shares are subscribed for wholly in cash and are fully paid up at the time of issue.

2.3. The shares are issued to raise money for the purposes of a qualifying business activity carried on by the issuing company or a qualifying 90% subsidiary[13] and before the end of the three year period beginning with the issue of the shares all of the money raised is spent for the purposes of the Qualifying Business Activity (*see paragraph* 8 *below*).

2.4. The issuing arrangements must not include arrangements:

a) to repurchase, exchange or disposal of the shares or other shares in the issuing company;

b) for the cessation of any trade being carried on or to be carried on by the issuing company or a connected person;

c) for the disposal of the assets (or of a substantial amount in terms of value of assets) of the issuing

---

[8] ITA section 257DG

[9] ITA section 257DH

[10] ITA section 257DL

[11] ITA section 257DL

[12] ITA section 257CS

[13] ITA sections 257CB and 257CC

company or of a person connected with the company;

   d)   to provide partial or complete protection for the investing person by means of any insurance, indemnity or guarantee.[14]

3.   Gross Assets Test

3.1.   Their value for a single issuing company must not exceed £200,000 immediately before the SEIS shares are issued and in the case of a parent company the same limit applies to the group assets.[15]

4.   Number of Employees

4.1.   The Company or Group must have less than 25 full-time employees (which include directors) or equivalent part-time employees at the time of issue of the SEIS Shares.[16]

5.   Qualifying Subsidiaries

5.1.   The subsidiary is a 51% subsidiary and no person other than the relevant company or another of its subsidiaries has control of the subsidiary and there are no arrangements in existence whereby these conditions would cease to be met[17] (other than a property management subsidiary – *see paragraph 5.2 below*).

5.2.   A property managing subsidiary whose business is wholly or mainly holding or managing land must be a Qualifying 90% Subsidiary of the Company.[18]

6.   Qualifying 90% Subsidiary[19]

6.1.   The holding company:

   a)   owns at least 90% of its issued share capital;

   b)   owns at least 90% of its voting power;

   c)   will receive at least 90% of its assets on winding-up;

   d)   has beneficial entitlement to at least 90% of profits available for distribution; AND

   e)   no other person has control of the subsidiary and no arrangements are in place whereby the above conditions will cease to be met.

7.   Qualifying trade[20]

7.1.   The trade is conducted on a commercial basis with a view

---

[14] ITA section 257CD

[15] ITA section 257DI

[16] ITA section 257DJ

[17] ITA section 191 by virtue of ITA section 257HJ

[18] ITA section 257DN

[19] ITA section 190 by virtue of ITA section 257HJ

[20] ITA section 189 by virtue of ITA section 257DA

to the realisation of profits and does not at any time during the three year period beginning with the issue of the SEIS shares consist wholly or as to a substantial part in carrying on excluded activities (*see paragraph* 9**Error! Reference source not found.** *below*).

8. Qualifying Business Activity

8.1. It is either

    a) the carrying on of or preparing to carry on a new qualifying trade by the issuing company or a 90% subsidiary at the date of issue of the SEIS shares; or

    b) carrying on or preparing to carry on research and development by the company or a qualifying 90% subsidiary at the date of issue of the SEIS shares and at that date it is intended that a new qualifying trade will be derived therefrom, or in respect of which a new qualifying trade being carried on by the company or 90% subsidiary will benefit.

8.2. A new qualifying trade is a trade which does not begin to be carried on by the issuing company or any other person during the two year period prior to the issue of the SEIS shares (the *pre-investment period*) and at no time before the relevant company begins to carry on the trade was any other trade being carried on by the issuing company or by a 90% subsidiary.

8.3. A qualifying trade is one which is conducted on a commercial basis with a view to realise profits and which does not at any time during the three years beginning with the issue of the SEIS shares consist wholly or substantially in carrying on excluded activities.

9. Excluded Activities[21]

9.1. Dealing in land commodities or futures or in shares, securities or other financial instruments;

9.2. Dealing in goods otherwise than in the course of an ordinary trade of wholesale or retail distribution;

9.3. Banking, insurance, money-lending, debt-factoring, hire-purchase financing or other financial activities;

9.4. Leasing, including letting ships on charter;

9.5. Receiving royalties or licence fees;

9.6. Shipbuilding;

9.7. Producing coal;

9.8. Producing steel;

---

[21] See ITA sections 192 to 199 for detailed provisions

9.9. Providing legal or accountancy services;

9.10. Property development;

9.11. Farming or market gardening;

9.12. Holding, managing or occupying woodlands, any other forestry activities or timber production;

9.13. Activities (other than R&D) carried on otherwise than in the course of a trade;

9.14. Operating or managing hotels or comparable establishments or managing property used as an hotel;

9.15. Operating or managing nursing homes or residential care homes or managing property used as a nursing home or residential care home

9.16. The subsidised generation or export of electricity; and

9.17. Providing services to another company where the other company's trade consists to a substantial extent of Excluded Activities.

10. Qualifying Investor

10.1. Neither the investor nor an associate of the investor may, at any time for the three year period beginning with the issue of the shares, be an employee of the issuing company or of any qualifying subsidiary of that company.[22]

10.2. A director of the issuing company or of any qualifying subsidiary will not be treated as an employee for these purposes.

10.3. The investor must at no time during the three year period beginning with the incorporation of the issuing company have a substantial interest in it, namely owning or being entitled to acquire more than 30% of the ordinary share capital, 30% of the issued share capital or 30% of the voting power in the company;[23] nor have any linked loan during that period; nor subscribe for the shares as part of an arrangement which provides for another person to subscribe for shares in another company in which the investor has a substantial interest.[24]

10.4. The maximum investment for which tax relief will be available per investor is £100,000

10.5. The investor must make a claim for SEIS relief, being a tax reduction at a rate of 50%.

---

[22] ITA section 257BA

[23] ITA sections 257BB and 257BF

[24] ITA section 257BC

THE TAX SCHEDULE

Appendix 11. VCT CHECKLIST

	Statutory Ref.
Requirements of a VCT	ITA ss.259 &
1. Not a close company	274;
2. Approved by HMRC	ITA 280B and
3. Its ordinary shares have been or will be admitted to trading on a regulated market	292A(1)
4. Its income has been or will be derived wholly or mainly from shares or securities	
5. It does not retain more than 15% of its income from shares or securities	
6. No holding in any company, other than a VCT or would qualify as a VCT save for the listing requirement, represents more than 15% by value of its investments	
7. At least 70% by value of its investments will be shares or securities (qualifying holdings)	
8. At least 70% by value of its qualifying holdings will be eligible shares	
9. Investments made by the company must not breach investment limits – namely total annual investment not exceeding £5 million (the maximum amount raised annually through risk capital schemes requirement)	
Qualifying holdings	ITA ss. 286 to
10. Share or securities first issued to the VCT company satisfying the following requirements (mirroring EIS company criteria):	313
a. UK permanent establishment	
b. Financial health	
c. Does not exceed the maximum investment requirement raised by the investment company (£1 million)	
d. No guaranteed loan	
e. Eligible shares represent at least 10% by value of total shares or securities of the investee company	
f. Trading	
g. Carrying on a qualifying activity (namely not an exempted activity)	
h. Control and independence	
i. The maximum amount raised annually through risk capital schemes does not exceed £5 million	
j. If an SEIS investment has been made at least 70% of the money raised has been spent before the issue	
k. Gross assets not greater than £15m before the issue and not greater than £16m immediately after the issue	
l. Fewer than 250 full time employees	

	Statutory Ref.
m. The use of the issue monies for a qualifying activity n. There are no disqualifying arrangements under ITA s299A	
Eligibility for investee relief 11. The VCT issues eligible shares to an individual at least 18 years old 12. The share issue raises money 13. The individual subscribes for the shares on his or her own behalf 14. The share issue and subscription are for genuine commercial reasons and not for tax avoidance 15. There are no linked loans	ITA s.261
Investee Tax Reliefs 16. A gain or loss on a qualifying disposal of ordinary shares in a VCT is not a chargeable gain or an allowable loss 17. The maximum amount of income tax relief for any tax year for an individual is £200,000 18. The amount of the relief is a 30% tax reduction 19. No income tax on VCT dividends 20. The tax relief will be withdrawn if the VCT shares are sold within five years of their issue	TCGA s.151A, ITA ss.260, 262, 263 & 266
Loss of investee tax reliefs 21. The individual disposes of the shares within five years of their issue 22. On a disposal made otherwise than by way of an arm's length bargain	ITA s.266
23. No entitlement to relief where there is a linked sale	ITA s.264A
24. No entitlement to relief if there is a linked loan during the relevant period	ITA s.264
25. If approval of the company as a VCT is withdrawn including because conditions for approval were not met at time of approval	ITA ss.268, 281 & 282

Appendix 12.   PENALTIES AND ERRORS

Wrongdoing	Statutory Reference	Definitions	Penalties[1]		
Tax return containing inaccuracy - tax understatement, an inflated loss or a false claim to tax repayment due to carelessness or deliberate error – Covers PAYE, VAT, Income Tax, CGT, CIS, corporation tax, VAT, IHT, ATED, SDLT, petroleum revenue tax, landfill tax, climate change levy, air passenger duty, alcohol and tobacco duties, excise duties, betting, bingo, lottery, gaming	FA 2007 Schedule 24 (*Penalties for errors*) Paras 4 & 4A for amount of penalties; Paras 9 & 10 for reductions in penalties for disclosure		Cat.1[3]	Cat 2[4]	Cat 3[5]
		'Careless'[2] - failure to take reasonable care or failure to inform HMRC of an inaccuracy	30% of potential lost revenue	45% of potential lost revenue	60% of potential lost revenue
		'Deliberate but not concealed'[6] - a deliberate inaccuracy but no concealment	70% of potential lost revenue	105% of potential lost revenue	140% of potential lost revenue
		'Deliberate & concealed'[7] – a deliberate inaccuracy which is concealed	100% of potential lost revenue	150% of potential lost revenue	200% of potential lost revenue

---

[1]Subject to reductions in the penalties for unprompted disclosure under Schedule 24 paragraph 9

[2] Schedule 24 paragraph 3(1)(a)

[3] Category 1 involves a domestic matter; or an offshore matter either in a category 1 territory or the tax is other than income tax or CGT

[4] Category 2 involves an offshore matter in a category 2 territory and the tax is income tax or CGT

[5] Category 3 involved an offshore matter in a category 3 territory and the tax is income tax or CGT

[6] Schedule 24 paragraph 3(1)(b)

[7] Schedule 24 paragraph 3(1)(c)

Wrongdoing	Statutory Reference	Definitions	Penalties[1]		
and general betting duties, & NIC					
			Cat 1	Cat2	Cat 3
Failure to make a return Covers all taxes as set out above	FA 2009 Schedule 55 Paras 3 to 6 for delays of 12 months or more	Deliberate & concealed	The greater of £300 & 100% of the tax	The greater of £300 & 150% of the tax	The greater of £300 & 200% of the tax
		Deliberate but not concealed	The greater of £300 & 70% the tax	The greater of £300 & 105% of the tax	The greater of £300 & 200% of the tax
		In any other case	the greater of £300 & 5% of the tax		
	Paras 3 to 5	Failure to make a return on or before a filing date	£100 for initial failure, £10 each day for continued failure during 90 day period following a notice & the greater of 5% of tax liability or £300 for continued failure after end of 6 months from the penalty date		
Penalty for failure to make payments on time Covers all taxes as set out above	FA 2009 Schedule 56 Para 3 for majority of taxes, separate provisions for PAYE & CIS		Para 3 penalties 5% of unpaid tax, and a further 5% if unpaid after 5 months of the penalty date, and a further 5% at end of 11 months		
Failure to keep records	TMA s 28B(5) & Sch 1A Para 2a(4); FA 1998 Sch 18 para 23		Up to £3,000		
			Cat 1	Cat 2	Cat 3
Failure to notify HMRC of a tax obligation Covers income tax, CGT, VAT corporation tax	FA 2008 Schedule 41 Para 6 for standard penalties	Deliberate & concealed	100% of lost revenue	150% of lost revenue	200% of lost revenue
		Deliberate but not concealed	70% of lost revenue	105% of lost revenue	140% of lost revenue

Wrongdoing	Statutory Reference	Definitions	Penalties[1]		
and other levies and duties		In any other case	30% of lost revenue	45% of lost revenue	60% of lost revenue
Failure to comply with HRC information & inspection powers	FA 2008 Schedule 36 (*Information & Inspection Powers*) Paras 39 to 44	Failure to comply or obstruction	£300 plus daily default penalties not exceeding £60 per day		
		Inaccurate information from carelessness or failure to inform HMRC	Not exceeding £3000 for each inaccuracy		
		Failure to pay a penalty	A tribunal may impose an additional amount not exceeding £1,000 per day		
		Continued failure to comply or continued obstruction resulting a tax saving	A tribunal may impose a penalty which it decides in addition to any other penalties (as above)		
PAYE – failure to make a return under the regulations	TMA s98A (c)		depending on the number of persons included in the return, £100 per month for fifty persons or less, or where number is greater £100 for each fifty persons and an additional £100 where the number is not a multiple of fifty;		
CIS – failure to make a return	TMA s98A(2)(b)(ii); FA 2004 s 70 & 71		Failure to file – penalty not exceeding £3,000; for making a false return a penalty not exceeding £3,000		
DOTAS - failures involving promoters to comply	TMA s 98C ; SI 2007/3104		£600 per day for failure to provide info to HMRC; £5,000 for all other failures i.e. to provide reference numbers/details to clients, failure to respond to an enquiry		
DOTAS –failure to notify use of notifiable scheme re VAT	VATA Schedule 11A para 11		£5,000 for failure to notify a notifiable scheme which is not a designated scheme; failure to notify a designated		

Wrongdoing	Statutory Reference	Definitions	Penalties[1]
			scheme is 15% of the VAT saving
Fraudulent evasion of income tax	TMA s 106A	Knowingly concerned	On summary conviction – imprisonment net exceeding 12 months or fine not exceeding statutory maximum or both On conviction on indictment, to imprisonment not exceeding 7 years or a fine or both
Employment related securities: Failure to file an annual return & reportable events	ITEPA s 421JC	Required to be filed electronically on or before 6 July in the following tax year	Initial failure – £100; failure continues for 3 month – £300; a further £300 if failure continues for 6 months; after 9 months and HMRC gives notice then daily penalty of £10 as determined by HMRC
Employment related securities: Filing incorrect information	ITEPA 421JD	Information contains a material inaccuracy which is deliberate or careless	A penalty decided by HMRC not greater than £5,000

Appendix 13. DOTAS legislation[1]

Tax	Commencement Date	Details	Statutory reference HMRC guidelines
VAT See **VAT Warranties** for further details	the original provisions came with effect from 1.8.2004; listed schemes 9 & 10 became reportable with effect from 1.8.2005	A 'designated/listed' scheme under Sch 11A para 3– see Sch 1 SI 2004/1933 (to date 10 are 'listed') with turnover of £600,000 or more; and a 'notifiable' scheme under Sch 11A para 5 set out in Sch 2 of SI 2004/1933 with any of the eight hallmarks and turnover of £10 million or more – requiring disclosure to HMRC	VATA Sch 11A ; SI 2004/1929; SI 2004/1933; SI 2005/2010; VAT Notice 700/8
SDLT	1.8.2005; from 1.11.2012 disclosure extended to cover schemes intended to be used for non-residential and/or residential property	Steps A to F set out in Schedule in SI 2005/1868 are excluded arrangements in themselves, requiring all other arrangements involving tax avoidance which haven't been grandfathered to be disclosed	FA 2004 ss 306 to 325; SI 2004/1863; SI 2004/1543(information Regs); SI 2005/1868; SI 2012/2396
ATED	1.10.2013	Applies where residential property worth more than £1m from 1.4.2015 and £500,000 from 1.4.2016 is owned by a corporate and there are transfers between parties (subject to exemptions)	SI 2013/2472
Income tax, capital gains tax and corporation tax	1.8.2006	Prescribed arrangements ('Hallmark' of schemes): • confidentiality involving a promoter; • confidentiality not involving a promoter;	SI 2006/1543 (Prescribed description of arrangements)

---

[1] See also HMRCF DOTAS Guidance (latest being November 2015 at the time this book was updated) and FA 2004 sections 306 to 319; the legislation is rapidly expanding and regularly being updated

Tax	Commencement Date	Details	Statutory reference HMRC guidelines
		<ul><li>involving a 'premium fee';</li><li>standardised tax product;</li><li>loss arrangement schemes;</li><li>leasing arrangements</li><li>employment income provided through 3rd parties[2]</li></ul>	
NIC	1.5.2007	Notifiable arrangements & notifiable contribution proposals as under s 306 FA 2004	SSAA s. 132A ; SI 2007/785
IHT	6.4.2011	there are prescribed arrangements if property becomes relevant property an a main benefit is an advantage obtained re a relevant property charge	SI 2011/170

[2] With effect from November 2013

Appendix 14. COMPANIES ACT 2006 – Part 28, Chapter 3

"SQUEEZE-OUT" AND "SELL-OUT"

Takeover offers

974 Meaning of "takeover offer"

(1) For the purposes of this Chapter an offer to acquire shares in a company is a "takeover offer" if the following two conditions are satisfied in relation to the offer.

(2) The first condition is that it is an offer to acquire—

   (a) all the shares in a company, or

   (b) where there is more than one class of shares in a company, all the shares of one or more classes,

   other than shares that at the date of the offer are already held by the offeror.

   Section 975 contains provision supplementing this subsection.

(3) The second condition is that the terms of the offer are the same—

   (a) in relation to all the shares to which the offer relates, or

   (b) where the shares to which the offer relates include shares of different classes, in relation to all the shares of each class.

   Section 976 contains provision treating this condition as satisfied in certain circumstances.

(4) In subsections (1) to (3) "shares" means shares, other than relevant treasury shares, that have been allotted on the date of the offer (but see subsection (5)).

(5) A takeover offer may include among the shares to which it relates—

   (a) all or any shares that are allotted after the date of the offer but before a specified date;

   (b) all or any relevant treasury shares that cease to be held as treasury shares before a specified date;

   (c) all or any other relevant treasury shares.

(6) In this section—

   "relevant treasury shares" means shares that—

(a) are held by the company as treasury shares on the date of the offer, or

(b) become shares held by the company as treasury shares after that date but before a specified date;

"specified date" means a date specified in or determined in accordance with the terms of the offer.

(7) Where the terms of an offer make provision for their revision and for acceptances on the previous terms to be treated as acceptances on the revised terms, then, if the terms of the offer are revised in accordance with that provision—

(a) the revision is not to be regarded for the purposes of this Chapter as the making of a fresh offer, and

(b) references in this Chapter to the date of the offer are accordingly to be read as references to the date of the original offer.

975 Shares already held by the offeror etc

(1) The reference in section 974(2) to shares already held by the offeror includes a reference to shares that he has contracted to acquire, whether unconditionally or subject to conditions being met.

This is subject to subsection (2).

(2) The reference in section 974(2) to shares already held by the offeror does not include a reference to shares that are the subject of a contract—

(a) intended to secure that the holder of the shares will accept the offer when it is made, and

(b) entered into—

(i) by deed and for no consideration,

(ii) for consideration of negligible value, or

(iii) for consideration consisting of a promise by the offeror to make the offer.

(3) In relation to Scotland, this section applies as if the words "by deed and" in subsection (2)(b)(i) were omitted.

(4) The condition in section 974(2) is treated as satisfied where—

(a) the offer does not extend to shares that associates of the offeror hold or have contracted to acquire (whether unconditionally or subject to conditions being met), and

(b) the condition would be satisfied if the offer did extend to those shares.

(For further provision about such shares, see section 977(2)).

976 Cases where offer treated as being on same terms

(1) The condition in section 974(3) (terms of offer to be the same for all shares or all shares of particular classes) is treated as satisfied where subsection (2) or (3) below applies.

(2) This subsection applies where—

(a) shares carry an entitlement to a particular dividend which other shares of the same class, by reason of being allotted later, do not carry,

(b) there is a difference in the value of consideration offered for the shares allotted earlier as against that offered for those allotted later,

(c) that difference merely reflects the difference in entitlement to the dividend, and

(d) the condition in section 974(3) would be satisfied but for that difference.

(3) This subsection applies where—

(a) the law of a country or territory outside the United Kingdom—

(i) precludes an offer of consideration in the form, or any of the forms, specified in the terms of the offer ("the specified form"), or

(ii) precludes it except after compliance by the offeror with conditions with which he is unable to comply or which he regards as unduly onerous,

(b) the persons to whom an offer of consideration in the specified form is precluded are able to receive consideration in another form that is of substantially equivalent value, and

(c) the condition in section 974(3) would be satisfied but for the fact that an offer of consideration in the specified form to those persons is precluded.

977   Shares to which an offer relates

(1) Where a takeover offer is made and, during the period beginning with the date of the offer and ending when the offer can no longer be accepted, the offeror —

(a) acquires or unconditionally contracts to acquire any of the shares to which the offer relates, but

(b)   does not do so by virtue of acceptances of the offer,

those shares are treated for the purposes of this Chapter as excluded from those to which the offer relates.

(2) For the purposes of this Chapter shares that an associate of the offeror holds or has contracted to acquire, whether at the date of the offer or subsequently, are not treated as shares to which the offer relates, even if the offer extends to such shares.

In this subsection "contracted" means contracted unconditionally or subject to conditions being met.

(3)   This section is subject to section 979(8) and (9).

978 Effect of impossibility etc of communicating or accepting offer

(1) Where there are holders of shares in a company to whom an offer to acquire shares in the company is not communicated, that does not prevent the offer from being a takeover offer for the purposes of this Chapter if —

(a) those shareholders have no registered address in the United Kingdom,

(b) the offer was not communicated to those shareholders in order not to contravene the law of a country or territory outside the United Kingdom, and

(c) either —

(i)   the offer is published in the Gazette, or

ii)   the offer can be inspected, or a copy of it obtained, at a place in an EEA State or on a website, and a notice is published in the Gazette specifying the address of that place or website.

(2) Where an offer is made to acquire shares in a company and there are persons for whom, by reason of the law of a country or territory outside the United Kingdom, it is impossible to

accept the offer, or more difficult to do so, that does not prevent the offer from being a takeover offer for the purposes of this Chapter.

(3) It is not to be inferred—

    (a) that an offer which is not communicated to every holder of shares in the company cannot be a takeover offer for the purposes of this Chapter unless the requirements of paragraphs (a) to (c) of subsection (1) are met, or

    (b) that an offer which is impossible, or more difficult, for certain persons to accept cannot be a takeover offer for those purposes unless the reason for the impossibility or difficulty is the one mentioned in subsection (2).

"Squeeze-out"

979   Right of offeror to buy out minority shareholder

(1) Subsection (2) applies in a case where a takeover offer does not relate to shares of different classes.

(2) If the offeror has, by virtue of acceptances of the offer, acquired or unconditionally contracted to acquire—

    (a) not less than 90% in value of the shares to which the offer relates, and

    (b) in a case where the shares to which the offer relates are voting shares, not less than 90% of the voting rights carried by those shares,

he may give notice to the holder of any shares to which the offer relates which the offeror has not acquired or unconditionally contracted to acquire that he desires to acquire those shares.

(3) Subsection (4) applies in a case where a takeover offer relates to shares of different classes.

(4) If the offeror has, by virtue of acceptances of the offer, acquired or unconditionally contracted to acquire—

    (a) not less than 90% in value of the shares of any class to which the offer relates, and

    (b) in a case where the shares of that class are voting shares, not less than 90% of the voting rights carried by those shares, he may give notice to the holder of any shares of that class to which the offer relates which the offeror has not acquired or unconditionally contracted to acquire that he desires to acquire those shares.

(5) In the case of a takeover offer which includes among the shares to which it relates—
   (a) shares that are allotted after the date of the offer, or
   (b) relevant treasury shares (within the meaning of section 974) that cease to be held as treasury shares after the date of the offer,
   the offeror's entitlement to give a notice under subsection (2) or (4) on any particular date shall be determined as if the shares to which the offer relates did not include any allotted, or ceasing to be held as treasury shares, on or after that date.

(6) Subsection (7) applies where—
   (a) the requirements for the giving of a notice under subsection (2) or (4) are satisfied, and
   (b) there are shares in the company which the offeror, or an associate of his, has contracted to acquire subject to conditions being met, and in relation to which the contract has not become unconditional.

(7) The offeror's entitlement to give a notice under subsection (2) or (4) shall be determined as if—
   (a) the shares to which the offer relates included shares falling within paragraph (b) of subsection (6), and
   (b) in relation to shares falling within that paragraph, the words "by virtue of acceptances of the offer" in subsection (2) or (4) were omitted.

(8) Where—
   (a) a takeover offer is made,
   (b) during the period beginning with the date of the offer and ending when the offer can no longer be accepted, the offeror—
       (i) acquires or unconditionally contracts to acquire any of the shares to which the offer relates, but

  (ii) does not do so by virtue of acceptances of the offer, and

(c) subsection (10) applies,

then for the purposes of this section those shares are not excluded by section 977(1) from those to which the offer relates, and the offeror is treated as having acquired or contracted to acquire them by virtue of acceptances of the offer.

(9) Where—

 (a) a takeover offer is made,

 (b) during the period beginning with the date of the offer and ending when the offer can no longer be accepted, an associate of the offeror acquires or unconditionally contracts to acquire any of the shares to which the offer relates, and

 (c) subsection (10) applies,

then for the purposes of this section those shares are not excluded by section 977(2) from those to which the offer relates.

(10) This subsection applies if—

 (a) at the time the shares are acquired or contracted to be acquired as mentioned in subsection (8) or (9) (as the case may be), the value of the consideration for which they are acquired or contracted to be acquired ("the acquisition consideration") does not exceed the value of the consideration specified in the terms of the offer, or

 (b) those terms are subsequently revised so that when the revision is announced the value of the acquisition consideration, at the time mentioned in paragraph (a), no longer exceeds the value of the consideration specified in those terms.

980 Further provision about notices given under section 979

(1) A notice under section 979 must be given in the prescribed manner.

(2) No notice may be given under section 979(2) or (4) after the end of—

(a) the period of three months beginning with the day after the last day on which the offer can be accepted, or

(b) the period of six months beginning with the date of the offer, where that period ends earlier and the offer is one to which subsection (3) below applies.

(3) This subsection applies to an offer if the time allowed for acceptance of the offer is not governed by rules under section 943(1) that give effect to Article 7 of the Takeovers Directive.

In this subsection "the Takeovers Directive" has the same meaning as in section 943.

(4) At the time when the offeror first gives a notice under section 979 in relation to an offer, he must send to the company—

(a) a copy of the notice, and

(b) a statutory declaration by him in the prescribed form, stating that the conditions for the giving of the notice are satisfied.

(5) Where the offeror is a company (whether or not a company within the meaning of this Act) the statutory declaration must be signed by a director.

(6) A person commits an offence if—

(a) he fails to send a copy of a notice or a statutory declaration as required by subsection (4), or

(b) he makes such a declaration for the purposes of that subsection knowing it to be false or without having reasonable grounds for believing it to be true.

(7) It is a defence for a person charged with an offence for failing to send a copy of a notice as required by subsection (4) to prove that he took reasonable steps for securing compliance with that subsection.

(8) A person guilty of an offence under this section is liable—

(a) on conviction on indictment, to imprisonment for a term not exceeding two years or a fine (or both);

(b) on summary conviction—

(i) in England and Wales, to imprisonment for a term not exceeding twelve months or to a fine not exceeding the statutory maximum (or both) and, for continued contravention, a daily default fine not exceeding one-fiftieth of the statutory maximum;

(ii) in Scotland or Northern Ireland, to imprisonment for a term not exceeding six months, or to a fine not exceeding the statutory maximum (or both) and, for continued contravention, a daily default fine not exceeding one-fiftieth of the statutory maximum.

Appendix 15. The Takeover Code Rule 15

Appropriate offer for convertibles etc.

(a) When an offer is made for voting equity share capital or for other transferable securities carrying voting rights and the offeree company has convertible securities outstanding, the offeror must make an appropriate offer or proposal to the stockholders to ensure that their interests are safeguarded. Equality of treatment is required.

(b) The board of the offeree company must obtain competent independent advice on the offer or proposal to the stockholders and the substance of such advice must be made known to its stockholders, together with the board's views on the offer or proposal.

(c) Whenever practicable, the offer or proposal should be sent to stockholders at the same time as the offer document is published but, if this is not practicable, the Panel should be consulted and the offer or proposal should be sent as soon as possible thereafter. A copy of the offer or proposal should be sent to the Panel at the time of publication.

(d) The offer or proposal to stockholders required by this Rule should not normally be made conditional on any particular level of acceptances. It may, however, be put by way of a scheme to be considered at a stockholders' meeting provided that, if the scheme is not approved at that meeting, or is not sanctioned by the court, the offeror shall immediately make an offer or proposal to stockholders which is not conditional on any particular level of acceptances or approval.

(e) If an offeree company has options or subscription rights outstanding, the provisions of this Rule apply mutatis mutandis.

NOTES ON RULE 15

1. When conversion rights etc. are exercisable during an offer All relevant documents, announcements and other information sent to shareholders of the offeree company and persons with information rights in connection with an offer must also, where practicable, be sent simultaneously to the holders of securities convertible into, rights to subscribe for and options over shares of the same class as those to which the offer relates. If those holders are able to exercise their rights during the course of the offer and to accept the offer in respect of the resulting shares, their attention should, where appropriate, be drawn to this in the relevant documents, announcements and other information.

2. Rules 9 and 14

If an offer for any convertible securities is required by Rule 9 or Rule 14, compliance with the relevant Rule will be regarded as satisfying the obligation in Rule 15(a) in respect of those securities.

THE TAX SCHEDULE

Index